MW00778910

*A Guide to*
# ASIAN PHILOSOPHY
# CLASSICS

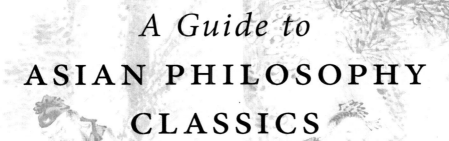

# A Guide to
# ASIAN PHILOSOPHY
# CLASSICS

# PUQUN LI
## WITH ARTHUR K. LING

broadview press

© 2012 Puqun Li

All rights reserved. The use of any part of this publication reproduced, transmitted in any form or by any means, electronic, mechanical, photocopying, recording, or otherwise, or stored in a retrieval system, without prior written consent of the publisher — or in the case of photocopying, a licence from Access Copyright (Canadian Copyright Licensing Agency), One Yonge Street, Suite 1900, Toronto, Ontario M5E 1E5 — is an infringement of the copyright law.

Library and Archives Canada Cataloguing in Publication

Li, Puqun
    A guide to Asian philosophy classics / Puqun Li with Arthur K. Ling.

Includes bibliographical references and index.
ISBN 978-1-55481-034-5

    1. Hindu philosophy.  2. Buddhist philosophy.  3. Philosophy, Confucian.  4. Taoist philosophy.  I. Ling, Arthur K  II. Title.

B121.L5 2012             181             C2012-902635-2

Broadview Press is an independent, international publishing house, incorporated in 1985.

We welcome comments and suggestions regarding any aspect of our publications — please feel free to contact us at the addresses below or at broadview@broadviewpress.com / www.broadviewpress.com.

| North America | UK, Europe, Central Asia, Middle East, Africa, India and Southeast Asia | Australia and New Zealand |
|---|---|---|
| Post Office Box 1243 Peterborough, Ontario Canada K9J 7H5 | | NewSouth Books c/o TL Distribution 15-23 Helles Ave. |
| 2215 Kenmore Ave. Buffalo, New York USA 14207 tel: (705) 743-8990 fax: (705) 743-8353 customerservice @broadviewpress.com | Eurospan Group 3 Henrietta St., London WC2E 8LU, UK tel: 44 (0) 1767 604972 fax: 44 (0) 1767 601640 eurospan @turpin-distribution.com | Moorebank, NSW Australia 2170 tel: (02) 8778 9999 fax: (02) 8778 9944 orders@tldistribution.com.au |

Copy-edited by Robert M. Martin

Broadview Press acknowledges the financial support of the Government of Canada through the Canada Book Fund for our publishing activities.

Book design by Michel Vrana

This book is printed on paper containing 100% post-consumer fibre.

Printed in Canada

To my father Zhongbang Li (李中榜) and my uncle Zhongshan Li (李中山) who taught me to strive to be a *junzi* (君子), or exemplary person

CONTENTS

# ACKNOWLEDGEMENTS

This book has one author but many contributors; it has benefited from many hands. First of all, I want to thank Professor Bruce Morito from Athabasca University for trusting and encouraging me to write this book in 2001, and my PhD supervisor Professor Andrew Lugg from the University of Ottawa for his untiring support, and for his comments on part of an earlier draft.

Second, I would like to thank particular individuals who have contributed in various ways to the writing of this book: Bert Plant, Frank Abbott, Dr. Rajesh Shukla, Dr. Wenliang Zhang, Dr. Michael Hunter, and Dr. Wayne Fenske. I am indebted to Sophia Veale for carefully commenting on the entire manuscript from a student's perspective. I particularly want to thank my friend Carol Shillibeer whose constructive suggestions have saved me from many mistakes and awkward expressions in part of an earlier draft.

Special thanks are due to Professor Arthur Ling, who kindly read the entire manuscript, suggesting many corrections, and mending my English. Like Socrates' midwife, Professor Ling helped me to articulate my thoughts in his work on my manuscript and in his role as a knowledgeable and delightful conversation partner regarding Asian philosophy, religion, and teaching strategies. What I've learned from our numerous lengthy discussions has greatly contributed to the production of this book. I have the feeling that it was God, *Brahman*, or Buddha who sent Professor Ling to assist me in the completion of the book.

Another midwife at the birth of this book who deserves special thanks is my copy editor Professor Robert Martin. His gentle but extremely careful professional touch on my manuscript saved me from many unclear points, inconsistencies, and awkwardness.

If there is any infelicity still in the text, it shows that I need to work harder on my writing and continue learning from colleagues such as Professor Martin.

My gratitude also goes to my colleague Professor Jonathan Katz and to Professor Arthur Ling for supporting me in my faculty scholarship application at Kwantlen Polytechnic University in 2006. Thanks to the Philosophy Department and the Faculty of Humanities at Kwantlen for generously granting me course release time while I was writing this book. The Kwantlen Library staff provided me with invaluable assistance in responding to my interlibrary loan requests and my new library collection suggestions. Their help directly facilitated the writing of this book, and I thank them for their friendly and efficient support in this regard.

I want to thank all my students through the years both in my Asian Philosophy course at Kwantlen Polytechnic University and in the Introduction to Philosophy: West and East course at Athabasca University. I thank them for providing me with the opportunities to try out and refine my exposition of the Asian philosophy classics, and for prompting me constantly to explore better and more effective ways to make Asian philosophical ideas accessible to beginners, particularly those coming from a Western *weltanschauung*. This book represents a work in progress that has come about through this process of ongoing exploration of the texts with my students.

I want to thank my son Star and daughter Sophie for demonstrating to me how three-year-olds can "play-in-the-moment"; it was their "timeless" and wandering style of play when they were small that helped me understand the Zen and Daoist practices of "wandering-in-the-world" and "living-in-the-present." I also want to thank my son for assisting me in preparing the figures and pictures in this book.

Ultimately, I am deeply grateful to my beloved wife, Ying Xu, who has been a quiet but unfailing support to me. Without her support, I would not have been able to complete this book.

# PREFACE

This is not a book on the history of Asian philosophy, but a guide or companion to ten representative Asian philosophy classics—the Upanishads, the Dhammapada, the *Fundamental Verses on the Middle Way* (*Mulamadhyamakakarika*), the *Analects*, the *Mengzi* (*Mencius*), the *Xunzi* (*Hsun Tzu*), the *Daodejing* (*Tao Te Ching*), the *Zhuangzi* (*Chuang Tzu*), the Platform Sutra, and the *Shobogenzo*.[1] These texts are selected because they provide an entry into some major schools of Asian philosophy—Hinduism, Buddhism, Confucianism, Daoism (Taoism), and Chan/Zen.

For many English speakers whose first contact with Asian philosophy was through graphic novels, movies, or TV, the exotic wisdom of Asian philosophy can be very intriguing and fun to ponder. But, for those who have tried to delve into the primary Asian philosophy texts (in translation), the story may be very different: these are not easy fun; rather, they can produce frustration and bewilderment. Encouragement and orientation are necessary for overcoming the cultural barriers these texts present. That is precisely the purpose of this guide: to make sense of the ideas in the chosen texts, to draw local conceptual maps, and to compare and contrast ideas from the philosophical

---

1     Two versions of the Chinese names are given in this list and elsewhere; the reason is that there is a traditional way of romanizing these names (i.e., of rendering the Chinese sounds into the Roman alphabet) and a way that uses the "pinyin" system that is now official and generally used. I'll be using pinyin throughout, but occasionally I'll also give a traditional romanization (in parentheses), to aid readers who may have seen this version elsewhere. The one substantial departure from pinyin romanization in here is the name "Confucius," too solidly entrenched for English speakers to ignore. For a very rough guide to pronunciation of pinyin romanizations, see Appendix 4 of this book.

traditions of the East and the West—in short, to help English speaking readers get their bearings when they first approach the Asian philosophy classics.[2]

A classic is a classic. This is not merely a tautology. A classic probes into the depths of human existence and the ultimate concerns of life. It inquires into fundamental issues such as the character of the self, the reality of suffering, the mystery of life and death, the nature of right and wrong, and the path to happiness. The greatness of a classic lies in its enduring significance across space and time. While a classic emerged in a particular time and culture, it has the power to address people in diverse social locations and times. This is not to suggest that every utterance of a classic—Asian or Western—is always directly relevant to the life of contemporary readers.[3] But, on the whole, when a classic is skilfully reinterpreted, it can continue to speak afresh to each generation, often beyond its native cultural contexts. In that sense, the import of a classic is truly trans-cultural and trans-temporal. Our experience of rapid globalization has rendered Rudyard Kipling's (in)famous remark, "Oh, East is East and West is West, and never the twain shall meet," grossly obsolete, if not blatantly false. If an Indian, Chinese, Japanese, or Korean interested in philosophy should read and can comprehend Plato's *Republic* and Aristotle's *Nicomachean Ethics*, a French, German, American, or Canadian with a similar passion for philosophy should read and can appreciate Confucius's *Analects* and Laozi's *Daodejing*.

There is still much we can and should learn from the ancient philosophy classics— from both the West and the East. While we may know much more about science and nature than the ancient philosophers (Asian or Western), we do not necessarily understand as much as they did about the good life. It is presumptuous of us to think that we are smarter and wiser than the ancient philosophers in all respects simply because of the fact that we have grasped more scientific knowledge. Echoing the comment of Jean-Jacques Rousseau (1712–78) cautioning against the development of science and technology, Alan Wallace has pointed out that "[t]he expansion of scientific knowledge has not brought about any comparable growth in ethics or value. Modern society has become more knowledgeable and powerful as a result, but it has not grown wiser or more compassionate."[4]

In some cases, the classical philosophers of the East and the West can be likened to the folks of two neighbouring villages who are digging a well in their respective villages. While they started at different places, they may eventually drink from the same fount. By analogy, an Asian philosophy classic should taste similar to a comparable Western philosophy classic—compare reading the *Analects* and the *Nicomachean Ethics*.

In other cases, however, ideas from one tradition may appear radically alien to people embedded in other traditions. For example, try to savour the Buddhist idea of

---

2    This guide aims at making sense of ideas in the Asian philosophy classics, not at offering definitive interpretations of those ideas.

3    Consider, for example, chapter 80 of the *Daodejing*, where Laozi suggests that people live in small, primitive, agrarian villages, not use boats, carts, armour, and weapons even if they have them, but return to the use of knotted cord for counting, and never travel beyond their villages.

4    B. Alan Wallace, *Contemplative Science—Where Buddhism and Neuroscience Converge* (New York: Columbia University Press, 2007), 2.

emptiness (no self-nature) or the Daoist idea of change (transformation of things) with our "taste buds" that are used to Parmenides' "Being" and Plato's "Forms." What we will probably experience is something insipid, if not downright distasteful. Fortunately, however, our "taste buds" are not fixed, nor are our minds imprisoned. This guide intends to sharpen readers' "taste buds" and open their minds so that they will be able to better taste alien ideas and better understand them.

In helping readers think through ideas in the select primary texts, this guide adopts three heuristic strategies of interpretation.

*The first strategy is to situate a text in its philosophical context.* A text that seems obscure at first glance can often be made more intelligible once it is appropriately contextualized as a part of a larger philosophical conversation. As we are reading a difficult text, it is often helpful to identify the author's interlocutor(s) or opponent(s). For instance, in order to understand the Buddhist philosopher Nagarjuna's notion of "emptiness" (no self-nature) in the *Fundamental Verses on the Middle Way*, it is helpful to see that he was responding to an interlocutor who believed that self-nature was real and substantive. In order to understand the Confucian philosopher Xunzi's thoughts, it is beneficial to read them against the backdrop of the competing ideas presented in the *Analects*, the *Mengzi*, the *Mozi*, the *Daodejing*, and the *Zhuangzi*. Understanding this background will help us appreciate Xunzi's role as a synthesizer of these diverse schools of thought and hence his unique contribution to Chinese philosophy.

*The second strategy is to ascertain the internal connection of ideas in a text in order to gain an understanding of how they constitute a coherent vision.* For example, this guide explores the interconnection of core ideas—*ren* (humanness), *li* (ritual), *junzi* (exemplary person), *zhong* (loyalty or conscience), *shu* (reciprocity/empathy)—in the *Analects*, so that readers can appreciate Confucius' vision on the training of *junzi* through *ren*, *li*, *zhong*, and *shu* and on how that training can contribute to the establishment of a harmonious society.

In adopting the first two strategies, I have sought to present each chapter of this volume as relatively self-contained as well as related to others. Thus readers may choose to focus on a particular chapter first, and then to relate it to other chapters both chronologically and conceptually.

*The third interpretive strategy is to bring some of the ideas in the select primary texts into dialogue with Western philosophy.* This conversation with Western thoughts allows readers to appreciate the currency of Asian philosophy classics. The relevance of the *Analects* to virtue ethics, the contribution of the *Mengzi* to the discussion of moral psychology, and the comparability of ideas in Dogen's *Shobogenzo* and ideas in Heidegger's *Being and Time* are but a few themes that illustrate the aliveness of the Asian philosophy classics in contemporary philosophy discussion.

Many readers of this guide may already have some familiarity with the Western philosophical tradition, and it is natural for them to compare the two traditions. In some cases, they may (understandably) read Western philosophical ideas into the Asian texts. Addressing potential problems in comparing ideas in the two traditions, I want to provide two caveats.

The first caveat is that comparison across traditions is best made on an idea-and text-specific basis, namely, between specific texts or ideas, rather than between entire traditions. Thus, the comparisons I make in this book are local rather than global. I am sceptical of the value of feeding novice students of Asian philosophies (or, for that matter, philosophy in general) with global comparative statements, which are often too general and, in some cases, vacuous. Such statements may also be misleading and mistaken. Consider, for example, this popular comparative remark: "Compared with Western philosophy, Asian philosophy is not argumentative." This remark may be both mistaken and misleading. The truth of the matter is that the Chinese classics of the *Mozi* and the *Xunzi*,[5] and especially the Indian Mahayana Buddhist masterpiece *Fundamental Verses on the Middle Way*, are all argumentative, and in this regard comparable to Plato's dialogues.

Another example of a global comparative statement concerns the contrast between the West's quest for "truth" and the Chinese search for the "Way" or *dao*. In spite of its intuitive appeal, this simplistic dichotomy has to be cautiously qualified and properly understood. According to David Hall, first of all, Chinese philosophers such as Confucius and Laozi do care about truth, but they focus on the "pragmatic" understanding of it, or on the issue of how to realize it, whereas Western philosophers like Plato and Aristotle apparently concentrate on a representational understanding of truth. Secondly, Mozi has speculations on "truth," "falsity," and "confirmation," and so on, but he does not hold a bifurcation between things as they are and things as they are represented. Thirdly, American pragmatism understands truth in a pragmatic way that is very similar to how Confucius and Laozi understand it. And finally, even Plato's or Aristotle's search for truth itself was ultimately aimed at creating proper social order to ensure a meaningful and harmonious existence for individuals.[6] Therefore, the line between the West's quest for "truth" and the Chinese search for the "Way" is not as sharp as many would think it is.

As a rule of thumb, then, readers should make sure not to lose sight of the nuanced distinctions between apparently similar ideas across traditions, and even within a tradition. Within the Chinese tradition, for example, different philosophers draw subtle distinctions when they use the same term. While both the *Analects* and the *Daodejing* appropriate the term *dao*, they do not use it in the same way or in the same sense. Therefore, in the light of this rule, I urge those who are embarking on a journey into Asian philosophy to first focus on specific philosophers, ideas, and concrete arguments, rather than on alleged neat global patterns. I urge them to get back "to the rough ground."[7]

---

5    The *Mozi* is not introduced in this guide, but some ideas in the *Mozi* will be discussed in chapter 5 of this volume in relation to corresponding ideas in the *Mengzi*.

6    See A.C. Graham, *Disputers of the Tao* (La Salle, IL: Open Court, 1989), 3; and David L. Hall, "The Way and the Truth," in *A Companion to World Philosophies*, Eliot Deutsch and Ron Bontekoe, eds. (Oxford: Blackwell, 1997), 214–23.

7    To borrow a phrase from Ludwig Wittgenstein, *Philosophical Investigations* (Oxford: Blackwell, 1958), I, §107.

The second caveat is that comparison should be made not merely for the sake of pointing out similarities and differences between two comparable texts or ideas across traditions, but for the purpose of explicating the implications of the similarities and especially of the differences, which in turn should prompt dialogue, engagement, and fresh learning. The outcome of such comparative exercise is likely an invitation to further exploration. For example, both Aristotle and the Chinese Buddhist Hui Neng have discussed the importance of "seeing," but they differ radically in what they mean by the term. The former uses it in an epistemic sense, the latter, spiritual. An appreciation of this difference can greatly enhance our understanding of the two philosophers' respective philosophical projects (see chapter 9 on the Platform Sutra).

Finally I want to offer a word of advice on how to read Asian philosophy classics. First, do not read the Asian philosophy classics as if they were scientific treatises. My experience with beginning students of Asian philosophy is that they sometimes approach Asian philosophy texts, unconsciously or subconsciously, as if they were works of natural science. They presume that the statements found in these texts are factual claims, and they demand scientific proof for them. I believe that this way of reading is premised on a mistaken understanding of the genre of the Asian philosophy texts. These texts were not written to report scientific facts or demonstrate scientific hypotheses, but rather to offer urgent prescriptions on living that pertain to issues of life and death. Thus, I think that we should focus on the moral and social visions articulated in the texts and on their practical implications. It seems wrongheaded, for instance, to treat the notion of Buddha-nature (as found in Nagarjuna's *Fundamental Verses on the Middle Way*, Hui Neng's Platform Sutra, and Dogen's *Shobogenzo*) as part of a scientific theory about the make-up of a human being or of any sentient being. Understood in its literary and philosophical contexts, the notion is an example of skilful means (*upaya*), the meaning of which is "metaphorical, analogical, evocative, and expressive."[8] In this understanding, the idea of Buddha-nature does not refer to some entity in the physical world, but performs the function of moral empowerment and evokes a certain moral equality in the religious practitioner. Whatever the term may refer to factually or cognitively, if it does so at all, is only of secondary importance.

To be sure, philosophers (Asian or Western) almost never deny scientific facts, but they make different interpretations of them. For example, both Zhuangzi and Socrates acknowledge that the physical body of a person is going to die or is mortal, but they differ in their *interpretation* of what mortality consists in: the former interprets it as a transformation of energy, *qi*, whereas the latter sees it as the liberation of the soul. None of the Chinese philosophers (Confucius, Laozi, and Mozi, etc.) denied the fact that ancient China at that time was in social chaos, but they proposed divergent solutions to it. Thus, what is philosophically interesting is the manner in which different philosophers make different interpretive "spins" on the same fact. In short, to demand scientific proof of a philosophical idea is to misunderstand the very nature of

---

8    Philip J. Ivanhoe, *Readings from the Lu-Wang School of Neo-Confucianism* (Indianapolis: Hackett, 2009), 4, note 5.

philosophical statements as interpretations, suggestions, and recommendations; it is to mistake non-cognitive expressions for attempted statements of facts.

This, of course, does not mean that all philosophical statements are equally plausible and practical. The study of philosophy involves precisely the task of understanding these interpretations, suggestions, and recommendations as they are, and critically evaluating their plausibility and practicality.

Second, do not assume that an Asian philosophical term has the same meaning as its English translation suggests on the surface. While comparison and contrast, made properly, can be helpful, it is crucial not to fall into the temptation of imposing a Western philosophical paradigm on an Asian classic text. When we read in translation such familiar terms as "time," "self," "mind," "death," "emptiness," "nature," and "non-action," we should not assume that they mean the same thing as they do in Western philosophy or in common usage, for they are naturally coloured by the cultures and traditions that produced them.[9] The term "non-action" (*wuwei*) in the *Daodejing* and the *Zhuangzi* does not mean "doing nothing at all." Nor does "nature" (*zi-ran*) in the *Daodejing* and the *Zhuangzi* simply mean external Nature out there. Nor does "emptiness" in *Fundamental Verses on the Middle Way* signify "sheer nothingness" or "complete annihilation." Therefore, to avoid misreading Asian philosophical classics, we need to meet Asian philosophy terms and ideas on their own turf.

To illustrate the importance of the above advice, consider the following quotes from our select Asian philosophy classics.

Quote 1:
It moves. It moves not. / It is far, and It is near. / It is within all this, / And It is outside of all this (*Isha Upanishad*, 5).

Quote 2:
Don't get selfishly attached to anything, for trying to hold on to it will bring you pain. When you have neither likes nor dislikes, you will be free (the Dhammapada: 211).

Quote 3:
Your life has a limit but knowledge has none. If you use what is limited to pursue what has no limit, you will be in danger. If you understand this and still strive for knowledge, you will be in danger for certain! (the *Zhuangzi*, section 3: "The Secret of Caring for Life").

---

9    However, I suggest that beginning students should in general trust translations of Asian classics. To play the cynical card that translation will never capture the original meanings of an ancient text can be unhealthy and tends to dampen a novice reader's interest in Asian philosophy classics, or, for that matter, in any classic that comes down to us through translation. Yet, my suggestion does not imply that all translations of an Asian classic are equivalent. Sometimes we can judge a translation by its coherency, or by whether it is likely to lead to unnecessary problems and erroneous interpretations. In this book, I address translation issues only when doing so can clarify things and can help avoid misunderstandings.

No doubt beginners will find these quotes hard to understand, bizarre, and even non-sensical. Isn't quote (1) saying that "something" is both A and NOT A—a contradiction? It appears to be saying something like "It is raining and it is not raining"— all in one breath! Who (and in what context) would say anything like that? What does "It" refer to anyway? The bewilderment here is analogous to Carnap's reaction to Heidegger's statement (in "What Is Metaphysics?") that "The Nothing nothings itself." But maybe the quote is onto something more than meets the eye, and maybe we should not read it from a strictly analytical mindset. (To understand this quote read chapter 1 on the Upanishads.)

If quote (1) seems illogical, quote (2) seems completely counterintuitive. Students in my Asian philosophy course complain that if they had neither likes nor dislikes they would be either unconscious (yet still alive, as in sleeping or as in being a vegetable) or totally dead. How can one be "free" in such a state? But the long history and the enduring influence of the Dhammapada make it unlikely that we can simply dismiss this apparently bizarre idea as nonsensical. It is necessary to suspend our initial judgment and patiently dig deeper into the text. (To understand this quote read chapter 2 on the Dhammapada.)

Doesn't quote (3) suggest that we should give up the pursuit of knowledge? Doesn't it contradict a long cherished value in the West, championed by such great thinkers as Socrates, Plato, Aristotle, Descartes, Bacon, Galileo, Newton, and Kant?[10] Isn't quote (3) providing an excuse for intellectual laziness? On this reading of Zhuangzi, one may argue, "Look, the Chinese Daoist Zhuangzi said it is dangerous to pursue knowledge, and because my life is limited and knowledge is not, I'm not going to bother trying anymore." Before jumping to this conclusion, it is perhaps advisable to first ascertain what kind of knowledge Zhuangzi is talking about in the quote. (To understand this quote read chapter 7 on the *Zhuangzi*.)

These three examples illustrate that we should be careful not to dismiss a text too quickly simply because it appears at first glance strange, opaque, counterintuitive, or illogical. In most cases, it is precisely the strange and opaque passages that reveal the distinct or unique features of the text in question. If you have studied a foreign language, you can probably appreciate this point readily. You may have encountered sentences or expressions in a foreign language that just do not make sense to you; you may have also learned that it is these sentences and expressions that reveal the fascinating features of the language you are studying.

I have selected the three quotes above in order to highlight the challenge of interpretation. However, I am not suggesting that all sentences in the Asian philosophy classics are as puzzling as those in the quotes. Many, or perhaps most, statements in the Asian philosophy classics are straightforward, or at least no more difficult than those found in the Western philosophy classics. I don't want anyone to be intimidated.

A guide is only a guide; this volume is not at all intended to replace the primary texts. Thus, readers still have to chew on the primary texts themselves. It is true that

---

10   It is noteworthy that they each pursued knowledge in their distinctive ways and that what they mean by "knowledge" may not be exactly the same.

they are sometimes hard to get your teeth into, but my suggestion is simple: don't be discouraged. When a person wants to climb up a high mountain, the climbing itself is a test of the climber's seriousness, strength, courage, and patience. Similarly, the persistent pondering of a text is in itself that which trains and shapes the mind. Japanese Zen Master Dogen's idea that "practice and enlightenment are one" provides a helpful way for seeing the process of engaging the Asian texts. The practice of wrestling with the Asian philosophy classics is in itself a quest for self-understanding. Hopefully, this guide will make your wrestling a bit easier and more fruitful. Just remember, if you are reading the Asian philosophy classics, you are already a keen student and learner.[11]

---

11    See the *Analects* 7:8, the *Daodejing* chapter 41, the Dhammapada 164, and the story of Naciketas in the *Katha Upanishad*.

CHAPTER 1

# The Upanishads

SUGGESTED PRIMARY READING

*Isa, Kena, Katha, Chandogya, and Brihadaranyaka Upanishads* in *A Source Book in Indian Philosophy*, Sarvepalli Radhakrishnan and Charles A. Moore, eds. (Princeton: Princeton University Press, 1967).

LEARNING OBJECTIVES

By the time you have worked through this chapter, you should be able to

- Describe the ideas of *Atman* and *Brahman*
- Explain the identification of *Atman* with *Brahman* and its implications
- Describe how the karma theory works
- Describe the path from transmigration (*samsara*) to liberation (*moksha*)

KEY WORDS

*Atman, Brahman,* karma, *samsara, moksha*

## GUIDING QUESTIONS

The following questions may seem far removed from practical, everyday concerns. But in the ancient Indian philosophical classic, the Upanishads, these questions are seen as of ultimate importance—questions that everyone has to confront in life.

1.  Is life simply what meets the eye—a process of birth, living, and death? Is death the ultimate end? Am I just this physical body, which lasts only a finite period of time? Do I have a true Self beyond my physical body?

2.  Are there moral laws governing human activities? Are we free in making ethical choices?

3.  Why is there universal suffering? Why do people suffer sometimes for no apparent reason?

4.  Is it possible to be free from suffering in this life? What should one do in order to be released from suffering?

The Upanishads not only ask these profound philosophical questions, but also provide answers to them. If we accept these answers, we could radically transform ourselves.

## INTRODUCTION

Indian philosophy springs from the fountainhead of the Upanishads, which is made up of a vast number of verses collected between approximately 1000 and 500 BCE. They are the concluding sections of four earlier collections of verses called the Vedas.[1] Scholars generally agree that the Vedas first took shape when the Sanskrit-speaking Aryan people migrated to the Indus Valley in approximately 1500 BCE and began to integrate into the aboriginal civilization which had been there since around 2500 BCE.[2] The Vedas consist of hymns or incantations for pantheistic nature worship. Natural forces, such as the sun, wind, storm, rain, fire, earth, and heaven, were worshipped as powers of life. It

---

1   The word "veda" literally means "knowledge" or "wisdom." There are four Vedas: *Rig Veda*, *Yajur Veda*, *Sama Veda*, and *Atharva Veda*; each of them contains four layers: Mantras or Samhitas (chanting hymns), Brahmanas (the authoritative explanation or elaboration of a Brahmin—a functional equivalent of a priest), Aranyakas ("forest books," hermits' reflections on the meaning of sacrificial rituals), and the Upanishads. A note on our typography: conventionally, all book titles appear in italics except for names of old major revered works of scripture (e.g., the Bible, the Qur'an). On this basis, "Vedas," "Upanishads," and "Dhammapada" will appear unitalicized (except when referring to a particular modern published edition or translation, or to a particular one of the Upanishads, e.g., *Katha Upanishad*). Rather than argue about whether the other books that I will discuss are "major revered works of scripture," I'll merely follow the usual (but not invariable) practice of italicizing their names. It's also conventional to insert the unitalicized word "the" preceding the names of these works (e.g., "the *Daodejing*").

2   Some figurines found in the Indus Valley show that gods and goddesses were worshipped. Indus Valley seals sometimes show the swastika symbol, which is also found in later Indian Hinduism, Buddhism, and Jainism. One famous seal represents a figure in what was later called the lotus position in Yoga. All these suggest that the Indus Valley Civilization contributed to India's later religion and philosophy.

is believed that by reciting, chanting, and singing verses from the Vedas one can obtain sacred energy from the powers of life. Although there were many gods in the Vedas,[3] there was already a tendency towards a monotheistic synthesis. Belief in the existence of the gods was not argued for, but simply assumed in sacrificial practices. Thus, the Vedas are more of the genre of nature mythology than of philosophy.

The Upanishads, by contrast, consist of predominately speculative and exploratory philosophical material, rather than cultic or ritualistic texts. Strictly speaking, they are not systematic philosophical treatises, and they even appear to be self-contradictory at times. But they seek to present a series of reasoned philosophical visions and ways of life. The dominant vision is that suffering (within a seemingly endless cycle of birth and death) is pervasive, due to one's ignorance of the true Self. Fortunately, however, the seemingly endless cycle of suffering is escapable if one realizes one's true Self.

Compared to the earlier layers of the Vedas, a significant "inward turn" (from ritual to self-contemplation) can be detected in the Upanishads: "the gods recede into the background, the priests are subordinated, sacrifices are looked down upon, contemplation takes the place of worship and the acquisition of divine knowledge takes precedence over the performance of rites and ceremonies."[4] Unlike Ecclesiastes in the Hebrew Bible, which looks to a transcendent God as the answer to the vanity of life under the sun,[5] the Upanishads urge all earnest seekers of truth to turn inward to their deep inner Self for answers to the problem of suffering.[6]

The path of inward exploration, or meditation, leads to liberation, but to ensure efficacy, the practice must be carried out under the guidance of qualified spiritual teachers—gurus. Indeed, the term "Upanishad" is derived from *upa*, near, *ni*, down, and *sad*, to sit, which altogether means a "secret doctrine" or "profound teaching" that pupils receive from their gurus.[7] While spiritual teachings are open to all, the gurus insist that in practice only keen and dedicated students are receptive to them.

The preoccupations of the Upanishads are predominately metaphysical—about ultimate release from suffering. In contrast to the Vedas, which focused on worldly goals, such as material benefits and pleasure, the Upanishads see the worldly goals as all transient. "Centenarian sons and grandsons," "cattle, elephants, gold, and horses," "wealth and long life," "lovely maidens with chariots, with lyres"—that is, all the

---

3    The major gods include Brahma (creator), Vishnu (sustainer), Shiva (destroyer), Indra (a deity of the thunderstorm or rain), and Agni (the god of fire). However, Lord Shiva is seen by many as the Godhead who is the creator, preserver, and the final destroyer of all things.

4    D.S. Sharma, *Hinduism through the Ages* (Bombay: Bharatiya Vidya Bhavan, 1973), 6. Also see Eknath Easwaran, *The Upanishads* (Tomales, CA: Nilgiri Press, 2007), 301–02.

5    See Ecclesiastes 12:13–14.

6    See *Katha*, II.1–5, and v.8–12. Notice, however, that the sacrificial and ritualistic Vedic practice continued to exist in Hindu tradition alongside the more speculative and philosophical Upanishadic teachings.

7    There is a different interpretation of the word "Upanishad": "*upa*" means "near," "*ni*" means "perfectly," and "*sad*" means "shatter" or "destroy." Thus, "Upanishad" altogether means knowledge that shatters human miseries and sufferings (see M. Bannerjee, *Invitation to Hinduism* [New Delhi: Arnold Heinemann, 1978], 35).

Moksha - liberation

Self/True nature over worldly possessions

commonly cherished goals of the ancient Indian world—are simply "ephemeral."[8] So long as one is ignorant of one's true nature, these worldly attainments can at best be of secondary importance.

Upans. fountain of later Indian thought

The Upanishadic sages inspired much of later Indian philosophies. Recurring motifs in the Indian philosophical traditions, such as the search for the true Self as deep consciousness, the pursuit of liberation (*moksha*) from transmigration—endless reincarnation (*samsara*)—and the principle of karma (deeds), are all traceable to the Upanishads. Thus, it is not an exaggeration to say that the Upanishads are the fountainhead of later Indian thought. In this regard, our study of the Upanishads will pave the way for an investigation of Indian Buddhism as found in the Dhammapada (Chapter 2 of this book) and the *Fundamental Verses on the Middle Way* (Chapter 3) and two later incarnations of Buddhist thought: Chinese Chan in the Platform Sutra (Chapter 9) and Japanese Zen in the *Shobogenzo* (Chapter 10).

authoritative Upanishads

Of the large number of Upanishads,[9] the following ten, called "principal Upanishads," are considered authoritative: *Isa, Kena, Katha, Prasna, Mundaka, Mandukya, Taittiriya, Aitareya, Chandogya,* and *Brihadaranyaka*. To ensure an adequate treatment of the select classics within the length of this guide, our discussion will be confined to only five of the principal Upanishads: *Isa, Kena, Katha, Chandogya,* and *Brihadaranyaka*.[10] Occasional references to the rest of the principal Upanishads will be made when it is necessary.

---

**DOING PHILOSOPHY**
*Are the Upanishads Philosophy Texts?*

Response (1): The Upanishads are not philosophy texts.

Eknath Easwaran: "Yet the Upanishads are not philosophy. They do not explain or develop a line of argument. They are *darshana*, 'something seen,' and the student to whom they were taught was expected not only to listen to the words but to *realize* them: that is, to make their truths an integral part of character, conduct, and consciousness."[11]    → apply truths into character

---

8  *Katha*, 1.23–26, in *A Source Book in Indian Philosophy*, Sarvepalli Radhakrishnan and Charles A. Moore, eds. (Princeton: Princeton University Press, 1967). Unless otherwise noted, further quotations from the Upanishads will be from this translation.

9  The traditional number is 108, though it may very well be more than that.

10  The literal meanings for the titles of these Upanishads are respectively "the ruler of the self" (*Isa*), "by whom and what" (*Kena*), "after death" (*Katha*), "the uprising of sacred song" (*Chandogya*), and "teachings from the great forest" (*Brihadaranyaka*). It is uncertain which individual sages authored the Upanishads—ancient Indians in general had less concern for authorship and chronology than for the content of thoughts. The truths revealed in them are believed to be universal and eternal; whoever formulated them is generally considered irrelevant.

11  *The Upanishads*, trans. Eknath Easwaran (Tomales, CA: Nilgiri Press, 2007), 22–23.

Response (2): The Upanishads are philosophy texts.

Joel Kupperman: "The Upanishads also are highly serious philosophy. They develop a sophisticated and (on the whole) highly consistent world picture, a metaphysics that in some respects parallels that developed much later by Baruch Spinoza in the West. As in Spinoza's case, the metaphysics generates an ethics. What the world really is like tells you what the best way is to live."[12]

Kupperman added that the Upanishads are texts of philosophy because they present "arguments, which may be explicit or implicit, [and they do not merely offer] an appeal to faith or devotion (or to reliance on the authority of the religious text) but instead an argued set of views that then is open to counterargument.[13]

Are the Upanishads philosophical texts? Are Easwaran and Kupperman in conflict in their views on the nature of the Upanishads? Is the defining characteristic of a philosophical text that of an explicit or implicit argument? Is "philosophy" rather a family resemblance concept which does not have one essential feature among its variety of uses? Can philosophy take many faces? (Similar questions will re-surface when we later explore the nature of Chan or Zen in Chapters 9 and 10 of this book.)

## WHO AM I, REALLY?—THE SEARCH FOR *ATMAN*

French biologist Jacques Monod (1910–76) wrote, "We would like to think ourselves necessary, inevitable, ordained from all eternity. All religions, nearly all philosophies, and even a part of science testify to the unwearying, heroic effort of mankind desperately denying its own contingency."[14] Indeed, the idea that our existence may be contingent, or entirely due to chance, can be a very unsettling thought. For this reason, human beings have expended much intellectual effort to resist this notion. The Upanishads reflect precisely such a heroic effort. The Upanishadic sages assure us that while we may be mortal and contingent, and thus suffer, the "I" that is mortal is but an illusion; it is not the ultimate "I." The ultimate "I" is that which we can realize, and once we realize it, we will no longer suffer. Thus, the *Chandogya* issues the invitation, "Come! Let us search out that Self, the Self by searching out whom one obtains all worlds and

---

12 Joel J. Kupperman, *Classic Asian Philosophy: A Guide to the Essential Texts* (New York: Oxford University Press, 2001), 3.
13 Kupperman, 4.
14 Jacques Monod, *Chance and Necessity*, Austryn Wainhouse, trans. (New York: Vintage Books, 1972), 44.

*we lack skills that needed to be taught and were taught, therefore have established incorrect / bad habits of how to handle life*

*overcome Demons*

all desires!"[15] The most important among the desires is to be "liberated from the mouth of death."[16] So the essential question is "Who am I, *really*?"

*Diff. between who am I & who are you*

The question "Who am I?" is very different from the question "Who are you?" While you may encounter the second question from time to time in everyday life, the first question rarely occurs to you, except perhaps when you are in a pensive mood. When asked "Who are you?" you generally respond by giving your name, occupation, social roles, and so on. You may even reply, "I am *this* physical body," while pointing to yourself. However, when a guru asks the question, "Who are you?" he is not after the sorts of responses you may give in an everyday conversation. He is challenging you to seriously consider the first question—"Who am I, *really*?" That is, what is the subject or the experiencing agent that makes my experience (or anyone else's) possible?

Unlike the run-of-the-mill responses to the second question, the answer to the first question does not come easily. Normally, you all have a strong sense of an enduring "I," even though you are aware that you are undergoing constant change, physically and mentally. But when you attempt to specify what you are by filling in the blank, "I am _____," you may find that the real "I" keeps eluding you. No matter what information you insert in the blank, the resultant statement is still nowhere close to capturing the experiencing agent that you know as "I." Since the filling-in-the-blank tactic merely looks at the "I" from an outsider's, or non-reflexive, perspective,[17] it paradoxically dismisses the true experiencing "I" altogether, and renders the "I" into a "he," "she," or "it."

*example of story*

This paradoxical dismissal of the "I" from a non-reflexive perspective is aptly illustrated in a humorous tale. Once upon a time in ancient China, a monk had been found guilty of a crime and was sentenced to a jail confinement in a remote town. He was being transported to the remote town by a slow-witted warden. Aware of his own absent-mindedness, the warden conscientiously made a list of everything he had to take care of, which reads "the verdict document, an umbrella, the wooden pillory (for the monk), the key to the pillory, the monk, and myself." Proud of being so organized this time, the warden gleefully said to himself while putting the note in his pocket, "This time I am not going to leave behind anything." Half way into their journey, they stopped at a restaurant for a short break. The cunning monk talked the warden into ordering some wine. Soon the warden drank more than he could absorb and collapsed at the table. The monk quickly lifted the warden's key and unlocked his wooden pillory. Being the prankster that he was, the monk shaved the warden's head before slipping away! When the warden came around, he immediately retrieved his note to see if anything was missing. He checked the items on the list one by one, "the verdict document, the umbrella, the wooden pillory (now around his own neck), the key to the pillory, and ... where's the monk?" Puzzled, he scratched his head. But to his horror, he felt a clean shaven head and let out a scream, "Heavens! Where is *I*?"

---

15  *Chandogya*, VIII.vii.2; see VIII.xii.6 and *Brihadaranyaka*, II.iv.6.

16  *Katha*, III.15.

17  A sword cannot cut itself, and a finger cannot touch itself. We call the sword and the finger "non-reflexive."

In asking "Who am I?" the "I" is performing a reflexive action, in which the "I" is simultaneously the speaker and the addressee, or the asking-"I" and the addressee-"I" respectively. Since the asking-"I" and the addressee-"I" are one, the asking-"I" becomes eclipsed at the utterance of the question. The situation is analogous to the seeing-eye that can never be in the field of vision and thus can never see itself.[18] The precondition of seeing is a duality where the one seeing and the one seen are not the same, as remarked by one Upanishadic sage, "For where there is a duality (*dvaita*), as it were (*iva*), there one sees another.... where, verily, everything has become just one's own self ... then whereby and whom would one see?"[19] What makes the tale of the slow-witted warden humorous is his complete failure to grasp the reflexive nature of the question—that the addressee-"I" and the asking-"I" are in fact one.

The question "Who am I?" is then much more profound than it appears. Appreciating the reflexive nature of the question, as already suggested, is the first step toward getting a grip on it. Further, the question calls for a different kind of "knowing" (where the subject and the object are dissolved into one), not a "knowing" of what one is, outwardly and temporally, but a knowing of what one-in-itself is—that is, the true nature of the asking-"I" that persists through time and change, which the Upanishads call *Atman*.[20] As mentioned earlier, the Upanishads reflect a heroic effort to go beyond our contingency, that is, our outward and temporal "I."

In this regard, the philosophical quest for the true self articulated in the Upanishads is quite similar to the philosophical visions found in the West, such as Parmenides' idea of Being, Plato's theory of Forms, and Kant's notion of the "Thing-in-itself." All these philosophers of the West subscribe to a dualism of appearance versus reality. For the two ancient Greek sages, the world of appearance is characterized by change and the world of reality by permanence, or constancy. For Kant, the dualism translates into the distinction between a *phenomenon* (a thing as it appears to us) and a *noumenon* (a thing-in-itself)—that is, between that which is within the limit of ordinary human knowledge and that which transcends it.

But how do the Upanishads establish the existence of *Atman,* or the unchanging Self? In the *Brihadaranyaka,* the answer to this question is given in an array of analogies: "As there can be no water without the sea, no touch without the skin, no smell without the nose, no taste without the tongue, no form without the eye, no sound without the ear, no thought without the mind, no wisdom without the heart, no work without hands, no walking without feet, no scriptures without words, so there can be nothing without

---

18  See Wittgenstein: "For the field of sight is not a form like this"

Eye—

(Ludwig Wittgenstein, *Tractatus Logico-Philosophicus*, Bertrand Russell and C.K. Ogden, eds. [New York: Cosimo Classics, 2010], 5.6331).
19  *Brihadaranyaka*, II.iv.14.
20  *Atman* literally means "breath"; etymologically it may be related to the German term *atmen* meaning "breath."

the Self" (II.iv:11). This verse enumerates a series of pairs: water/sea, touch/skin, smell/ nose, taste/tongue, form/eye, sound/ear, thought/mind, wisdom/heart, work/hands, walking/feet, and scriptures/words. The point is that the second element of each pair is that which gives rise to the first element, or that the existence of which is presupposed by the first element.

Is this argument compelling? Surely we may agree that "there can be no smell without the nose, no taste without the tongue" and so on, but we need not concede that "there can be nothing without the Self." Logically, it is quite possible that the alleged Self may simply be the aggregate of effects produced by the skin, the nose, the tongue, the eye, the ear, the mind, and so on. In other words, once we have listed the skin, the nose, the tongue, the eye, and so on, along with their corresponding effects, we may have already exhausted our description of our selves. There may be nothing above or beyond the items on the list.

---

### DOING PHILOSOPHY
#### "I" (Atman) or Not "I": Is There a Subject behind Consciousness?

The idea of *Atman* in the Upanishads finds certain echoes in the West. Descartes (1596–1650) contends "*Cogito ergo sum*" ("I think, therefore I am") because for him the act of doubting (a kind of thinking or consciousness) itself implies a subject that doubts.

However, by sharp contrast, Hume (1711–76) argues that actually our conception of a self is merely "a bundle of experiences." And in the same spirit with Hume's, Wittgenstein (1889–1951) questions the idea of a transcendent Self with the analogy of the eye and the field of sight: "Where in the world is a metaphysical subject to be found? You will say that this is exactly like the case of the eye and the visual field. But really you do not see the eye. And nothing in the visual field allows you to infer that it is seen by an eye."[21]

Which view is more plausible? The Upanishads', Descartes', Hume's, or Wittgenstein's? Does the proposition "It is raining" imply that the "It" must refer to an agent/subject that is raining? Should we understand "I" (in "I think, therefore I am") in the same way as we understand the "It" (in "It is raining")? More importantly, what implications would answers to these questions have on cognition, self-identity, and meaning of life?

---

In *Chandogya*, one of the oldest and best-known Upanishads, the search for the true Self at one point has gone through a long list of possibilities: Name, Speech, Mind (*manas*), Conception (*samkalpa*), Thought (*citta*), Meditation (*dhyana*), Understanding

---

21  *Tractatus* 5.633.

*Chandogya – an upanishad.* [handwritten]

(*vijnana*), Strength, Food, Water, Heat, Space, Memory, Hope, and Life (*prana*, breath).[22] The list contains physical elements as well as mental elements, but because of the briefness of the verses, the connections between these elements are rather obscure. It appears that the sages of the *Chandogya* were still groping for some ultimate element that could be regarded as the true Self.

At another place in the same text, Indra's story of progressive search for the *Atman* is elaborated on.[23] The story opens with a conversation between Prajapati, the lord of creatures, and his two disciples, Indra and Virochana, after they have been living with him for thirty-two years. Prajapati asks them why they have been with him so long. In reply, they say that they had heard of his inspiring teachings and wanted to realize the Self.

Now, taking advantage of this teachable moment, Prajapati provides further instructions on the nature of the true Self. Prajapati asks them to look at their reflections in a pan of water and tell him what they see. They reply that they have seen the Self, even the hair and the nails. Then, Prajapati asks them to get dressed up and then look at their reflections again. This time they reply that they have seen the Self, well-dressed and well adorned. Virochana, who is from among the godless, concludes from this that the true Self is the body and its desires, so he goes to the godless and begins to teach them to indulge the senses and to find pleasure in this world. Indra, who is from among the gods, begins to question this view on his way to the gods. He sees a danger in identifying the Self with the body. He reasons:

> Just as, indeed, that one [i.e., the bodily self] is well-ornamented when this
> body (*sarira*) is well-ornamented, well-dressed when this is well-dressed,   *ornament*
> adorned when this is adorned, even so that one is blind when this is blind,    *perishes*
> lame when this is lame, maimed when this is maimed. It perishes immedi-       *no body*
> ately upon the perishing of this body. I see nothing enjoyable in this.[24]    *in this* [handwritten]

Therefore, unhappy with Prajapati's first response, Indra goes back to Prajapati for a second round of instruction. Impressed with Indra's insight behind his question, Prajapati invites him to live with him for another thirty-two years. Then he tells him that what moves about in joy in the dreaming state is the true Self. But Indra is still not satisfied with this answer. He reasons:

> In the dreaming state, it is true, the Self is not blind when the body is blind,
> nor lame when the body is lame, nor paralyzed when the body is paralyzed,
> nor slain when the body is slain. Yet in dreams the Self may appear to suffer
> and to be slain; it may become conscious of pain and even weep. In such
> knowledge I see no value.[25]

---

22  *Chandogya*, VII.1, VIII.1, ff.
23  See *Chandogya*, VIII.viii–xi.
24  *Chandogya*, VIII.ix.1.
25  *Chandogya*, VIII.x.1–2 (trans. Eknath Easwaran).

Indra returns to Prajapati for the third time and is invited to stay with his master for another thirty-two years. This time, the teacher tells Indra that it is in a state of dreamless sleep that the true Self is found. But Indra still questions the answer: "In the state of sleep one is not aware of oneself (*atmanam*) or of any other. The state of dreamless sleep is very close to extinction. In this knowledge I see no value."[26]

So Indra approaches to Prajapati for yet another answer, which (as you can guess by now) means another period of residency—five years this time. It is in this final round of instruction that Prajapati explains that the true Self is not the physical body, though it dwells in the body; instead it is the master and foundation of the body, and that the true Self can only be realized in a state of freedom from attachment:

> In that state, free from attachment, they [the metaphysical subjects or states of consciousness] move at will, laughing, playing, and rejoicing. They know the Self is not this body, but only tied to it for a time as an ox is tied to its cart. Whenever one sees, smells, speaks, hears, or thinks, they know it is the Self that sees, smells, speaks, hears, and thinks; the senses are but his instruments.[27]

Unlike the analogical argument we have seen in the *Brihadaranyaka*, the story of Indra is in fact a series of *ad absurdum* arguments couched in a narrative form. As the story unfolds, we see different ideas of the true Self presented and refuted. The Self is first identified with physical appearance or the body, but the problem with this view, as Indra soon realizes, is that the body (thus the Self) would perish when the body dies. Then, the Self is equated with a dream self, but as noticed by Indra, this dream self would still be subject to pain, suffering, and destruction. Next, the Self is identified with a self in an unconscious, dreamless state, which is not subject to pain, suffering, and destruction, but this self would not be aware of itself either. Finally, the answer is revealed: the Self is what makes possible all the preceding conceptions of self—namely, waking experience (in space and time), dreaming experience (not in space and time), and the dreamless self (all faculties unified).

The story of Indra shows that the "Upanishads refuse to identify the Self with the body, or the series of mental states or the presentation continuum or the stream of consciousness."[28] Instead, they maintain that the true Self must be the very metaphysical foundation for all physical and mental phenomena.[29] It is a state of unitive

---

26 *Chandogya*, VIII.xi.2 (trans. Eknath Easwaran).
27 *Chandogya*, VIII.xii.2 (trans. Eknath Easwaran).
28 Sarvepalli Radhakrishnan, *Indian Philosophy*, Vol.1 (London: George Allen &Unwin, 1958), 159.
29 A parallel transcendent foundation of the *prana* (a vital, life-sustaining force or energy of living beings and vital energy) is also found in the Upanishads (see *Chandogya*, V.1.6–12). As Deussen has pointed out, "The superiority of the *prana* to the other vital organs (eye, ear, speech, manas [mind], etc.) is illustrated by the parable of the rivalry of the organs, which forms a favorite theme of the Upanishads. In order to test which of them is the most essential, the *pranas* (eye, ear, speech, etc.) one after another leave the body, which nevertheless still continues to exist; but when the *prana* proposes to depart, they become conscious that none of them can exist without it." (Paul Deussen, *The Philosophy of the Upanishads*, A.S. Geden, trans. [Edinburgh: T & T Clark, 1908], 103–04).

consciousness where the experiencing (subject) and the experienced (object) are fused into one. It is believed to be an immortal bliss that is radically different from any common conditioned, object-directed, pleasure. In the language of the *Brihadaranyaka*, "this true Self is behind all sensing and knowing, it is an unseen Seer. He is the unseen Seer, the unheard Hearer, the unthought Thinker, the ununderstood Understander. Other than He there is no seer. Other than He there is no hearer. Other than He there is no thinker. Other than He there is no understander. He is your Self, the Inner Controller, the Immortal."[30]

In addition to the analogical argument and the *ad absurdum* argument we have explored, the notion of the true Self is also explained through allegories in the Upanishads. One such example is the allegory of the lord of the chariot found in the *Katha.* In this allegory, the body is likened to a chariot; the discriminating intellect the chariot driver; the mind the reins; the senses the horses; the selfish desires the roads; and the Self the lord of the chariot. The chariot, the chariot driver, the reins, and the horses are the interrelated components that are directly involved in the driving of the chariot. The lord of the chariot, however, is not directly involved in the driving itself, but merely issues commands to the driver and enjoys the ride. All the four components are really his instruments. The body, the intellect, the mind, and the senses are the things that make this earthly life possible, but they are subject to pleasure, pain, and sorrow. The Self, on the other hand, is undifferentiated consciousness. It is behind bodily existence, and thus beyond pleasure and sorrow, and free from the jaws of death.[31]

This structural analysis of the Self is similar to, though more sophisticated than, Plato's chariot allegory of the structure of the soul.[32] In Plato's chariot allegory there are two horses, a white one and a black one, and a charioteer. The unruly and hot-blooded black steed symbolizes one's desire or appetite; the white horse, one's spirit (animatedness); and the charioteer, one's reason. The key difference between the two allegories is that in the *Katha*, the Self is behind and beyond both physical and mental faculties (including reason), whereas with Plato it is reason that is reining in desire and spirit.

In sum, what is the Self or *Atman* according to the Upanishads? Five main points have emerged in our discussion on the nature of *Atman*:

1. *Atman* is not reduced to any particular thing or phenomenon, physical or mental.
2. *Atman* is not absolute void or nothingness either.
3. *Atman* is what makes possible the experiential self (senses and mental phenomena).
4. *Atman* is the invisible, eternal, and metaphysical agent.
5. *Atman* is a blissful, unitive state of consciousness where any duality is totally dissolved.

30  *Brihadaranyaka*, III.vii.23, also see *Brihadaranyaka*, III.viii.8, 11.
31  See *Katha*, I.iii.3–16.
32  See *Phaedrus*, sections 246a–254e.

If everything is fused together in *Atman*, then one may query: If *Atman* does not have any individuating properties—that is, concrete properties that allow us to distinguish one person from another—wouldn't we plunge right into the abyss of contradiction when we realize our true Self—for we lose our individual identity just when we realize our true Self? How could a featureless Self be *my* true Self? Wouldn't the notion of *Atman* negate altogether the legitimacy of the problem of personal identity, which is a major preoccupation in the philosophical tradition of the West? These are all important questions that invite further engagement. To be sure, for the Upanishadic sages, the existence of a metaphysical Self is unquestionable, so they ask confidently, "If he [Self] were not there, who would breathe, who live?"[33] They are convinced that there is a subject in us "which is awake even in our sleep."[34] But are they correct? Given that this true Self is unknowable in any subject-object dualistic way, how can they be so confident that it is eternal, blissful, etc.?

### WHAT IS THERE, *ULTIMATELY*?—THE SEARCH FOR *BRAHMAN*

The question of "What is ultimately there?" is no less philosophical than the question of "Who am I, *really*?" According to the Upanishads, the answers to both questions converge in the conclusion that the "I" (*Atman*) is identified with Ultimate Reality (*Brahman*)—that is, the essence of an individual is also the essence of Ultimate Reality; each person belongs to the Ultimate Reality just as any other does. Before delving into the issue of what it is to say the *Atman* is identified with *Brahman*, we need to first explore the notion of *Brahman, or Ultimate Reality*. So, what is ultimately there?

Is the world a mechanical amalgamation of diverse objects or events as they ordinarily appear to us? Or is there an underlying unity or oneness to diversity and change? This is one of the key questions that the Upanishads asked. Following the monotheistic tendency in the Vedas, the Upanishads see a unitary reality behind the apparent diversity and constant change in the world. The sages of the Upanishads do not merely wonder at the existence of the universe; they wonder at the unity that lies in its ultimate foundation—*Brahman*. "The term *Brahman* comes from the Sanskrit root *brh* meaning 'to burst forth' and suggests the concept of the *Ground of all Being* from which everything emanates."[35]

Like the search for *Atman*, the search for *Brahman* in the Upanishads also has an exploratory quality. In the *Brihadaranyaka*, for example, *Yajnavalkya* explains to his pupil *Gargi* that the diverse phenomena in the world are all ultimately dependent upon *Brahman* as the ground of their existence. Indeed, the world is "woven" from successive elements: water, wind, atmosphere-worlds, Gandharvas (male nature spirits), the sun, the moon, the stars, the Hindu gods Indra and Prajapati, and ultimately *Brahman*.[36] The *Chandogya* presents a similar, though much more sophisticated, view

---

33  *Taittiriya*, II.vii.1.
34  *Katha*, II.ii.8.
35  Jeaneane Fowler, *Hinduism—Beliefs and Practices* (Eastbourne, UK: Sussex Academic Press, 1997), 114.
36  See *Brihadaranyaka*, III.vi.

that incorporates both mental and physical elements: Name—Speech—Mind (*manas*)—Conception (*samkalpa*)—Thought (*citta*)—Meditation (*dhyana*)—Understanding (*vijnana*)—Strength—Food—Water—Heat—Space (*akasa*)—Memory—Hope—Life (*prana*, breath)—*Brahman*.[37] While the manner in which various elements are linked in the two places may seem speculative and obscure to us, they clearly illustrate the Upanishadic belief of an underlying ultimate reality and the intensity of the quest to understand it.

But what does understanding *Brahman* consist in? To understand *Brahman* (Reality-in-itself) is not merely to understand any or even all particular things in the world. Reality-in-itself is that which underlies all particular things; it is the "common ground," as it were, of all that exists. This type of understanding calls for conceptual abstraction.

To illustrate how abstraction works, let us consider a particular thing like an apple. What is an apple? One way of responding to this question is to name the class of things to which an apple belongs, hence the statement "An apple is a fruit." This way of thinking that reasons from a particular thing to its class membership is called abstraction. Should we iterate the process, we can ask "What is a fruit?" to which we may respond "It is a kind of food." To take it to the next level of abstraction, we can inquire, "What is food?" If we keep iterating the process of abstraction, we probably will come to say that a particular thing is merely a *thing*. Once we reach this point, we may wonder if there may still be another level of abstraction. Many people believe that there is not, but some would argue that underlying the innumerable things or beings in the world is the ultimate level of abstraction—"Being."

Some readers might have already noticed that, at each escalation of abstraction, the extension of a term, or the number of objects covered by the term, broadens while the number of features or attributes required to define the term diminishes. The concept of food, for example, is characterized with fewer features than the concept of fruit; however, the term "food" denotes more edible things than does the term "fruit." Following this line of reasoning, we can conclude that the concept of Being, which is the highest level of abstraction, should be "featureless" yet have maximal extension. For example, Being does not have any concrete or specific attributes as does a particular object like an apple. If we accept this view, it would be odd to say that Being is as sweet as an apple, for Being is a "no-thingness." The Upanishadic concept of *Brahman* resembles the notion of Being in precisely this respect: it is without attributes, or *nirguna*. The cognition of Being does not seem to yield any concrete, discursive knowledge, for the latter calls for identification and distinction. To have concrete knowledge of a particular thing implies that we can say what it is and how it differs from other things. No wonder Hegel, in his Preface of *The Phenomenology of Spirit*, called the cognition of the Absolute [Being] vacuous, like watching cows in dark night: since all cows are black no articulated cognition is possible.[38]

But is this the only way of understanding Being? Must Being be conceived of as no-thingness? An alternative understanding is possible. If we take Being to be the Ultimate Reality that underlies every particular thing in the world, then it is equally reasonable to

---

37  See *Brihadaranyaka*, iii.ix.9 and *Chandogya*, vii.i.5 ff.
38  See *Hegel's Phenomenology of Spirit*, A.V. Miller, trans. (Oxford: Clarendon Press, 1977), 9.

conclude that Being encompasses all the features found in the particular things in the world, and in a deep (non-discursive) sense, whatever feature a particular object possesses is at the same time a feature of Being. Now, we must be careful not to conclude that Being is defined by or confined to the attributes of the particular things in the world. In other words, we may affirm that Being is red, blue, white and so on without saying that Being is defined by or confined to these attributes.

*Brahman* is like Being in this second understanding. Thus, *Brahman* has *saguna*, attributes. It is positively described as "bright," "pure," "wise," "intelligent," "encompassing," and "self-existent."[39] It is also described as "immortal" and with "unlimited freedom."[40]

But *Brahman* is not merely the sum of all particular objects or characteristics. To avoid equating *Brahman* with the particulars, the Upanishads tend to speak of *Brahman* in terms of negations (i.e., saying what it is not) rather than positive attributions (i.e., saying what it is). For example, *Brahman* is described as not open to the senses, "[n]o one soever sees Him [*Brahman*] with the eye, not by speech, not by mind, not by sight."[41] According to another verse, *Brahman* is "soundless, touchless, formless, imperishable."[42] And according to *Yajnavalkya*, *Brahman* is unbound, not injured, and not seized.[43]

In addition to the method of negation, the Upanishads also employ paradoxes, or apparently contradictory statements, in describing *Brahman*.[44] For example, in *Isha* 5 we find the following paradoxical pairs:

[1] It moves. It moves not.
[2] It is far, and It is near.
[3] It is within all this, and It is outside of all this.

How should we make sense of these pairs? A common reaction may be a sense of puzzlement. These verses simply defy the ordinary principles of logical reasoning. For example, let us substitute "It" with a particular object, say a car, and see what happens. Verse [1] will then read, "The car moves. [And] It moves not."—a conjunction. Now, if we take this conjunction to be describing two events happening at the same time, then we end up with a contradiction: "The car moves and does not move."[45] (Similar analysis can be made about [2] and [3].)

In religious discourse, paradoxes are commonly used to talk about divine or ultimate reality, which transcends ordinary experience. Paradoxes tease the mind in affirming

---

39  *Isha*, 8.

40  *Katha*, VI.1 and *Chandogya*, VII.xxiv.1, *Chandogya*, VII.xxv.2.

41  *Katha*, VI.9, 12.

42  *Katha*, III.15.

43  *Brihadaranyaka*, v.ii.3.

44  Both negative description and contradictory expressions are appropriated by Nagarjuna in expounding and defending the foundational insight of the Buddha—interdependent-arising. See chapter 3 of this book on Nagarjuna's *Fundamental Verses on the Middle Way*.

45  Contradictory expressions in language are not always unintelligible. Consider an everyday example when one expresses an ambivalent feeling: "I love him (her) *and* I hate him (her)."

that something both is and is not, in order to show up the inadequacy of common linguistic expressions to ascribe definitively any positive but limited qualities to the divine. Since *Brahman* is Ultimate Reality, it is not a concrete object and is thus boundless and non-objectified. Any linguistic expression that is used to describe concrete objects (call it "thing language") cannot adequately capture what Being is.

Or, perhaps we can see these apparently contradictory pairs as being both true, in different senses. Let me illustrate this point with the water cycle on earth. The water on earth "moves" in the sense that it constantly changes its forms and states. However, it "moves not" in the sense that the total amount of water on this planet remains constant over time. Thus, we can say that the water on this planet both "moves" and "moves not." By the same token, we can say that the water ("Being") on this planet is here (in a particular lake, for example) and not here (beyond this lake), it is near and far, and it is everywhere.[46]

---

**DOING PHILOSOPHY**
*More Contradictory Verses*

Here is another example of apparently contradictory verses from the Upanishads:

Smaller than a grain of rice, smaller than a grain of barley, smaller than a mustard seed, smaller than a grain of millet, smaller even than the kernel of a grain of millet is the Self. This is the Self dwelling in my heart, greater than the earth, greater than the sky, greater than all the worlds.[47]

How do you customarily respond to contradictory verses? Can you explain how they may be meaningful? Why do you think the authors of the Upanishads employ such apparently contradictory verses? Can they speak of Ultimate Reality without using such contradictory verses? Are there any other ways of approaching and understanding Ultimate Reality?

---

If *Brahman* is everywhere, why is it not seen, known, or realized? The Upanishads argue that this is the case because we customarily mistake specific things (appearance) for *Brahman* (Reality), and because we use dualistic thinking to understand *Brahman*—which is beyond all forms of duality. (Dualistic thinking is a mode of thought that separates the experiencing subject from what is experienced. Dualistic thinking refers to the notion that the subject can observe or think about that which is not the subject

---

46 If the water cycle illustration makes sense, then the Upanishads seem to subscribe to a mythic version of the law of conservation of energy—the conservation of cosmic spirit, awareness, or life power (*Brahman*).
47 *Chandogya*, III.14.3.

from a completely detached point of view.) The following two passages from the Upanishads can illustrate the point.

> A. Where one sees nothing else, hears nothing else, understands nothing else—that is a plenum [a complete fullness]. But where one sees something else—that is the small. Verily, the plenum is the same as the immortal; but the small is the same as the mortal.[48]

> B. Him [*Brahman*] they see not, for [as seen] he is incomplete. When breathing, he becomes breath by name; when speaking, voice; when seeing, the eye; when hearing, the ear; when thinking, the mind: these are merely the names of his acts. Whoever worships one or another of these—he knows not; for he is incomplete with one or another of these. One should worship with the thought that he is just one's self, for therein all these become one. That same thing, namely, this self, is the trace of this All, for by it one knows this All ... He finds fame and praise who knows this ...[49]

According to passage (A), *Brahman* is a plenum—one unitary whole, not isolated and fragmented pieces. But the whole is not commonly perceptible or realized. What can commonly be seen is "something else," namely the particular things or objects that are small or partial. As long as we are only looking at the small or the partial, we cannot know the underlying whole. In other words, if we know only the small, which is mortal or changing, we cannot understand the whole, which is immortal or constant. It is only through "seeing" or realizing the immortal whole in a unitary state of consciousness that one can expect true knowledge and salvation. Seeing the small is like a number of blind people each touching different parts of an elephant, but each naively trusting that the part they touch is the true shape of the elephant.

Passage (B) makes it more explicit why *Brahman* is not usually seen. Using anthropomorphic language, the passage states that all particulars are but manifestations of the great all-pervading *Brahman*, and all the manifestations are merely the names of *Brahman*'s acts. When people are distracted by the limited, particular manifestations or the names, they do not see the unitary whole or the ultimate agent beneath all the various manifestations. The right thought one should have is to penetrate the surface illusion (*maya*) of particular manifestations—because they do not have independent existence without being grounded in *Brahman*. One will then realize *Brahman* directly.

As mentioned earlier, the "small," the "incomplete," and the "names" issue from dualistic thinking, but in order to properly understand *Brahman*, an entirely different way of thinking is called for. This alternative way of thinking relies on introspection, rather than sensory perception. Thus the *Katha* explains,

---

48  *Chandogya*, VII.xxiv.1.
49  *Brihadaranyaka*, I.iv.7.

The Self-existent pierced the openings [of the senses] outward;
Therefore one looks outward, not within himself.
A certain wise man, while seeking immortality,
introspectively beheld the Self face to face.[50]

It is clear that the sages of the Upanishads are less interested in the study of external physical objects for the purpose of knowing them objectively, and they are more interested in introspectively knowing one's true Self. In the Upanishads, the dualistic way of knowing things is not the sole way of knowing, nor the most important way of knowing.

**DOING PHILOSOPHY**
Brahman *versus God (in the Hebrew Bible)*

Is *Brahman* the same as God in the Hebrew Bible? Here are some points of comparison and contrast:

1. Like God, who is sometimes characterized as the Ground of Being, *Brahman* is the ultimate principle and source of the world. "On it all the worlds do rest; and no one soever goes beyond it."[51] It is "[o]n a part of just this bliss [from *Brahman* that] other creatures have their living."[52] It is as if all things and events in the world were like the innumerous rays of the sun, while the sun itself is the ground, source, the uniting-point of all the rays.[53]
2. Just as no question can be legitimately asked about who or what had created God, so is it the case with *Brahman*.[54]
3. It is possible and necessary to realize that the "I" is *Brahman* in the Upanishads;[55] it is not possible nor allowed to say the "I" is God in the Hebrew Bible.

God created the world *ex nihilo* whereas *Brahman self-created* itself from Being. At one place in the Upanishads, the beginning of the world was said to be just "Being (*sat*), one only, without a second," who procreated himself.[56] At another, the world in the beginning was first "Self (*Atman*) alone in the form of a Person" and then fell into "two pieces"—a husband and a wife. And the rest of

---

50 *Katha*, IV.1.
51 *Katha*, v.8; see also *Katha*, VI.1.
52 *Brihadaranyaka*, IV.iii.32.
53 See *Brihadaranyaka*, II.iv.11.
54 See *Brihadaranyaka*, III.vi.
55 See *Isha*, 16.
56 *Chandogya*, IV.ii.1–3; see also *Aitareya*, I.i.1–4.

procreation was all from this couple.[57] In a similar vein, the seeming emptiness (non-thingness) in the seeds of the nyagrodha (banyan) tree does not mean complete void. It actually contains all the life, the source, the producing power of the tree. It is from the seed's "hidden essence" that "a whole nyagrodha tree will grow."[58] By analogy, the Self (*Brahman*), though unperceived, is the First Cause,[59] the ground of existence,[60] and the source of life for all creatures.[61]

## WHAT I AM "IS" WHAT THERE IS—*ATMAN* "IS" *BRAHMAN*

In the Upanishads, the search for the true Self and the search for Ultimate Reality eventually converge, hence the most important claim of the entire Upanishads: "That Thou Art" (*Tat Tvam Asi*), or *Atman* "is" *Brahman*.[62] While we have treated *Atman* and *Brahman* as provisionally separate in the preceding sections, it is time now to see in what sense they are identical to each other.

To make sense of the identification of *Atman* with *Brahman*, it is important to first clarify the notion of identity as expressed through the different uses of the verb "is" in the formula of "A is B."[63] The following examples, though not exhaustive, illustrate the diversity of meanings carried by the verb "is":

(1) 2 plus 2 is 4 (equating).
(2) The rose is red (attributing/predicating).
(3) Mr. Li is from Beijing (indicating origin).
(4) Toronto is in Ontario (indicating location).
(5) John is Peter's brother (associating).
(6) This book is Jonathan's (possessing).
(7) A bear is an animal (classifying).
. . . .
(x) *Atman* "is" *Brahman* (?)

What is the crucial difference between the use of "is" in (x) and in the other uses on the list? It is that in cases (1) to (7), on both sides of the "is" are particular, separate things or beings, whereas in case (x), both "A" and "B" are Being itself, albeit with two

---

57  In *Brihadaranyaka*, I.iv.1–5.
58  *Chandogya*, VI.xii.2.
59  *Shvetashvatara*, I.2.
60  *Shvetashvatara*, I.7.
61  *Isha*, 16.
62  *Chandogya*, VI.ix.4, VI.xii.3.
63  In a negative statement of the form of "A is not B," "is not" can have different senses too. For example, the ancient Chinese logician Gong Sunlong's (c. 279–248 BCE) famous proposition "A white horse is not a horse" can mean (1) "A white horse (concept) is not identical to a horse (concept)"—as the latter clearly is wider in extension, including black horse, red horse, etc., or (2) "A white horse is not a kind of horse," which is obviously a nonsensical expression. Gong Sunlong intended to use the proposition in the first sense.

different names. So, to say "*Atman* 'is' *Brahman*" is not to say that *two* things are identical, but to say that two different names of Being refer to the same Being, analogous to the example, "The Morning Star is the Evening Star," where both names refer to Venus. Just as "the Morning Star" and "the Evening Star" are numerically identical, so are *Atman* and *Brahman*.

In the claim "*Tat Tvam Asi*," if "*tat*" (that) is taken to refer to *Brahman* and "*tvam*" (thou) is taken to refer to *jiva* (embodied self or ego),[64] then it is obviously false to equate the *tat* (*Brahman*), which is limitless, with the *tvam* (*jiva*), which is subject to the limitation of being embodied self. However, if "*tat*" is understood as *Brahman*, and "*tvam*" is also understood as Being that underlies the embodied self, then it is possible and meaningful to speak of the absolute identity between the two apparently different "things." In this understanding, that is, if we treat "*tat*" and "*tvam*" as two things, they are qualitatively identical. However, they are not really two things, and to say that "*Atman* 'is' *Brahman*" is not to affirm some kind of part-whole relationship, where *Atman* is conceived of as a part of *Brahman* spatially or functionally (see case [4] and [7] above). Rather, it is to say that *Atman* and *Brahman* are in essence not two different things, and therefore numerically identical.

Let's illustrate the identity of *Atman* and *Brahman* with a different analogy, the analogy of $H_2O$ and its three states—solid, fluid, and vapour. If we take $H_2O$ to symbolize *Brahman*, and take ice, water, and vapour to represent embodied selves (*jiva*), then due to the limitation of ice (solid state), there is no identity between $H_2O$ and ice, since $H_2O$ embraces more states than just that of solidness, and since ice may not "realize" its true nature of $H_2O$ness—because it is confined to its superficial and accidental feature of solidness. But if we look at the true nature of ice, it is nothing other than $H_2O$. Thus, in this latter sense, it is possible to make an identity statement: "Ice (water, or vapour) is $H_2O$." Conversely, it is also possible to make an identity statement: "$H_2O$ is 'realized' ice (water, or vapour)."[65]

The ancient Indian sages maintain that people may not realize that their true Selves are in fact of the same nature as *Brahman* because of egoistic thinking, which focuses on their particular body, form, location, vision, knowledge, and so on. However, when people transcend such thinking, they are in the position to realize that their true Self "is" in fact *Brahman*—hence "*Atman* 'is' *Brahman*." "[T]hey see themselves in everyone and everyone in themselves"[66]—"the indivisible unity of life."[67] This, I think, is the real significance of "*Atman* is *Brahman*."[68]

---

64  The embodied self or the individual self is the *Atman* coupled with the bodily senses (see *Chandogya*, VIII.xii.3). According to Eliot Deutsch, *jiva* is either taken to be a mirror or reflection of *Atman*, or as a limitation of *Atman*. Yet in both cases, "*Jiva* qua *jiva* is an illusory appearance" (Eliot Deutsch, *World Philosophies* [Upper Saddle River, NJ: Prentice Hall, 1997], 28).

65  By the same token, rain water, well water, lake water, tap water, sewer water, toilet water, and even urine and diarrhea, are all forms of water. Equally illuminating is the analogy of clay in explaining the identity of *Atman* with *Brahman*. While a lump of clay can be made into a pot, a jug, or a plate, it is essentially and always clay (see *Chandogya*, VI.1).

66  *Brihadaranyaka*, IV.23; see also *Katha*, I.ii.8.

67  *Brihadaranyaka*, II.iv.14.

68  Compare this with Jesus' remark: "I [an enlightened self] am the way and the truth and the life" (John 14:6, New International Version).

The relationship of *Atman* and *Brahman* can be illustrated in yet another way. Think of an empty bottle. The air inside the bottle is exactly the same as the air outside the bottle. Of course, one can get fixated on the fact that the air inside the bottle is trapped in the bottle, and the fact of its confinement may mislead one to conclude that the air in the bottle is different from the air outside. This mistaken belief is analogous to the error that mistakes the *jiva* (embodied self) for the true Self—an error of limited vision that prevents one from seeing that there is an underlying reality to the *jiva*—the true Self, which is also *Brahman*. The failure to properly realize the true Self or *Brahman* is traceable to our ignorance and limited vision. Thus, in order to realize the insight that "*Atman* is *Brahman*," the bottle has to be broken; ignorance and limited vision have to be removed. Once the bottle is broken, the air inside the bottle is set free to unite with the air outside. By the same token, once our ignorance and limited vision are removed, we can see the essential sameness between *Atman* and *Brahman*.

The idea that the true Self, *Atman*, is also *Brahman* is empowering. It suggests that at the deepest level of existence all things or beings are equal in spite of their apparent differences. It reveals the tendency of the Upanishads to synthesize diversity or multiplicity (e.g., races, languages, and occupations) in India into a unified whole. It also has important ethical implications. It serves as an ethical calling which asks people to see their lives as a unified whole and to live accordingly. While the Judeo-Christian tradition advocates neighbourly love on the grounds that all human beings are created in the image of God and are therefore of equal worth, the Upanishads anchor the same spirit of love on a different—and rather counterintuitive—premise that the conventional dichotomy between one's self and others is but illusory, for all beings are the same at the deepest level of reality.

### KARMA AND TRANSMIGRATION

The idea of karma is a unique and fundamental component in the Upanishads. The term "karma" literally means "action" or "deed." The theory of karma affirms that all events are effects of certain preconditions and at the same time causes of certain effects. This universal principle of causality is held to be valid in all realms of existence—physical, psychological, and moral. The Upanishads, however, emphasize its workings in the domain of human moral actions. The *Brihadaranyaka* proclaims, "Verily, one becomes good by good actions, bad by bad action."[69] The theory of karma not only maintains that good actions and bad actions produce rewards and punishments respectively, but also that the ultimate balance of rewards and punishments is absolutely just. As Hiriyanna has explained, "whatever we knowingly do, will, sooner or later, bring us the result we merit; and there is no way of escape from it. What we sow, we must reap, that is, the karma doctrine signifies not merely that the events of our life are determined by antecedent causes, but also that there is absolute justice in the rewards and punishments that fall to our lot in life."[70]

---

69  *Brihadaranyaka*, III.ii.13; see also IV.iv.5 and 6.
70  M. Hiriyanna, *The Essentials of Indian Philosophy* (London: George Allen & Unwin, 1948), 46.

The idea of absolute retributive justice of karma, however, does not seem to entail a quantitative interpretation according to which the amount (or the manner) of punishment or reward one will receive is exactly the same as the amount (or the manner) of harm or good that one has done. For example, the idea does not imply that if you kicked a person three times, then, sooner or later you would get three kicks from someone.[71] It only means that good deeds will *necessarily* lead to reward and bad deeds to punishment.[72]

However, injustices occur routinely in the world, and the theory of karma seeks to account for them by speculating into how cause-and-effect relationships are maintained across lifetimes. Thus, the theory raises the issue of what may become of us after death. The answer to this question in the Upanishads is not annihilation, not eternal blessing in heaven, nor eternal punishment in hell, but the transmigration of the *jiva* along a scale of higher and lower beings: "those who are of pleasant conduct ... will enter a pleasant womb, either the womb of a *Brahmin* (priest), or the womb of a *ksatriya* (warrior), or the womb of a *vaisya* (merchant or artisan). Those who are of stinking conduct ... will enter a stinking womb, either the womb of a dog, or the womb of a swine, or the womb of a *candala* (outcaste)."[73] When one dies, everything bodily dissipates. What persists is only *jiva* with karma—the effects of one's actions.

The exact origin of the idea of transmigration is uncertain, though it may be inspired by the observation of the cycles of plants and animals. The *Katha* says, for example, "see how it was with those who came before / How it will be with those who are living / Like corn mortals ripen and fall; / Like corn they come up again."[74]

The theory of karma raises some interesting questions about whether the caste to which a person belongs is entirely determined by factors outside the person's control in present life. On one interpretation, people are simply born into their respective castes, as determined by the principle of karma, and the working of karma is beyond their control. India's notorious caste system (which is to some extent still alive in India today) has sometimes been interpreted through this deterministic understanding of karma.[75] However, on another interpretation, people belong to their respective social castes because of the actions they performed in their previous lives. In this view,

---

71 Similarly, the principle of "an eye for an eye" in the Hebrew Bible (see Leviticus 24:19–21, Exodus 21:22–25, and Deuteronomy 19:16–21) need not be taken literally.

72 The principle of karma assumes that the happiness and suffering we experience are in exact proportion to our good deeds and bad deeds respectively. Such a principle was not seen in *some* parts of the Hebrew and Christian Bibles. Job, for example, suffered greatly but not because he had committed corresponding sins. Jesus was tortured and killed for no sin of his own. To be sure, in both cases, Job and Jesus suffered for some cause (Job because of Satan; Jesus for the sake of others' redemption), but their suffering does not trace back in proportion to *their* respective misdeeds.

73 *Chandogya*, v.x.7.

74 i.i.6.

75 "The idea of *varna* (often translated as 'caste') originally may have been about one's propensities or temperaments (unactive/*Sattvika*, active/*Rajasika*, and inactive/*Tamasika*), not about one's social status or division of labour." See Satyavrata Diddhantalankar, "A Defence of Varna (Caste)," (excerpt) in *The Philosophical Quest: A Cross-Cultural Reader*, Gail M. Presbey, Karsten J. Struhl, and Richard E. Olsen, eds., second edition (New York: McGraw Hill, 1999), 591–95.

people's life circumstances and social status are not fixed once and for all: those born in a low caste could, through diligent practice of their respective duties, be reborn in a higher caste and vice versa.[76]

The theory of karma, then, is not to be equated with determinism or fatalism. According to the Upanishads, while the embodied *jiva* self is largely shaped by karma, the true Self is not. "The deed adheres not on the man [*Atman*]."[77] "He [*Atman*] does not become greater by good action, nor inferior by bad action. He is the lord of all, the overlord of beings, the protector of beings...."[78] Thus, the *jiva* self and the true Self represent two different layers or understandings of an individual, illustrated in the diagram below:

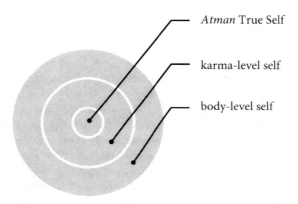

*Atman* True Self

karma-level self

body-level self

VARIOUS LEVELS OF A PERSON. *This diagram should not be understood purely spatially. The true Self is not an object hidden in the inner core of a person, as a walnut kernel hidden in its shell. The three levels of self are better seen as three levels of awareness of an individual.*

On the outermost layer is the body-level self that interacts with the physical world. In the intermediate layer is the karma-level self, which is subject to the principle of karma. In the innermost layer is the true Self. The true Self, in this conception of the human personality, is not subject to the chains of karma. While the karma-level self is likened to a bird on the tree of life that tastes its sweet and bitter fruits, the true Self (*Atman*) is like another bird on the same tree who "calmly observes" the other bird yet without being attached to or bothered by what she observes.[79]

From this perspective, the theory of karma does not contradict our intuitive faith in free will. This point has been aptly illustrated by Radhakrishnan with an analogy of a

---

76  Adding to the complexity of karma's operation, one's good or bad karma may also be transferred to another person under certain circumstances. For example, it is believed that "if someone lets a guest depart unfed, the guest will take away the host's good karma and leave behind his own bad karma" (Wendy Doniger, *The Hindus—An Alternative History* [New York: Penguin Press, 2009], 169).

77  *Isha*, 2.

78  *Brihadaranyaka*, IV.iv.22.

79  *Mundaka*, III.i.1.

card game. He remarks, "[t]he cards in the game of life are given to us. We do not select them. They are traced to our past karma, but we can call as we please, lead what suit we will, and as we play, we gain or lose. And there is freedom."[80] The cards can symbolize bodily and mental make-up (even social status) that we inherited from a previous life, but how we employ such inheritance in the form of moral and spiritual decisions is completely up to us.

The theory of karma has important religious and practical implications. On the one hand, it rationalizes whatever is happening in one's life as the just reward or punishment of what one did in a previous life. It allows people to cope with experiences of hardship and suffering which do not seem to have any apparent or reasonable explanations. However, a potential pitfall of such rationalization is that it may legitimate passive acceptance of violence and social injustice. For example, an abused spouse may be coaxed into believing that she deserves to be abused because of the wrongs she had committed against the abuser in a previous life. Therefore, the "absolute justice" of karma does not automatically cohere with our intuitive demand for social justice in this present life. On an institutional level, the doctrine has also been used to justify a fixed, hereditary interpretation of the caste system.

On the other hand, the theory of karma has served the dual purpose of directing moral actions and inspiring moral aspirations. Those who are enjoying a life of ease may be encouraged to tell themselves to continue to do good if they want to continue to enjoy a good life now and hereafter. Those who are enduring hardship may be comforted by the thought that a good life awaits them either in the near future or in the next life as long as they continue to do good. Karma does not just work in this life, but across lifetimes.

Our ordinary experience indicates that we neither remember what happened in our past life nor foresee what will happen in our future life (if there are indeed past and future lives). Does this fact of our ordinary experience falsify the karma principle? One may argue that the karma principle, being analogous to a natural law, simply works on its own whether one accepts it or not. In other words, karma's validity does not depend on one's verification of it by comparing and contrasting one's memory of past life, foreknowledge of future life, and what is happening in one's present life.

Furthermore, perhaps we should not take "past life" and "future life" in too literal a sense. Instead, we should take them metaphorically: "past life" simply means whatever happened in the past (e.g., yesterday, last month, two years ago) rather than a time before our birth; and "future life" simply means whatever will happen in the future (tomorrow, next month, or two years later) rather than a time after our death. On this metaphorical understanding of "past life" and "future life," then, we can reasonably assume that normal people do have a memory of recent past events and some kind of foreknowledge of what is to happen in their life (especially in the near future).

The important point with regard to karma's validity is that, once we subscribe to it, we will *interpret* events in our life as following what karma principle prescribes. We *see* a bad thing that happens in our life *as* a result of what we did before, and we also *see* a good thing that happens in our life *as* a result of what (something else) we did

---

80  Sarvepalli Radhakrishnan, *The Hindu View of Life* (London, George Allen & Unwin, 1927), 54.

before. In other words, we hold fast to the karma theory as an interpretive "frame-work" or "paradigm." Thus, the validity of karma principle hinges on our subjective commitment, not on memory of the past and foreknowledge of the future, nor objec-tive verification.

---

**DOING PHILOSOPHY**
*Karma versus God: Are They Compatible Ideas?*

Is the karma theory just a projection of human expectation? Is it just a para-digm (or metaphor) the sages of the Upanishads have arbitrarily adopted to see the world in a certain way? Does karma in the Upanishads work autono-mously, or does it require a supernatural judge that possesses consciousness, personality and a will? In dispensing this absolute justice, karma seems to work autonomously and self-sufficiently without the need of any gods. "If karma alone is to determine irrevocably the future of a man, shaping the course of his after life in one or the other species, then he himself becomes the architect of his fortune. All rituals, sacrifice, priests and gods cease to be indispensable."[81]

Do you agree with this interpretation of the theory of karma? Philosophically, is there a way to decide which belief is better: to believe in an eternal retribu-tion in heaven and hell, to believe in annihilation after death, or to believe in transmigration and in some cases emancipation from transmigration? Despite their differences, is it possible for all these to lead to similar moral teachings?

---

## MOKSHA—THE WAY OF LIBERATION

While the Upanishads are generally regarded as the fountainhead of Indian philoso-phy, they are also (together with the earlier layers of the Vedas) considered religious texts of Hinduism, the dominant faith in India in its long history. It is important to be reminded that the line between philosophy and religion is not clear-cut in the Indian tradition, as it is clear-cut in the typical case of Kant in Western philosophy. Indeed, if we rather liberally take "emancipation from some lower state of being to a higher state of being" as the defining characteristic of religion, then all the Asian philosophy classics covered in this book can be read as religious texts, in that they each recognize the need for and point to a path to emancipation.

Emancipation, or *moksha,* is the ultimate objective of the Upanishads.[82] The Upanishads see the unenlightened life as an endless cycle of birth and death, or *samsara,*

---

81 Kashi Nath Upadhyaya, *Early Buddhism and the Bhagavadgita* (Delhi: Motilal Banarsidass, 1971), 76–77.
82 In Hinduism *dharma* (righteousness), *artha* (wealth), *kama* (physical pleasures), and *moksha* (lib-eration) are prescribed as the four goals to be striven for in life, by every person. Accordingly, there are

which is also an endless cycle of suffering. According to the sages of the Upanishads, *samsara* stems from one's ignorance of one's true Self and one's attachment to an elusive, egoist self; even pains and sufferings caused by diseases and natural disasters are seen as ultimately derived from one's ignorance of the true Self. The physical self gets born and dies, but not the true Self, *Atman*. When one takes the physical self as one's true Self, one will constantly worry about one's demise, and this can go on across lifetimes, thus *samsara*, the endless cyclic suffering.

While in Western philosophy there is no clear counterpart to the idea of *samsara*, there are stories in Greek mythology that are in some ways similar to the idea of cyclic suffering: the suffering of Prometheus who has his liver eaten by a great eagle and has it grow back overnight to be eaten again the next day, and of Sisyphus who painstakingly rolls a boulder up a hill, only to watch it roll back down, and to repeat this throughout eternity. Both scenarios highlight the perpetual or cyclic nature of suffering. To be sure, *samsara* is not exactly the same as the suffering of Prometheus and Sisyphus, in that the idea of *samsara* does not call for any punitive deities. Nonetheless, it is fair to say that the idea of *cyclic* suffering is found in both traditions.

These sages also believe that it is possible to be liberated from *samsara* through realizing that true Self (*Atman*) is *Brahman*. As shown in the preceding pages, "*Atman* is *Brahman*" is not merely a proposition that states a fact, nor a tautology or empty formula. It is rather an invitation, a calling, an urge, or a command to a way of life, which is intimately linked to salvation. The "is" in "*Atman* is *Brahman*" indicates a practice, an action of realization.

When we realize the identity of *Atman* and *Brahman*, we are divested of any individuality, and we are free from any sense of possession, loss, or gain. However, the result is not an absolute void or death, or a passionless life. As Radhakrishnan poetically puts it, the "self is not annihilated any more than the ray of the sun is lost in the sun, the wave of the sea in the ocean, the notes of music in the one harmony. The song of the individual is not lost in the music of the world march."[83] In other words, the union is rather like a river flowing into the ocean, which gives up its individuality while gaining at the same time a new, immortal and infinite life. In the colourful language of *Chandogya*, rivers, once running towards east or west, when they have flowed into the sea, "know not 'I am this one,' 'I am that one.'"[84] Or to use still another analogy, the union of *Atman* and *Brahman* is like a lump of salt completed dissolved in water. The lump of salt is no more an individual object, but it is everywhere, all pervasive.[85]

The Upanishads maintain that, when a person has lost his individuality, "his body is no longer his body, his actions are no longer his actions; whether he still continues

---

also four stages of life. In childhood and early youth, one learns *dharma*; in youth one gets married and enjoys *artha* and *kama*; when one reaches middle age (the third stage) and old age (the fourth stage), one should strive to attain *moksha*.

83  Radhakrishnan, *Indian Philosophy*, 241.
84  *Chandogya*, VI.x.1
85  See *Chandogya*, VI.xiii.1–3; *Brihadaranyaka*, II:iv.12.

to live and to act or not is, like everything else, a matter of indifference."[86] Calling *Brahman* a creator, the *Katha* further remarks that liberation occurs "when through the grace of the Creator" a person "beholds the greatness of the Self" and "becomes freed from sorrow":[87] one will then enjoy "eternal happiness,"[88] and will be "liberated from the mouth of death."[89] This does not mean that one's body-level self will not physically die. Rather, it means that one who has realized the nature of one's true Self will no longer fear death, as a drop of water does not "fear" its "death" when it merges with the ocean.

While the Upanishads argued that *Atman* is essentially *Brahman*, they did not argue that every individual automatically can realize the identity of the two. According to Radhakrishnan, while it is true that *Atman* is *Brahman*, it still requires each individual's effort to personally attain that knowledge. As he puts it, "[s]imply because it is said that God [*Brahman*] is in man, it does not follow that with it there is an end of all endeavour. God is not in man in such an obvious fashion that he can possess Him absentmindedly and without effort or struggle. God is present as a potential or a possibility. It is man's duty to lay hold of Him by force and action."[90]

Now a practical question arises: What should we do in order to experience the identity of *Atman* and *Brahman*? The Upanishads have suggested several concrete ways which may facilitate the attainment of the union or liberation: to seek the help and instruction of a guru; to practice yoga meditation and to chant OM (or AUM); to control one's senses and desires; to sacrifice; to be virtuous; to will release; to give; and to cultivate compassion.[91] It is clear that the union or liberation is not merely cognitive ("knowing" *Atman* is *Brahman*), but also emotional (e.g., feeling compassion) and actional (giving).[92]

### DOING PHILOSOPHY
*Whose Emancipation?*

If emancipation means the complete dissolution of one's self into *Brahman*, many people may wonder what the point of this emancipation is, given that any immortality, peace, joy, or whatever, will have nothing to do with "me." How would the ancient sages respond to this question? Or would they consider this very wonder wrong-headed?

86  Deussen, 409.
87  *Katha*, II.21 (trans. Eknath Easwaren); see also *Katha*, IV.iv.
88  *Katha*, v.12 (trans. Eknath Easwaren).
89  *Katha*, III.15 (trans. Eknath Easwaren).
90  Radhakrishnan, *Indian Philosophy*, 209.
91  See *Chandogya*, I.i.1, I.i.5, and II.xxiii.1; *Katha*, I.ii.8, I.ii.9, II.ii–iii, II.xxiii–xxiv, VI.x, and VI.xi; *Brihadaranyaka*, III.v, IV.iv.6, IV.iv.22, and v.ii.3; and *Isha*, I.
92  The idea of seeing liberation in these three ways (cognitive, emotional, and actional) comes from Kalidas Bhattacharyya (see his "The Status of the Individual in Indian Metaphysics," in *The Indian Mind—Essentials of Indian Philosophy and Culture*, ed. Charles A. Moore [Honolulu: University of Hawaii Press, 1967], 311ff).

Two features about emancipation are notable in the Upanishads. First, it is believed to be possible at any moment, including within this present life. The *Chandogya* claims, "[t]hose who know this [Self] live day after day in heaven in this very life."[93] There is no need to wait till death before one can be liberated—that is, to experience the identification of *Atman* with *Brahman*.[94] As Klostermaier puts it, "Liberation, then, is not 'going somewhere' or 'leaving the world,' but the realization of a condition which always existed, but was unrecognized."[95] Clearly, this view stands in stark contrast with Socrates' view of the liberation of the soul, which is only possible after death when the soul separates from the body.[96]

Second, liberation relies on one's own effort and exertion, in that it is by virtue of one's own effort that one is saved.[97] No deity is summoned to make the salvation possible, though spiritual teachers (gurus) are believed to be crucial. Karma, as a law of the universe, once triggered, works automatically; it is not programmed or controlled by an external deity. Rather, it is triggered by individuals' multitudes of desires. It is the true Self (*Atman*) that is to be inwardly realized, not an external and transcendental deity that is to be worshipped. *Brahman*, which is also *Atman*, is transcendent but immanent.[98] As we shall see in later chapters, both these features were carried over, *mutatis mutandis*, to Buddhism, particularly Chinese Chan and Japanese Zen.

## CONCLUDING REMARKS:
## THE INFLUENCE OF THE UPANISHADS

We have pointed out that the thoughts in the Upanishads serve as a philosophical reservoir for later Indian philosophies. Now it is time to elaborate on this point. The Indian philosophies after the Upanishads can be roughly classified into two groups. One group accepts the authority of the Upanishads. All the philosophers in this group hold, in one way or another, that *Brahman* and *Atman* are eternal and permanent. In this group, Six Systems have been developed: the mind-matter dualistic school (*Sankhya*), the meditative school (*Yoga*), the logical school (*Nyaya*), the empiricist and atomistic school (*Vaisheshika*), the anti-ascetic and anti-mysticist school (*Mimamsa*), and the non-dualistic school (*Vedanta*). They are called the orthodox schools. Thanks to the

---

93  *Chandogya*, 8.3.3 (trans. Eknath Easwaren).

94  It is also very important to notice that *Atman* differs radically from Socrates' soul in another aspect: while Socrates' soul is, presumably, still, individual-specific, *Atman* is deemed as devoid of any individual characteristics, like a drop of water when it melds with the ocean.

95  Klaus Klostermaier, *A Short Introduction to Hinduism* (Oxford: Oneworld Publications, 1998), 93.

96  Consider Joseph Campbell's following remark: "One of the problems in our [Judeo-Christian] tradition is that the land—the Holy Land—is somewhere else. So we've lost the whole sense of accord with nature. And if it's not here, it's nowhere."

97  It seems paradoxical that it is precisely by virtue of the self's effort that one's self is overcome or transcended. The paradox becomes even more striking when later in the final chapter of this book we read Dogen's following remarks: "To study the Way is to study the self. To study the self is to forget the self. To forget the self is to be enlightened by all things. To be enlightened by all things is to remove the barriers between one's self and others."

98  See *Isha*, i.vi–vii; and *Brihadaranyaka*, iii.viii.15.

work of Shankara (788–820 CE), *Vedanta* came to be the dominant current of Hinduism at the beginning of the ninth century.

The "heterodox" schools, on the other hand, reject the authority of the Upanishads. They include Jainism, Buddhism, and Cârvâka, (a materialist school that died out in the fifteenth century).

Jainism (from the word *jina*, meaning "conqueror" of worldly limitations or ignorance), founded by Vardhamana Mahavira (c. 599–c. 527 BCE), maintains that *jiva* (soul) is a subtle eternal substance which animates the body, and the soul has atomic-like constituents. It also teaches that in its original pure state, the soul has omniscient knowledge, but it is obscured or blocked by the karmic matter that embodies it, including the body, senses, mind, intelligence, and so on. Jainism thus has a more developed doctrine of karma and transmigration of the soul, which leads to the conviction that all living things are equal, and violence or harmful actions are therefore never acceptable.

According to Buddhism, developed by Siddhartha Gautama, known as "the Buddha," (c. 563–483 BCE), nothing (including especially *Brahman* and *Atman*) is permanent; everything comes into being as a result of interdependent-arising. As a fundamental principle of the universe, interdependent-arising applies both to the physical and the spiritual. While the ideas of karma and *samsara* are found in Buddhism, they have also been transformed by it. In the next two chapters, we will examine two Buddhist scriptures, the Dhammapada and the *Fundamental Verses on the Middle Way*, to see how the ideas in the Upanishads have been reshaped by Buddhism.

## WORK CITED AND RECOMMENDED READINGS

1. Bina Gupta and William C. Wilcox, "'*Tat Tvam Asi*': An Important Identity Statement or a Mere Tautology," *Philosophy East and West* 34:1 (January 1984): 85–94.
2. Sarvepalli Radhakrishnan, *The Hindu View of Life* (London: George Allen and Unwin, 1957).
3. Sarvepalli Radhakrishnan, *Indian Philosophy*, Vol. 1 (New York: Oxford University Press, 1997).
4. Franklin Edgerton, *The Beginning of Indian Philosophy* (Cambridge, MA: Harvard University Press, 1965).
5. Surendranath Dasgupta, *A History of Indian Philosophy* (Cambridge: Cambridge University Press, 1963).
6. Jeaneane Fowler, *Hinduism: Beliefs and Practices* (Eastbourne, UK: Sussex Academic Press, 1997).
7. Arvind Sharma, *Classical Hindu Thought: An Introduction* (New York: Oxford University Press, 2000).
8. Klaus K. Klostermaier, *A Short Introduction to Hinduism* (Oxford: Oneworld Publications, 1998).
9. *The Upanishads*, trans. Eknath Easwaran (Tomales, CA: Nilgiri Press, 2007).
10. Whitley R.P. Kaufman, "Karma, Rebirth, and the Problem of Evil," *Philosophy East and West* 55:1 (January 2005): 15–32.

# CHAPTER 2

# The Dhammapada

## SUGGESTED PRIMARY READING

*The Dhammapada: Verses on the Way—A New Translation of the Teaching of the Buddha, with a Guide to Reading the Text*, Glenn Wallis, trans. and ed. (New York: The Modern Library, 2004).

## LEARNING OBJECTIVES

By the time you have worked through this chapter, you should be able to

› Describe the philosophical landscape in India during the time of the Buddha
› Explain the importance of mind as the cause of suffering and the basis for liberation
› Explain how the Buddha's emphasis on experience reflects a transformation of the key ideas in the Upanishads
› Explain how different ontologies in the Upanishads and in the Dhammapada may lead to similar ethical teachings

## KEY WORDS

karma, no-self (*anatman*), mind, suffering (*dukkha*), nirvana

## GUIDING QUESTIONS

Just as the Upanishads are concerned with the delivery (*moksha*) from suffering (*samsara*) that is caused by ignorance of one's true Self (*Atman*), the Dhammapada focuses on liberation (*nirvana*) from suffering (*dukkha*) that is caused by ignorance of the true nature of things, including especially the self. In particular, the Dhammapada can be seen as trying to answer the following questions:

1. Why is life imperfect and unsatisfactory? Why do we experience emotional and spiritual suffering?
2. Why do we cling to pleasure, enjoyment, and even happiness, but to no avail?
3. Medicine can sometimes alleviate our physical pain, but what can alleviate or even eliminate emotional and spiritual suffering?

In response to these questions, the Buddha argues that the root cause of the unsatisfactoriness of life (*dukkha*) is our unwillingness to accept the impermanent nature of things, especially the impermanent nature of self. Accordingly, he maintains that a life without suffering is a life that accepts and embraces impermanence.

## INTRODUCTION

The Dhammapada, perhaps the most popular early Buddhist scripture, summarizes the basic teachings of Buddhism.[1] Compiled in the third century BCE, about 200 years after the death of Gautama Siddhartha (the Buddha, also known as Sakyamuni, the sage of the Sakya clan in northern India), the scripture is traditionally regarded as an authentic, though not necessarily verbatim, record of his teachings. Several versions of it have survived, the most popular among them being the version in the Pali language.[2] The scripture is a foundational text of Theravada ("teachings of the elders") Buddhism—an early school of Buddhism that later flourished in Sri Lanka, Laos, Cambodia, Burma, and Thailand. It is also widely studied and revered in virtually all other schools of Buddhism.

The word "*dhammapada*" is a compound formed by "*dhamma*" and "*pada*," both of which have multiple connotations. The word "*dhamma*" means "elements," "phenomena," "patterns," and "laws." The word "*pada*" means "foot," "step," "footstep," "path," "word," or "verse." The compound word "*dhammapada*" thus means "right path" or

---

1   The Four Noble Truths are mentioned in verses 190–92 and 273, the Eightfold Path in Chapter 20, and the doctrine of no-self (nothing is permanent or substantial) is in verses 277–79.

2   For information about other versions of the scripture, see John Ross Carter and Mahinda Palihawadana, *The Dhammapada* (New York: Oxford University Press, 2000), Introduction, xi ff. For our purposes, however, the important point is that although "the Dharmapada [Sanskrit counterpart of the Pali 'Dhammapada'] texts of the different schools varied in language, size, and chapter arrangement, there were hardly any differences among them [in content]" (Ross and Palihawadana, xix).

"verses on the way." Interestingly, both "dhamma" and "pada" have affinities to the Chinese word *dao* (道), which connotes the right way or right path.

The Pali version of the Dhammapada is composed of 423 verses, organized loosely into 26 themes or chapters.[3] For example, Chapter 3 is about the importance of a tamed mind, Chapter 10 deals with the topic of violence, and Chapter 26 describes the characters of *brahmana*, the superior person or the truly awakened. The verses in the Dhammapada are metrical; this feature probably serves as a mnemonic device.

The content of the Dhammapada reads like a training manual or guidebook for the Buddhist way of life. Each verse is like a nugget of wisdom, both instructive and inspirational. Gautama's teachings in this scripture focus on the nature of *dukkha* (which is often translated as suffering) and its cessation. Compared with the Confucius of the *Analects*, who advocates a vision of life shaped by one's familial and state-political contexts, the Gautama of the Dhammapada commends a way of life that connects ethics and well-being with the mind regardless of one's familial and state-political particulars. For Gautama, distress stems from a polluted mind, whereas a happy life comes from a clean mind.

The Dhammapada offers in most cases straightforward and down-to-earth moral instructions.[4] This may come as a surprise to those who expect to find in it sophisticated teachings, or perhaps divine and theistic revelations. The directness of the Dhammapada is evident in the following verses:

> In this world / hostilities are *never* / appeased by hostility. / But by the absence of hostility / are they appeased. / This is an interminable truth. (verse 5)[5]

> The refraining from all that is harmful, / the undertaking of what is skilful [good], / the cleaning of one's mind—that is the teaching of the awakened. (verse 183)[6]

> [P]reserving in what should be done, / do not do what should not be done. (verse 293; also see verses 117–18, 313–14, 337–38, and 346)[7]

---

3   Some chapters (e.g., Chapters 4 Flowers and 23 Elephant) use metaphorical symbols rather than points of doctrine as titles.

4   According to the Theravada Buddhist tradition, each verse in the Dhammapada was occasioned by a different episode in which only one or a few specific persons were addressed. For this reason, the scripture is sometimes accompanied by about 300 tales that give further details to the originating episodes. An example of such a compilation is Narada Thera, trans., *The Dhammapada, Pali Text and Translation with Stories in Brief and Notes* (Taipei: The Corporate Body of the Buddha Educational Foundation, 1993).

5   *The Dhammapada: Verses on the Way—A New Translation of the Teaching of the Buddha, with a Guide to Reading the Text*, Glenn Wallis, trans. and ed. (New York: The Modern Library, 2004). Unless otherwise noted, all the quotations from the *Dhammapada* will be from this translation.

6   What this verse says can be seen as universally shared by all the great world religions.

7   For more specific moral admonitions, see verses 325 (about eating and sleeping) and 246–47 (about drinking, adultery, and stealing).

Win over an angry person with poise. / Win over a mean one with kindness. / Win over a greedy person with generosity, / and one who speaks
falsely with honesty. (verse 223; also see verses 197, 389, and 406)

The accessibility of the scripture, however, does not imply that the teaching in it
is easy to put into practice. In fact, just the opposite is true.[8] Juan Mascaro clearly
noticed this point when he told the following story: "It is said that once a man of arms
undertook a long journey to see a holy follower of Buddha, and asked if the message
of Buddha could be taught to him. The answer was: 'Do not what is evil. Do what is
good. Keep your mind pure. This is the teaching of Buddha.' 'Is this all?' said the man of
arms; 'Every child of five knows this.' 'It may be so, but few men of eighty can practice
it,' he was told."[9]

## THE PHILOSOPHICAL LANDSCAPE IN GAUTAMA'S TIME

In order to understand Gautama's teachings, we need to understand the philosophical
landscape in India in his time, for his teachings are embedded in the Indian tradition,
and emerged as an innovative alternative to the then existing rival religious doctrines
and practices. One such important influence was Brahmanism, which based its doctrine
and practice on the authority of the Vedas and the privilege of the *Brahman* (Brahmin)
caste. This tradition, however, was in decline in Gautama's time, for "the Brahmans had
become mere repeaters of texts, not creative thinkers or 'meditators.'"[10] In addition,
several schools of wandering philosophers (*shramanas*) were actively questioning the
authority of the Vedas and the privilege of the *Brahman* caste. The world-renouncing
lifestyle of such philosophers posed a direct challenge to the pre-determined rights and
obligations prescribed in the caste system.[11]

The rival theories proposed by Brahmanism and by the wandering philosophers
centre on two important issues. (1) Is there an enduring Self? and (2) Is there moral
causality (karma)? The rival schools arrived at different answers, with very different
ethical implications. The table below contrasts in a quick glance the rival views of Self
and moral causality in Gautama's time.

---

8  In this connection, readers of the *Daodejing* would be quick to find some echoes: "When the best
scholars hear about the Way, / They assiduously put it into practice. / When average scholars hear
about the Way, / They sometimes uphold it and sometimes forsake it. / When the worst scholars hear
about the Way, / They laugh at it! / If they did not laugh at it, it would not really be the Way" (Laotse,
*The Daodejing of Laotse*, Philip J. Ivanhoe, trans. [Indianapolis: Hackett, 2002], Chapter 41), and "My
teachings are easy to understand and easy to implement; / But no one in the whole world has been able
to understand or implement them" (Chapter 70).

9  Juan Mascaro, trans., *The Dhammapada* (London: Penguin, 1973), Introduction, 21–22.

10  A.K. Warder, *Indian Buddhism* (Delhi: Motilal Banarsidass Publishers, 2000), 30.

11  The flourishing of the rival schools is in some way analogous to the situation in China around
Confucius' time when the rituals and systems of the Zhou Dynasty were disintegrating and hundreds
of schools vied for superiority. The difference however is that in India the central concern of all the
rival schools was not about how a state should be ruled, but about how a human being as such is to be
liberated from suffering, regardless of social and political contexts.

| SCHOOLS/ISSUES | IS THERE AN ENDURING SELF? | IS THERE MORAL CAUSALITY? |
| --- | --- | --- |
| Brahmins (Brahmanas) | Yes | Yes |
| Materialists (Cârvâkas) | No | No |
| Ascetics | Yes | No |
| Sceptics | Judgment withheld | Judgment withheld |
| Jains | Yes | Yes |
| The Buddha | No | Yes |

## A. THE BRAHMINS (*BRAHMANAS*)

The Brahmins believed in both an enduring Self and moral causality. But the existence of an enduring Self may not seem verifiable by direct first-person experience. Is there indeed such an enduring Self? What if one is obsessed with the enduring Self that is only putatively there? Might belief in this putative Self lead one to egoistic attachments?

## B. THE MATERIALISTS (*CÂRVÂKAS*)

One group of wandering philosophers in the Buddha's time were the *Cârvâkas* or the Materialists. These philosophers believed neither in an enduring Self nor in moral causality. They argued that it was pointless to worry about moral responsibility, moral consequences, or afterlife, for at death the elements (some take there to be four—earth, fire, air, and water, while others take there to be more than four) would simply come apart, and there was no such thing as an enduring Self. For instance, the wandering teacher Kakuda Kātyāyana argued that there were seven elements in the world—earth, water, fire, wind, pain, pleasure, and life. Since these seven elements were unchanging, Kakuda argued, killing a person with a knife was simply a matter of putting the knife into the spaces between the elements. Thus, killing was of no moral consequence.[12] According to the materialists, then, there is absolutely nothing special about being human; everything is reduced entirely to the fortuitous combination and separation of elements.[13] For these philosophers, the meaning of life is simply free pursuit of sensual pleasure.

---

12 See Hirakawa Akira, *A History of Indian Buddhism: From Sakyamuni to Early Mahayana*, Paul Groner trans. and ed. (Honolulu: University of Hawaii Press, 1990), 17.
13 Compare with Socrates' criticism, in Plato's *Phaedo*, of the Pre-Socratic philosopher Anaxagoras, who tried to explain human actions totally in terms of material forces, air, ether, and water. According

One might ask these Materialists: Must human life be understood on a level that is different from the level of elements? Does the mind (subjectivity) have any place in their materialist system? Should we care about the social consequences of such a doctrine if people indeed follow it in real life? Can the doctrine serve as a healthy guide?

## C. THE ASCETICS

The Ascetics denied moral causality but believed in an enduring soul. They argued that "the supposed choice of action had no real effect whatsoever on men's condition of life, here or hereafter."[14] According to them, "[all] that happened within the universe took place within a totally closed causal system in which all events were completely and unalterably determined by cosmic principles over which there was no control [...] what appears as the act of a man, who is the supposed actor, is no act at all, and there is therefore no question of choice of action and, therefore, no moral choice."[15] They maintained that practicing asceticism is the last stage leading to the final peace in human destiny.[16]

This asceticism is clearly fatalism *par excellence*, which rendered human effort and human life futile and meaningless. It is conservative (to say the least), as it advises people to accept the status quo.

## D. THE SCEPTICS (AGNOSTICS)

The sceptic philosophers of the time suspended any judgment concerning the Self, afterlife, and moral causality; they did not commit themselves to any positive or negative positions regarding the two questions. And it is extremely questionable what kind of positive guidance to life this doctrine can provide.

## E. THE JAINS

The Jains affirmed the existence of both an enduring Self (*jiva*, or the soul) and moral causality. The goal of the Jains is "to free the soul by overcoming the instincts and

---

to Socrates, the fact that he ended up in prison cannot be simply reduced to his body movement, the structure and combination of his bones, sinews, flesh, and skin. "To call those things causes," said Socrates, "is too absurd. If someone said that without bones and sinews and all such things, I should not be able to do what I decided, he would be right, but surely to say that they are the cause of what I do, and not that I have chosen the best course, even though I act with my mind, is to speak very lazily and carelessly. Imagine not being able to distinguish the real cause from that without which the cause would not be able to act as a cause. It is what the majority appear to do, like people groping in the dark; they call it a cause, thus giving it a name that does not belong to it" (*Phaedo*, 99a–b. Translated by George Maximilian Anthony Grube, *Five Dialogues* [Indianapolis: Hackett, 2002]). It is Socrates' philosophic beliefs and the accusations against him that led him to prison.

14   Trevor Ling, *The Buddha: Buddhist Civilization in India and Ceylon* (London: Maurice Temple Smith, 1973), 79.

15   Ling, 79.

16   See Ling, 79.

desires that arise from the physical body."[17] Thus, Jainism prescribed the practice of severe austerities to weaken the physical needs of the body. Compared to the other schools, Jainism is close to Buddhism in some respects (recognizing karma—though Jainism considers karma as a kind of matter that is made of tiny imperceptible particles—and recommending non-violence, etc.), yet different from Buddhism in that it accepts an eternal soul and embraced severe austerities.

## F. GAUTAMA'S ALTERNATIVE

Gautama Siddhartha was different from all the above philosophers. His answer to the two questions was that there is no enduring Self but there is moral causality. Based on his answers to these two questions, he proposed a way of life that is practical and responsible. He wanted to seek genuine solutions to problems that beset humanity in the immediate present rather than engage in airy metaphysical debate (for example, debates about whether there is an eternal soul and about whether the universe is finite).

Gautama Siddhartha was born a prince around the sixth century BCE in a small state in the Himalaya foothills, in present day Nepal. He married and had a son. As a member of the royal household, he lived in luxury. His life took a turn in his late twenties when he came to observe the poignant reality of the life events of sickness, aging (decaying), and death. His observations disturbed him so profoundly that he was determined to seek peace of mind. How can suffering in life be eliminated? Haunted by this question, Gautama renounced his family life and experimented with the ascetic path under the guidance of several teachers. For six years, he practiced meditation and mortification. However, he eventually became dissatisfied with their teachings and their ascetic practice. He left his teachers and went on to pursue his own practice of deep meditation. One day, while meditating under a Bodhi tree, he attained enlightenment. Gautama thus became venerated later by his followers as the Enlightened One, or the Buddha.

Central to the Buddha's enlightenment is his realization that the way to liberation and inner peace is a "middle way" that avoids extremes, including those of luxury versus asceticism (both of which he had practiced), fatalism versus fortuitism (which the Ascetics and the Materialists respectively maintained), and eternalism (the Brahmins and the Jains) versus nihilism (the Materialists). The Buddha taught that all cravings need to be extinguished. Unlike the Materialists who indulged in desires or the ascetics who tried to forbid them, the Buddha advocated controlling them. For the Buddha, neither self-indulgence nor self-abnegation eliminates egoistic attachment; in fact, both strengthen it.

Most crucial to the Buddha's experience of enlightenment is his realization that there is no empirical basis for any permanent self-identity (see Dhammapada verse 279). You may recall that in the Upanishads the existence of *Atman* is only inferred by

---

17  Hirakawa Akira, *A History of Indian Buddhism: From Sakyamuni to Early Mahayana*, Paul Groner, trans. and ed. (Honolulu: University of Hawaii Press, 1990), 18.

the analogy that a sense experience is to its corresponding sense organ as all of consciousness is to *Atman* (*Brihadaranyaka* II.iv.11). However, the Buddha did not accept this analogy, but taught that there is only consciousness, without an agent lurking behind it—that is, there can be action without an agent. Thus, the Buddha advises: Don't think (imagine), but experience yourself! Then you will realize that *Atman* (if taken as an external agent) does not really exist.

The Buddha's idea that there is no self but that there is moral causality would have appeared intuitively difficult or even impossible to his contemporaries. One may ask the Buddha: How can there be thought without a thinker, consciousness without a Self, and moral causality without a responsible agent? In responding to this question, the Dhammapada was compelled "to justify any moral choice in the context of a doctrine of impermanence and non-substantiality allowing no room for a permanent and eternal self and still account for man's responsibility."[18] We shall see later in this chapter whether the justification is plausible.

## MIND—THE ROOT CAUSE OF SUFFERING AND THE BASIS FOR EMANCIPATION

In Greek mythology, humans differ from the gods in that only the latter enjoy immortality. This difference between humans and the gods points to our sense of dissatisfaction with life that stems from our temporal finitude. A similar theme is echoed in the myth of Adam and Eve in the Hebrew Bible, in which death (and hence mortality) was introduced to the human race as a result of their eating from the Tree of Knowledge of good and evil. These myths give us the impression that both the ancient Greeks and the ancient Hebrews attributed human unhappiness to human temporal finitude. However, it can be argued that, on closer inspection, both traditions merely saw temporal finitude as a derivative instead of the root cause of unhappiness. In the Greek tradition, human unhappiness stems from the awareness that gods enjoy immortality. In the Hebrew tradition, the root cause of human unhappiness is human's wilful disobedience of God.

Like these two traditions, the Dhammapada is also interested in the root cause of human suffering, which it traced to the human mind—indeed, a polluted mind. The notion of polluted mind resembles the awareness of human mortality as the root cause of suffering in the Greek tradition and the wilful disobedience against God's will in the Hebrew tradition in that all regard the mind as the root cause of suffering. However, unlike the Greek and Hebrew traditions, the Dhammapada sees suffering as stemming from a mind that is ignorant of true reality as impermanence, a mind that clings to the products of its own imagination.

The purpose of the Dhammapada, then, is to help people realize the harmfulness of mental clingings and turn from them by radically disciplining and retraining their minds. The path of mental training, according to the Dhammapada, will eventually

18   David J. Kalupahana, trans., *A Path of Righteousness: Dhammapada* (Lanham, MD: University Press of America, 1986), 59.

lead to the dissolution of suffering and to a happy life. This central theme of the Dhammapada is succinctly summarized in the opening verses of the work:

> Preceded by mind [*mano*] / are phenomena, / led by mind, / formed by mind. / If with mind polluted / one speaks or acts, / then pain follows, / as a wheel follows the draft ox's foot. (verse 1)

> Preceded by mind / are phenomena, / led by mind, formed by mind. / If with mind pure / one speaks or acts, / then ease follows, / as an ever-present shadow. (verse 2)

A few points in these two verses need clarification. (1) What is the Buddha's understanding of the mind? (2) What is a polluted mind? (3) How does one clean the polluted mind? (4) What is a pure or tamed mind? Let's tackle these questions in sequence.

### 1. The Buddha's Understanding of the Mind

The Buddha sees the mind (*mano*) as a faculty along with other sense faculties: eyes, ears, nose, tongue, and body. The eyes, the ears, the nose, the tongue, and the body each have their respective objects: material form, sound, smell, and tangibility. And the mind has ideas and concepts as its objects. But unlike the eyes, the ears, the nose, the tongue, and the body, each of which focuses on its own objects, the mind can intervene in the faculties of seeing, hearing, smelling, tasting, and feeling, and it can significantly shape the performance of these faculties.

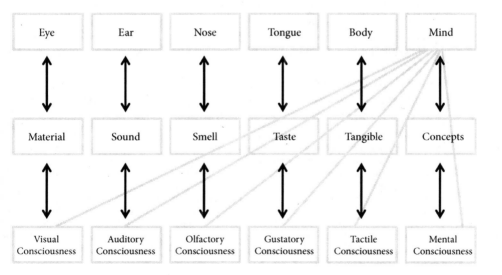

In other words, for the Buddha, mind plays a crucial, regulatory role in shaping one's *lived* world, not only cognitively, but also emotively and conatively.[19] It is the "generative condition" and "predominant factor" regarding how we see, feel, and react to the world and to other people.[20] In short, our mind can "pollute" the other five senses, but it can also "purify" them.

For example, if my mind mistakes a rope for a snake, then I would see, feel, and react to the rope as if it were a snake. On the other hand, if my mind perceives a rope as it is, I will see, feel, and react to it in a totally different way. By the same token, if my mind takes my self to be a permanent and independent entity, I will see, feel, and react to the world in a self-centred or grasping way. On the contrary, if my mind takes my self to be interdependent upon all that is around me, then I will see, feel, and react to all that is around me in a more compassionate way. Imagine seeing people around you as members of your family, or even parts of your body. Are you likely to want to injure or harm them?

According to the Dhammapada, then, in order to live a happy life, it is absolutely essential to alter the habits of a mind that is usually unruly, easily agitated, and confused. The Dhammapada says: "Whatever a rival may do to a foe, / or a vengeful person to the one he hates, / a wrongly applied mind would do more damage to him than that. / Nothing that a mother, father, or other relative might do would do more good for him than a mind well controlled" (verses 42–43; cf. verses 103–05).

### 2. The Polluted Mind

The polluted mind is one that fails to realize that nothing is permanent in the world. This mind, failing to realize the impermanence of things, mistakes illusions and delusions for reality and then clings to them. The clinging makes the mind easily agitated, tense, and unhappy; it also leads to bad deeds and speech that cause hardship for others. This, according to the Buddha, is the working of the polluted mind—the root cause of suffering. (Suffering and the cause of suffering are the subject matters of the first and second Noble Truth, see verse 191.)

The working of the polluted mind can manifest itself in many ways in our everyday actions. One common symptom is not being willing to accept change. Suppose my car breaks down on my way to an important meeting, and I get out of my car and kick

---

19  Although the Buddha emphasizes the role of mental training as a path of liberation, he does not think that the mind has the capacity to create any idea directly and willfully. As Kalupahana has noticed, "it is true that *mano* exerts an enormous influence on ideas (*dhamma*). Yet it is not true that all ideas are generated by the mind. Ideas of cognition (*vinnana*) are not mere products of the mind, even though they can be influenced by the mind. They are also conditioned by the objects of perception. Ideas of reflection, on the contrary, are the products of the mind. Hence [for the Buddha] it is the mind that is primarily responsible for metaphysical ideas such as soul, self and substance, and these latter are without objective support" (Kalupahana, trans., 157). On the other hand, the fact that our minds are conditioned and dependent upon other factors does not mean that we are completely determined, in which case moral choices would be impossible.

20  See *The Dhammapada*, John Ross Carter and Mahinda Palihawadana, trans. (New York: Oxford University Press, 1987), 90, 93.

it in a fury. My action might be a form of catharsis, but from the Buddhist point of view it stems from my inability to accept that change (or impermanence) is the very nature of things; any composite thing, my car included, is subject to change and hence breakdown. In life we of course want outer conditions (my car included) to be always optimal, but they are never in our complete control. Therefore, we will often be irritated by uncontrollable conditions.

Another symptom is that we stick to our expectations and take them as a fixed criterion of judgment and thus refuse to accept anything that does not meet them. Suppose that I am behind a cautious driver, who brakes as the light turns yellow, when I am quite convinced that there would have been sufficient time for both his vehicle and mine to drive through. So, I sound my horn, screaming at the same time, "Come on, I have an important appointment and I am already late!" Again, my fit of rage might be cathartic, but it is also an expression of the polluted mind in Buddhist psychology, in that I am judging things from an ego-centred perspective, demanding that the world (particularly the driver in front of me) should cater to my interests, because "I am more important than others!" I falsely expect everything to orbit around me or my activities![21] As a popular song declares, "I believe that the world should revolve around me!" In this way, my polluted mind judges the world from my ego-centred eyes, blaming everything and everyone else except myself. The Dhammapada provides a vivid portrait of such an ego-centred person: "He berated me! He hurt me! / He beat me! He deprived me!" / "For those who hold such grudges, / hostility is not appeased" (verse 3). Such polluted minds are fault-finding: "they find fault with one who sits silently, / they find fault with one who speaks much, / they find fault with one who speaks but little. / There is no one in this world who is not faulted" (verse 227; cf. verses 252–53).

A third symptom of a polluted mind is that we fail to realize that nothing is isolated and independent and that the world is like an infinite, interconnected, multidimensional and centreless web or net in which every knot is directly and indirectly dependent upon and reflective of every other knot. An example of this interconnected view of life and the world is that my being able to write this book is dependent directly and indirectly upon countless number of conditions, including those who taught me Asian philosophy; those who trained me in Western philosophy; the opportunity I had to teach both Western and Asian philosophies; the many Asian classics that are available both in their original languages and in English translation and the great number of books on Asian classics that have been made available; the support of my family, colleagues, and the university where I teach; the fact that I live in a part of the world that is not in total chaos, etc., etc. We can even go as far as to say that, in an ultimate sense, my writing of this book is connected to the conditions of the whole world. A failure to recognize the interdependence of things may result in arrogance or self-aggrandizement, in that I may believe that my success in writing this book is due solely to *my* own effort (see verse 74).

---

21  Read a similar idea in the *Zhuangzi*: a "completed mind" (*chengxin*, 成 心) judges things from an ego-centred point of view.

If, according to the Buddha, nothing is permanent or independent, and everything is constantly changing and always interconnected, then there should be no substantial Self. But why does an individual feel strongly that he or she has one substantial Self? The reason is that our thinking (including memory and imagination) fabricates that "feel." In the Introduction of his translation of the Dhammapada, Eknath Easwaran offers a nice explanation of how the "feel" of Self occurs. He explains: "A movie screen does not really connect one moment's image to the next, and similarly there is no substrate beneath the mind to connect thoughts. The mind *is* the thoughts, and only the speed of thinking creates the illusion that there is something continuous and substantial."[22] It is the memory of past images and the anticipation of future images that create the "feel" of a continuous "thing" running through the images.

In a similar fashion, when you are watching a 3D movie, actually only two sets of images are shown on the screen. However, through the filters of a pair of 3D glasses, one set of the images enters your left eye and the other your right eye. Your mind integrates the two sets of images so you feel objects flying off the screen towards you and creepy characters reaching out to grab you. All this magical effect is the result of mental fabrication!

By the same token, it is the memory of one's past experience and the anticipation of one's future experience that construct the "feel" of a Self. All in all, the "feel" of a Self is just a product of mental construction, normally sustained by linguistic reification of words like "I," "me," "my," and "mine."

The problem with the constructed "feel" of Self is that through a process that involves ignorance, craving, and attachment, it gives rise to suffering. For example, due to ignorance we come to believe falsely that things are permanent—which prompts us to crave things. If we can get them, we stick to them, worrying about losing them; if we cannot get them or lose them, we feel sorrow or resentment. This is how we suffer, whether we get things we want or not. In the Buddhist scholar Edward Conze's words, "we flounder alternatively in vain hopes or despairs."[23]

## DOING PHILOSOPHY
### Hume versus the Buddha: No-Self Similar Theories, Different Practical Implications

It is easy for those who read both Buddhism and Hume to notice their similarities regarding the idea of no-self. However, it is perhaps more important to see that in spite of their similarities, they have inspired different moral practices. As Troy Wilson Organ noted, "David Hume and Siddhartha Gautama arrived at approximately the same conclusions about the nature of the self. But after reaching this conclusion Hume lived as he did before, i.e., his

---

22 *The Dhammapada*, trans. Eknath Easwaran (Berkeley, CA: Blue Mountain Center of Meditation, 2007), Introduction, 82.
23 Edward Conze, *Buddhist Thought in India* (Ann Arbor: The University of Michigan Press, 1967), 40.

lifestyle continued as though he believed in the reality of a substantial ego. But Gautama's lifestyle changed radically after he came to this conclusion. Hume's conclusion started a round of arguments which we still continue in the West; Gautama's conclusion began a lifestyle which has shaped East Asia for 2,500 years. Hume taught how to think about personal identity in the absence of belief in a substantial ego; Gautama taught how to live a selfless life."[24]

Why do you think that the Buddha and Hume developed such different ways of life in spite of their shared idea that there is no permanent self?

### 3. To Clean the Polluted Mind

It is indeed a formidable task to try to clean the polluted mind (see verse 33), because we habitually fall into the trap of mental attachment. Nevertheless, the Buddha contends that, through a variety of trainings and practices (see Chapter 20 on the Eightfold Path), the polluted mind can be cleansed (see verse 191).

To clean the mind is not to deny all the physical senses, survival instincts, or physical needs. The Buddha practiced asceticism before attaining enlightenment, but he realized that asceticism is not the right path to enlightenment. To clean the mind is to remove the "afflictions" or "defilements" of the mind (verse 88)—that is, to restrain and eliminate attachments or cravings through disciplining all the faculties—eyes, ears, nose, tongue, body, and even mind itself. "Restraint of the eye is beneficial. / Beneficial is restraint of the ear. / Restraint of the nose is beneficial. / Beneficial is restraint of the tongue. / Restraint of the body is beneficial. / Beneficial is restraint of speech. / Restraint of the body is beneficial. / Restraint of the mind is beneficial. / Beneficial is restraint all around. / Restrained all around, the practitioner / is released from all pain" (verses 360–61).[25]

But how do we discipline the faculties? One essential step is meditation.[26] According to the Buddhist scholar Walpola Rahula, early Buddhism had actually developed many specific meditation techniques,[27] but for our purposes here, it suffices to explain one such technique, called "calm observation." This technique involves observing, in a nonjudgmental manner, the coming and going of mental content. Rahula explains:

Say you are really angry, overpowered by anger, ill-will, hatred. It is curious, and paradoxical, that the man who is in anger is not really aware, not

---

24  Troy Wilson Organ, *Western Approaches to Eastern Philosophy* (Athens, OH: Ohio University Press, 1975), 20.

25  Cf. the *Analects* 12:1.

26  Buddhist meditation was derived from ancient Indian Yoga, neither of which is merely for physical fitness and health as is commonly understood in the West. Rather, both are essentially techniques for mind training and self-transformation.

27  See Walpola Rahula, *What the Buddha Taught* (New York: Grove Press, 1974), 68–75.

mindful that he is angry. The moment he sees his anger, it becomes, as if it were, shy and ashamed, and begins to subside. You should examine its nature, how it arises, how it disappears. Here again it should be remembered that you should not think "I am angry," or of "my anger." You should only be aware and mindful of the state of an angry mind. You are only observing and examining an angry mind objectively. This should be the attitude with regard to all sentiments, emotions, and states of mind.[28]

We can see from this quote that the key in the technique of "calm observation" is objective examination of mental content. To illustrate this point, let's consider the reactions of students and victims' families in the Virginia Tech massacre. On April 16, 2007, Seung-hui Cho, an undergraduate student at Virginia Polytechnic Institute and State University in Blacksburg, Virginia, killed 32 people and wounded 25 others in a shooting rampage. When Cho was cornered by law enforcement officers, he shot himself and died.

What would be a survivor's habitual reaction to Cho and the massacre? How would the victims' families react to Cho and the massacre? We might think that *all* of them would be outraged and overwhelmed by grief, anger, and hatred. But part of what happened after the massacre was hard to believe: while many were indeed angry, some were calm and even compassionate to Cho and his family. A student added a rock for Cho to a stone memorial placed on the main campus lawn. One Blacksburg resident (who went to campus to memorialize all the people killed, including Cho himself) said, "Forgiveness is part of being freed from anger."[29] In the following days, when more information about Cho, including his severe anxiety disorder (known as selective mutism) and his serious depressive disorder since middle school, came to light, more people began to calm down and come to terms with the massacre. For many the coping process was not easy.

How might calm meditation help in a situation such as this? A calm observation of the incident can make us realize that the massacre is not simply Cho's problem—Cho is not an unchanging and independent entity—it is, in the deep sense of interconnectedness, *our* problem. And such realization can prevent us from being swept away by our strong emotional reactions, so that we may be released from our urge to seek revenge, for example, from any impulsive thought to hunt down Cho's family members and make them pay (cf. verses 231–34). (Of course, keeping a calm mind toward the Virginia massacre does not mean denying the reality and gravity of Cho's crime.) It can also help us channel our efforts to seriously look for ways to eliminate conditions that may lead to similar tragedies in the future. In short, "calm observation" can help us see and understand things as they are, i.e., constantly changing and always interconnected. In this way, people can act wisely and judiciously regardless of the situation they are in.

---

28  Rahula, 74.
29  See <http://www.kdhnews.com/news/story.aspx?s=15578>.

Can meditation and calm observation have such powerful effects on emotions and behaviours? Many people accept that physical training matters to the body and hence to the development of physical skills, but remain sceptical about the efficacy of meditation in managing or altering emotions. Richard Davidson, a University of Wisconsin brain and behaviour scientist, points out: "There is a tremendous lacuna in our worldview, where training is seen as important for strength, for physical agility, for athletic ability, for musical ability—for everything *except* emotions. The Buddhists say these are skills, too, and are trainable like any others."[30] While the precise mechanism of the impact of meditation on emotion is still being studied, mostly notably through the cooperation of Tibetan Buddhist monks, cognitive scientists and philosophers around the world, the evidence emerging thus far in such collaborative research shows that negative emotions (such as hatred and jealousy) can be deactivated and positive emotions (such as happiness, compassion, and joy) cultivated through long hours of meditation.[31] Cognitive scientists have recognized the connection between meditation and brain change, one variety of neuroplasticity (brain and nervous system alteration as the result of input from the environment). Science writer Sharon Begley explains:

> [T]he mental training that lies at the core of meditative practice can alter the brain and thus the mind in an enduring way—strengthening connections from the thoughtful prefrontal lobes to the fear- and anxiety-generating amygdala, shifting activity in the prefrontal cortex from the discontented right side to the eudaemonic left side. Connections among neurons can be physically modified through mental training just as a biceps can be modified by physical training. Much as sustained attention can turn up activity in regions of the motor cortex that control finger movements in the virtual piano players, so might it damp down activity in regions from which negative emotions emanate and at the same time dial up activity in regions devoted to positive emotions.[32]

Thus, it seems that neuroplasticity applies not just to cognitive aspects of the mind, but also to emotional aspects. With proper mental training, one can develop one's capacity for such positive emotions as empathy and compassion.[33]

---

30 Sharon Begley, *Train Your Mind, Change Your Brain—How a New Science Reveals Our Extraordinary Potential to Transform Ourselves* (New York: Ballantine Books, 2007), 231.
31 The Buddha's mental training techniques can be seen as a form of psychotherapy that is very different from Freud's psychoanalysis. Psychoanalysis aims at restoring psychologically abnormal people to their normal states (called by Buddhists as "worldling" states), but such normal states are still far from what Buddhists call the enlightened state.
32 Begley, 241.
33 Interested students can watch a fascinating talk entitled "The Habits of Happiness" by French biologist and Buddhist monk Matthieu Ricard at <http://www.ted.com/talks/matthieu_ricard_on_the_habits_of_happiness.html>.

### 4. The Pure Mind

When our mind is entangled with what happens around us, we can become easily agitated. When we experience life as a flow of tumultuous events, our mind may be running like a wild horse. But the Dhammapada promises us that, with a pure, tamed mind, one will enjoy "ease" (verse 35), and be liberated from "the bonds of Mara," that is, the bonds of "craving, discontent, and passion."[34]

What is the state of ease and freedom from "the bonds of Mara" like? The Dhammapada further explains that it is a state that goes beyond gain and loss (verses 39, 267, 412), a state "unshaken by praise and blame" (verse 81), a state not attached to "what is pleasing," nor "to that which is unpleasing" (verse 210). It is this point that many may find difficult to understand: how is such a mental state possible? To highlight the difficulty, let's start with a few English translations of verse 39:

> He whose mind is not soaked (by lust), he who is not affected (by hatred), he who has transcended both good and evil—for such a vigilant one there is no fear. (Thera translation)

> For one who is awake, / Whose mind isn't overflowing, / Whose heart isn't afflicted / And who has abandoned both merit and demerit, / Fear does not exist. (Fronsdal translation)[35]

> There is no fear for the wide awake— / the one who has let go of gain and loss, whose mind is not moistened by passion, / whose thoughts are unassailed. (Wallis translation)

> They are wise whose thoughts are steady and minds serene, unaffected by good and bad. They are awake and free from fear. (Easwaran translation)

What does it mean to say that an awakened mind can "transcend both good and evil" ("abandon both merit and demerit," or "let go of gain and loss," or be "unaffected by good and bad")? Does it mean that a pure mind is an indifferent, affectless, and apathetic mind? Does it mean that a pure mind is in a vegetative state, or in a coma? These questions are understandable since for many the very meaning of human life partly consists in the ability to distinguish loss from gain, good from evil, and the ability to pursue for gain (good) and to avoid loss (evil). Many would argue that a human life is impossible without being affected by gain and loss, good and evil.

It seems totally wrong, however, to think that the Buddha is trying to train people to be indifferent, affectless vegetables, because in many places in the Dhammapada the Buddha urges people to live "a life of good conduct" (verse 168), to do "no evil," to engage in "what is skilful [good]" (verse 182), to select "what's good and avoid what's

---

34  Wallis, 119, note 37.
35  Gil Fronsdal, *The Dhammapada* (Boston: Shambhala, 2005).

evil" (verse 269), and to love one's mother and father (verse 332). If the Buddha had intended to train people to be affectless vegetables, he would not have been true to his intention in offering these exhortations. Therefore, it seems extremely implausible to think that both the Buddha and the compilers of the Dhammapada—fine thinkers that they were—would have overlooked such a glaring contradiction.

If a mind untroubled by loss and gain (or good and evil) is not an indifferent, affectless mind, then what is it? A story about the Bible commentator, Matthew Henry (1662–1714), may shed some light on the idea of such a mind. Having been robbed, he wrote: "I thank Thee [God] first because I was never robbed before; second, because although they took my purse they did not take my life; third, because although they took my all, it was not much; and fourth because it was I who was robbed, and not I who robbed."[36] Would Matthew Henry have thought that it was a good thing to be robbed? Definitely not. But, once the robbing had occurred, there was nothing he could have done to reverse the event. So he adopted an attitude of calmness toward a situation usually considered unacceptable. For Matthew Henry, then, every day is a "good" day, and every moment a "good" moment. I think this is what it means to have a calm mind,[37] like the deep ocean. Such a mind is not punctuated by the ups and downs of emotional waves that are caused by the vicissitudes of life.

### DOING PHILOSOPHY
*A Life of Excitement versus a Life of Calmness*

A life of excitement can be seen as a life of tease. It constantly teases you to satisfy your cravings (not just your basic needs, which are limited and easily met) yet never allows you to remain constantly satisfied. Thus your mind is always in a turbulent state. This is why it is extremely difficult to have a calm mind like that revealed in the Matthew Henry story. This fact prompts some to argue that, if one follows the Buddha's way of life, not to be bothered by gain and loss, good and bad, etc., then one's life would be boring, for there would be no excitement or interesting ups and downs. As one of my students put it in a weekly commentary in my Asian philosophy class, "an emancipated person can no longer be considered human, as it goes against what it is to be human to be free from sorrow and be eternally happy."

Do you agree with this argument? Do humans have a fixed nature? Could we argue that while there may be (in some sense) a difference between

---

36 This widely repeated quotation (see, for example, <http://thinkexist.com/quotes/matthew_henry/>) may be a misquotation (see <http://en.wikiquote.org/wiki/Matthew_Henry>). In any case, it's the attitude projected here that's of interest to us.

37 See a similar idea in Confucius' *Analects*: "He that is really Good can never be unhappy." *The Analects of Confucius*, Arthur Waley, trans. (New York: Macmillan, 1938), 9:28.

extraordinary human beings (such as Socrates, Jesus, the Buddha, and Confucius) and ordinary human beings, their greatness does not render them any less human? Moreover, if the Buddha after enlightenment has a motivation to liberate others from sufferings (which are caused by cravings), would his own motivation be considered a craving, perhaps the last craving to end all cravings?

## THE BUDDHA'S EMPHASIS ON EXPERIENCE

The Buddha emphasizes direct experience—not the authority of a teacher, such as the Buddha himself, or of a text, such as the Vedas or the Upanishads—as the source and content of his teachings. As the Buddhism scholar A.K. Warder noted, the Buddha "rejected all authorities except experience: the student should experiment for himself and see that the teaching is true, not accept it because the Buddha says so."[38]

The Buddha's enlightenment and consequently his teachings are grounded in his experience of meditation, not the sort of ordinary perceptual experience we have when awake. In an ordinary perceptual episode, or even in a series of contiguous perceptual episodes that span a short period of time (say, a week), we see very little if any change in externals or in ourselves. Even when we do notice that we have changed over a longer period of time (say, two years), we may still think of the change as only applying to our appearance and not to our self-identity, or the core of our Self.

The Buddhist meditative experience can lead one to experience (realize) the impermanence of things, especially the impermanence of one's self.[39] While the attachment to an imaginary Self may generate ills of selfish desire, craving, hatred, conceit, pride, and egoism, the realization of the impermanence (or interdependence) of the self helps cure these ills.

In stressing the importance of direct experience, the Buddha encourages his followers to focus on questions that are answerable experientially, and to avoid unfruitful metaphysical speculations. Metaphysical questions—such as "Is the Universe eternal?" "Is the soul the same as the body?" "Does the Buddha exist after death?"—are intellectually enticing, but the Buddha considers them counter-productive speculations. These questions are neither experientially answerable nor consequential to our urgent and practical concern—the elimination of suffering. The Buddha presses home this point with a parable:[40] A man had been wounded by an arrow thickly smeared with

---

38  Warder, 35.

39  Buddhism is no ordinary empiricism. Hoffman has explained it this way: "In Buddhism, although the doctrine is a 'come and see' doctrine, it will not be falsified by the assiduous meditating monk who meditates and yet does not 'see' rebirth. If such a monk were ever dull enough to conflate meditation with a scientific hypothesis capable of falsification if false, then he will face the meditation teacher's unrelenting remonstrations to go and meditate more. At no point will the meditation teacher agree that the student has falsified the doctrine in case the student came and did not see" (Frank J. Hoffman, *Rationality and Mind in Early Buddhism* [Delhi: Motilal Banarsidass, 1987], 98).

40  See Huston Smith and Philip Novak, *Buddhism—A Concise Introduction* (New York: HarperCollins, 2003), 26–27.

poison. When a surgeon arrived, the wounded man stubbornly insisted that he would not have the arrow pulled out until he knew by what man he was wounded, or until he knew what the bow was made of. However, before knowing all this, that man would have died.[41]

In line with his reliance on experience, the Buddha uses terms like "deities" and "spirits" as mere posited entities. As Wallis has pointed out, "Nowhere, the Buddha insisted, were the kinds of powers, forces and beings that are posited in the narratives of theistic traditions really observable—nowhere, that is, outside the narratives themselves."[42] While the Buddha still preserved many terms used in the Vedic tradition that may be read in a reified or theistic way, he radically changed the senses of the terms he appropriated. In other words, he (mostly) used the "old bottle" but put into it completely "new wine."

To see how the Buddha put "new wine" into the "old bottle," we need to understand his non-reified understanding of some key terms that were prevalent in India at his time: karma, death, and nirvana.

### KARMA

As we know from the previous chapter, "karma" means "action" or "deed" in the Upanishads. In the Brahmanism that is based on the Vedas and the Upanishads, karma was primarily understood outwardly and ritualistically, with a fixation on the outcome or result of an action or ritual. Due to this fixation, as noted earlier, ritual practice in the Buddha's time had slipped into sheer formalism. To counteract this external focus, the Buddha traced the sources of deeds or actions to the mind.[43] He emphasized the volition of actions (verse 1)—whether mental, verbal, or physical.[44]

By reinterpreting karma as a matter of volition, the Buddha had undermined the hereditary basis of the caste system (see *Chandogya*, V.10.7). According to the Buddha, a Brahmin could not be said to have been determined by birth; rather, one's moral and social status is determined by one's volition. In other words, one *is* what one intends or one *is* one's intentions—the line between intentions and actions has been dropped. In emphasizing the oneness of intentions and actions, the Buddha would agree with Jesus' view that "anyone who looks at a woman lustfully has already committed adultery with her in his heart" (Matthew 5: 28).[45]

---

41  Given the Buddha's doctrine of interdependent-arising and his acceptance of karma theory, we may infer that he would not be against science per se; for example, he would not be against astronomy, but it seems that he would not think the subject of astronomy as urgent and important as ethical practice and meditation.

42  Wallis, Foreword, xii.

43  See Nikunja Vihari Banerjee, *The Dhammapada* (New Delhi: Munshiram Manoharlal Publishers, 1989), Introduction, 7.

44  Thus, involuntary, unintentional, or unconscious actions, though technically deeds, do not count as one's karma; such actions may result in criminal responsibility, not karmic responsibility. However, this understanding of karma may raise the following question: should killing a terminally ill patient with the intention of ending her excruciating pain count as a good intention, hence good karma?

45  It is necessary to point out that in many cases "commit a crime in one's heart" is very different from "commit a crime in reality." Without the distinction, probably every teenager in the world should go to

If we understand karma outwardly, we may be tempted to see karma as an impersonal, blind, ruthless, and unstoppable force, and thus slip into a sense of helplessness in the face of it. However, the Buddha's new understanding of karma opens up a much more positive outlook on life: once we realize how karma stems from our volition, we can learn to dwell consciously on good intentions that allow good karma to take effect and at the same time avoid ("starve") ill intentions that generate bad karma.

> In this world / hostilities are *never* / appeased by hostility. / But by the absence of hostility / are they appeased. / This is an interminable truth. (verse 5)

Thus, the Buddha's teaching on karma encourages a positive approach to living that takes our intentions seriously.

> A destructive act is better undone, / for it consumes one with regret afterwards. / But a constructive act, / doing which one does not regret, / is better done. (verse 314)

> For the person of respectful character / who always honours his elders, / these four qualities increase: / life span, appearance, happiness, and strength. (verse 190)

> Whoever harms with violence / those who are gentle and innocent, / to one of these ten states / that person quickly descends: he would beget / severe suffering; / deprivation and fracturing / of the body; or grave illness, too; / mental imbalance; / trouble from the government; / cruel slander; / loss of relatives; or destruction of property. / Or a raging fire burns his dwellings. / After the dissolution of his body / the unwise one falls into the lower world. (verses 137–40)

> Whoever destroys life in the world / or speaks wrongly, / takes what was not given, / or goes to another's wife, or a person who / drinks intoxicating liquors, / digs up his own root / in this very world. (verses 246–47; cf. verses 309–10)

> The person who wishes ease for himself / through causing pain to others, / contaminated by contact with hostility, / he is not released from hostility. (verse 291)

For example, when one pursues another's wife, even though they (the man and another's wife) have enjoyed some "petty pleasure," they will suffer from "a loss of self-

---

jail. "Do not commit any crime in your heart" reflects a moral exhortation or commitment; "Do not commit any crime" may be just a legal injunction.

worth," "disturbed sleep," "disgrace," "harsh punishment from the government," and transmission to "the lower world [hell]" (verses 309–10).

To those who doubt the working of karma, the Dhammapada suggests that they need to be more patient, for the consequence of an intention/action appears instantly as well as in a temporal sequence. Well-intentioned actions lead to rewards and ill-intentioned actions lead to self-harm, sooner or later. It can be defended that this is indeed how moral causality works in the grand scheme of things even though the consequence of an intention/action may not be obvious to us at the individual or micro-level of experience over a short period of time.

> Even a person who acts to his / own detriment has good fortune / as long as his misdeed has not matured. / But when the misdeed has matured / then that person experiences misfortunes. (verse 119)

> One should not think slightly of injury— / "that will not come to *me*." / With drops of falling water / even a water pot is filled. / The childish person is full of injury / gathered day by day. (verse 121)

> One should not think slightly of value [good acts]— / "that will not come to *me*." / With drops of falling water / even a water pot is filled. / The wise person is full of value / gathered day by day. (verse 122; cf. verses 13–39, 67–69, 127, 131–32)

## DEATH AND NIRVANA (*NIBBANA*)

One can see death as the end of existence, a total annihilation, or one can see it as a phase leading to reincarnation or resurrection. The first may be called annihilationism, and the second eternalism (which postulates either an eternal soul that is to be reincarnated or an enduring personality that is to be resurrected). The Buddha teaches a middle way according to which the effects of a person, namely the person's deeds, survive, without positing any enduring personal identity or soul.

The Buddha's view on death is often illustrated with an analogy of the transmission of a flame from one candle to another. In this analogy, no enduring candle is required in order to keep the flame burning. The first candle burns out, which passes its flame to the next candle in a row, and so the sequence continues. There is no permanent candle running through the whole sequence. In the same manner, the Buddha's view on death is that the *effects* of a person's life can survive, but there is no permanent Self. As Rahula has explained, for the Buddha, "even now during this life time, every moment we are born and die [in the sense that we change constantly], but we continue. If we can understand that in this life we can continue without a permanent, unchanging substance like Self or Soul, why can't we understand that those forces themselves can continue without a Self or a Soul behind them after the non-functioning of the body?"[46]

---

46 Rahula, 33.

For the Buddha, birth and death are not to be understood as end points that mark the beginning and end of a line called "life," but as perpetual events that occur at *any* moment within and without "life." According to this understanding, any change or any moment can be seen as "birth" *and* "death." If any moment within and without this "life" is equally seen as both "birth" and "death," then there is neither the birth of an identity nor the death of it.

The idea that "in this life we can continue without a permanent, unchanging substance like Self or Soul" may be troublesome for ethics, as ethics seems to assume self-identify across time. For example, we believe that if a man who committed a crime ten years ago is caught by the police now, he should be judged and convicted—despite the fact that much about him (such as his job, name, height, personality, etc.) may have changed. We believe that he is still the *same* person. But in what sense is he the "same" person? Do we have to assume a metaphysical (permanent and independent) self-identity to make moral or legal judgements? It seems that as long as there is sufficient evidence of wrongdoing by the earlier person, and of his continuity with the present one (for example, bodily continuity, continuity provided by memories, continuing similarities in personality, and identical DNA), a conviction can be secured. In this case, there is no need to assume (metaphysically) that the suspect has an enduring Self or Soul. The various continuities mentioned above are linguistic devices that do not assume any metaphysical agent behind the continuities. These linguistic conventions do not refer to what philosophers take to be the enduring Self or Soul.

The lack of an enduring identity, however, does not release us from our moral responsibility. A criminal, for example, cannot argue (convincingly) to the jury that, since he lacks an enduring Self or Soul, and he is not the same person that he was at the time the crime was committed, he should not be held responsible for the crime. Therefore, for the Buddha, as long as moral causality is granted, we can accept the notion of moral responsibility without having to assume a permanent self-identity. Ethics, according to the Buddha, is not based on metaphysical assumptions (such as the existence of *Atman* as a permanent agent), but on human empathy and sympathy. "All tremble before violence. / All fear death. / Having done the same yourself, / you should neither harm nor kill. All tremble before violence. / Life is held dear by all. Having done the same yourself, / you should neither harm nor kill" (verses 129–30).

If, in the face of death (the ceasing of brain activity followed by the decay of the body) we seek comfort from the Dhammapada, we are likely to feel disappointed. Instead of promising that there is an "I" that survives after death, the Dhammapada candidly admits that death is necessary and inevitable. The following verses may sound particularly disheartening for those of us who yearn for immortality:

Soon, for certain, / this body will lie on the ground, / cast away, without consciousness, / like a useless log. (verse 41)

Worn out is this body, / a frail nest of disease. / This festering mass breaks apart, / for life has death as its end. (verse 148)

Like gourds / cast off in autumn / are these grey bones. / Seeing them as such—what joy? (verse 149)

## DOING PHILOSOPHY
*The Buddha's Death versus Jesus' Death*

We are told in the *Nirvana Sutra* that Gautama addressed his disciples just before his death with the following words: "Although I may die, you must not for that reason think that you are left without a leader. The teachings and precepts I have expounded to you shall be your leader. Therefore if any of you have any doubts, now is the time to question me about them. You must not lay yourself open to regret later on, when you may say, 'why didn't we ask him while he was still alive!' Shortly after, he said, 'Decay is inherent in all composite things. Work out your salvation with diligence.'"[47]

According to Hoffman, the Buddha's teachings could still be valid even if Gautama did not exist. However, the core teachings of Christianity would collapse if Jesus did not exist, or if one denied the literal resurrection of Jesus Christ, which Christians traditionally believe to have occurred. Hoffman argues, "[f]or the Buddhist path or doctrine does not depend on the historicity of Gotama [Gautama] in the way that Christianity depends on the historicity of Jesus and on his resurrection. Buddhism 'depends on' Gotama in the sense that he is viewed as the turner of the wheel of doctrine in the present eon. But Gotama is not viewed as the first such Buddha, nor the last ... Jesus' existence is logically a pre-condition for his undergoing a resurrection, as Gotama's existence is logically a pre-condition for his becoming a Buddha. Yet whereas if it could be shown that the Biblical Jesus did not exist Christianity would be undermined, if it could be shown that Gotama did not exist, Buddhism would not be undermined. So it is not the historicity of Gotama which supports Buddhism, unlike the situation with Christianity."[48]

Do you agree with Hoffman? Why or why not? Can we argue that the moral teachings of Jesus would still be valid even if he had not been literally resurrected? Should we rather understand Jesus' resurrection in a metaphorical sense? You may want to consult what St. Paul says in 1 Corinthians 15:13–19. (Hint: Disciples of a great spiritual teacher often have a strong inclination to divinize their teacher. To turn a great historical spiritual teacher into a divine being can make his / her teaching more attractive and more authoritative to later followers. But it can also make people, particularly the sceptical-minded, doubt the whole business of divining embellishment.)

---

47  Daisaku Ikeda, *Buddhism: The First Millennium*, Burton Watson, trans. (New York: Kodansha International, 1977), 16.
48  Hoffman, 6.

Given the above verses, it is indeed puzzling to read statements about death in the Dhammapada that seem to affirm a diametrically opposite view—the view that one can reach a deathless state of being. Verses on this view are many: "Diligence is the path to the deathless ... The diligent do not die" (verse 21), death can be mastered (verses 44–45), and it is possible to "walk beyond the sight of the king of death" (verse 46). If the Dhammapada is not contradicting itself about death, the word "death" in these verses must be used in a different sense from its conventional sense. In these verses, "death" must not be taken as referring literally to the end of a physical life. Rather, according to Gil Fronsdal, it must be taken to mean the *deadly forces* in life and in experience, such as fear, anger, and clinging.[49]

Thus, in the Dhammapada, death as a natural phenomenon is not denied; what is denied is that it absolutely matters to us humans—we can cultivate our mind so that death (the end of our physical life) does not bother us anymore. A legend in the Buddhist tradition illustrates the point.

A mother once came to the Buddha for help because her only son was dying due to an incurable disease. The Buddha advised her to get a handful of mustard seeds as medicine from a house where no one had lost a child, husband, parent, or friend. With great expectation, the mother went from house to house in the village, but to no avail. There was not a single house which had never lost a child, husband, parent, or friend.

And soon the son died, but the mother had learned an object lesson, and a hard one, from the Buddha's advice: death is common to all, and in the face of it, one needs "the courage to be" (to borrow a phrase from theologian and Christian existentialist philosopher Paul Tillich). Eventually the mother buried her son and took refuge in the Buddha's teaching. The message in the legend is clear: the emancipation that the Buddha is preaching is based on a profound recognition and acceptance of the certainty of physical death (see verses 46, 170).

The Upanishads argue that one's true Self, *Atman*, cannot be touched by death, because *Atman* is essentially different from the empirical self that is susceptible to change and death. But the Dhammapada denies that we have two selves: the empirical self and the transcendental Self, *Atman*. For the Buddha, the empirical self is the only self there is. Since there is no constant or enduring Self, or "I," then, logically, death cannot touch "I." That is, if I am not an enduring entity (but like froth, a mirage, or a burned log) in the first place, there is no death of *me* (as a substance)! Once I have realized that there is no enduring "I" (this sounds paradoxical), death cannot touch "me" (verses 62, 367).

---

49 Fronsdal, Introduction, xxvi; also see Thera, 51 who interprets "death" in verse 46 as "life's sorrow, born of passion."

## DOING PHILOSOPHY
*Self-Reliance versus Other-Reliance:*
*The Dhammapada, Mahayana Buddhism, and Christianity*

Does emancipation rely on one's self-effort, on others, or on external forces, such as divine beings? The Dhammapada emphasizes self-reliance. For example, verse 165 claims that "By oneself is damage done: / by oneself is one defiled. / By oneself is damage not done: / by oneself is one purified. / Purity and impurity come from oneself. / No one can purify another." Again, verse 276 and verse 380 reiterate the message: "It is up to you to strive ardently. / The Buddhas are those who make known the way. / Those who follow, practicing meditation, / are released from Mara's bond." "You, indeed, are the master of yourself. / You, indeed, are your own refuge. / So, restrain yourself, / like a merchant restrains a fine horse" (cf. verses 50, 58–59, 80, 103–05, 145, 160, 181, and Chapter 12, "Oneself," of the Dhammapada).

Self-reliance, however, does not negate the need for enlightened beings (i.e., Buddhas) or spiritual teachers. Self-reliance means that whether a person follows a particular path ultimately depends on that person, but it acknowledges the contribution that external forces can make towards that person's emancipation.

The Mahayana school of Buddhism later developed a faith in divine-like bodhisattvas (especially in popular Buddhist practice) that strengthened the importance of external help. Concerning the idea of external help, Christianity went even further: it stressed that without divine grace, including the sacrifice of Jesus, no matter how hard we try, we would not be able to save ourselves.

Buddhists generally admit that external forces (called skilful means, *upaya*) can certainly be helpful, encouraging, and inspiring. (Just think of the effect that the utterance "Santa Claus is watching you!" may have on a child before Christmas. A simple mention of Santa Claus, an imagined figure notwithstanding, can indeed make children behave.) But Buddhists also warn us that external forces can be abused or misused when one relies on them exclusively, without making serious self-effort. Thus Buddhists stress that it is only when external factors are coupled with self-effort and self-change that they can contribute to emancipation.

The idea of self-reliance in the Dhammapada is based on a non-theistic understanding of the law of karma. Christmas Humphreys explained this point nicely: "An understanding of the law of Karma leads to self-reliance,

for in proportion as we understand its operation we cease to complain of
our circumstances, and cease from turning with the weakness of a child to a
man-made God to save us from the natural consequences of our acts. Karma
is no God, for the gods themselves are subject to its sway. Only the ignorant
personify Karma, and attempt to bribe, petition or cajole it; wise men understand it and conform to it."[50] Do you agree with Humphreys that only "the
ignorant personify Karma"?

The deathless state that is discussed throughout the Dhammapada is called nirvana.[51] Nirvana can be seen as a Buddhist counterpart of *moksha* that is discussed
in the Upanishads, but nirvana does not assume anything eternal, either *Atman* or
*Brahman*. Nirvana is not a promised union of the individual self with a universal Self
(*Brahman*), but the absence of suffering, or the absence of deadly forces such as greed,
hatred, and confusion.

Many Western readers tend to unwittingly regard nirvana as the Buddhist counterpart to resurrection—being in a different time (future), a different location (Heaven).
But this reading is a misunderstanding. The word "nirvana" literally means "blow
out," as in the extinguishing of a fire by the exhaustion of the fuel. In the Buddhist
context, it means extinguishing the fire of lust, hatred, and delusion. It can also mean
"unbinding," indicating a state that is not bound by cravings or attachments.[52] It is not
something that only happens in one's future (afterlife).

Nor is nirvana a simple change of location. To be in nirvana is not as simple as
to go from one room to another, though sometimes changing a location can help
one alter one's mental state and habits. A mere change of location, according to the
Dhammapada, is not enough for liberation. "People who are anxious with fear / often
go for refuge to mountains and forests / to tree shrines in pleasant groves. / This is
not a secure refuge. / This is not the best refuge. / Arriving at that refuge, / a person
is not released from all pain" (verses 188–89). Rather, nirvana or liberation has to do
with a change of one's state of being. When a person reaches nirvana, sometimes it is
said as if that person *went to* the other shore (verses 85, 414). But this is not to be taken
literally or spatially. When we say "John *went to* sleep," we do not mean John literally
"went anywhere"—another city, for example. We simply mean that without changing
physical location, John's state of being changes from "being awake" to "being asleep."
Therefore, an enlightened one and an ignorant one may live in the same place, but
live in totally different states, with the former "gazing down," "as if standing on a
mountain," "on the sorrowing people" or "the childish ones below / standing on the
ground" (verse 28).

50  Christmas Humphreys, *Buddhism: An Introduction and Guide* (New York: Penguin Books, 1962),
102–03. See also Warder, 151–52.
51  See verses 21, 23, 32, 75, 89, 114, 126, 134, 184, 203, 204, 218, 226, 285, 289, 369, 372, and 411.
52  See Wallis, 113–15, note 23.

## CONCLUDING REMARKS:
## THE INFLUENCE OF THE DHAMMAPADA

As a classic of Buddhism, the Dhammapada is often contrasted with the Upanishads—the classic texts of Hinduism. They are sometimes seen as proposing directly opposing views about life and practice. For example, ontologically, the Upanishads maintain that both the Self (*Atman*) and the world (*Brahman*) are permanent, whereas the Dhammapada insists that nothing is permanent and there is no Self. However, it will be going too far to conclude from this ontological difference that concerning ethics the Dhammapada is in direct opposition to the Upanishads. On the contrary, as far as ethics is concerned, these two texts share many similarities.

First, the purpose of identifying *Atman* with *Brahman* in the Upanishads is to teach people not to be egoistic or selfish, so too is the purpose of the Buddhist doctrine of no-self (*anatman*) in the Dhammapada. *Atman*, though sometimes translated as Self, does not stand for ego-centredness, but for non-individualistic Self. While Atman is commonly taken to be a permanent agent, it is perhaps better seen as a non-ego-centred consciousness. Second, both the Upanishads and the Dhammapada accept the idea of karma or moral causality (see *Brihadaranyaka*, IV.xxxviii.5 and Dhammapada verse 1). Third, both texts hold a conviction in human capacity for self-realization or self-emancipation.

There are indeed ideas (or interpretations of ideas) in the Upanishads that the Dhammapada did not accept. First of all, the Dhammapada did not accept the idea of *Atman* as an immortal agent on the basis that the idea is experientially baseless and that breaking through the ego-self does not have to lead to an immortal *Atman*. Instead of arguing for an immortal Self, the Dhammapada replaced it with a non-identical but continuous awareness. It would seem, in the view of the Dhammapada, that the presupposition of *Atman* may unwittingly encourage people to identify it with a putative *jiva* (personal soul) and thus make them attach to egoistic cravings. Second, the Dhammapada rejects the caste system that may be implied in certain interpretations of ideas in the Upanishads that divides people into a hereditary and rigid hierarchy. The Dhammapada argues that all human beings are equal, regardless of caste, gender, or anything else. It seems to have resolved the tension between social distinction as entailed in the caste system and the idea of equality taught in the Upanishads (as in the claim "*Atman* is *Brahman*") by discarding the former. In this connection, the Dhammapada proposed a way of emancipation that is open to everyone, in contrast with the teachings of the Upanishads which seem to be (at least in practice) accessible only to sages and Brahmins.

Given the above comparison between the Dhammapada and the Upanishads, it is better to see the Buddha not as a destroyer of the teachings of the Upanishads, but as an innovative interpreter of what he saw as the true message of the Upanishads. In this light, it is better to see the Dhammapada and the Upanishads not as two opposing texts but as two equally beautiful spiritual guides—both of which aim at helping people to live effectively and free from suffering.[53]

---

53 It must be noted that the metaphysical assumption of the indestructible and immutable Self (*Brahman* or *Atman*) may be used to justify violence and killing. In the Bhagavadgita, which has been

Since many of the ideas in the Dhammapada also appear in other Buddhist scriptures, it is difficult to trace this scripture's precise influence on later development of Buddhism. However, it is safe to say that, as a Buddhist classic and a handbook for practitioners, it has had a great general impact on the spread and development of Buddhism. Indeed, even if all the voluminous scriptures of Buddhism were lost, as long as we have the Dhammapada, we would still have the quintessence of the Buddha's teachings.

A survey of the major ideas in the Dhammapada also explains why Buddhism was able to spread beyond the borders of India, and take root in South East Asian and East Asia, particularly in China. First, according to the Buddha's teachings, all are equal, and people should be judged not by their birth, appearance, or social status, but by their moral character. This idea is appealing to the Confucian thinkers in China as it resonates well with Confucius' idea that an exemplary person (*junzi*) is to be judged by character rather than birth. Second, the Buddha's emphasis on the importance of self-reliance in order to free oneself from suffering accords nicely with Confucius' stress on moral self-cultivation. Third, the Buddha's ethical teachings are just as humanistic (or non-theistic) as Confucius' teachings. Finally, the Buddha's sensitivity to the impermanent nature of the world chimes well with the Chinese Daoist idea of change and transformation of things. Therefore, it is no accident that Buddhism came to be an important influence on the Chinese mentality.

## WORKS CITED AND RECOMMENDED READINGS

1. Gil Fronsdal, trans., *The Dhammapada, A New Translation of the Buddhist Classic, with Annotations* (Boston: Shambhala, 2005).
2. Narada Thera, trans., *The Dhammapada, Pali Text and Translation with Stories in Brief and Notes* (Taipei: The Corporate Body of the Buddha Educational Foundation, 1993).
3. A.L. Herman, *An Introduction to Buddhist Thought—Philosophic History of Indian Buddhism* (New York: University Press of America, 1983).
4. Frank J. Hoffman, *Rationality & Mind in Early Buddhism* (Delhi: Motilal Banarsidass, 1987).
5. Walpola Rahula, *What the Buddha Taught* (New York: Grove Press, 1974).
6. Steven Collins, *Selfless Persons* (Cambridge: Cambridge University Press, 1982).
7. Heinrich Zimmer, *Philosophies of India*, ed. Joseph Campbell (Princeton: Princeton University Press, 1969).
8. Charles A. Moore, ed., *The Indian Mind—Essentials of Indian Philosophy and Culture* (Honolulu: The University Press of Hawaii, 1967).

---

seen as the quintessence of the Upanishads, Arjuna was exhorted to slay his enemies in view of the metaphysical knowledge of the indestructible and immutable Self. (See Bhagavadgita, II.)

# CHAPTER 3

# The *Mulamadhyamakakarika*
## (The *Fundamental Verses on the Middle Way*)

SUGGESTED PRIMARY READING

Selected sections of Nagarjuna's *Mulamadhyamakakarika*, from *The Fundamental Wisdom of the Middle Way*, Jay L. Garfield, trans. (New York: Oxford University Press, 1995): Dedicatory Verses, Chapter I: Examination of Conditions, Chapter IV: Examination of the Aggregates, Chapter XIX: Examination of Time, Chapter XXIV: Examination of the Four Noble Truths, and Chapter XXV: Examination of Nirvana.

### LEARNING OBJECTIVES

By the time you have worked through this chapter, you should be able to

- Explain Nagarjuna's notion of "emptiness" (as interdependent-arising)
- Describe Nagarjuna's critique of substantial and nihilistic theories of causality
- Describe Nagarjuna's critique of substantial conceptions of time
- Explain Nagarjuna's "Middle Way"
- Explain Nagarjuna's identification of *samsara* and *nirvana*

### KEY WORDS

interdependent-arising (*pratîtyasamutpâda*), emptiness (*shunyata*), middle way, dependent designation, self-essence (*svabhava*), conventional and ultimate truths, *samsara* (birth-death cyclic existence), *nirvana*

## GUIDING QUESTIONS

Despite the Buddha's warning against the two extremes of substantialism and nihilism, his insight of interdependent-arising (*pratîtyasamutpâda*) has been misinterpreted either substantially or nihilistically. A substantial reading of it leads to a belief that all things arise out of basic, changeless elements called *dharmas*. A nihilist reading takes "interdependent-arising" itself as simply meaning "non-being," or "total void." In defending the Buddha's insight against the above misinterpretations, Nagarjuna, one of the best known Buddhist philosophers in history, asked the following questions:

1.  What are the dangers of the substantial and nihilistic misinterpretations of the Buddha's insight?
2.  How do we reconcile our common intuition that things exist and the Buddha's deep insight that no thing (as entity with self-essence, *svabhava*) exists?
3.  From the perspective of emptiness (interdependent-arising), how do we understand important ideas in Buddhism, such as time, samsara and nirvana?

In answering these questions, Nagarjuna closely followed the Buddha's steps by walking a subtle "Middle Way."

## INTRODUCTION

The *Fundamental Verses on the Middle Way* was written by Indian Buddhist philosopher Nagarjuna (second century CE),[1] the founder of the Middle Way school (*Madhyamaka*) of Mahayana Buddhism.[2] It is arguably the most important and most influential philosophic classic in Mahayana Buddhism, as evidenced by its tremendous influence on various Mahayana schools of Buddhism in China, Tibet, and Japan. We shall see its impact on Chinese Chan, as exemplified in Hui Neng's Platform Sutra (see Chapter 9), and on Japanese Zen, as seen in Dogen's *Shobogenzo* (see Chapter 10).

---

1    Little is known about Nagarjuna's life except that he was born in a Brahmin family in southern India and later converted to Buddhism when he migrated to northern India, then a centre of Buddhist-activity.
2    The Mahayana ("Great Vehicle") tradition arose around 200–100 BCE in India. In contrast with the Theravada or Hinayana ("Small Vehicle") tradition which followed the Buddha's original teachings, the Mahayana tradition universalizes or generalizes the Buddha's teachings. First, Mahayana tradition treats Gautama, the historical Buddha, as merely one of the innumerable "buddhas"—that is, the enlightened ones. Secondly, it regards laypersons (not solely the monks and nuns) as fully capable of attaining enlightenment. More importantly, unlike the Theravada tradition which emphasizes individual liberation, the Mahayana tradition stresses an ideal of becoming a Bodhisattva (an enlightenment-being) aiming at ending the suffering of all humans and even all sentient beings. This last point particularly explains how the tradition got its name Mahayana ("Great Vehicle"), because it is dedicated to carrying all humans on the Great Vehicle of Buddhist teachings from the sea of suffering to the other shore of nirvana.

The *Fundamental Verses on the Middle Way* contains twenty-seven chapters, which Garfield organizes into four interrelated thematic groups: Chapters i-vii on the Buddhist understanding of reality; Chapters viii-xiii on the nature of self and subjective experience; Chapters xiv-xxi on the external world and the relation of the self to objects; and Chapters xxii-xxvii on the soteriology (the doctrine of salvation) of Buddhism.[3]

In order to see the interconnection of these groups, we can interpret the *Fundamental Verses on the Middle Way* as making a thorough investigation of the notion of "emptiness" (*sunyata*)—an equivalent to the Buddha's insight of interdependent-arising (*pratityas-amutpâda*)—as well as of its ontological and soteriological implications. First, based on the perspective of "emptiness," the text investigates important philosophical topics such as causality, self, time, and samsara and nirvana. Second, it explicates the Buddha's insight of interdependent-arising (achieved by direct experience) and its dynamic, mutually penetrating relationship with the idea of conventional existence (arrived at by conceptual understanding). Third, it argues that, since conceptual construction (reification) is the cause of our cravings and attachments that result in all kinds of suffering, dissolving conceptual construction makes possible the release from suffering.

A challenge that confronts readers of the work—novices and seasoned students alike—is that it is written in a rather terse, cryptic, and paradoxical style, and it is replete with technical terms (e.g., self-essence and nirvana) and idiosyncratic usage (for example, the word "emptiness" for Nagarjuna does not mean "nothingness" as it might suggest to the uninitiated).

A prime example of Nagarjuna's thought-stopping rhetorical device is his use of successive negations and apparent contradictions, neither of which appears to lead anywhere. In the dedicatory verses, he speaks of the interdependently arisen as "unceasing, unborn; unannihilated, not permanent; not coming, not going; without distinction, without identity."[4] This long series of negations is baffling, in that it does not seem to offer anything particularly informative about what exactly interdependent-arising is.[5] His exposition of samsara and nirvana serves as a good illustration of his notorious use of contradictions: "There is not the slightest difference / Between cyclic existence [samsara] and nirvana. / There is not the slightest difference / Between nirvana and cyclic existence" (xxv, verse 19).

How is it that there is not the slightest difference between samsara and nirvana? Are we actually inclined to think of them as poles apart like heaven and hell (against the backdrop of Christianity)? Just imagine how absurd it would sound if one insisted, "There is not the slightest difference / Between heaven and hell. / There is not the slightest difference / Between hell and heaven."

When we approach Nagarjuna's text, it is important not to dismiss these negations and contradictions as trivial language games no matter how odd they may appear to us

---

3   Jay. L. Garfield, trans., *The Fundamental Wisdom of the Middle Way: Nagarjuna's Mulamadhyamaka-karika* (New York: Oxford University Press, 1995), 91–92.
4   Garfield's translation. Unless noted, further quotations from Nagarjuna are from the same translation.
5   See also Chapter xxv verse 3 for a similar list of negations on nirvana.

at first glance.[6] As we will see below, these mind-boggling expressions (when properly contextualized) can be seen as deliberate rhetorical vehicles for truths that are otherwise not easily conveyed, or likely to be misunderstood. They disrupt the conventional and reifying uses of language, which Nagarjuna considered to be the primary source of philosophical errors.

We may find three interpretive rules of thumb helpful when approaching the text. First, we will do well to observe Nagarjuna's idiosyncratic usage of terms. As mentioned earlier, for example, the term "emptiness" (*sunyata*) in Nagarjuna's usage does not mean "nothingness." Second, we have to unpack Nagarjuna's terse verses slowly and carefully to see the reasoning behind them. Third, we need to note that the import of Nagarjuna's theoretical analysis is ultimately soteriological and is intended to guide people to the path of liberation from suffering.

## FROM GAUTAMA BUDDHA TO NAGARJUNA

In the Dedicatory Verses of the work, Nagarjuna declares that it is the Buddha's insight of interdependent-arising that he aims to enunciate and defend: "I prostrate to the Perfect Buddha, the best of teachers, who taught [interdependent-arising]." Therefore, in order to understand Nagarjuna's project, it is necessary to first recapitulate what Gautama Buddha taught about interdependent-arising.[7]

The core of Gautama Buddha's teaching consists in the Four Noble Truths: (1) Life (if ignorantly lived) is suffering (*duhkha*); (2) The cause of suffering is ignorance about the true nature of existence (which leads to cravings for permanence and separateness);[8] (3) Destroying ignorance and craving will eliminate suffering; (4) There are practical paths to eradicate suffering. These practical paths, or spiritual practices, are further delineated in the teaching of the Eightfold Path. The first practice included in the Eightfold Path is that of Right View.[9] Since Nagarjuna's thoughts can be seen as an exposition of what the Right View of reality consists in, it is important to first clarify the notion of Right View before examining Nagarjuna's other ideas. This clarification will also

---

6    D.T. Suzuki pointed out (at the risk of over generalization), "the Western mind abhors paradoxes, contradictions, absurdities, obscurantism, emptiness, in short, anything that is not clear, well defined, and capable of determination" (D.T. Suzuki, "Basic Thoughts Underlying Eastern Ethical and Social Practice," in *Philosophy and Culture—East and West*, Charles A. Moore, ed. [Honolulu: University of Hawaii Press, 1962], 429).

7    What we'll call "interdependent-arising" is also translated in the literature as "dependent-arising" and "interdependent origination."

8    The ignorance discussed in the Buddha's teachings is much more fundamental and universal (concerning the very nature of existence) than any ordinary ignorance, for example, ignorance of computer knowledge. One could be very knowledgeable in computer science, or any other science for that matter, yet still be ignorant of the very nature of existence, which, according to the Buddha, is interdependent-arising. However, this is by no means to say that Buddhism is at odds with science (see discussion on conventional and ultimate truths below).

9    The other seven paths are: right intention, right speech, right action, right livelihood, right effort, right mindfulness, and right concentration.

help bring into focus Nagarjuna's role as a faithful follower and defender of Gautama Buddha's teachings.

We commonly see the world as an amalgamation of innumerable objects with different durations, from fleeting moments to eternity. We may observe and believe that these objects are somehow related to one another, but we may also incline to think that they are intrinsically separate from each other, each having its unique independent identity. In a similar fashion, we also tend to view ourselves as autonomous entities, and to assume that our lives are both independent and everlasting in some way. There seems to be an enduring ego that persists through my experiences, and my experiences seem to be *owned* by and to rotate around me as a unitary subject.

### DOING PHILOSOPHY
*From Descartes' Wax to Whitehead's Process: The Pursuit of True Reality*

Descartes argues against the reliability of sense perception as a source of knowledge. To illustrate this point, he speaks of the colour, shape, texture, and smell of a piece of wax. He argues that these features of the wax are subject to change as the wax is heated, but the substance of the wax itself remains unchanged. Thus, our senses alone do not yield true knowledge. Descartes' example here has a great deal of intuitive appeal because it represents how we tend to think about everyday objects. In psychology, thanks to the work of Swiss psychologist Jean Piaget (1896–1980), we know that even young children perceive objects as if they preserve their identity through change—a phenomenon known as cognitive "conservation."

Our use of language fuels the tendency as well. For instance, although there are many different kinds of games, we are tempted to believe that there must be a core common essence ("gameness" or "gamehood") shared by all the games, simply because we use the same word "game" in referring to them.

By the same token, we habitually assume that "I" must refer to an identity core since *I* use it in addressing myself in different situations. But as Wittgenstein has potently argued, the word "game" is a family resemblance concept. It does not represent a core essence of "gameness" or "gamehood," and "I" is an indexical (like "this" and "that") which does not presume a metaphysical identity.

Inspired by quantum mechanics and relativity theory, Alfred Whitehead (1861–1947) rejected the notion that the world consists of static, independent entities, called material objects. His view of reality is that it is as a network of interdependent, dynamic collections of momentary events—the core of his process philosophy. The idea of events or processes is close to the Buddhist notion of interdependent-arising.

The Buddha and Nagarjuna did not deny that such psychological tendencies constitute the tacit assumptions underlying our everyday activities, but they regarded these tendencies as potentially detrimental to our ethical and spiritual life. For the Buddha and Nagarjuna, the problem is that such psychological tendencies may cause us to cling to the *deemed* or *posited* independence and eternity of an object or of the self, which in turn leads to a self-centred outlook on life. It is precisely this clinging to self-centredness that keeps us in the state of ignorance. Thus enlightenment is not possible until this self-centred clinging is destroyed. An important way to overcome such self-oriented clinging is the practice of meditation, through which one can come to see the truth that things are in fact empty of any independently existing essence. This is the truth of interdependent-arising, which is also the Right View.

Interdependent-arising means that everything is constantly changing and is dependent on a variety of conditions. In other words, it means that nothing is permanent, nothing exists independently of conditions, and nothing is self-sufficient. A person, seen from the perspective of interdependent-arising, is only a collection of ever-changing physical and mental processes or events. This understanding of personhood is summed up in the Buddhist teaching of five aggregates, namely the five physical and mental processes that constitute a person, including matter (bodily processes), sensations, perceptions, mental formations (volitions), and consciousness. There is no permanent self or identity behind or above these aggregates, just as there is no independent entity called a "university" behind and beyond its campus facilities and the activities that go on there. To say a person is not permanent is *not merely* to say that that person is going to die one day (though it is true), but also that *at every instant* that person is constantly changing and constantly dependent (both physically and mentally) on conditions.

It is one thing to assent to the belief that there is no independent, permanent self; it is quite another to live by it, for our default disposition is to act as if we *do* have independent, permanent selves. One may think, for instance, that "my life achievement is solely mine"—such thinking leads to arrogance. One may also think that "others' problems are theirs, not mine"—such thinking leads to apathy. Furthermore, in order for a person (say, Peter) to hate or even kill another person (say, John), Peter has to first treat John as an "other," one that is completely separated from Peter, rather than as an integral part of Peter's life.

All these—arrogance, apathy, hatred, and killing—arise from a false belief in a separate and permanent self. And it is Gautama Buddha's belief that *realizing* the ultimate truth of interdependent-arising will enable people to eliminate the craving for permanence and independency, and thereby to lead a selfless and compassionate life.

Gautama's insight of interdependent-arising raises some interesting philosophical questions. For example, if things have interdependently arisen from certain conditions, how should we construe the conditions themselves? Are they to be seen as ultimate constituents of the world, like atoms—minute, indivisible, and independent particles? Or are they to be seen also as interdependent-arising phenomena?

The Sarvastivada (sarva means "all"; asti "exist"; vada "saying") schools—founded around the third century BCE, and influential for centuries—viewed the principle of interdependent-arising as operating on atom-like constituents. They argued that while commonly observed things exist, they exist merely as constructions composed of basic, ultimate, self-existent constituents, called *dharmas*.[10] The idea of interdependent-arising, according to the Sarvastivadins, can be explained with an example of a jigsaw puzzle and its pieces: the puzzle as a whole is a construction made up of its pieces, but the pieces themselves are fundamental, ultimate, and not arising from anything else. In other words, for the Sarvastivadins, interdependent-arising is at work at the level of the puzzle as a whole, but not at the level of its constituent pieces.

In positing *dharmas* as the ultimate building blocks of the world that possess a self-existent essence (*svabhava*),[11] the Sarvastivadins did not push the idea of interdependent-arising to all levels of existence, for they saw a danger in doing so. They worried that if there were no ultimate real (self-existent) constituents, then everything would be foundationless, and nothing could exist. They worried that the aggregates that constitute a person would also have no reality, and thus the person would not really exist at all, because neither the identity of a person nor the continuity of personal identity would be conceivable.

A fatal implication of this view is that there would be no real Gautama Buddha, let alone his teachings! The goal of Buddhist practice would be completely unattainable, for there would not be a person with an enduring identity to practice the path and to obtain enlightenment. In short, the Sarvastivadin metaphysicians feared that if some sort of ultimate, self-existent constituents were not posited, all of the Buddha's teachings would collapse into nihilism. However, in positing these self-existent dharmas, the Sarvastivadins elicited a disguised version of substantialism, not unlike the way in which *Atman* and *Brahman* were often understood in the Upanishads. Indeed, the idea of dharmas can be seen as a "reincarnation" of the idea of *Atman* in that both claim permanence.

It is against the Sarvastvadins' interpretation of interdependent-arising that Nagarjuna proposed an alternative interpretation, which aims to dissolve the Sarvastvadin's posited ultimate constituents. The Dedicatory Verses expressly connect Nagarjuna's teaching of interdependent-arising to that of the Buddha. For Nagarjuna, the Sarvastivadin metaphysicians suffered from a grave logical inconsistency in holding that on the one hand commonly perceived objects are the function of interdependent-arising and on the other hand that there are ultimate constituents, which are *not* subject to interdependent-arising. To avoid this inconsistency, Nagarjuna maintained that

---

10  These fundamental elements are similar to atoms ("particles that are indivisible") understood by Pre-Socratic atomist Democritus (c. 460– c. 370 BCE) in the sense that they are fundamental, self-sufficient, and unchangeable.

11  According to Paul Williams, the concept of *svabhava* originally "seems to indicate the defining characteristic of a *dharma*. It is that which makes a *dharma* what it is, as resistance or hardness is the unique and defining characteristic of an earth dharma, for example....The concept of the essence (*svabhava*), however, seems to undergo a subtle shift in meaning in the Madhyamaka. It comes to signify generally 'inherent existence' in the sense of independent real existence. For *x* to have inherent existence is for *x* to exist in its own right" (Paul Williams, *Mahayana Buddhism—The Doctrinal Foundations* [London: Routledge, 1989], 60).

interdependent-arising, properly understood, entails that there are no self-existent constituents.[12] We'll see in a moment how he answered the objections to this position.

Now that we have given a background setting for Nagarjuna's work, let's turn our attention briefly to Nagarjuna's arguments. Contrary to many people's general and often misleading impression about Asian philosophy being non-argumentative, Nagarjuna stood out as a master of logical argumentation by any standard. Indeed, it is precisely through his skilful employment of the tool of logic that he was able to deconstruct the substantialist and the nihilistic misunderstandings of Gautama Buddha's teachings.

Nagarjuna's two major logical techniques merit particular emphasis. The first one is his use of the *reductio ad absurdum* (RAA) method. For example, in his effort to refute substantialism and nihilism, Nagarjuna first assumed that these positions were true and proceeded to deduce from them conclusions that turned out to be contradictions, which then became grounds for rejecting those positions. This technique is an effective way of disarming the defences of those who are sympathetic to the views being refuted. At the time of the writing of the *Fundamental Verses on the Middle Way*, the two positions Nagarjuna set out to refute had already enjoyed much popularity (see Chapters XXIV and XXV), so the use of *reductio ad absurdum* would have been particularly timely.

The second major logical technique that Nagarjuna employed is tetralemma. A tetralemma consists of four mutually exclusive and jointly exhaustive logical alternatives:

| a) Affirmation | P | "P is the case" (X is Y) |
|---|---|---|
| b) Negation | Not P | "P is not the case" (X is not-Y) |
| c) Affirmation of both (a) and (b) | P and Not P | "P is the case" and "P is not the case" (X is both Y and not-Y) |
| d) Negation of each of (a) and (b) | Not P, and Not Not P | "P is not the case," and "P is not not the case" (X is neither Y nor not-Y) |

Nagarjuna analyzed what he considered to be the false metaphysical views pertaining to topics such as interdependent-arising, conditions, and nirvana (see Chapter XXV) in the form of a tetralemma. Then, he proceeded to show that none of the alternatives in the tetralemma are viable.

---

12   For an interpretation of Nagarjuna's project that is similar to what we make here, see Kalupahana 5–7. For a different interpretation, see David Burton, *Emptiness Appraised—A Critical Study of Nagarjuna's Philosophy* (London: Curzon Press, 1999), Preface, x–xi.

## WHAT "EMPTINESS" REALLY MEANS FOR NAGARJUNA

The *Fundamental Verses on the Middle Way* can be read, as a whole, as an explication of how the idea of emptiness bears upon a variety of topics in the Buddha's teachings. It is Nagarjuna's belief that a proper understanding of emptiness serves to dispel all the misunderstandings and criticisms of the Buddha's teachings. As he puts it: "For him to whom emptiness is clear, / Everything is clear. / For him to whom emptiness is not clear, / Nothing becomes clear" (Chapter xxiv.14).

Therefore, to understand Nagarjuna's "Middle Way," it is crucial to first understand his use of the term "*sunyata*," most commonly translated as "emptiness." As an approximation to the term "*sunyata*," "emptiness" can be misleading. It may lead people to think that "*sunyata*" means "nothingness" or "void."

In order to get a proper understanding of the sense in which Nagarjuna uses the term "*sunyata*" ("emptiness"), let's consider how the word "empty" is used in the following statements:

1.  "Nobody is in the room; the room is empty."
2.  "Life is meaningless; it is empty."
3.  "I am stunned at the crime scene—my mind is empty."
4.  "John has practiced Buddhist mindfulness for 30 years and now his mind is empty (i.e., he has realized emptiness)."

In statement (1), that the room is empty means that nobody is in the room. But the room may be full of other things, say, desks and chairs. In other words, the room is not absolutely (or metaphysically) empty. Similarly, in statement (2), that life is empty does not mean that nothing whatsoever happens in life; it means that life does not have permanent values or purposes that one would hope it to have, or it is empty—devoid of certain expected values or meanings. In statement (3), "my mind is empty" simply means that my mind is not thinking of a particular idea, or my mind is in a mess, or I do not know what to do. But none of the three uses of "empty" in statements (1), (2), and (3) pertains to Nagarjuna's technical notion of "emptiness."

Nagarjuna uses "emptiness" as an equivalent to the Buddha's notion of interdependent-arising. In this equivalence, "emptiness" means "absence of substantial entities" or "absence of any form of reification in consciousness." If we follow Nagarjuna's use of the word "emptiness," we will have to understand the above statements very differently.

With regard to statement (1), when we say a room is "empty," we are saying that the room is not some self-existent substance, but an "arising" that comes out of a configuration of interdependent conditions. Even though the room may be full of ordinarily construed objects, such as desks, chairs, and persons, the room (and indeed everything in it) is still empty of self-existent essence. Similarly, with regard to statement (2), when we say life is empty, we are saying that life is empty (devoid of substance) regardless of whether we believe life has a meaning or not. In other words, even if we believe life has a meaning, life is still absent of self-existent substance.

The empty state of mind addressed in statement (3) is very different from the empty state of mind addressed in statement (4). As explained above, in statement (3), "my mind is empty" means that my mind is not thinking of a particular idea, or that my mind is in chaos. But this does not mean that my mind has realized emptiness (inter-dependent-arising). When John in statement (4) has realized emptiness, even though he still has ideas in mind (thus his mind is *not* "empty" in the normal sense of the word, including such meanings as hollowness, deadness, and meaninglessness), he has realized the non-substantial nature of these ideas, that is, he does not reify them.[13]

To understand Nagarjuna's notion of emptiness, it will help if the idea is put against the backdrop of substantialism and nihilism. Substantialism maintains that the world consists of permanent entities, and nihilism holds that the world is nothing but an illusion, a metaphysical void. Against these two extreme views of existence, Nagarjuna argues that the true nature of things is neither substantial nor void, but "unceasing, unborn, unannihilated, not permanent, not coming, not going, without distinction, without identity" (Dedicatory Verses).

Given the identification of emptiness with interdependent-arising, Nagarjuna's Dedicatory Verses can be paraphrased as follows: "[What-arises-interdependently] does not cease from putative self-essence or nothingness, nor is it born of self-essence or nothingness. Similarly, [what-arises-interdependently] neither exists nor becomes non-existent because of a putative self-essence. It does not come from self-essence or nothing, nor does it change into self-essence or nothing. It is not intrinsically distinc-tive, nor does it intrinsically have an identity." In other words, the Dedicatory Verses meant to convey that what-arises-interdependently cannot be characterized by prop-erties attributed to things with self-essence, such as "ceasing," "born," "annihilated," "permanent," "coming and going."

For Nagarjuna, neither nihilism nor substantialism offered a coherent explanation of the phenomenon of change. On the one hand, if existence is seen as absolute noth-ingness (by nihilism), then what undergoes change? On the other hand, if existence is seen as consisting of substantial entities (by substantialism), then how could change happen to these entities?

In trying to understand true reality in a way other than the two extremes of nihil-ism and substantialism, one may take Plato's route of dualism, which argues for two levels of existence: the phenomenal existence that changes all the time, and the ultimate existence of Forms that does not change at all. In everyday life we seem to be operating (though unconsciously) with a version of Plato's dualism, in that we tend to accept the developmental changes we experience through our lifespan and yet believe that there is an enduring part of us (the "real" Self) that stays the same through these changes. For Nagarjuna, however, there is no need to postulate a realm of Forms, and the ever-changing existence is the only existence. He would argue that the postulation of a realm of Forms may instigate our craving for permanency.

---

13  In order to properly understand Nagarjuna's notion of emptiness, we also have to guard against our habitual tendency of reification with regard to negative nouns like emptiness, nothing, or nobody. For example, the statement "Nobody is watching the show" does not mean that there is such a person called "Nobody" who is watching the show.

## THE FIRST VERSE OF CHAPTER I (ON CONDITIONS)

In the very first verse of Chapter I, Nagarjuna demonstrates the incoherency of the substantialist and the nihilistic theories on causation. He advances four claims, each of which is a denial of a particular theory of causation: "Neither from itself nor from another / Nor from both, / Nor without a cause, / Does anything whatever, anywhere arise."

"Neither" and "nor" in this verse indicate a rejection of the theories stated after them. These four statements can be paraphrased as follows:

It is wrong to hold that a thing is self-caused (i.e., "from itself").
It is wrong to hold that a thing is not self-caused (i.e., it is other-caused, "from another").
It is wrong to hold that a thing is self-caused and not self-caused (i.e., "from both").
It is wrong to hold that a thing is neither self-caused nor not self-caused (i.e., "without a cause").

It becomes clear that the four causal theories that Nagarjuna attacks are:

1. A thing is self-caused,
2. A thing is other-caused,
3. A thing is both self-caused and other caused,
4. A thing is neither self-caused nor other-caused—i.e., is uncaused.

Now, let us use the example of a hatching chick to illustrate what it is that Nagarjuna is rejecting in these four claims. According to the rejected theories, the hatching chick can be conceptualized causally in one of the following ways:

a) The chick is self-caused,
b) The chick is other-caused,
c) The chick is both self-caused and other-caused,
d) The chick is neither self-caused nor other-caused (i.e., "The chick is uncaused").

In these four theories, Theory (b) seems to have some intuitive appeal since we do conventionally take an egg and a chick as two distinct things. Thus it makes good sense to say that the chick is other (egg)-caused under relevant conditions for the hatching (temperature, etc.). On the other hand, Theory (d) has the least intuitive appeal since by claiming that the chick is uncaused, it amounts to a wholesale denial of causality, which clearly defies common sense.

It is extremely important to note that the word "cause" (or "caused") is used in a way very different from the way it is used in our everyday language. In our everyday language, we do not say a chick is self-caused. Moreover, when we say that a chick is other-caused, we probably refer to a hen (or, more precisely, a hen's laying) as the other / external cause, not to an egg as the other / external cause. In everyday language, we consider an egg as a (material) *condition* for the hatching, but not a cause. On the other hand, the meaning of the word "cause" (or "caused") in the above four theories that Nagarjuna is addressing is based on a substantial assumption which takes a cause as one substance and its effect as another. Under this understanding of the word "cause" (or "caused"), substantialistic philosophers insist that a chick can be said to be self-caused, or other-caused (by an egg). And what Nagarjuna is trying to do with these theories is to show that, given the substantial assumption, these theories lead to logical inconsistencies.

Despite the appeal of Theory (b), Nagarjuna categorically rejected *all* four causal theories above. For him, the first three Theories (a, b, c) are wrong because they are versions of substantialism on causality, and Theory (d) is also wrong because it amounts to a form of nihilism on causality. Let's unpack Nagarjuna's criticisms of the four theories one by one.

I. *An effect arises from itself (as cause).* This view runs into the following problems:

(1) On this view, an effect must be identical to its cause. For example, an egg (a cause) can only produce the same egg (an effect) itself. But this contradicts our understanding that any act of production implies a numerical, if not qualitative, distinction between the producer and the produced. The egg's reiterative self-reproduction does not explain how an egg can become a chick.

(2) If an effect is identical to its cause, then, when we understand the chick we should also apprehend the egg. But that is not the case.

(3) If it is possible for an egg (a cause) to become a chick (an effect), how does an egg still keep its self-essence (*svabhava*) once it has in fact become a chick?

(4) It is against our everyday experience to maintain that an egg and a chick have the same nature. In fact, we would have trouble carrying out such common tasks as food shopping or cooking if we did not observe the difference between the two.

(5) If production begins and ends with the self (*svabhava*), the product, the producer, the act of producing, and the agent will all be identical. But this is impossible. (A snake will not be able to grow or reproduce by biting off its own tail!)

II. *An effect arises from something other than itself (as cause).* This view encounters the following problems:

(1) If an effect is essentially different from its cause, how is it possible that there is a causal link between them? For instance, we do not expect to get a chick to hatch from a rock because we view a rock and a chick as essentially different.[14]

---

14 Compare this with the Cartesian dualistic predicament—if the mind and body are essentially different, how do they interact with each other?

(2) In order for an effect to be inherently different from its cause, both of them should be present simultaneously so that we can compare them to see they are different, but an egg and the hatching chick from the egg do not exist simultaneously, so how do we know that they are inherently different?

(3) The effect (the chick) can be construed in a manner of tetralemma as (i) inherently existent, (ii) non-existent, (iii) both (i) and (ii), and (iv) neither (i) nor (ii).

(3.1) Against (i): If the effect (the chick) were inherently existent, then there would be no need at all for the cause (an egg) to produce it.

(3.2) Against (ii): If the effect (the chick) were non-existent, the cause would be a cause for nothing and thus no cause.

(3.3) Against (iii): If the effect (the chick) were both existent and non-existent, then what could act as a cause for this chick that is both "existent and non-existent"?!

(3.4) Against (iv): If the effect (the chick) were neither existent nor non-existent, nothing could act as a cause for this chick.

iii. *An effect arises both from itself (as a cause) and something else (as another cause).* This alternative is impossible for the simple reason that neither production from self nor from other can be individually established (see points i and ii above).

iv. *An effect arises without any cause.* If a thing were uncaused (i.e., not from itself, nor from others), then it could randomly come into being under any conditions. For example, a chick could just magically emerge from a rock. This of course amounts to a complete demolition of causal connection. Therefore, "an effect arises without any cause" is also a wrong way to understand cause-effect phenomena.

On the surface, Nagarjuna's rejection of the four cause-effect theories sounds like a negation of change or causation altogether. However, he specifically rejects only the substantialistic account that takes causes as possessing inherent nature, and the nihilistic account that views causes as nothingness—he does not deny causal phenomena or conditions (see Chapter 1, verse 2). What he brings to light, critically, is our tendency to cut up reality (for example, the "egg-chick" continuum) into separate entities (egg and chick) and then to wonder how such entities can link together in a causal way. We habitually trap ourselves in a conceptual cocoon we created and then ask seriously why it happened. What Nagarjuna tries to do is simply to pierce the cocoon and free us from the trap.

### EXAMINATION OF THE AGGREGATES: NO-SELF

The insight of interdependent-arising leads to the realization that the nature of self is, paradoxically, no-self. According to the insight, a person emerges out of five aggregates (*skandhas*): the form (individual's physical body),[15] feelings (sensations),

---

15  The physical body is further broken down into its four great elements: earth, water, fire, and wind.

discriminations (clinging to characteristics), dispositions (will to act), and consciousness (awareness). Beyond or behind these aggregates, there is no ego or agent. Contrary to the Sarvastivadin metaphysicians, Nagarjuna argues that even these five aggregates themselves are empty of self-existent essence, or self-nature.[16]

DOING PHILOSOPHY
*To* Become *a Human*

Great thinkers think alike. One view that many thinkers have arrived at is that a human is not defined or fixed by birth, caste, location, race, etc., but by deed. Here are a few examples:

Martin Luther King: "I have a dream that my four little children will one day live in a nation where they will not be judged by the color of their skin, but by the content of their character" ("I have a dream," speech delivered on August 28, 1963).

The Buddha: "It is not matted hair nor birth that makes a Brahmin, but truth and the love for all of life with which one's heart is full. What use is a deer-skin on which to sit for meditation, if your mind still seethes with lust?" (The Dhammapada, The Brahmin Verse 26: 393–94, trans. Easwaran).

Confucius: "The Master said, 'Only common people wait till they are advanced in ritual and music [before taking office]. A gentleman [son of a ruler] can afford to get up his ritual and music later on.' Even if I accepted this saying, I should still be on the side of those who get on with their studies first" (the *Analects* 11:1, Waley's translation).

Xunzi: "Although a man may be the descendant of kings, dukes, or high court ministers, if he cannot adhere to ritual principles, he should be ranked among the commoners. Although a man may be the descendant of commoners, if he has acquired learning, is upright in conduct, and can adhere to ritual

---

16 The logical thoroughness revealed here is typical in Mahayana Buddhism. Other examples of logical thoroughness include: (1) if compassion for others is good, then we can extend it to all living beings, or even all beings; (2) if all humans have potential (Buddha nature) to be enlightened, then we can extend it to believe that all living beings (even all beings) have that potential; (3) if the historical Buddha was a great man who seems to have magical powers to help people, then it is better to believe that the historical Buddha is just one instance of some transcendental, eternal Buddha, who can manifest himself in different persons past, present, and future. Some of these examples are related to Chinese Chan and Japanese Zen (see Chapter 9 on Hui Neng's Platform Sutra and Chapter 10 on Dogen's *Shobogenzo*). Notice, however, that the developments of Buddhism shown in these examples are not always easy to reconcile with the Buddha's teaching of interdependent-arising.

principles, he should be promoted to the post of prime minister or high court official" ("The Regulations of a King").[17]

Employing the aggregate of form as an illustration, Nagarjuna argues that form (matter) arises from an interdependent relationship with its cause. Thus, neither form nor its cause possesses self-essence.

Now, let us turn to his argument for this view: "Apart from the cause of form, / Form cannot be conceived; / Apart from form, / The cause of form is not seen" (verse 1). In this opening verse, Nagarjuna states the thesis of the mutual dependence of form and its cause.

Then, he proceeds to unpack his argument for the thesis in the succeeding verses: "If apart from the cause of form, there were form, / Form would be without cause, / But nowhere is there an effect / Without a cause" (verse 2). We can paraphrase verse 2 in a *reductio* argument:

1. If form/effect existed apart from its corresponding causes (Assumption).
2. There would exist a form/effect without cause (Inference from 1).
3. But by convention cause and effect come in a pair (Axiom).
4. 2 and 3 are in contradiction.
5. Therefore, it is not the case that form/effect exists apart from its cause (negation of 1. RAA, 1–4).

The next verse also employs the *reductio* argumentative strategy: "If apart from form / There were a cause of form, / It would be a cause without an effect. / But there are no causes without effects" (verse 3). The argument is rephrased as follows:

1. If a cause of form exists apart from its effect (namely, form) (Assumption).
2. There would exist a cause without an effect (Inference from 1).
3. But by convention cause and effect come in a pair (Axiom).
4. 2 and 3 are in contradiction.
5. Therefore, it is not the case that a cause of form exists apart from its effect/form (negation of 1. RAA from 1–4).

The next verse recapitulates the conclusions of verses 2 and 3: "When form exists [i.e., has self-essence], / A cause of the arising of form is not tenable. / When form is non-existent [i.e., nothingness], / A cause of the arising of form is not tenable" (verse 4). Whether form/effect and cause are taken as either inherently existent or non-existent, the consequence in either case is a complete denial of the mutual dependence of cause

---

17 Xunzi (whose name is sometimes rendered as Hsün Tzu) is a Chinese Confucian philosopher we'll introduce in Chapter 8 of this book. This quotation is from Burton Watson's translation, *Hsün Tzu: Basic Writings* (New York: Columbia University Press, 1964), 35–36.

and effect. First, if form/effect exists inherently, then a cause for the arising of form is not possible. Second, if form/effect is nonexistent (absolute nothingness), a cause for the arising of form/effect is not possible, either. Thus, in verse 5, Nagarjuna urges us not to "construct theories about form," that is, not to reify form (as possessing substance) nor to take it as nothingness.

Now, Nagarjuna takes the analysis one step further by arguing that a cause and its effect are distinct (though mutually dependent). "The assertion that the effect and cause are similar / Is not acceptable. / The assertion that they are not similar / Is also not acceptable" (verse 6). His argument can be unpacked as follows:

1. The assertion that the effect/form and cause are (substantially) the same is not acceptable, because if they were the same, then we would not even be able to state a cause-and-effect relationship, and we would be holding a circular view that form causes form to arise.
2. Nor is the assertion that they are not (substantially) the same acceptable, because if they were substantially different (as, for example, matter and immaterial things), it is inconceivable how they would interact with each other.
3. Either way, the assertion would lead to a denial of the mutual dependence of cause and effect.

By the same token, according to Nagarjuna, the arguments employed in the analysis of form and its cause can be extended to other aggregates as well (verse 7), so that no elements (no matter how basic or fundamental) possess self-essence. The self too is neither the different aggregates conceived of individually or separately (otherwise one person would have several selves), nor is it merely a random collection of the aggregates. Instead, the self arises interdependently from the aggregates that are themselves empty of self-essence.

This understanding of a person is reminiscent of the analysis of the true nature of a seed in the *Chandogya* (vi.xii.1), in which the putative essential features of a seed are stripped away one by one until the seed is shown to consist in nothing. While this anatomy of a seed may appear to facilitate an understanding of emptiness as interdependent-arising, there is a crucial difference between the seeming nothingness that lies behind the seed and the emptiness of the seed as interdependent-arising. The nothingness of the seed is shown only *after* the seed has been completely anatomized whereas the emptiness of the seed as interdependent-arising can be realized at any moment, *even if the seed is not dissected.*

## EXAMINATION OF TIME (CHAPTER XIX)

What is time? We know pretty well what it is in everyday life, and we take it for granted, never questioning its existence. We commonly conceptualize time as consisting of past, present, and future. However, if we pause to think over this conception, the putative reality of time quickly eludes us, for the past is already gone, the future has not yet come, and the immediate present is constantly fleeting even as we speak. Like the aggregates, time also does not possess self-essence.

In everyday life, time is usually measured according to the movement of the clock hands. In science, time is measured by the movement of celestial bodies or of electrons. In such cases, time is not mysterious: it is public, interpersonal, and as if objectively, "out there." While Nagarjuna may not doubt the usefulness of such conceptions of time in everyday life and in science, he did or would question that such conceptions of time can proffer insight on our understanding of the meaning of life and death.

Nagarjuna critically examines two salient features in our ordinary understanding of time. The first feature is that our ordinary conception of time is divided into three segments—past, present, and future. This feature can be illustrated in the way we describe how a seed grows into a tree. Suppose we are looking at a tree sprout *now*. At some point *in the past*, the tree sprout was a seed. If the sprout continues to grow, it will become a tree *in the future*. Or to use another example, a person's lifespan is often linearized in the same way: John was a small child *in the past*; *now* he is a middle-aged man; and he will become an old man *in the future*. The second feature of our ordinary conception of time is that time is spatialized and taken as a container. For example, we say flowers blossom *in* spring, and leaves fall *in* autumn.

Both these features of our ordinary conception of time may be hijacked by metaphysicians. Drawing from our ordinary conception of time, metaphysicians may reify time and treat it as substantially containing three segments and treat it as a substantial container. But for Nagarjuna, such reifications of time are incoherent and untenable. In Chapter XIX, he launches three arguments against these inaccurate views of time.

Verses 1–3 comprise Nagarjuna's first argument. Here he tackles the three-segment view of time, which treats each segment of time as having self-essence: "If the present and the future / Depend on the past, / Then the present and the future would have existed in the past" (verse 1). This is a *reductio* argument, which can be unpacked as follows:

1. The present and the future [substantially] "depend on" the past (Assumption).
2. The present and the future would have existed in the past (An inference from 1).
3. By convention the present and the future are not in the past; otherwise, the present and the future would be identical to the past, and time would be impossible (Axiom).
4. 2 and 3 result in a contradiction (Conjunction of 2 and 3).
5. Therefore, it is not the case that the present and the future [substantially] "depend on" the past[18] (RAA from 1–4).

---

18 It goes without saying that following the same pattern of reasoning, Nagarjuna could reach other possible permuted conclusions: the past and the future do not depend on the present; the past and the present do not depend on the future.

Verse 2 also follows a *reductio* argument: "If the present and the future / Did not exist there, / How could the present and the future / Be dependent upon it?"

1.  Suppose that the present and the future do not (conventionally) depend on the past (Assumption).
2.  Then any interaction between the present, the future with the past would be impossible (An inference from 1).
3.  Time would be impossible (Inference from 2).
4.  Therefore, it is not the case that the present and the future do not (conventionally) depend on the past. Or in other words, time must not be understood as having three independent segments (RAA from 1-3).

The argument continues: "If they are not dependent upon the past, / Neither of the two would be established. / Therefore neither the present / Nor the future would exist" (verse 3). This can be unpacked as follows:

1.  Suppose that the present and the future are not (conventionally) dependent upon the past (Assumption).
2.  Neither the present nor the future would be established (An inference from 1). (How could one talk about the present and the future without a comparison with or a reference to the past? Notice that a *discourse* about the present, the past, and the future does not necessarily imply a reification of any of them.)
3.  Therefore, neither the present nor the future could exist as independent segments (Inference from 2).

In sum, Nagarjuna argues that these three modes of time (present, past, and future) do not truly exist as three independent segments. The conception of time as three independent segments is just a creation of our thoughts. In the same vein, he argues that "upper, lower, middle" do not exist as reified independent locations, nor do "unity and diversity" exist as substantially independent or separate (verse 4).

In verse 5 Nagarjuna launched his second argument against substantial understanding of time. His argument is that neither a static nor a nonstatic view of time is coherent: "A nonstatic time is not grasped. / Nothing one could grasp as / Stationary time exists. / If time is not grasped, how is it known?"

To explicate this verse, three points can be made:

1.  If time is conceived as nonstatic, that is, if time is constantly and instantly changing, so too are the past, the present, and the future. Then, time becomes unintelligible.
2.  If time is conceived as stationary, then it would no longer count as time. That is, according to our conventional understanding, time flows from the past to the present and to the future. So time that does not flow is not possible. Stationary "points" are not what we mean by "time."

3.  Either way (whether as "nonstatic" or as "stationary"), time does not have self-essence.

Finally in verse 6 Nagarjuna proposes his third argument, which tackles the view of time as an entity. The argument proceeds from the premises that being and time are *substantially* distinct, and that paradoxically the latter depends upon the former: "If time depends on an entity, / Then without an entity how could time exist? / There is no existent entity. / So how can time exist?" This is a *reductio* argument:

1.  Suppose that time is a container (Assumption).
2.  Then it has to rely on entities to exist—that is, to make sense (otherwise the container would be empty) (Inference from 1).
3.  There is no entity (according to interdependent-arising) (Axiom).
4.  The conjunction of 2 and 3 results in a contradiction (from 2 and 3).
5.  Therefore, time as conceived in (1) is baseless and does not exist (RAA from 1–4).

It is paramount to note that in these arguments Nagarjuna does not deny or reject temporal phenomena. What he argues against is the substantial conception of time that treats it as consisting of three independent segments and as an independent container (or substratum), because such misconceptions make change and nonsubstantial causal phenomena unintelligible and impossible. Moreover, these misconceptions also render Buddhist practice (any practice, for that matter) futile, in that if past, present, and future are (substantially) independent of each other, what is the point of moral practice in the present? What is the point of planting a seed of oak *in the past*, if it has nothing to do with its germination *at the present*, and if it has nothing to do with its growing into an oak tree *in the future*? We shall see later (in Chapter 10 on Dogen's *Shobogenzo*) that Dogen's view on time and being is in complete accord with Nagarjuna's.

Nagarjuna's nonsubstantialist understanding of time has significant practical implications. First of all, in this view, past, present, and future, when understood nonsubstantially, are ontologically equal, in that no instant or moment has more value than any other. Just imagine how this view could change the way we view ourselves if we did not judge time from a self-centred point of view: if every moment is equal, then my birthday and your birthday enjoy the same ontological status. Neither is more special than the other.

More importantly, if time is seen as nonsubstantial, every moment is open to us for liberation. Liberation does not necessarily require a lengthy period of time. Long-time practitioners have no reason to be proud of themselves, and novices do not have to feel inferior to other experienced practitioners.[19] Liberation/nirvana can happen at any time. This does not imply that human volition alone can bring about liberation when-

---

19  See Khenpo Tsültrim Gyamtso, *The Sun of Wisdom: Teachings on the Noble Nagarjuna's Fundamental Wisdom of the Middle Way*, Ari Goldfield, trans. and ed. (Boston: Shambhala, 2003), 126–27.

ever one wants; it means only that one should not foreclose the possibility of liberation at any time. Accordingly, efforts are always appropriate. With this understanding of time in mind, the saying of later Zen, "Every day is a good day" makes perfect sense.

### EXAMINATION OF THE FOUR NOBLE TRUTHS (CHAPTER XXIV): THE TWO TRUTHS AND THE MIDDLE WAY TRIANGLE

Chapter XXIV is the most important chapter of the whole *Fundamental Verses on the Middle Way*, as it spells out the system of the middle way. It explicates not only the important distinction between conventional truth and ultimate truth, but also the interconnectedness of interdependent-arising, emptiness, and dependent designation.

If emptiness is not understood as interdependent-arising, but as absolute void, certain questions arise naturally: Are the Four Noble Truths and the three jewels (Buddha, Dharma, and Sangha/Buddhist spiritual community) void as well? Would there be a contradiction in the belief that everything is void (no Dharma) and the view that there is conventional truth (Chapter XXIV: 1–6)? Moreover, would nirvana also be void (Chapter XXV: 1)? These questions, all stemming from a nihilistic construal of emptiness as nothingness, pose a serious challenge to the Buddha's teachings.

In response to this nihilistic construal of these foundational Buddhist teachings, Nagarjuna argues that the Four Noble Truths and nirvana should not be construed as nothingness, but as "empty" of self-essence, and that it is precisely because the Four Noble Truths and nirvana are "empty" of self-essence that they are possible. "Whoever sees dependent arising / Also sees suffering / And its arising / And its cessation as well as the path" (verse 40, also see verses 7, 11–15).

Nagarjuna's rebuttal of nihilism encompasses several interpenetrating layers. First, according to him, if everything were perceived as having essence or self-essence (see verse 16), there would be no perception of causes and conditions, and thereby interdependent-arising would be impossible. Viewed this way, the Four Noble Truths would be without causes and conditions and thus nonexistent (verse 20). In particular, if suffering possessed self-essence, it would be impossible for suffering to arise or cease; likewise, the path of liberation, the practice, and the three jewels would all be inconceivable (verses 21–32). For if we were substantially enlightened, what would be the point of practicing the Buddha's teachings?[20] On the other hand, if we were substantially in ignorance, there would be no way to remove the ignorance, and any practice would simply be futile. Moreover, right action and wrong action would all be rendered impossible, because if things were not empty of self-essence (i.e., not interdependent-arising), there would be no free choice (verses 33–35, 37).

Second, Nagarjuna claims that the Buddha's teachings are based on two truths—the truth of worldly convention and the ultimate truth. "The Buddha's teaching of the Dharma / Is based on two truths: / A truth of worldly convention / And an ultimate

---

20  This was the question that puzzled Dogen so much when he plunged into Buddhism. See Chapter 10 of this book on the *Shobogenzo*.

truth" (verse 8). "Those who do not understand / The distinction drawn between these two truths / Do not understand / The Buddha's profound truth" (verse 9).

According to the tacit convention in our everyday lives, trees, tables, books, cars, houses, money, and "I" exist, which Nagarjuna takes to be "a truth of worldly convention."[21] For him, there is nothing wrong with acknowledging this truth of worldly convention itself, but it is wrong to consciously or subconsciously regard these things as permanent and self-sufficient entities and then cling to them. Such clinging reveals a failure to understand "the ultimate truth," or the ultimate nature of reality, namely that everything arises interdependently.

In order to better illustrate what Nagarjuna meant by the two kinds of truth, let's imagine a three-dimensional coordinate system. And let's further imagine an object, O, (e.g., an animal, a person, a missile, or a rock) to be moving along a trajectory along the X, Y, and Z axes, such that at any instant the position of the object O can be specified as a (X, Y, Z) point. This description of the movement of the object is useful and necessary in our everyday life. However, in an ultimate sense, this coordinate system does not truly capture the object's movement itself, for what it characterizes is merely a collection of discrete, static points. Notice that in the coordinate system, time, space, and the object O may be taken as three distinct and independent things, but in truth the actual movement of the object *is* at once all three of them—the continuum of space-time-object. The distinction of space, time, and the object is already an abstraction.

Our whole conceptual apparatus (convention) is functionally like such a coordinate system—though human convention is much more complicated than this simple coordinate system. Just as we must not mistake the static points *about* the movement of an object for the object's actual movement, we must not take whatever our conceptual apparatus has described and fixed as true reality.[22]

The ultimate reality (emptiness) is like the actual movement of an object. It can be alluded to by language but cannot be truly apprehended by language. A basket (conceptual apparatus) cannot hold water (reality). However it can be apprehended through direct personal experience. "The fish knows by itself whether the water is cold or warm," as later Zen masters often like to say. The ultimate reality is beyond all categorization or conceptualization, but not mysterious. To borrow an example from Wittgenstein, we

---

21  According to Jay L. Garfield and Graham Priest, "conventional truth (reality)" for Nagarjuna may encompass three meanings. "On the one hand, it can mean *ordinary*, or *everyday*. In this sense a conventional truth is a truth to which we would ordinarily assent—common sense augmented by good science. The second of these three meanings is *truth by agreement*. In this sense, the decision in Australia to drive on the left establishes a conventional truth about the proper side of the road. A different decision in the USA establishes another. Conventional truth is, in this sense, often quite relative. (Candrakirti argues that, in fact, in the first sense it is also relative—relative to our sense organs, conceptual scheme, etc. In this respect he would agree with such Pyrrhonian skeptics as Sextus.) The final sense of this cluster is *nominally true*. To be true in this sense is to be true by virtue of a particular linguistic convention. So, for instance, the fact that shoes and boots are different kinds of things here, but are both instances of one kind in Tibetan—*Iham*—makes their co-specificity or lack thereof a nominal matter" ("Nagarjuna and the Limits of Thought," *Philosophy East and West* 53:1 [January 2003]: 5).

22  A similar theme on the limits of language appears in Chapter 1 of the *Daodejing*.

*feel* that the aroma of coffee is in some sense beyond description, but it is not mysterious. One only needs to smell it to know what it is like.[23]

There are two ways to respond to conventional truths: either to cling to them or to transcend them. If we cling to them, we will be trapped in illusions. If we transcend them, we will experience true reality. To illustrate, consider the example of a finger that points to the moon. In terms of our realizing the truth—seeing the moon, the finger can be either revealing or concealing. It can be revealing if we "transcend" the finger to see the moon; however, it can be concealing if we "cling to" the finger itself. This seems to be exactly what Nagarjuna is saying in verse 10: "Without a foundation in the conventional truth, / The significance of the ultimate cannot be taught. / Without understanding of the significance of the ultimate, / Liberation is not achieved."

Furthermore, Nagarjuna relates the idea of independent-arising to both emptiness and dependent designation (i.e., conventional truth), and he calls the mutually dynamic relationship among them "the middle way" (verse 18)—the heart of the whole *Fundamental Verses on the Middle Way*: "Whatever is dependently co-arisen / That is explained to be emptiness. / That, being a dependent designation, / Is itself the middle way."

The interdependent relationship among interdependent-arising, emptiness, and dependent designation can be illustrated with an equilateral triangle diagram below.

Interdependent-arising

Emptiness                    Dependent designation

In this triangle, the middle way entails three equivalences: (i) Interdependent-arising is equivalent to emptiness; (ii) emptiness is equivalent to dependent designation; and (iii) interdependent-arising is equivalent to dependent designation. The equivalences can also be represented in a formula: Interdependent-arising = Emptiness = Dependent Designation.

Much has been said about the first equivalence (i), so let us turn to the second (ii) and the third (iii) equivalences. The second equivalence (which equates emptiness with dependent designation) avoids two extreme views: first, it avoids nihilism, because emptiness is not nothingness. Second, it avoids substantialism. With dependent designation we (provisionally) use thing-language to express conventional truth, but we will not subscribe to permanent, independent entities.

A similar analysis could be made regarding (iii). Since dependent designation is equivalent to interdependent-arising, and since the latter is not nothingness, the former does not entail an ontological commitment that there are permanent and independent

---

23  See Ludwig Wittgenstein, *Philosophical Investigations* (Oxford: Basil Blackwell, 1958), I, §610.

things. For Nagarjuna, the three relationships of equivalences are equally important. They function like the legs of a three-leg table. If any leg is missing, the table will fall. In the same way, denying any of the equivalence relationships will result in the collapse of the other two: "If [inter]dependent arising is denied, / Emptiness itself is rejected. / This would contradict / All of the worldly conventions" (verse 36).

### EXAMINATION OF NIRVANA (CHAPTER XXV): SOTERIOLOGICAL IMPLICATION OF THE MIDDLE WAY

In spite of its abstract and theoretical content, Nagarjuna's *Fundamental Verses on the Middle Way* is a treatise of spiritual teaching which aims at a soteriology. Indeed, Nagarjuna's spiritual concerns implicitly run through the whole text and culminate in Chapter XXVI, Examination of the Four Noble Truths, and especially Chapter XXV, Examination of Nirvana.

Chapter XXV can be divided into three sections (1–3, 4–18, and 19–24). The first section states that nirvana is neither empty (absolute void) nor not empty (substantial). The second section elaborates the point stated in the first section through an application of the tetralemma method. And finally the third section clarifies the point that nirvana and samsara are not ontologically different. To throw into sharp relief Nagarjuna's view on samsara and nirvana, we might do well to focus just on the first and third sections.

The first section explains the idea of nirvana. As you may recall from the previous chapter, the idea of nirvana is the *summum bonum* of Buddhism. It literally means "blowing out" (a fire or flame) or "cooling down" by cutting off the fuel to a fire. It has been characterized as a state of extinction of ignorance, attachment, and craving. When attachment and craving are destroyed, suffering ceases and one becomes liberated from *samsara*.

Nagarjuna's discussion starts with a challenge to the idea of nirvana. The challenge goes like this: if everything, including nirvana, were empty (in the sense of "absolute void"), then arising (suffering) and passing away (end of suffering) would be impossible. Therefore, nirvana is impossible (verse 1).

In response to this challenge, Nagarjuna argues that the situation is exactly the opposite. If everything is nonempty (i.e., with self-essence), then no arising or passing away is possible. Specifically, if a person has a self-essence of being ignorant, then he/she would never be able to remove his/her ignorance and enter nirvana. On the other hand, if a person has a self-essence of not being ignorant—which means he/she is already in nirvana—what is the point of Buddhist practice for him or her? In short, if everything *is* with self-essence, then nirvana becomes impossible (verse 2).

Countering the challenge, Nagarjuna argues that suffering is interdependent-arising, and because it is interdependent-arising liberation becomes possible and the Buddhist practice meaningful. If suffering is understood as interdependent-arising, it can be removed by changing the conditions that lead to it. If nirvana is understood as interdependent-arising (emptiness), it becomes possible by cultivating the conditions that lead to it.

In the third section (verses 19–24), Nagarjuna argues that, in an ultimate sense, samsara is the same as nirvana—there is no ontological difference between the two: "There is not the slightest difference / Between cyclic existence and nirvana. / There is not the slightest difference / Between nirvana and cyclic existence" (verse 19). "Whatever is the limit of nirvana, / That is the limit of cyclic existence. / There is not even the slightest difference between them, / Or even the subtlest thing" (verse 20).

These are probably the most perplexing verses in Chapter xxv. What is Nagarjuna getting at? Is it true that there is absolutely no difference at all between samsara and nirvana? If so, why even bother talking about prasticing Buddha's teaching and transforming from *samsara* to nirvana? To answer these questions, let's first start with the following picture.[24]

What is it? Is it a duck? Is it a rabbit? Many of us tend to answer: It is both. It is a duck if you see it *this* way; it is a rabbit if you see it *that* way (and we may even trace the contour of a duck or a rabbit as we speak).

Suppose that person A has never seen a duck or a picture of it, but has only seen a rabbit or a picture of it, would he or she perceive a duck? Conversely, suppose that person B has never seen a rabbit or a picture of it, but has seen a duck or a picture of it, would he or she see a rabbit? It stands to reason that person A is probably not disposed to seeing a duck and person B a rabbit.

Now show person A a duck and then the above picture. This time person A is most likely to see the picture as depicting a duck even though not an iota of the picture has changed. What has changed is the *way* person A sees the picture.

The Buddhist experience of awakening is similar to this, in that it consists in a new way of seeing and experiencing things. An awakened person sees the world not as reified objects, or things with self-essence, but as interdependent-arising. However, while the two ways of seeing the picture are equally valid, it is not so with the reified and non-reified ways of seeing and experiencing the world. According to Nagarjuna, the non-reified way, or the awakening way, is obviously preferred.

Another analogy—the analogy of a rope—may better illustrate the difference between ignorance and awakening. Suppose person A saw a piece of rope on the ground and mistakes it for a snake, and person B sees the same thing and recognizes it as it is, a rope. The Buddhist would say that person A is suffering from delusions, for he/she fails to see the rope as it is, whereas person B not only sees the rope as it is, but also understands what it is like to see it as a snake (person B is much like the philosopher who returns to

---

24 Wittgenstein uses this picture to illustrate the idea of "seeing an aspect" in *Philosophical Investigations* II, §xi.

the Platonic cave and sees the shadows on the wall but does not deem them as reality). What actually is there (the rope) is the same to both A and B, but what it *means* to each of them is radically different. So the change from illusion to awakening lies in one's consciousness—which can culminate in a change of one's whole existential being, not the things that he/she deals with. As Garfield put it, to "be in samsara is to see things as they appear to deluded consciousness and to interact with them accordingly. To be in nirvana, then, is to see those things as they are—as merely empty, dependent, impermanent, and nonsubstantial, but not to be somewhere else, seeing something else."[25] Liberation does not take one to a new world beyond this world; rather, it enables one to adopt or realize a radically new perspective.[26]

Here is a Zen story that illustrates the similarities and differences between heaven (enlightenment) and hell (illusion) in Buddhism.

> Once upon a time there was a Japanese warrior who was suspicious of views about heaven and hell. One day, the warrior encountered a Zen master and he took the opportunity to ask about heaven and hell:
> "Master, is there really a heaven and a hell?"
> The master, instead of answering the question, asked,
> "What do you do?"
> "I am a warrior," replied the warrior proudly.
> "You look like a beggar, not a warrior!"
> Hearing this, the warrior was furious, and he quickly pulled his sword:
> "How dare you insult me—I will kill you!"
> "See, the gate of hell is opening," said the Master calmly.
> A sudden flash of light dawned on the warrior. Throwing away his sword, he knelt down to salute to the master.
> The Master, with a gentle smile, responded, "See, the gate of heaven is opening."

Spiritual awakening, then, is more than an aspect change in seeing, a mere cognitive change, for example, from seeing a duck in the duck-rabbit picture to seeing a rabbit in it, even though the change may be a big gestalt shift. It is a profound awareness that penetrates the very being of one's self and things around one. It consists in a complete reorientation of life, a radical change in all one's interaction with the world.

Doesn't such change of mind or change of living count as a difference between samsara and nirvana? I think Nagarjuna would have to count it as a difference—albeit only a difference in the conventional or nominal sense. However, he would insist that, ultimately, both samsara and nirvana are interdependent-arising. It is precisely in this

---

25  Garfield, 332.
26  Chinese Chan Buddhists often express the same point, but more vividly. They say that before enlightenment "mountains and waters are mountains and waters," and after enlightenment "mountains are (just) mountains and waters are (just) waters."

sense that for him there is *not* the slightest (substantial) difference between samsara and nirvana. "The very same world is samsara or nirvana, dependent upon one's perspective. When one perceives the constant arising and ceasing of phenomena [entities with self-essence], one perceives samsara. When all reification is abandoned, that world and one's mode of living in it, becomes nirvana."[27]

It is important to note that, for Nagarjuna, the identity of samsara with nirvana is not a simple expression of the law of identity (nor is it the case with the identity of *Atman* and *Brahman*), but should be taken as a command or a warning not to treat samsara and nirvana as substantially different; otherwise it would be impossible to change from samsara to nirvana.

## CONCLUDING REMARKS: THE INFLUENCE OF THE *FUNDAMENTAL VERSES ON THE MIDDLE WAY*

The *Fundamental Verses on the Middle Way* not only explicates the Buddha's insight of interdependent-arising, but deconstructs all metaphysical theories that try to explain the world in terms of fixed substances. It seriously questions some metaphysical interpretations of causality, identity, time, language, and so forth.

Due to the contribution of the *Fundamental Verses on the Middle Way* (and Nagarjuna's other works) to the Buddhist tradition, Nagarjuna is often regarded by many Buddhists of the Mahayana tradition as "the second Buddha" or "Nagarjuna bodhisattva." In Chinese Chan and Japanese Zen traditions, he is considered the fourteenth patriarch of the Indian lineage.

Nagarjuna's *Fundamental Verses on the Middle Way* has inspired many commentaries in Sanskrit, Tibetan, Chinese, and Japanese. The best known commentary is Chandrakirti's (c. 600–50 CE) "The Entrance to the Middle Way" (*Madhyamakavatara*). In 409 CE Kumarajiva (344–413 CE) translated the text into Chinese and its subsequent influence on Chinese thinking was extensive. Chinese Buddhist schools, such as San Lun, Tian Tai, and Chan, drew heavily upon intellectual and spiritual sources from the text and the thoughts of the Middle Way School. To a great extent, Chan and Zen are practical applications of the *Madhyamika* thought.

### WORKS CITED AND RECOMMENDED READINGS

1. Khenpo Tsultrim Gyamtso, *The Sun of Wisdom: Teachings on the Noble Nagarjuna's Fundamental Wisdom of the Middle Way*, Ari Goldfield, trans. and ed. (Boston: Shambhala, 2003).
2. David J. Kalupahana, *Nagarjuna: The Philosophy of the Middle Way* (Albany, NY: State University of New York Press, 1986).
3. Jay L. Garfield, trans. and commentary, *The Fundamental Wisdom of the Middle Way*, *Nagarjuna's Mulamadhyamakakarika* (New York: Oxford University Press, 1995).

---

27  Garfield, 328.

4. John P. Keenan, *The Foundational Standpoint of Madhyamika Philosophy*, Gadjin Nagao, trans. (Albany, NY: State University of New York Press, 1989).

5. Hsueh-Li Cheng, "The Roots of Zen Buddhism," *Journal of Chinese Philosophy* 8 (1981): 451–78.

6. Paul Williams, *Mahayana Buddhist—The Doctrinal Foundations* (Oxford: Routledge, 1989).

7. Jay L. Garfield and Graham Priest, "Nagarjuna and the Limits of Thought," *Philosophy East and West*, 53:1 (January 2003).

8. Jay L. Garfield, *Empty Words—Buddhist Philosophy and Cross-Cultural Interpretation* (New York: Oxford University Press, 2002).

9. The Dalai Lama, *The Middle Way*, Thupten Jinpa, trans. (London: Wisdom Publications, 2009).

CHAPTER 4

# The *Analects*

PRIMARY TEXT READING SUGGESTION

Arthur Waley's translation of *The Analects of Confucius* (New York: Vintage Books, 1989).

## LEARNING OBJECTIVES

By the time you have worked through this chapter, you should be able to

- ▸ Describe Confucius' ethical and political vision
- ▸ Understand Confucius' idea of *ren* as a moral demand and as practice
- ▸ Identify Confucius' sensitivity to moral nuances
- ▸ Describe Confucius' non-theistic and humanistic understanding of ethics

## KEY WORDS

humanness (*ren*), ritual propriety (*li*), the Way (*dao*), exemplary person (*junzi*), loyalty or conscience (*zhong*), empathy or consideration (*shu*)

## GUIDING QUESTIONS

In a time of social and moral chaos, Confucius had to respond to the following urgent questions—questions that faced virtually all the philosophers of ancient China around Confucius' time:

1.  How does a society in chaos get back on track? How does society go about rebuilding a sense of moral order?
2.  Are heavy-handed law enforcement and severe punishment effective means of (re)building society?
3.  Must the existence of God be presupposed in restoring social and moral order? In other words, is ethics possible without God?

In response to these questions, Confucius' *Analects* proposes that the restoration of social harmony must begin with the training of exemplary persons (*junzi*), and that heavy-handed law enforcement (despite its temporary, superficial gains) eventually will not work, and that ethics can be humanistic—need not be sanctioned theologically.

## INTRODUCTION

Confucianism, the school of philosophy based on the teachings of Confucius (Kongzi, Master Kong, 551–479 BCE), was the primary shaping force in the historical development of Chinese philosophy and Chinese culture, with its emphasis on ethics, family, moral self-cultivation, and the value of this life. Although three doctrines—Confucianism, Daoism, and Buddhism—come together in Chinese philosophy, Confucianism stands out as dominant. Comparatively speaking, Daoism and Buddhism as philosophies focus more on spiritual concerns and appeal only to some, mainly the intellectual elites,[1] whereas Confucianism focuses on political matters, and the practical concerns of everyone's daily life. Thus, Confucianism enjoys a universal appeal.

Confucius was born into an impoverished family[2] in the state of Lu (now Qufu city, Shangdong province), which was a vassal state of the Zhou Dynasty (1046–256 BCE). He was a capable autodidact, managing to acquire by his own effort a wealth of knowledge about the history and culture of his land.[3] He briefly held several minor government posts in his home state.

Realizing the importance of education, he took it upon himself to offer lessons to pupils from all walks of life. This was indeed an unprecedented practice, in that only

---

1   Daoistic philosophy (*daojia*) was later (in the first century CE) adapted in the development of *religious* Daoism (*daojiao*). The word "Daoism" is thus ambiguous, obliterating the distinction between Daoism as a philosophy and Daoism as a religion. The word "Buddhism" has traditionally been used to designate a theory and a practice that is both a philosophy and a religion.
2   See 9:6 (all passage numbers follow Arthur Waley's translation of *The Analects of Confucius* [New York: Vintage Books, 1989], unless otherwise specified).
3   See 5:28, 7:1.

the ruling class enjoyed access to education prior to his educational initiative. For this he has been revered as the first teacher and educationist in the history of China.[4]

Confucius was also a philosopher with a profound sense of social concerns. He lived in a time of social turmoil when Zhou culture was in decline and its vassal states were constantly fighting. In response to this social distress, he made it his mission to travel from state to state, in the hope of persuading rulers to adopt his teachings on social reform. His teachings, in a nutshell, advocated humanness (*ren*) and ritual propriety (*li*), and their importance in the making of exemplary persons (*junzi*) at all levels of society, especially among the rulers. Although Confucius' effort to transform the rulers of his time was not a success, he was certain that his teachings would eventually inspire and transform his students, and consequently transform society at large through their influence.[5] Confucius was revered by his students as a man who could enable people to live in harmony.[6] The portrait of Confucius reflected in the *Analects* epitomizes his vision and mission.[7]

The *Analects* (*Lunyu*, literally, "*Selected Sayings*") consists primarily of sayings and dialogues attributed to Confucius, with sporadic remarks by some of his prominent disciples.[8] Scholars generally agree that the work was probably authored by Confucius' immediate disciples and edited by followers of later generations.[9] This fact notwithstanding, the work as a whole is still the most reliable source of Confucius' teachings.

The *Analects* is a potpourri of discussions on various aspects of life—ethics, politics, education, family value, economy, and so on. It is a text with an intricate web of interconnected and intertwined moral concepts, cardinal among which are *ren* (humanness), *li* (ritual propriety), and *junzi* (exemplary persons or gentlemen), *zhong* (loyalty or conscience), and *shu* (empathy or consideration). The text contains twenty books, almost none of which seems organized around a unified theme.[10] Instead, remarks on different topics crisscross each book, so much so that first-time readers of the text may have difficulty locating in it a coherent, overarching vision. But one must not think of the philosophy of the *Analects* as a mere patchwork of random thoughts.[11] Those who are

---

4  Confucius was more than a teacher in the ordinary sense of the word; he had a broad vision of education which focused more on training character or how to be a good person than on vocation (see 1:7), and he taught a wide variety of subjects, including the Six Classics (Book of Documents, Book of Odes, Book of Rituals, Book of Music, Book of Changes, and Spring and Autumn Annals) and Six Arts (ritual propriety, music, archery, charioting, calligraphy, and calculation). Some of the Classics may have been compiled and/or edited by Confucius himself.

5  For Confucius' own interest in and his encouragement of his students to take office, see 9:12, 15:7, 17:1, 18:7, 19:13.

6  19:25; also see 5:26.

7  Regarding Confucius' sense of mission, see 7:23, 9:5.

8  Book 19 contains sayings exclusively from Confucius' disciples.

9  See Waley, 21–26, and E. Bruce Brooks and A. Taeko Brooks, *The Original Analects: Sayings of Confucius and His Successors* (New York: Columbia University Press, 1998), Appendix 1: "The Accretion Theory."

10  The only exception is Book 10 where the theme is clearly ritual propriety and how Confucius observed it in a variety of circumstances.

11  Confucius explicitly says that there is one thread connecting everything in his teachings (4:15, 15:3). The question of how to interpret the "thread" forms an important and controversial issue in Confucius'

willing to think through the text with Confucius will eventually be able to detect its integrated vision and may even come to appreciate its appeal.

To appreciate the *Analects*, it is helpful to bear in mind that Confucius' sayings are advice and instructions occasioned by concrete situations and addressed to specific individuals, even though in many cases the exact situations or contexts are not explicitly given in the text. In this sense, the Confucius in the text is like a "doctor of the soul" (or, to use a more contemporary term, a "life coach"), who is called upon in a variety of circumstances to diagnose moral problems and prescribe appropriate cures. Thus, Confucius should be regarded as a philosopher of life rather than a theoretical philosopher.[12]

Another important rule of thumb when reading the *Analects* is to study it topically. For instance, we can collate all the remarks on humanness (*ren*), ritual propriety (*li*), and exemplary person (*junzi*) together and then examine them group by group. Through comparison and synthesis, this approach of lateral reading may help bring order to the unsystematic material.

## CONFUCIUS' ETHICAL-POLITICAL VISION

For Confucius, the first few centuries of the Zhou Dynasty signified a period of peace and order. During this period, the Zhou kings (called "sons of Heaven") developed a feudal system in which the sons of the ruling family were enfiefed—that is, provided land for the establishment of their own states, under the condition that they acknowledge the Zhou king's ownership of the land and pay tributes to the king's court. The Zhou Dynasty had inherited from the two previous dynasties, Xia (2205–1766 BCE) and Yin or Shang (1766–1050 BCE), a sophisticated system of ceremonies and rituals that served to regulate the hierarchical and patriarchal relationships in society, including those between the king and the lords of the states, between the king and ministers, and between parents and sons. Since the social hierarchy was based on blood-relationships, the ruling family (*jia*) and the state (*guo*) were intrinsically connected. To a large extent, Zhou society was characterized by peace and order. However, by Confucius' time, conflicts among the vassal states led to perennial wars, which in turn weakened the Zhou king's central control. Eventually the king ruled in name only, and Zhou society deteriorated into a state of chaos.

A symptom of the social chaos at this time was the collapse of the ritual system that had been integral to the fabric of Zhou society. The ministers, for example, were

---

scholarship. See Bryan W. Van Norden, "The Dao of Kongzi," *Asian Philosophy* 12:2 (2002): 157–71.

12   At least in terms of writing style (if not totally in philosophical content) philosophers can be roughly classified into two categories: system-building philosophers, such as Plato, Spinoza, Kant, and Hegel; and non-system-building philosophers, such as the Pre-Socratics, Marcus Aurelius, Confucius, Pascal, Kierkegaard, Nietzsche, and the later Wittgenstein. Regarding the issue of whether Chinese philosophy in general is systematic or not, see Fung Yu-lan, *A History of Chinese Philosophy* Vol. 1 (Princeton: Princeton University Press, 1983), 4. See also Kwong-Loi Shun, *Mencius and Early Chinese Thought* (Stanford, CA: Stanford University Press, 2000), 5–6.

flouting the ritualistic conventions that defined their hierarchical relationship with the king. A prominent instance is that of the powerful *Ji* family in Confucius' home state Lu, which took the liberty of making offerings to the spirit of Tai Mountain. In performing the ritual, the family had symbolically usurped the authority of the Zhou king, for by convention no one but the Zhou king had the right to make the offerings.[13] While the system of rituals was still in place, it had degenerated into mere formality. Rituals were performed without reverence; mourning was observed without grief.[14] As a result, the Zhou king was no longer respected as the "Son of Heaven." The demise of centralized control allowed the lords of the states to contend for power. Naturally, the more powerful states now became the *de facto* rulers of the land. The entire social order had collapsed; the king was no longer a king in reality, and the ministers were no longer ministers. Even within a royal family, the patriarch/filial relationship was no longer honoured.[15]

For Confucius, ritual propriety is rooted in the virtue of humanness, which denotes respect and concern for others, and the appropriate performance of the rituals is meant to bring out people's humanness. Thus, the collapse of ritual propriety in Zhou, as Confucius saw it, was symptomatic of a dire spiritual condition in society where people (especially rulers) had lost their moral capacity to treat one another with respect and care.

For Confucius, Zhou society at his time had abandoned the Way of its forebears and was therefore in urgent need of reform.[16] He was confident that he could help restore Zhou society to its former days of glory.[17] Although at times Confucius appeared exasperated in the process of carrying out his mission, he had never doubted the rightness of his project.[18]

How can social order and harmony be restored? According to Confucius, the essential point is to institute moral renewal at all levels of the society, particularly among members of the ruling class, through the cultivation of morally exemplary persons. When people live up to such a moral ideal as fathers and sons, there will be order and harmony among families. When rulers and ministers live up to such an ideal, there will be harmony in the state they govern, and this social peace may even spread to the whole world. But how are exemplary persons cultivated? For Confucius, the key rests upon summoning people to respond to the fundamental moral demand of humanness—being and becoming human.

---

13  See 3:6; also see 3:1, 3:2, 3:22, 6:25.

14  See 3:26; also see 3:3, 3:10, 4:13. J.L. Austin calls illegitimate performance of rituals "void, or given in bad faith, or not implemented, or the like" (J.L. Austin, *How to Do Things with Words* [Cambridge, MA: Harvard University Press, 1967], 11).

15  See 12:11, 18:7.

16  See 3:24, 16:2; also see 1:12.

17  See 3:24, 17:5.

18  In this regard he was seen as a "wooden bell" of Heaven that can wake up the people to a doctrine that will bring the world back to order (9:5, 7:23).

## HUMANNESS (REN) AS A MORAL DEMAND

The Chinese word "*ren*" (仁) comprises two parts: the left half signifies a "person" ( 亻 ) and the right half designates "two" (二). Etymologically the word seems to refer to being or becoming human in a model person-to-person relationship. Thus, we will translate "*ren*" as humanness.[19]

The precise meaning of "*ren*" is context dependent. In the *Analects*, the term is used prescriptively (one ought to be/do *ren*) and descriptively (a person or an act is *ren*). Moreover, it is used for a range of moral concepts, including will or motive, moral demand or duty, moral ideal or orientation, moral action (means), and moral practice. This versatile use of the word makes it the most complicated and sometimes elusive notion in the whole *Analects*. But it is also the most important idea in the book.

The word "*ren*" rarely appeared in pre-Confucian literature, but it occurrs 105 times (in fifty-eight of the 499 verses/sections) in the *Analects*, more frequently than any other central Confucian concept, for example *li* (ritual propriety, seventy-two times), *xin* (being true to one's words, thirty-six times), and *xiao* (filial piety, eighteen times). This concept is so prominent in Confucius' teachings that it has become the hallmark of his humanism. Although Confucius claimed that he was merely transmitting the Way of the former kings without proposing anything new, the idea of humanness was indeed his innovation.[20]

Confucius takes humanness to be the ultimate moral demand that applies to every person in society, regardless of the person's position in the social hierarchy.[21] As a moral demand, humanness requires that one care for others. When one of his pupils asked about the nature of humanness, Confucius replied: "Care for others."[22] This type of care is first expressed in the respect and concern one has toward others as persons. Confucius maintains that humanness as an ultimate moral demand is based on the value of the human person and the sanctity of human life.

A story illustrates Confucius' high regard for human life. He had been away from home at the state court; when he returned home, he saw that his stables had all burned down. Immediately he asked whether any person had been hurt, instead of inquiring about his horses and material things.[23] According to the *Mengzi* (another Confucian classic named after the Confucian philosopher Mengzi), Confucius had also vehe-

---

19  Other translations of "*ren*" include "goodness" (Waley), "authoritative conduct" (Roger T. Ames and Henry Rosemont, Jr., trans., *The Analects of Confucius—A Philosophical Translation* [New York: Ballantine Books, 1998]), and "perfect virtue" or "benevolence" (James Legge, trans., *Confucian Analects*. In James Legge ed., *Confucius* [New York: Dover, 1971. (Reprint from the second revised edition published 1893.)]).

20  See 7:1. This is perhaps why Confucius' disciples often enquired about what "*ren*" means and how to practice it, as they were new to Confucius' employment of the term. See Ames and Rosemont, Introduction, 50.

21  Our modern conception of social equality is alien to Confucius. It is probably unfair to expect him to transcend the ethical limitations of his era.

22  12:22.

23  10:17.

mently condemned the practices of human sacrifice and figurine sacrifice;[24] he said that the inventor of tomb figurines did not deserve to have any offspring![25] In addition, this type of care is expressed in the consideration of the feelings, needs, and overall well-being of others. As Confucius puts it, "A man of humanness, wishing to establish his own character, also establishes the character of others, and wishing to be prominent himself, also helps others to be prominent."[26]

According to Confucius, humanness as a moral demand is both a constant demand and a life-long demand. It is constant in that it applies to every moment of life, so a person of humanness would not ignore the demand of humanness even "for the space of a meal."[27] It encompasses life-long, serious duties that do not end until one's death.[28] While Confucius was fully aware that in reality very few actually lived by humanness constantly, he still insisted on its necessity and its urgency as a moral ideal. He believed firmly that everyone had the capacity to act according to humanness.[29]

Confucius' idea of humanness is akin to Kant's idea of moral duty or moral obligation, which demands one's constant and persistent commitment. According to Kant, the moral imperative of treating others as an end (and not merely as means) applies to everyone, and its universal validity is derived from pure practical reason—a faculty that every normal human being possesses. In a similar view, Confucius considers it an essential human characteristic to seek humanness. However, unlike Kant who bases the moral duty exclusively on pure practical reason, Confucius seems to ground the moral demand of humanness on the natural affective bonds between parents and children, as well as between siblings. As one disciple of Confucius puts it, "Filial piety and brotherly respect are the root of humanness."[30] The root metaphor is very significant since it suggests the idea of a constant growing and flourishing from the root upward.

For Confucius, ethically speaking, one is not born with certain substantive properties that make one a human being. Instead, one becomes or develops into a human being by acting in response to the moral demand of humanness. As Ames and Rosemont put it, it is a matter of what one makes of one's life that gives rise to one's humanness. Thus, they claim that humanness is "not an essential endowed potential, but what one is able to make of oneself given the interface between one's initial conditions and one's natural, social, and cultural environments."[31] In this sense, biologically, one can be a member of the *homo sapiens* species without being an authentically human person if one fails to live by humanness. A man can be a biological father, too, without being an authentic father if he neglects his duty as a father. A ruler or a minister can also be one in name

---

24 Figurine sacrifice is a sacrificial ritual in which carved or moulded figures are used.
25 See the *Mengzi*, 1A4.
26 Wing-tsit Chan's translation slightly modified—where Chan translated "*ren*" into "humanity," I rendered it "humanness" (*Sourcebook in Chinese Philosophy* [Princeton: Princeton University Press, 1993], 6:28).
27 4:5.
28 8:7.
29 See 4:6, 6:7.
30 1:2, Chan's translation.
31 Ames and Rosemont, Introduction, 49.

only if he does not exemplify humanness in his respective capacity. What makes one an authentic human being is the *practice* of humanness, which is determined contextually according to one's social and moral roles.[32]

There is another difference between Kant's idea of moral duty and Confucius' view of the demand of humanness. In Kant's ethics, human beings are theoretically isolated from real life situations; they are stripped of all contextual details and are reduced—as it were—to nothing but featureless atomistic entities. Factors such as their social positions, family backgrounds, personality traits or dispositions, feelings and emotions are all suspended or bracketed out. The "one" in a formulation of Kant's Categorical Imperative—one should never act in such a way that one treats humanity, whether in one's self or in others, as a means only, but rather always as an end in itself[33]—is a person that is stripped of all personal, particular features. It appears to Kant that unless all these factors are suspended, no universal moral principle is possible. In contrast, Confucius' demand of humanness, while applying to everyone, does take into account the specific factors mentioned above. Confucius' attention to these specific factors stems from the fact that humanness as a moral demand is not about the application of a formal rule, but about caring for others in particular circumstances.[34] For humanness to be possible, one must attend to all the specificities of life.[35]

What does it mean for a person to respond to the call of humanness? First, it means attending to one's duties of care as defined by one's social roles and contexts: as a son or daughter, one should practice filial piety to one's parents; as a younger sibling, one is required to show brotherly (or sisterly) respect to one's elder brothers (and sisters); when relating to friends, one should be faithful to one's words; and when serving the government, one should be loyal to one's post. A ruler should love his ministers by treating them with ritual propriety, and he should show affection to the common people, for instance, by not exploiting their labour when they ought to be working in the fields.[36] In terms of moral training and moral cultivation, filial piety and brotherly respect are seen as more fundamental than other duties of care.[37] In Confucius' vision, the different duties of care are complementary, like the musical notes that make up a chord. The diverse socially defined obligations are seen as different ways of showing

---

32  See *Analects* 12:11, 13:3.
33  Immanuel Kant, *The Fundamental Principles of the Metaphysics of Morals*, paraphrased.
34  See 1:5, 1:6, and 17:4.
35  Our contrast between Confucius and Kant here is by no means to downplay the importance of Kant's insight on impartial principles. Some scholars have argued that Confucian ethics may, in practice, degenerate into injustice and unfairness in the form of favouritism, nepotism, and even despotism (see Robin R. Wang, "The Principled Benevolence: A Synthesis of Kantian and Confucian Moral Judgment," in *Comparative Approaches to Chinese Philosophy*, Bo Mou, ed. [Aldershot, UK: Ashgate, 2003], 122–43), and Eske Møllgaard, *An Introduction to Daoist Thought—Action, Language, and Ethics in Zhuangzi* [London: Routledge, 2007], 117). I doubt, however, that this is an expected consequence of Confucius' ethics. First of all, Confucius did offer impartial guidelines (see 6:28 and 15:23, quoted below). And secondly, it may be argued that the degeneration actually happens when one misuses or abuses Confucius' guidelines. It is true that selfish inclinations can sometimes slip in so that Confucius' guidelines for caring for others are not followed, but so is the case when selfish inclinations lead people to ignore Kant's impartial principles.
36  See 1:5, 3:19.
37  See 1:2, 1:6.

care and concern for others. Thus, social harmony results when people faithfully fulfill their respective social roles and obligations.[38]

Second, following the call of humanness means to observe one's ethical priorities. Confucius recognizes that it is not possible for a person to care for everyone *to the same degree*, so he advocates caring first for one's family members and loving them with more intensity than those outside the family. The ethical priority of family members is natural and realistic because it is based on blood ties and gives full consideration to one's limited resources (such as time, money, energy, etc.).

In normal situations, the act of spending all one's money helping total strangers far away while leaving one's own family to starve does not seem to accord with our moral intuition.[39] However, the act of spending *some* of one's money in helping total strangers—even though that would amount to reducing the living standard of one's own family to a limited extent—seems perfectly consistent with our common moral intuition. While Confucius stresses the ethical priority of caring for one's family members, he does not argue that one should simply restrict one's care for others within family. Indeed, he advocates that one should care for the multitude broadly.[40]

To some readers, Confucius' ideas of filial piety and brotherly respect may appear to entail non-reciprocal relationships, with parents and elder siblings being the respective beneficiaries. This asymmetry may cause us to wonder whether filial piety and brotherly respect are truly consistent with the idea of humanness. Shouldn't notions such as love and care imply mutuality? For Confucius, the one-sidedness of filial piety and brotherly respect is only apparent, for in his social vision, the hierarchical structure of a family unit—and for that matter any social unit—does not imply a top-down *power* structure, where those lower in the hierarchy are to blindly submit to their superiors, nor are they expected to be treated with disrespect by their superiors. Although in practice filial piety may be abused to encourage blind obedience, this is more of an unfortunate distortion than an essential element of Confucius' ideal of filial piety. When Confucius said that in practicing filial piety one should "never disobey,"[41] he was not suggesting that one should never disobey the commands of one's parents or that one should never disapprove of their actions. Rather, he was advocating that one should never disobey one's duty of serving parents as prescribed in the rules of ritual propriety, which entails taking care of them when they are alive, burying them when they die, and offering sacrifices to them regularly as part of ancestral worship after their death.[42] It is important to note that, rather than urging blind obedience, Confucius actually advises a son sometimes to gently remonstrate with his parents: "In serving his father and mother a man may gently remonstrate with them. But if he sees that he has failed to change their opinion, he should resume an attitude of deference and not thwart them; he may feel discouraged, but not resentful."[43]

---

38  Oddly, the *Analects* is silent on romantic love and on respect between wife and husband.
39  For more on this point, see Peter Singer's book, *The Life You Can Save—Acting Now to End World Poverty* (New York: Random House, 2009).
40  See 1:6 and 6:30.
41  See 4:18.
42  See 2:5.
43  See 4:18.

On the other hand, Confucius also maintains that parents ought to win their authority and their children's respect by fulfilling their obligations as parents, such as loving their children and nurturing them physically, emotionally, and morally. For example, Confucius encouraged his son to learn traditional rituals, and to study the Book of Odes (*Shi Jing*, the earliest existing collection of poems and songs, dating from the eleventh to the sixth centuries BCE), as they were seen as keys for proper speaking and behaving.[44]

In the same vein, while Confucius stresses an administrative hierarchy between the king and the ministers, he believes the moral relationship between them should be reciprocal. A ruler must be morally upright and treat his ministers and the general populace with respect, for it is his moral uprightness and respect that command the obedience of those he leads. Confucius says: "If those above them love ritual, then among the common people none will dare to be disrespectful. If those above them love right, then among the common people none will dare to be disobedient. If those above them love good faith, then among the common people none will dare depart from the facts."[45] In another verse, Confucius explains that the observance of ritual propriety is integral to a ruler's relationship to his minister; he says, "Rulers should employ their ministers by observing ritual propriety, and ministers should serve their lord by doing their utmost."[46] These texts suggest that while Confucius accepts that society is hierarchically structured, reciprocity is also an implicit principle that regulates the relationships across levels of the hierarchy. This is true of the relationship between a father and a son, and the relationship between a ruler and his ministers. The parents and rulers are addressed more prominently than sons and ministers, probably because in Confucius' time (even in our time) the former exerted more social influence and were perceived to have been entrusted with greater moral responsibilities than the latter.

Third, to respond to the call of humanness involves living by a principle that distinguishes right from wrong. Humanness therefore includes moral integrity. Numerous cases in the *Analects* show that Confucius takes an ethical stand.[47] The following is a typical example:

> Zigong inquired, saying, "What do you think about someone who is loved by everyone in his village?" "It is not enough," said the Master. "What if everyone in the village despises a person?" "It is not enough. It would be better that the best villagers love, and the worst despise, this person."[48]

The point Confucius is driving at seems to be that we should be suspicious of the crowd pleasers, for there is a good chance that they are merely opportunists who do not stand for any principles.[49] Thus, Confucius urges us to "look into the matter carefully"[50]

---

44  See 16:13.
45  13:4; also see 2:20, 15:33.
46  3:19, Ames and Rosemont's translation; also see the *Mengzi* 4B3.
47  See 6:5, 17:21.
48  13:24, Ames and Rosemont's translation; also see 4:3, 17:13.
49  Also see the *Dhammapada* verse 228.
50  15:28, Ames and Rosemont's translation.

whenever someone is loved or despised by everyone. In such cases, there is good chance that the person thus loved or despised may have compromised her moral integrity. We should certainly be suspicious of the moral integrity of a mayor—or for that matter any politician—who promises to or has indeed taken actions to make virtually *everyone* in a jurisdiction happy (including drug dealers, bank robbers, and rapists)!

Confucius does not suggest that one should blindly "be nice" to all regardless of the situation. Rather, he suggests that one should be sensitive to the principle that distinguishes right from wrong, and that one should respond to right and wrong in different ways:

> Someone said, "What do you think of repaying hatred with virtue?"
> Confucius said, "In that case what are you going to repay virtue with?
> Rather, repay hatred with uprightness and repay virtue with virtue."[51]

Imagine three options that one might face when encountering hatred: one could "repay hatred with hatred," "repay hatred with virtue,"[52] or "repay hatred with upright-ness." The first option appears wrong to Confucius, because it will lead to a vicious circle, and it is contrary to his general teachings of humanness. The second option may be noble, but may also be naïve, since it implies that the victim in question makes no discrimination between his/her dealing with virtue and with ill will, and that would amount to abandoning moral justice. In reality this second option may express itself in blind forbearance in the face of ill will. For Confucius, the most practical option is the third option—"repay hatred with uprightness."

## DOING PHILOSOPHY
### Hatred and Virtue: Some Proposals

How do we respond to ill will and hatred? Great thinkers from the East and the West have made various proposals:

Socrates: "One must never in any way do wrong willingly.... Nor must one, when wronged, inflict wrong in return, as the majority believe, since one must never do wrong" (Crito, 49a, b).

Old Testament: "Show no pity: life for life, eye for eye, tooth for tooth, hand for hand, foot for foot" (Deuteronomy 19:21, New International Version).

New Testament: "But I tell you, Do not resist an evil person. If someone strikes you on the right cheek, turn to him the other also" (Matthew 5:39). "But I tell

---

51  14:36, Chan's translation.
52  See the Dhammapada verse 197 and the *Daodejing* Chapter 79.

you: Love your enemies and pray for those who persecute you, that you may be sons of your Father in heaven. He causes his sun to rise on the evil and the good, and sends rain on the righteous and the unrighteous" (Matthew 5: 44–45). "Do not repay anyone evil for evil. Be careful to do what is right in the eyes of everyone. If it is possible, as far as it depends on you, live at peace with everyone. Do not take revenge, my dear friends, but leave room for God's wrath, for it is written: 'It is mine to avenge; I will repay,' says the Lord" (Romans 12:17–19) (All New International Version).

The Buddha: "For hatred can never put an end to hatred; love alone can. This is an unalterable law" (the Dhammapada, verse 5).

Laozi (Lao Tzu): "Repay resentment with Virtue" (the *Daodejing*, Chapter 63).

Mahatma Gandhi: "An eye for an eye makes the whole world blind."[53]

Martin Luther King, Jr.: "But there is something that I must say to my people, who stand on the warm threshold which leads into the palace of justice: In the process of gaining our rightful place, we must not be guilty of wrongful deeds. Let us not seek to satisfy our thirst for freedom by drinking from the cup of bitterness and hatred. We must forever conduct our struggle on the high plane of dignity and discipline. We must not allow our creative protest to degenerate into physical violence. Again and again, we must rise to the majestic heights of meeting physical force with soul force.
   The marvellous new militancy which has engulfed the Negro community must not lead us to a distrust of all white people, for many of our white broth-ers, as evidenced by their presence here today, have come to realize that their destiny is tied up with our destiny. And they have come to realize that their freedom is inextricably bound to our freedom" (from his "I Have a Dream" speech, Washington DC, 28 August 1963).

Mencius (Mengzi): "Here is a person who is harsh to me. A gentleman in this situation will invariably examine himself, saying, 'I must not be benevolent. I must be lacking in propriety. How else could this situation have come upon me?!' If he examines himself and *is* benevolent, and if he examines himself and *has* propriety, yet the other person is still harsh, a gentleman will invariably examine himself, saying, 'I must not be loyal.' If he examines himself and

---

53   This quotation (or a variation on it) is widely attributed to Gandhi (and is spoken by the actor Ben Kingsley, playing him in the 1982 movie *Gandhi*), but there is no record of his having said it. It does appear in Martin Luther King, Jr.'s *Stride Toward Freedom: The Montgomery Story* (New York, Harper & Brothers, 1958).

*is* loyal, yet the other person is still harsh, a gentleman says, 'This person is simply incorrigible! What difference is there between a person like this and an animal?! What point is there in rebuking an animal?'" (4B28, also see 7A4).

Which proposal do you want to adopt? Why? Is there anything in common in all these proposals? Are there similarities among them?

In order to explain Confucius' point "repay hatred with uprightness," consider the following scenario. Suppose John has been maliciously harassed at work by some colleagues because of his ethnic background. They have been hurling insults at him persistently and frequently. How should John respond?

Confucius, it seems, would not consider it acceptable for John to be nasty to those who have insulted him. Such action would only exacerbate the situation. Should John then simply have treated them with respect and care (i.e., repaying hatred with virtue) as if nothing had happened? There is no denying that his colleagues might be moved by his kindness and stop harassing him. However, since they had been harassing John persistently, the chance of such a drastic change of heart may be very slim. More importantly, a further problem with this response is that the moral wrongness of the actions of John's colleagues is not addressed. While "turn the other cheek" or "love your enemy" may sound noble, to follow such advice in the above scenario appears too naïve and perhaps even dangerous. Blind forbearance and tacit consent to persistent insult may simply send the wrong message to the perpetrators that their abusive acts are acceptable.

In the light of the difficulty with the second option, Confucius would very likely advise John to make it clear that his colleagues' abusive insults are morally wrong, but how he should confront them or communicate this message to them will depend on various particular factors in the situation—he might try to discuss the matter seriously with them, or call the police, or file a written complaint with the company manager, or sue his colleagues, for example. Whatever he chooses to do, he will be doing it in the spirit of "uprightness."

### DOING PHILOSOPHY
*Are Force and War Sometimes Necessary*
*and Morally Justifiable in Response to Evil?*

In us President Barack Obama's Nobel Peace Prize ceremony speech (Oslo, Norway, December 10, 2009), he expresses admiration of Martin Luther King's and Gandhi's creed of non-violence, but he says it "may not have been practical or possible in every circumstance." Obama argues that "There will be times when nations—acting individually or in concert—will find the use of force not only necessary but morally justified." As an example, Obama cites, "A non-violent movement could not have halted Hitler's armies. Negotiations cannot convince al Qaeda's leaders to lay down their arms." He added that "force can be justified on humanitarian grounds, as it was in the Balkans, or in other places that have been scarred by war. Inaction tears at our conscience and can lead to more costly intervention later." However, he qualifies his point by saying "To say that force is sometimes necessary is not a call to cynicism—it is a recognition of history; the imperfections of man and the limits of reason.... the instruments of war do have a role to play in preserving the peace.... But war itself is never glorious, and we must never trumpet it as such."

Do you agree with Obama's view on the use of force in some circumstances? Do you think he should follow King and Gandhi instead? To what degree is Obama's "realistic" approach akin to Confucius' view of "repay hatred with uprightness"? (You may also want to compare Obama's reservations about the use of war with Laozi's view on war in the *Daodejing* [Chapter 31]: "Weapons are inauspicious instruments, not the instruments of a cultivated person. / But if given no choice, the cultivated person will use them. / Peace and quiet are the highest ideals; / A military victory is not a thing of beauty. / To beautify victory is to delight in the slaughter of human beings. / One who delights in the slaughter of human beings will not realize his ambitions in the world" [Ivanhoe's translation].)

Humanness as a moral ideal informs personal, social, and political actions. This ideal is personal, and requires a serious commitment and persistent effort. And this ideal includes others, therefore those who set humanness as an ideal should love the multitude and help others to "stand up" (*li*) and "advance forward" (*da*). And a ruler would confer wide benefits upon the common people and ease the lot of the whole populace.[54] This shows that humanness as a moral ideal is at once ethical and political; although the realization of humanness relies on the ruler's cultivation of virtues, the aim of such moral cultivation is good governance and the welfare of the people. Confucius predicted that a king who is committed to moral self-cultivation himself (i.e., the cultivation of humanness) would prevail in the world after a single generation.[55] A society of humanness is one in which people fulfill their specific moral obligations of caring for others. He even suggests that humanness is such a worthy goal that those committed to it are willing to give up their lives to achieve it: "A resolute scholar and a man of humanness will never seek to live at the expense of injuring humanness."[56]

---

54  See 1:6, 6:28, 14:42.
55  See 13:12.
56  15:8, Chan's translation adjusted.

## HUMANNESS AS PRACTICE

Humanness, in the *Analects*, is not a Platonic ideal that exists only in the heaven, nor, as Waley interpreted, a "mystic entity."[57] The moral idea of humanness constantly calls for one's existential and ethical response in concrete situations, so the pursuit of humanness entails concrete practices in real life. It is not a matter of talking, but a matter of doing.[58] As Chan explains it, humanness is "first and foremost an activity, not a state of mind."[59] Although Confucius did not explicitly argue that human nature is intrinsically good—an undertaking his spiritual follower Mengzi picked up more than a century later—he did assume that every normal human being has the moral capacity to respond to the call of humanness.[60]

It is interesting to see that Confucius' moral teachings do not rely on a definitive view of human nature. In fact, the *Analects* is notoriously vague about human nature. First, Confucius' disciple Zigong is reported to have mentioned that Confucius' pupils had not heard much of their master's view on people's "natural disposition."[61] This may suggest that human nature may not have been a topic of interest for Confucius. Second, there is indeed a remark by Confucius about human nature—"By nature [people] are alike; through habituation-learning [they] become apart."[62] Confucius here does seem to assume that there is a human nature, but what this nature consists in is still far from being clear. Is Confucius speaking of our "physical nature"? If so, how is it different from animal nature? Does he think that human beings, whose natures are alike, are essentially good? We shall see that it is precisely these questions that piqued the interest of Mengzi and his contemporaries. At any rate it seems safe to say that in the above quote human nature is at best ethically "neutral,"[63] and that it is possible to advocate moral teachings without a definite doctrine of human nature.

Consistent with his assumption that every normal person has the moral strength or power to practice humanness,[64] Confucius also believes that most people are teachable and malleable, even the petty, the morally inferior, and the barbaric.[65] This belief is certainly compatible with his assumption that humans are alike in their nature, whether human nature is essentially good or bad. Either view is compatible with the belief of human malleability and perfectibility. Either view would still support Confucius' vision and mission—to train people to be good and to establish harmony in families, states, and the world. If it turns out that human nature is essentially bad, the task of

---

57  Waley, 1989, 28.
58  See 1:3, 12:3, 17:17, 1:2, and 12:1.
59  Wing-tsit Chan, "The Evolution of the Confucian Concept of *Jen* [*Ren*]," *Philosophy East and West* 4 (1955): 309.
60  See 4:6, 12:1.
61  See 5:12.
62  17:2, my translation.
63  Chan translation, 46.
64  See 4:4.
65  See 12:19, 9:13.

moral training and cultivation will be arduous and may require coercion. Conversely, if human nature is essentially good, the task will be natural and relatively effortless. To be sure, Confucius was dissatisfied with the moral condition of his time, as he deplored the fact that people were fonder of physical beauty than moral excellence.[66] Yet he still seems to have been confident that with proper training and self-cultivation most people would have the capacity to put humanness into practice.[67] Later development of Confucianism in the Warring States period (475–221 BCE), while adhering to his conviction that humans are teachable, bifurcated into two branches: Mengzi and Xunzi. Mengzi argued that human nature is good and that moral training and moral cultivation are a matter of naturally realizing and extending this good nature. Xunzi on the other hand contended that human nature is bad and moral training and moral cultivation must be artificially imposed on humans.

### MORAL WILL

The impetus to practice humanness springs from one's moral will. Confucius says, to practice humanness depends on oneself, rather than on others.[68] Moreover, he argues that moral teachings alone without self-effort do not better a person morally; he says, "A man can enlarge his Way; but there is no Way that can enlarge a man."[69] Thus, moral behaviour stems from one's moral will, which one might regard as the "fountainhead" of moral practice. Without it moral behaviour is impossible. Confucius says that he cannot do anything with one who understands the call of humanness but simply does not want to carry it out.[70]

Like Kant, Confucius insists that moral will is more fundamental than the "gifts of nature" (such as intelligence and judgment) and "qualities of temperament" (such as resoluteness and perseverance) and "gifts of fortune" (such as power, riches, and honour). Lacking gifts of nature, qualities of temperament, or gifts of fortune does not necessarily put one in a disadvantageous position when practicing humanness. On the other hand, the moral demand of humanness does not require that everyone play the same social role, say, as a king—a role that demands the capacities and skills for managing and governing a domain, which only a few possess. The moral demand only requires that people practice humanness in accordance with their respective social roles. Therefore, for Confucius, social distinction and stratification do not necessarily prevent people from practising humanness; they are in fact the means through which

---

66 See 9:17, 15:12.
67 There are two other concepts that seem closely related to the idea of human nature: *de* (moral force or virtue) and *zhi* (uprightness, honesty, or straightness). Confucius uses *de* in a neutral sense as he referred to an exemplary person's (*junzi's*) *de* as well as a petty person's *de* (12:19). He also applied the concept of *de* to horses (14:33). So for him *de* does not define exclusively human nature. Nor does *zhi* do the job, because *zhi* was used by Confucius to designate a feature of personality (5:24, 6:17, 13:18), not the defining nature of being human.
68 See 12:1.
69 15:28.
70 See 9:23.

humanness is embodied in the world. People may have varying degrees of success in the practice of humanness, depending upon various personal and social conditions. However, inasmuch as they have the capacity to exert their moral will, they stand on equal footing. In this sense, neither one's natural endowment nor one's good fortune is relevant. Confucius says, "Is humanness far away? As soon as I [that is, any moral agent] want it, there it is right by me."[71]

Basing on the assumption that everyone has the strength or power to exert a moral will,[72] Confucius lectured his disciple Ranyou for not having even attempted to exert his moral will:

> Ranyou said, "It is not that your Way does not commend itself to me, but that it demands powers I do not sufficiently possess." The Master said, "He whose powers give out collapses during the course of the journey (the Way); but you deliberately draw the line [before you start]."[73]

Ranyou appeared to have claimed that his inability to exert a moral will stemmed from his lack of personal capacities. But Confucius maintained that Ranyou's deficiency, real or perceived, could only have been the lack of gifts of nature or gifts of fortune. Thus, for Confucius, Ranyou's excuse could not have been legitimate, for everyone has the capacity to exert moral will regardless of his or her natural abilities (or the lack thereof). The message of Confucius' rebuke is rather straightforward: Even if you think you lack gifts of nature or gifts of fortune, you still have to make an effort to *employ* whatever you have before determining whether you have what it takes to achieve your aim. If you are not even willing to make an attempt to practice humanness right from the start, your lack of initiative only indicates that you are in fact *unwilling*, rather than *unable*, to do so.

### RITUAL PROPRIETY (*LI*)

As we have seen, humanness is a matter of action, but it is not a matter of any action. Rather, it is a matter of doing things *appropriately*—that is, observing *li*, or ritual propriety. Before Confucius' time, *li* was primarily concerned with ceremonies or rituals used in ancestor worship, but Confucius uses the term in a much broader sense. He uses it to cover a variety of conventions, regulations, and codes of conduct in almost every facet of life, including rules regulating the practices of royal court proceedings, ancestor worship, and even table manners.[74] A crucial part of ritual propriety prescribes the duties and obligations of various social roles. For example, a father should take care of his family, and a son should respect his father and his elder brother. A ruler should employ the ministers with ritual propriety (respect) while

---

71　7:29, Chan's translation, modified. It is also in this sense that Mengzi claims that everyone can act as the legendary exemplary rulers Yao and Shun acted (see the *Mengzi*, 6B2).
72　See 4:4.
73　6:10, Waley's translation modified.
74　See 1:12, 2:5, and Book 10.

ministers should serve their rulers loyally.[75] According to Confucius, sincere and correct observance of ritual propriety embodies true humanness; to act in accordance with ritual propriety is to answer the call of humanness.[76]

When one of his disciples Yan Yuan inquired about the nature of humanness, Confucius said, "To master oneself and submit to ritual propriety is to practice humanness," and further explained that "submitting to ritual propriety" means "to look at nothing in violation of ritual propriety, to listen to nothing in violation of ritual propriety, to speak of nothing in violation of ritual propriety, never to take a move in violation of ritual propriety."[77]

Confucius maintains that as one develops physically, one should also grow in awareness of the call of humanness and respond to it accordingly, but this latter process can occur only through the learning and practice of ritual propriety. In learning and practicing ritual propriety, one comes to know where to "stand," that is, how to behave in particular situations so that one can show respect for others appropriately.[78] Confucius urges his son to learn ritual propriety and warns him that without it one cannot "stand up"[79]—that is, take an ethical stance. Just as infants have to learn to stand up physically and walk on their own, once they have grown up they have to learn to stand up ethically. Both cases require inculcation and acculturation, and call for the exercise of one's will and effort. In order to learn to stand up ethically, one needs the help of one's family in giving early training in ritual propriety. This is why the ritual practice of filial piety and brotherly respect is regarded as the root of humanness.[80] The practice of filial piety and brotherly respect takes place in a natural context, as small children learn to love their parents and their brothers at home. Once they have internalized the spirit of humanness at home, they can extend the spirit of humanness and apply it, once they have grown up, to a larger social context. This is why those who practice filial piety and brotherly respect at home are more likely to behave ethically and are much less likely to defy authority or initiate rebellion.[81]

Learning to stand up ethically, however, takes a long time and requires much more effort than learning to stand up physically. Confucius confesses that it was not until he was thirty years old when he was able to fully stand up ethically.[82] Learning to stand up ethically involves a process of internalization and socialization, in which one becomes increasingly mature in dealing with the demands of different social roles and social relationships.

---

75  See 3:19.
76  Rituals in the Vedas are very different from rituals in the *Analects*. In the Vedas, rituals are believed to make contact with gods whose powers are "borrowed" to benefit us humans; rituals in Confucius' sense focus more on the secular, human-to-human relationship.
77  12:1.
78  See 8:8, 16:13, 20:3.
79  See 16:13; also see 17:10.
80  See 1:2.
81  See 1:2.
82  See 2:4.

In the process of aiding individuals to stand up ethically, the rules of ritual propriety first serve to regulate one's behaviours.[83] The regulative function of ritual propriety expresses itself in two ways. First, the rules of ritual propriety *inform* young people about what proper behaviours are. They bring them from the state of moral ignorance to moral knowledge. Second, they *constrain* them when they are tempted to behave inappropriately or deviate from the social norms. The informative function of the rules is proactive, and the constraining or restrictive function of the rules is latent. In the latter case, young people simply take ritual propriety for granted.[84] In Confucius' time, because violations of the rules of ritual propriety were common, Confucius paid special attention to the constraining function of ritual propriety. He advised his disciple Yan Hui to follow ritual propriety in every way.[85]

Confucius' teaching about the proper observance of ritual propriety may sound rigid at times. However, he never viewed the rules of ritual propriety legalistically as if they were law codes, or *fa*, such as the criminal and penal codes. The word *fa* appears only twice in the whole text of the *Analects*, and neither use of the term implies severe punishment.[86] For Confucius, even though punishment itself may help reform or reha-bilitate the transgressor, it is not as good as moral training. For Confucius, punishment is at most an expedient instrument for governing the masses.[87]

In addition, Confucius is emphatic that the observance of ritual propriety is not merely a matter of formality. He says: "Ritual, ritual! Does it mean no more than pres-ents of jade and silk? Music, music! Does it mean no more than bells and drums?"[88] He emphasizes that the mere external performance of an act of ritual propriety without the accompanying inner attitude of humanness is not ritual propriety at all.[89] Someone who attends a mourning ceremony without expressing real grief is not actually observing ritual propriety.[90] Neither is a ruler doing so if he fails to respect (*rang*, literally "defer to") others.[91]

---

83  The training in ritual propriety can take many forms: including telling stories, watching traditional dramas, practicing ancestor worship, and attending traditional schools. It does not simply mean a rote memory of a list of rituals.

84  It is noteworthy and not coincidental that Confucius frequently addressed ritual propriety along with music (11:1, 11:26, 13:3, 14:12, 16:2, and 16:5; also see 17:18, 17:21). There are indeed parallels between learning to play (good) music and learning and observing ritual propriety. Both can be initially restric-tive and regulative; both have the functions of guiding and refining our behaviour and emotion; both are expressive (3:23); and finally both are self-rewarding (1.1). See Karyn Lai, "Confucian Moral Cultivation: Some Parallels with Musical Training," in Kim-chong Chong, Sor-hoon Tan, and C.L. Ten, eds., *The Moral Circle and the Self* (Chicago: Open Court, 2003). Confucius was aware that music can also be ethically corrupting when he remarked that the music of the state Zheng was licentious (15:11, 17:18).

85  See 12:1 quoted above; also see 1:12, 6:27, 9:11.

86  See 9:24, 20:1.

87  See 2:3 (a discussion of this passage is below).

88  17:11.

89  See 3:3.

90  See 3:4; also see 3:12.

91  See 4:13.

**DOING PHILOSOPHY**
*Are Rules of Ritual Propriety Fixed in Time?*

While humanness and ritual propriety share a symbiotic relationship, there is at times tension between them. If it is (stubbornly) believed that *only* a fixed ritual practice—say, that of three-year mourning (see 17:21)—can actualize a moral ideal humanness, in the form of filial piety, then the ritual practice becomes fossilized and loses its real spirit. If, on the other hand, the spirit of humanness is too flexibly construed, that is, if random actions are all taken to be embodiments of humanness, then unprincipled practice can creep in in the guise of flexibility. For the sake of flexibility, for example, one may argue that mourning for a deceased parent is not necessary for those who are busy with their jobs. While Confucius urged society to observe ritual propriety, he never assumed that all the rules of ritual propriety were fixed in time.[92] For him, the balance between humanness and ritual propriety is dynamic, not static, and is subject to ongoing adjustment.

A discussion of the tension between humanness and the rules of ritual propriety may trigger us to ask the following question: Should we follow the rules and moral injunctions in spiritual teachings (such as Judaism and Christianity) to the letter? Actually doing so may lead to absurd consequences. (See, in this regard, A.J. Jacobs's hilarious book, *The Year of Living Biblically—One Man's Humble Quest to Follow the Bible as Literally as Possible* [New York: Simon & Schuster, 2008].)

Despite his stern tone in insisting on the observation of the rules of ritual propriety, Confucius' real position is that ritual propriety is not passive adherence to social norms, but rather allowing the rules of ritual propriety to actively refine one's behaviour and emotions: "Courtesy not bounded by observing ritual propriety becomes tiresome; caution not bounded by observing ritual propriety becomes timidity; boldness unbounded by observing ritual propriety becomes rudeness."[93]

Confucius also advocates that a ruler should avoid coercing his people into obeying the law by merely imposing punishment on them, but should instead appeal to their "moral force" (*de*)—that is, the strength of their moral character. He reasons that the proper observance of ritual propriety can help keep people orderly by fostering in them a healthy sense of shame, which in turn motivates them to order themselves voluntarily.

The Master said: "Lead the people with administrative injunctions (*zheng*) and keep them orderly with penal law (*xing*), and they will avoid

92  See 2:23, 3:14, 8:20.
93  8:2, Waley's translation revised.

punishments but will be without a sense of shame. Lead them with moral force [or virtue] (*de*) and keep them orderly through observing ritual propriety (*li*) and they will develop a sense of shame, and moreover, will order themselves."[94]

Thus, for Confucius, an important aim of the observance of ritual propriety is the refinement of one's moral force. As Waley pointed out, the "Confucius of the *Analects* is not much concerned with the details of ritual, either public or domestic ... [but] ... with the general principles of conduct, with morality rather than manners."[95]

Confucius argues that ritual propriety sustains good governance and enables society to "stand up" ethically as well as politically. He insists that to govern properly is to govern in accordance with ritual propriety.[96] He says that when rulers follow ritual propriety, the common people will be less likely to be disrespectful, so that they will be easy to govern.[97] Conversely, a heavy-handed approach that employs harsh coercive force may produce, at best, some short-term gain, but it is short-sighted and can be ineffective and dangerous in the long run. For Confucius, while physical force and punishment may stop people from doing wrong temporarily, they will not eradicate evil. In fact, it may even lead to more resentment and hatred on the part of the punished, which may in turn incite revenge. He thinks that the heavy-handed approach is inferior to the moral persuasion/education approach because the former merely addresses antisocial behaviour superficially. It is as if in curing a disease one simply suppresses the symptoms but leaves the root cause untouched. He insists that anti-social behaviours will only be suppressed temporarily through coercion if the offenders are shameless about their deeds. For Confucius, the function of ethics is preventive (i.e., aiming to stop harm from occurring) whereas the function of laws is only remedial at best (i.e., aiming to ameliorate harm after it has been done). Since the former produces more good in society than the latter, Confucius considers moral education more foundational to good governance than law enforcement. Jean-Jacques Rousseau (1712–78) echoed this point more than two thousand years later; he wrote, "Force is a physical power; I do not see what morality can result from its effects. To yield to force is an act of necessity, not of will; it is at most an act of prudence."[98]

The penal law defines an unlawful behaviour, and it may even explain why the behaviour is unlawful, but it does not necessarily make an agent *feel* shame. One will feel shame only when one has a moral conscience and believes that she/he will be morally tarnished if she/he commits an unlawful act. Confucius believes that only moral training (including observing ritual propriety) enables people to develop a sense of honour and shame, and that people will abstain from unlawful acts voluntarily only when they have a sense of honour and shame. In advocating ethics over punishment, he expressed

94  2:3, Ames and Rosemont's translation revised.
95  Waley, 55; see also 67.
96  See 4:13, 11:26.
97  See 13:4, 14:41, 16:2.
98  Jean-Jacques Rousseau, *The Social Contract* (Orig. 1762; Ware, UK: Wordsworth Editions, 1998), 8.

his wish that society would rid itself of the need of law courts and the use of deadly force altogether.[99]

## HUMANNESS AND PRACTICAL WISDOM

Suppose that one understands the importance of the call of humanness, and is familiar with the rules of ritual propriety. Does it follow that one will know *a priori* exactly what to do in every concrete life situation? When we read a book of ethics, we hope it will tell us exactly what to do in any particular circumstance. However, this hope is premised on an assumption that underestimates the complexities and contingencies of the moral life and overestimates the efficacy of moral teachings or doctrines. Kant's ethics, for instance, would not be able to tell us exactly what one ought to do when moral duties come into conflict. Let's say I have a duty always to tell the truth and a duty to protect my friend. Now, suppose there is a madman waving a gun at me, demanding to know where my friend is. What should I do? Should I tell the truth? My two duties come into conflict here. To act in accordance with one duty will cause me to forsake the other: If I tell the truth, I will not be protecting my friend. If I decide to protect my friend by not telling the truth, I will not be fulfilling my duty always to tell the truth.[100] Nor can utilitarian ethics provide a determinate prescription regarding what one ought to do in a concrete situation, for it does not provide a definite way of calculating and weighing the consequences or utilities of a particular course of action.

However, failure to prescribe a definite course of action does not nullify the usefulness of an ethical theory. Both Kantian ethics and utilitarianism offer great ethical guidelines and insights for our moral deliberation, but they do not automatically translate into concrete prescriptions in a fixed and formulaic way. They do not offer ready-made solutions to concrete ethical problems. What is needed in making a moral choice and acting morally is moral sensitivity, which is what Aristotle called *phronêsis*, or practical wisdom. Confucius exemplifies precisely this quality. The following two remarks from the *Analects* illustrate this point clearly:

> The Master said, "Exemplary persons (*junzi*) in making their way in the world are neither bent on nor against anything; rather, they go with what is appropriate (*yi*)."[101]

> [After commenting on the moral characters of various people, Confucius concluded] "But I am different from all of these people in that I do not have presuppositions as to what may and may not be done."[102]

---

99 See 12:13, 12:19. Here one may ask the following question: Is Confucius' view regarding the transformative power of morality too naïve and too optimistic?

100 Kant in fact considers this case, and argues (implausibly, for many critics) that one should tell the truth. His short essay on this, "On a Supposed Right to Lie Because of Philanthropic Concerns," is published (among other places) in *Grounding for the Metaphysics of Morals; with, On a Supposed Right ...*, James W. Wellington, trans. (Indianapolis: Hackett, 1981).

101 4:10, Ames and Rosemont's translation.

102 18:8, Ames and Rosemont's translation.

In the first passage, Confucius advocates that an exemplary person does what is appropriate (*yi*). However, he does not go on to explain the criteria of appropriateness. How does one know what is appropriate and what is not? In some passages in the *Analects*, *yi* applies to how a ruler should employ and manage people.[103] In many others, it applies to profit or gain.[104] In fact, Confucius never offers any general definition of *yi* that specifies its necessary and sufficient conditions. Instead, he only urges people not to presuppose *beforehand* what may or may not be done, but to attend to what is right and wrong in a case by case manner, taking into consideration the particularity of each case. This lack of a definite description of *yi* seems to accord with the characterization of Confucius as someone who does not claim or demand absolute certainty.[105]

While ritual propriety prescribes characteristic virtues such as filial piety, brotherly love, and loyalty or conscience, it does not do so by specifying how they ought to be instantiated in *all* specific cases; it does not specify all the ethically relevant particularities, such as one's particular family situation, personality traits, interests, and capacities. In other words, for Confucius, the ethical life and moral practice are not definitively circumscribed by ritual propriety; they cannot be simply reduced to mechanical adherence to a set of inflexible rules. Van Norden explains Confucius' view:

> Kongzi [Confucius] is not interested in giving us a neat, rightly organized worldview, because he does not think that reality is neat and tightly organized. Instead, Kongzi thinks that we must develop a number of virtues: humanness, righteousness, wisdom, courage, loyalty, faithfulness and filial piety. To the extent that we have these character traits, we will have a subtle, *situational appreciation* that goes beyond any simple verbal rule, formula, or practice. This situational appreciation will allow us to respond appropriately to the complex and ever-changing world in which we live.[106]

For Confucius, then, the complexity of the ethical life and moral practice does not allow for any definitive, simplistic list of moral dos and don'ts that address all the eventualities of life. However, this does not mean that for him ethics is unhelpful, unteachable, or unlearnable. On the contrary, every verse of the *Analects* aims to help us develop the ability to deliberate on complex moral situations. In using the *Analects* as a resource for ethical thinking, three types of material are particularly helpful: first, the numerous individualized moral instructions and examples; second, the conceptual linkages among the virtues; third, the general guidelines or working strategies for moral deliberation.

First, the *Analects* supplies numerous individualized instructions and specific examples on how to practice humanness, how to become an exemplary person, how to avoid being a morally petty person, how to practice filial piety and brotherly love, and so on. The examples are not exhaustive, but suggestive of how the virtues can be instantiated. Regarding the teaching of humanness, for example, Confucius' individualized

---

103 See 5:16, 6:22, 13:4.
104 See 7:16, 14:12, 14:13, 16:10, 19:1.
105 See 9:4; also see 14:32.
106 Bryan W. Van Norden, "The *Dao* of Kongzi," *Asian Philosophy* 12:2 (2002): 166 (my emphasis).

instruction is characteristic: "Sima Niu asked about humanness. The Master [Confucius] said, 'The man of humanness is slow in speaking.' 'But is that all that humanness is?' Niu added. The Master said, 'Since practicing humanness is difficult, how can one but be slow in speaking [of it]?'"[107]

Confucius' instruction here is occasioned by the inquiry of Sima Niu, who has the habit of speaking rashly. Thus, Confucius' advice here pertains to a particular way of practicing humanness, which seeks to remedy Sima Niu's weakness. Unfortunately Sima Niu does not seem to comprehend that one can only learn to practice humanness by embodying it in one's concrete situation in life, so he asks further, "Is that all that humanness is?" Sima Niu wants to know the "true" nature of humanness because in his mind "slow in speaking" does not seem to be able to capture the "whole truth" about humanness. Underlying this question, however, is not only his ignorance of humanness, but more sadly his *un*willingness to act.

It is important to note that Confucius did not go on to say that humanness is much more than simply being "slow in speaking." Why did he not say so? A possible reason is that Confucius was aware that even if he further clarified humanness (by pointing out other aspects or ways of practicing humanness, and not by offering a universal definition) Sima Niu would still not work on what he truly needed to work on immediately—namely, correcting his tendency of speaking rashly. If this interpretation is correct, it suggests that, in this particular context, Confucius may have considered it futile to give a further explanation of humanness if Sima Niu was not willing to practice it in any event.[108]

When teaching his pupils, Confucius was attentive to their individual circumstances and personal dispositions. On one occasion, two of his pupils, Zilu and Ranyou, came to him with the same question—that is, whether one should act upon what one has learned. Confucius responded by urging Ranyou to go ahead and act upon it, yet telling Zilu to consult his father and elder brothers first before acting.[109] When asked why he gave such different recommendations to Zilu and Ranyou, Confucius explained that it was because Ranyou was diffident and thus had to be urged on, whereas Zilu had more than one person's energy so he had to be reined in. This example illustrates Confucius' pedagogical sensitivity to his pupils' particular personalities and capacities. One might think that Confucius' different answers to the same question indicate that for him moral instruction is totally arbitrary. However, the truth is that *in those particular contexts*, both of his answers were definite and appropriate.

Second, the *Analects* suggests a number of conceptual linkages among the wide range of moral concepts it introduces, including humanness (*ren*), ritual propriety (*li*), exemplary persons (*junzi*), morally petty persons (*xiaoren*), filial piety (*xiao*), loyalty or conscience (*zhong*), faithfulness (*xin*), appropriateness (*yi*), and wisdom (*zhi*). These concepts are often discussed in the text in connection with one another, either directly

---

107 12:3, my translation.
108 Sima Niu's attitude to Confucius' moral instructions was in sharp contrast with two other pupils of Confucius, Yan Yuan and Zhong Gong, who showed great eagerness to practise what Confucius urged them to do. See 12:1 and 12:2.
109 See 11:22.

or indirectly.[110] Thus, the idea of humanness is in a subtle way linked up with virtually all other basic Confucian concepts, and its relation to any of them is neither obscure nor mystical. As Tu Wei-ming has observed, "a systematic inquiry into each occurrence of the linkage problem should eventually yield the fruit of a coherent semiotic structure of *jen* [*ren*, humanness] ... through 'matching concepts' or more dramatically, through a series of wrestlings with the meanings of each pair of ideas in terms of comparative analysis, *jen*'s true face should not be concealed for long."[111] One example of the conceptual linkage is the relationship between humanness and ritual propriety, which has been explained in some detail in the previous pages.

Third, the *Analects* proposes a few general guidelines or working strategies that we need to consider when approaching a moral decision. Three such guidelines are as follows.

*Guideline 1: Filial piety and brotherly love are the root of humanness.*
"Exemplary persons concentrate their efforts on the root, for the root having taken hold, the way will grow therefrom. Filial piety and brotherly love are the root of [practicing] humanness."[112] This general guideline specifies the importance of moral cultivation in the context of family. Learning to fulfill one's responsibilities to one's parents and siblings is the root of morality. The metaphor of "root" can be understood both temporally and logically. In the temporal sense, the metaphor suggests that one must first cultivate filial piety and fraternal love *before* one can act ethically in public life. In the logical sense, filial piety and fraternal love provide the requisite conditions for understanding how to act ethically toward others.

*Guideline 2: (dubbed the Golden Rule): Carrying out your duty of humanness.* "A man of humanness, wishing to establish ... his own character, also establishes the character of others, and wishing to be prominent ... himself, also helps others to be prominent. To be able to judge others by what is near to ourselves may be called the method of realizing humanness."[113]

*Guideline 3: (dubbed the Silver Rule): Act with empathy.* "Do not do to others what you do not want them to do to you."[114]

---

110 Some examples of passages connecting *ren* with other moral concepts: with *junzi*, see 2:4–5, 6:26, 8:2, 12:24, 14:6, 17:21, and 20:2; with *li*, see 3:3, 8:2, 12:1, 15:33, and 17:21; with love/care, see 12:22, 17:21; with death, see 14:16, 14:17, 15:35, 18:1, and 15:9; with courage/bravery, see 8:2, 8:10, 9:29, 14:4, 14:28, and 17:8; with learning, see 7:8, 19:6; with the Way, see 1:2, 7:6; with wisdom, see 4:1, 4:2, 6:22, 6:23, 9:29, 14:28, 15:33, 17:1, and 17:8; with speech, see 1:3, 12:3, 13:27, 14:4, 17:17, and 5:5; with anxiety, see 9:29, 14:28, and 12:4; with saintliness, see 6:30, 7:34; with filial piety, see 1:2, 1:6; with appearance, see 1:3, 12:20, 17:17; with loyalty/conscience, see 5:19, 13:19. Any of these connections would make a good term paper topic for those who are passionate about the *Analects*.

111 Tu Wei-ming, "Jen as a living metaphor in the Confucian *Analects*," *Philosophy East and West* 31:1 (January 1981): 50.

112 1:2. Translation (revised) from Ames and Rosemont.

113 6:28 (Chan's translation adjusted).

114 12:2 (Chan's translation); also see 5:11, 15:24.

Both guidelines 2 and 3 emphasize the significance of love of others. Guideline 2 is positive or active whereas Guideline 3 is negative and restrictive. It is in this sense that they are often called the "Golden Rule" and the "Silver Rule" respectively. For Confucius, the optimal *ideal* is that one would follow Guideline 2, which aims to help one serve the interests of others as well as those of oneself, where the relationship between serving others and serving oneself is considered reciprocal. However, Confucius suggests that if Guideline 2 proves to be too demanding, one should at least follow Guideline 3, which ensures that one's behaviour is at least of no harm to others.

These general guidelines do not undermine the importance of being attentive to the particulars of a moral situation. As guidelines they cannot be applied to all moral situations in exactly the same way without taking into account the particulars of each situation. The application of Guideline 1, for example, relies heavily on a contextualized understanding of filial piety and brotherly love.[115] The applications of Guideline 2 and Guideline 3 are more complicated than they seem. For example, in applying Guideline 2, one may believe that one is carrying out one's duty when one is in fact imposing one's will on others. To illustrate, if I take it upon myself to persuade my friend to take philosophy courses simply because I like them and believe it is my duty to convert others to liking them, my action will be a form of imposition. What counts as "establishing" and "being prominent" is also indeterminate until one has taken into consideration all the relevant factors of a particular case. Guideline 3 is subject to abuse also when it is used as an excuse for not acting positively. For example, a father may justify not giving his children fresh fruits and vegetables on the grounds that he does not like it when others force him to eat them. Thus, Guideline 3 can degenerate into a passive ethics of indifference—that is, "I'll leave you alone because I want to be left alone." (A prison inmate might use Guideline 3 to petition for his release: "Since I do not want to be locked up, I do not wish to have another person locked up. So, if I were the judge, I would set myself free.") Again, what counts as "what you yourself do not want" is neither universal nor absolute, but contingent on a wide range of factors unique to a moral situation.

This context-dependency of moral deliberation, however, does not lead to moral relativism. When young people undergo moral training and learn to make ethical judgments in concrete real-life contexts, they gain certain skills and competencies in moral decision making. Just as parents in real life would not adopt the attitude of "anything goes" in their moral judgment, nor would their children. Like transferable skills, people's moral competencies enable them to deliberate on what they ought to do in novel situations. The moral resources provided in the *Analects*, namely the numerous examples, the links among moral concepts, and the general moral guidelines, do not automatically translate into a definitive moral decision. One still has to *reflect* on what one has learned and to put it into practice.[116] As we have seen earlier, Confucius instructed his favourite disciple Yan Hui to "act according to ritual propriety." This instruction should be understood in terms of acting in ways that show respect and concern for others,

---

115  See 1:2, 1:6, 1:11, 2:5, 2:6, 2:7, 2:8, 2:20, 2:21, 4:20, 8:21, 11:5, 13:20, 19:18.
116  See 1:1, 2:15, 2:11.

rather than as acting according to an exhaustive and fixed list of codes of conduct. The *Analects* is not a book that tabulates *all* the correct ways of looking, listening, speaking, and moving. For Confucius, a moral agent has a responsibility to deliberation on her/his moral decision in light of all the relevant factors of a particular context.

We may illustrate Confucius' emphasis of moral deliberation with an analogy that likens the moral life to driving. Even if we drive to and from work via the same route every day, we still have to be mindful of the actual road conditions, traffic patterns, and potential obstructions or hazards every time we drive on the route. The circumstantial factors relevant to driving are constantly changing, making each trip unique and requiring constant alertness and responsiveness to the presenting conditions of the road. There is no reason to expect that we will be able to find a universal law that governs invariably how a car should be driven each time. Such a law would be impractical and futile. Likewise, in the moral realm, there would be no reason to expect that we can have a universal rule book that tells us exactly what to do in each moral situation. Such a rule book would also be impractical. Worse still, it would encourage intellectual and ethical laziness.

We can also liken Confucius to a "life doctor" or "life consultant" who diagnoses specific life or ethical problems and then prescribes remedies accordingly. Indeed, he can be likened to a skilful traditional Chinese medical (TCM) doctor. Good TCM doctors always adjust their herbal prescriptions according to the particulars of each patient, even though patients may have the same disease. For a good TCM doctor, there is no such thing as a universal panacea or fixed formula for an illness. Just as a good TCM doctor is skilfully attentive to the particular details of the each patient and that patient's condition, Confucius was also skilfully attentive to the people he instructed, so his moral prescriptions were carefully tailored to their moral situations according to all relevant considerations.

## CONFUCIUS' NON-THEIST ETHICS

As we have seen above, Confucius' ethics are based on a strong conviction in humanness, which is grounded on the assumption that humans are generally teachable and perfectible. So ethics for Confucius seem autonomous, without the need for divine sanction. When we examine the *Analects* more carefully, we will find that Confucius' ethics is subtler than a straightforward humanistic ethics (for example, Mill's utilitarianism or Kant's deontology), even though it does not require a belief in a deity as its source or justification as do the Judeo-Christian and Islamic traditions.

Heaven and the mandate of heaven are recurrent ideas in the *Analects*.[117] Many instances of these terms in the text seem to point to a personal deity. For example, Confucius spoke of people committing a sin against heaven who will have no god to pray to. He intimated that the will of heaven was in control of the fate of a culture,

---

117 See 2:4, 3:13, 6:26, 7:22, 9:5, 11:8, 12:5, 14:37, 16:8, 17:19.

directly determining whether a culture will flourish or perish.[118] Lamenting that the rulers of his time had failed to understand him and his teachings, Confucius said, "Only the heaven knows me."[119] When his disciple Zilu was concerned that his master had done something immoral with Nanzi, (the consort of Lord Ling of Wei, and a woman of bad repute), Confucius declared, "If I had done anything improper, then let heaven forsake me!"[120] When his favourite student Yan Hui died, Confucius exclaimed, "Heaven is destroying me!"[121] These remarks easily conjure up images of some conscious divine being that resembles the God of the Judeo-Christian tradition. But is this indeed what Confucius meant by heaven and the mandate of heaven? Is Confucius' ethics premised on the existence of a deity and thus a theistic ethics?

A careful scrutiny of all the remarks about heaven and the mandate of heaven in the *Analects* reveals that the terms do not refer to a full-fledged personal or anthropomorphic God. First of all, nowhere in the *Analects* is Confucius said to have *communicated* with heaven even though he did speak of it many times. The word "heaven" was not used with a religious meaning in these contexts, as in a prayer. Confucius was not praying to a personal deity who would listen and respond to him. Rather, he was either expressing his confidence in the rightness of his conduct and his way of life or his frustration and sadness. It is true that in these remarks the word "heaven" appears to have an ethical connotation,[122] but the notion does not assume the existence of a deity.

Secondly, for Confucius, moral life is based on one's self-sufficiency, so there would be no need to rely on any external force or to petition a god for assistance. Once, when he was very ill, his disciple Zilu asked to pray for him to the gods of the heavens above and the earth below. In response, Confucius dismissed Zilu's request by remarking that he had been "praying" for a long time.[123] His dismissive reply seems to suggest that he saw no need for the rite of prayer and that the life he had lived was enough to show its worth and rightness.[124] Likewise, when Confucius spoke of people committing a sin against heaven who would have no god to pray to, he was underscoring the point that if one was not living a virtuous life, then praying would simply be futile.[125] The point is further supported by his disciples' observation that their master never talked about spirits.[126]

Thirdly, in the *Analects*, the word "heaven" is sometimes used to refer to the ways or the conditions of the natural world. When Confucius claimed that heaven does not

---

118 See 3:13; 6:26 and 11:8; 9:5 respectively.
119 14:36.
120 6:26.
121 11:8.
122 For more passages on heaven (*tian*) that have ethical connotations, see 3:13, 3:24, 7:23, 8:19, 9:5, 9:6, 9:12.
123 See 7:35.
124 See Waley, 131, note 3.
125 In Chinese folk faith people pray to various gods and saints, including legendary and historical figures that were apotheosized, not to one single God, as in monotheistic religions such as Christianity and Islam.
126 7:21.

*speak* anything and four seasons run their course,[127] he was implying that there is no personal deity governing the natural world, for heaven is silent. The natural cycle we observe in nature runs on the power of nature itself. On another occasion, "heaven" is used to refer to the sky. Confucius' disciple Zigong exclaims that it would be as hard to equal our Master as to climb up on a ladder to the sky.[128]

The expression "mandate of heaven" in Confucius' usage does not refer to some command issued by an anthropomorphic God, but to aspects of the world that are beyond an individual's control. For example, according to Confucius, great social change has its reasons and inevitability; whether the Way (i.e., the Way of early Zhou and of legendary rulers Yao, Shun, and Yu) is to prevail or not, it will not be prevented by a particular individual.[129] Offering a componential analysis of the expression *tianming* ("heaven"), Confucius' disciple Zixia explains: "Life/Birth and death are the mandate of heaven (*ming*); wealth and honour depend on heaven (*tian*)."[130] Here heaven and the mandate of heaven are described as some powers or courses of event that lie outside an individual's control. One cannot negotiate with *tian* and *ming*. For Confucius, while we may seek wealth and honour, whether we will succeed depends ultimately on external factors beyond our control, none of which are taken anthropomorphically as deities. When Confucius says that at fifty he realized the biddings of heaven (*tianming*),[131] he probably meant that he understood by then the general trend of events as well as his own capabilities and limitations, and not that he had finally come to know a personal God.

Confucius' acknowledgement of uncontrollable forces or courses of events does not necessarily lead to fatalism. Confucius believes that one can decide if one wants to behave ethically or not,[132] and one can also decide whether or not to observe rituals.[133] The practice and actualization of humanness and *dao* depend on one's own effort. In short, ethics for Confucius does not stem from an anthropomorphic divine being, but lies in each individual's conscious choice itself.

An agricultural image may shed some light on Confucius' view about the controllable and the uncontrollable. Weather conditions are what farmers have to accept and adapt to when they grow crops; they are not controllable (even though nowadays we may predict bad weather conditions, still we can do little to eliminate the conditions). On the other hand, growing crops requires much effort on the farmers' side: watering crops, fertilizing the land, weeding, and so on. And the latter is within their control. This is all they can and ought to do, and they have to do it with diligence and hope. In a similar way, Confucius insists that to lead an ethical life we should try to carry out what we ought to carry out. While we certainly hope for success, we also should realize that

---

127  See 17:19; also see 20:1.
128  See 19:25.
129  See 14:36; also see *Mengzi* 4A7.
130  12:5.
131  See 2:4.
132  See 4:6, 7:29, 15:28.
133  See 12:1.

without the cooperation of adequate conditions, there is no guarantee that our effort will be rewarded in exact proportion.[134]

In talking about heaven Confucius does not seem to be interested in speculating about the origin of the universe. In his view, the world we live in is a given, not created by some external deity or spiritual beings. For him, this mundane world we inhabit is the only real world we have; any other world below or beyond is simply fiction. To Confucius, there appears to be an absence of any mythology about a primordial fall from innocence, such as the myth of the fall of Adam and Eve, where transgression against God's will figures centrally. Human beings and the world are in an essential and primordial union and harmony; human beings are not estranged in the world. Therefore, there is simply no need for a salvation myth that involves reconciliation with a divine being.

This, however, is not to say that the society in Confucius' time was already a perfect place. Quite on the contrary: society was out of harmony and in a state of decline. But, for Confucius, such disorder and disharmony do not stem from a violation of God's will, but rather from society's abandonment of humanness and ritual propriety, which Confucius thought were perfectly exemplified in the early Zhou society.[135] In particular, Confucius was looking to exemplary persons (especially exemplary rulers) and an exemplary social system (Zhou li), rather than to a supernatural being, as the basis of moral inspiration and moral transformation.

Two points can be deduced from this world view. First, since the world is essentially or inherently harmonious or hospitable to its inhabitants, human beings were happy in their primordial state. Therefore, our basic attitude to the world should be that of acceptance. Confucius exemplifies this attitude, in that he did not curse heaven or blame others even when few understood or accepted him and his teachings.[136] Unlike Socrates, who believed that true happiness is only possible after death when our soul is set free from the body, Confucius sees happiness as firmly grounded in this life, and not in some spiritual state in another realm of existence. For him, happiness can be found in everyday activities. To learn and practice what one has learned is a pleasure; to have friends coming to visit you from afar is a happy occasion.[137] To observe rituals properly, to appreciate the wonder of musical harmony, to discuss the merits of others, and to be in the company of many wise friends are all happy things.[138] The meaning of life consists in carrying out one's specific roles in one's station in life, thereby contributing to the overall harmony of one's family, community, country, and the world.[139] Thus,

---

134 Compare our agricultural image with the popular Serenity Prayer: "God grant me the serenity to accept the things I cannot change, courage to change the things I can, and wisdom to know the difference."

135 Confucius also admired the legendary ages of rulers Yao, Shun, and Yu for their virtuous ruling (See 8:18, 8:19, 8:20, 12:22, 14:6, 15:5).

136 See 14:36.

137 See 1:1.

138 See 16:5.

139 See 5:26.

Confucius' moral and philosophical vision is thoroughly this-worldly. In that sense, there is no need for him to believe in a transcendent divine being who confers meaning to life and judges the world from above.

Secondly, for Confucius, the current world situation is not perfect, so we cannot simply sit idly or surrender ourselves to external circumstances. We must make every effort individually and collectively to reform it.[140] In other words, for him, happiness can only come about when we make an effort to better ourselves and the world. The first thing we should try to do is to get to know the Way (which encompasses broadly appropriate personal and social behaviours, including those that enable one to lead and govern a state). And in pursuing the Way, one should feel that the pursuit itself is rewarding; regardless of such external matters as material riches, social rank, public recognition, or fame;[141] one who really responds to humanness can never be unhappy.[142]

This life in this world is Confucius' concern, and it is reflected in his view on death as evidenced in an often-quoted passage:

> Tzu-lu [Zilu] asked about serving the ghost and spirits [*guishen*, dead ancestors]. The Master said, Till you have learnt to serve men, how can you serve ghosts? Tzu-lu then ventured upon a question about the dead. The Master said, Till you know about the living, how are you to know about the dead?[143]

It is tempting to conclude from this passage that Confucius has so emphasized the importance of serving the living that he has simply dismissed questions about spirits and death. However, as Tu Wei-ming has pointed out, the "assertion that knowing life is a precondition for knowing death by no means implies the rejection of the need for knowing death. On the contrary, precisely because one cannot know death without first understanding the meaning of life, a full appreciation of life entails the need for probing the meaning of death."[144] Confucius talks about the importance of offering sacrifice to one's deceased ancestors, but this does not assume the existence of an afterlife. In his view, in offering sacrifices to one's ancestors and the gods, one only needs to act "as if" (*ru*) they were present.[145] This suggests that he was agnostic about the afterlife, but still believed in the practical value of offering sacrifices to one's ancestors in shaping one's moral character. This interpretation is consistent

---

140 See 15:28.
141 See 1:15, 6:9, 15:31.
142 See 7:18, 9:29.
143 11:11
144 Tu Wei-ming, "Chinese Philosophy: A Synoptic View," in *A Companion to World Philosophies*, Eliot Deutsch and Ron Bontekoe, eds. (Oxford: Blackwell, 1997), 7.
145 See 3:12. Simon Blackburn, in defending what he called "quasi-realism," argued that in moral philosophy we make moral statements as if there were moral facts, and that we act as if there is an underlying ontology when there is in fact none. He calls this "projective metaphysics" and an "as-if" philosophy (*Essays in Quasi-Realism* [New York: Oxford University Press, 1993], 55). Confucius here seems to fit such an "as-if" characterization.

with what we know about Confucius' concern about living this life ethically in this world. It is not likely that Confucius had ever explicitly denied the existence of ghosts and spirits, or it would have rendered baseless his advice to his contemporaries to continue to practise the sacrificial rituals of ancestral worship. As Confucius' rival Mozi (c. 470–c. 391 BCE) pointed out, if there is no fish, what is the point in making fishing nets? If there is no guest, what is the point of conducting a welcome ceremony?[146] That said, there is still no need to assume that Confucius was in fact a "closet believer" of ghosts and spirits. If this had been the case, he would have been plagued by the question of how to prove their existence—a question that he would treat as impractical and irrelevant.

It does not really matter for him whether the deceased continues to enjoy some form of post-mortem existence. What really matters for him is how people regard death from an ethical point of view. Confucius claimed that when people show proper respect to the dead at the time of their passing and in an ongoing manner after they have long passed away, the strength of their moral character (de) will thrive.[147] In other words, Confucius seems to be suggesting that the practice of mourning the dead can become care for the living.

In the West, theists argue that God exists, so the rites, practices, and moral teachings associated with Him are meaningful. In contrast, many atheists argue that God does not exist, therefore the rites, practices, and moral teachings associated with God are baseless and meaningless. But is it possible to value the *idea* of God as pertaining to rites, practices, and moral teachings without subscribing to the existence of a personal God? Is it possible to regard Jesus as a historical figure and accept his teachings without believing that he is *literally* God or the son of God? Judging from his "as-if" attitude toward gods, ghosts, and spirits, Confucius' answer would likely be an enthusiastic "Yes!"

While Confucius regarded death as a serious matter, not to be handled recklessly,[148] he was not interested in the metaphysics of it, such as the issue of what will happen after death. Confucius accepts death as a natural event that is inevitable and beyond our control, and he advocated that we should calmly accept it, instead of fearing its coming.[149] However, Confucius also recognized with great regret and sympathy that some deaths are untimely or unnatural. Thus, he cautioned people not to risk their lives irresponsibly.[150] That said, Confucius was not completely against the idea of sacrificing one's life: he maintained that if death is a price one has to pay to preserve humanness, then one must accept death without hesitation.[151]

---

146 See the *Mozi*, section 48. *The Mozi: A Complete Translation*, Ian Johnston, trans. (New York: Columbia University Press), 2010.
147 See 1:9.
148 See 2:5.
149 See 11:12, 11:22, 14:6.
150 See 7:10, 8:13.
151 See 15:8, also see 4:8.

## DOING PHILOSOPHY
*Death: Confucius versus Heidegger*

Martin Heidegger (1889–1976) argues that human beings are beings-toward-death (that is, we human beings are perhaps the only sentient beings that are fully aware of our mortality), and that one does not exist authentically until one faces death as the ultimate possibility. One important implication of this view is that life, when viewed through the lens of death, takes on a sense of urgency, in which every minute counts and every moment of life is a gift to be cherished. Compared to Heidegger, Confucius appears not to have given the ultimate eventuality of death much attention.

Do you think that Confucius is being too short-sighted in setting aside the problem of death? Do you agree or disagree that one cannot live meaningfully without realizing one's mortality? Should we bear in our mind the inevitability of death every day? Would a constant awareness of death paralyze meaningful living?

## FROM EXEMPLARY PERSONS (*JUNZI*) TO A HARMONIOUS WORLD

We have seen that Confucius takes it upon himself to renew society by advocating the training of exemplary persons who serve as moral role models in society, and he sees the way of moral training as the only proper means of societal transformation in his time. The significance of the idea of exemplary persons in Confucius' view must not be underestimated. Ying-shih Yu claims that Confucianism is in fact the doctrine of becoming exemplary persons.[152]

The term "*junzi*," literally means "the son(s) of a ruler." It was initially used to refer to members of the upper class elite who enjoyed a high social and political status by virtue of blood-relationship or marriage. While occasionally using this term in its traditional sense, Confucius primarily uses it in a moral sense. Thus, in Confucius' usage, the notion of nobility has been given a moral, rather than social, definition; as Chan has remarked, for Confucius, "nobility was no longer a matter of blood but of character."[153] This shift to the moral meaning of nobility is illustrated in the *Analects*' glorification of the legendary practice of the king ceding his throne to a morally exemplary person (who is unrelated to the king by blood), instead of passing it on directly to his blood-related heirs.[154] The term "*junzi*" then does not refer to an *ad hoc* group of people who come to enjoy a noble status in society by birth or marriage, but

---

152 Ying-shih Yu, "The *Junzi* Ideal in Confucianism," in *Contemporary Interpretation of the Tradition of Chinese Thoughts* (Taipei: Lian Jing Publishing), 145.
153 Chan, 15; also see Waley, 34, Ying-shih Yu, 149.
154 See 20:1.

to individuals who have become noble in character by leading an exemplary life. The moral nuance of the term is faithfully captured in Ames and Rosemont's translation of it as "exemplary persons."

The characteristics of exemplary persons are described in contradistinction to another kind of person, xiaoren, which literally means "small person." The term xiaoren is used in both a moral sense and a social-political sense. In the moral sense, it refers to a morally inferior or deficient person, as reflected in the common translation "petty person." In the social-political sense, it designates the common people, the subjects ruled by a king. Exemplary and petty persons are juxtaposed in many passages in the Analects;[155] the idea of petty persons functions as a foil to bring out the qualities of exemplary persons.

According to Confucius, a general distinction between exemplary and petty persons lies in their attitudes and behaviours toward the call of humanness. Exemplary persons exert themselves in responding to the call of humanness.[156] By contrast, petty persons do not respond to the call of humanness properly.[157] Exemplary persons are morally active and self-motivated whereas petty persons are passive and lack moral initiative. In David S. Nivison's interpretation, petty persons are "cold" or "not warmed enough" to the moral call of humanness.[158] They are deficient in moral will. Exemplary persons regard humanness as their own obligation and responsibility; for the impetus to practice humanness originates from them rather than from others.[159] Confucius says: "Exemplary persons make demands on themselves, while petty persons make demands on others."[160]

Secondly, exemplary persons set their hearts upon moral character (de) and seek to do what is appropriate in particular circumstances (yi). They bring out the best in others whereas petty persons tend to bring out the worst in others.[161] Petty persons focus on their personal gains and may in fact sacrifice virtue and morality for the sake of material gain, fame, and power.[162]

---

155 See 4:11, 4:16, 6:11, 7:36, 12:16, 12:19, 13:4, 13:23, 13:25, 13:26, 14:7, 14:24, 15:20, 15:33, 16:8, 17:23, 19:8.
156 See 4:5.
157 See 14:6. The first half of 14:6, when translated literally, reads "There are junzi who are not ren," and understood thus this statement poses a puzzle as it seems in direct contradiction to 4:5 where the very meaning of junzi is one who always adheres to ren. One plausible way to unravel the puzzle is to point out that in 4:5 Confucius was talking about ren as a moral demand, whereas in 14:6 he refers to a practice of ren. In this sense, one who understands ren as a moral demand might in reality slip into not practicing it on some occasion. Another plausible interpretation is to take junzi in the sentence "There are junzi who are not ren" as only nominal: one may act as an exemplary person but in fact lack ren.
158 David S. Nivison, The Ways of Confucianism—Investigations in Chinese Philosophy, Bryan W. Van Norden, ed. (Chicago: Open Court, 1996), 81.
159 See 12:1.
160 See 15:21, Ames and Rosemont's translation. It bears relating that junzi would not ostracize petty persons, nor would they be subject to their negative influence (1:8). Junzi would try to have a positive influence on petty persons (12:19).
161 See 12:16.
162 See 4:11, 4:16, and 14:24.

In Confucius' ethics, the ideal of exemplary persons is what connects the task of moral cultivation and the goal of social transformation.[163] The ultimate aim of cultivation, in this view, is to benefit others as well as oneself. In other words, Confucius' ethics is constructed around the interplay between the self (individuals) and others (society). Thus, when a ruler practices moral self-cultivation as an exemplary person, the whole populace will ultimately benefit. Concerning this point, evidence abounds in the *Analects*:

> Tzu-kung [Zigong] said, "If a ruler extensively confers benefit on the people and can bring salvation to all, what do you think of him? Would you call him a man of humanity [humanness]?" Confucius said, "Why only a man of humanity? He is without doubt a sage. Even (sage-emperors) Yao and Shun fell short of it. *A man of humanity, wishing to establish his own character, also establishes the character of others, and wishing to be prominent himself, also helps others to be prominent.* To be able to judge others by what is near to ourselves may be called the method of realizing humanity."[164]
>
> Zilu asked about exemplary persons. The Master replied, "They cultivate themselves by being respectful."
> "Is that all?" asked Zilu.
> "They cultivate themselves by bringing accord to their peers."
> "Is that all?" asked Zilu.
> "They cultivate themselves by bringing accord to the people. Even a Yao or a Shun would find such a task daunting."[165]
>
> Chi K'ang Tzu [Ji Kangzi] asked Confucius about government, saying, "What do you think of killing the wicked and associating with the good?" Confucius replied, "In your government what is the need of killing? If you desire what is good, the people will be good. The character of a ruler [*junzi*] is like wind and that of the people is like grass. In whatever direction the wind blows, the grass always bends."[166]

According to these remarks, the moral self-cultivation of an exemplary person works in two ways: (a) from the inside out—that is, through transforming a person for the benefit of oneself and others, and (b) from the top down—that is, through transforming a ruler who in turn acts in the interest of society at large. In Confucius' view, ideally, the more exemplary persons there are in a society, the better off that society. However, he was particularly interested in having exemplary persons serve as rulers, presumably because they are in a more influential position than anyone else in society. Therefore, a ruler has all the more reason to live an upright life. As

---

163 The idea is similar to Plato's view of a real philosopher serving as a king or a king becoming a philosopher (see Plato's *Republic* v: 473c-d), and of the education of the philosopher-kings (vii 535a-540a).
164 6:28, Chan's translation; my emphasis.
165 14:42 (Ames and Rosemont's translation).
166 12:19 (Chan's translation).

Confucius says, "If the ruler himself is upright, all will go well even though he does not give orders. But if he himself is not upright, even though he gives orders, they will not be obeyed."[167] This, however, is not to say when a ruler is upright, his people must be morally good *ipso facto*, or that a bad ruler necessarily prevents his people from being morally upright individuals. Rather, Confucius' point seems to be that a good ruler, *as a general rule*, enables his people to be good.

In addition to emphasizing the priority of the ruler's moral character, Confucius also gives due attention to the skills of governing, such as "rectifying names," or *zhengming* (that is, ensuring that people know their roles in society),[168] promoting the upright,[169] using the labour of the peasantry only at proper times of the year,[170] ensuring that his state has sufficient food and sufficient arms, and gaining people's confidence in their rulers.[171]

### CONCLUDING REMARKS: THE INFLUENCE OF THE *ANALECTS*

Confucius and his *Analects* have had an unparalleled influence on Chinese philosophy and Chinese culture. Confucius' ethical vision, his emphasis on the value of family, and his focus on humanness and ritual propriety have made the *Analects* the "Bible" of Chinese ethical humanism.

Confucius' ideas were further developed by Mengzi and Xunzi in the Warring States period (476–221 BCE). By early Han Dynasty (206 BCE–220 CE), Confucius had become venerated as a deified figure, and Confucianism had become the orthodox philosophy of the state.[172] Despite a few brief periods of decline—including the Cultural Revolution (1966–76) when Confucius was officially maligned—the influence of Confucius and Confucianism has endured with remarkable persistence. Even when China (the Han people) was ruled by non-Han people in the Qing (1644–1912) Dynasty, Confucianism continued to be the official ideology of the state.[173] Proponents of Confucianism used to believe, rightly or wrongly, that a ruler would be able to keep his state in order if he had mastered and put into practice Confucius' teachings from even half of the *Analects*.

Confucianism eventually spread to Korea, Japan, and Vietnam, and has also become part of the ideological fabric of these countries. The economic boom in East Asia over the past three decades, coupled with the opening of mainland China to the world, has stimulated a resurgent interest in Confucius and Confucianism around the world.

---

167  13:6; also see 13:1.
168  See 12:11, 13:3.
169  See 2:19, 12:22.
170  See 1:5.
171  See 12:7.
172  Despite the fact that to a large extent rulers adopted Legalism in their actual ruling.
173  Yuan Dynasty (1271–1368), a period when the Han people were ruled by the Mongolian people, may be an exception.

## WORK CITED AND RECOMMENDED READINGS

1. *The Analects of Confucius*, Burton Watson, trans. (New York: Columbia University Press, 2007).
2. *The Analects of Confucius: A Philosophical Translation*, Roger Ames and Henry Rosemont, Jr., trans. (New York: Ballantine, 1999).
3. *Confucius: Analects with Selections from Traditional Commentaries*, Edward Slingerland, trans. (Indianapolis: Hackett, 2003).
4. Bryan W. Van Norden, ed. *Confucius and the Analects: New Essays* (New York: Oxford University Press, 2002).
5. Max Weber, *The Religion of China* (Orig. 1916), Hans H. Gerth, trans. and ed. (New York: The Free Press, 1964).
6. David L. Hall and Roger T. Ames, *Thinking Through Confucius* (Albany, NY: State University of New York Press, 1987).
7. Herbert Fingarette, *Confucius: The Secular as Sacred* (New York: Harper & Row Torchbook, 1972).
8. A.C. Graham, *Disputers of the Tao: Philosophical Argument in Ancient China* (La Salle, IL: Open Court, 1989).
9. Benjamin I. Schwartz, *The World of Thought in Ancient China* (Cambridge, MA: Harvard University Press, 1985).
10. Bryan W. Van Norden, *Virtue Ethics and Consequentialism in Early Chinese Philosophy* (Cambridge: Cambridge University Press, 2007).

CHAPTER 5

# The *Mengzi*

## SUGGESTED PRIMARY READING

Bryan W. Van Norden's translation of selections from *Mengzi*, in *Readings in Classical Chinese Philosophy*, Philip J. Ivanhoe and Bryan W. Van Norden, eds. (New York: Seven Bridges Press, 2001), 111–50.

## LEARNING OBJECTIVES

By the time you have worked through this chapter, you should be able to

> - Describe Mengzi's doctrine of human nature
> - Explain Mengzi's debate with rival theories on human nature
> - Describe Mengzi's view on moral cultivation
> - Explain Mengzi's development of Confucianism

## KEY WORDS

human nature (*xing*), four sprouts (*si duan*), heart (*xin*), extending affection (*tui en*)

## GUIDING QUESTIONS

Confucius observes that humans are by nature close to each other, and only through habit and learning do they become different, but he leaves open the issue of whether human nature is good, bad, or something else. In response to Confucius, the philosopher Gaozi argues that human nature is empty. The *Analects* argues that humanness starts with filial piety and brotherly love within the family. But Mozi criticized this argument by insisting that it merely promotes partiality, when in fact impartial care is preferable. Mengzi, the best known follower of Confucius' teachings in Chinese history, contended that Gaozi's view about human nature and Mozi's view about impartial love are threats to Confucius' authentic teachings. He responded to Gaozi and Mozi (and others) by considering the following questions:

1. Which is better, the belief that human nature is good or the belief that human nature is empty?
2. Which is morally preferable, partial care (graded care) or impartial care?

In response to these questions, Mengzi argues that human nature is not empty, but good, and that partial care is preferable to Mozi's impartial care.

## INTRODUCTION

The great Confucian philosopher Mengzi[1] was born in Zhou (in present-day Shandong province), a small state not far from where Confucius once lived. According to tradition, it is believed that Mengzi acquired his knowledge of Confucius' teachings from the disciples of Zi Si (492–431 BCE), who was himself a second-generation disciple, as well as grandson, of Confucius.

The *Mengzi* is a collection of his sayings and dialogues, compiled by his immediate and later followers. The work consists of seven books, each of which is subdivided into two parts (A and B). Each part is further broken down into short sections. For example, 2A6 refers to Book 2, part A, section 6. In contrast to the pithiness of the *Analects*, the *Mengzi* is composed of comparatively sustained passages, many of which are well contextualized and carefully argued.[2] Two focused portions of the text are Mengzi's discourse on benevolent ruling directed to the kings of the Warring States (Books 1–3) and his debate with rival theories on human nature (Book 6).

Mengzi took himself to be a faithful follower of Confucius. He not only upheld Confucius' basic teachings (most importantly, Confucius' faith in the transformational

---

1   His name is often found in the literature romanized to "Mencius."
2   A salient feature of its argumentation is its employment of analogical argument, which was highlighted in D.C. Lau's noted paper "On Mencius' Use of the Method of Analogy in Argument." Lau's paper first appeared in *Asia Major*, N.S. X (1963), and was reprinted as Appendix 5 in Lau's translation of Mengzi's work, *Mencius* (New York: Penguin Books, 1970).

power of morality), but also advanced them to a new stage. While Confucius did not attempt to build a theory of human nature, Mengzi developed such a theory, arguing that human nature is essentially good—that is, that all human beings are born with the potential and predisposition to be good. Mengzi also elaborated on the ideas of moral cultivation, love with distinction, and the priority of morality over gain (all of which were, by and large, implicit in the *Analects* in a less developed form). In addition, Mengzi extended Confucius' teachings of humanness more fully to its political application by emphasizing the notion of *yi* (righteousness). Due to his contributions to the defence and development of Confucius' teachings, Mengzi was venerated by later generations as the "Second Sage" in the Confucian tradition.[3]

Let's begin our survey of the thought of Mengzi with his influential theory of human nature.

### MENGZI'S THEORY OF HUMAN NATURE

A central concern of the *Mengzi* is the issue of human nature. The entirety of Book 6 deals with this issue, and additional coverage can be found explicitly and implicitly in other parts of the work. Why did Mengzi devote so much attention to discussing human nature? Why was the issue of human nature so urgent for him? To answer these questions, we need to examine the social and intellectual milieu of Mengzi's time.

Mengzi came on stage during the Warring States period (476–221 BCE) when China was not yet a unified country and the states that occupied the land that would eventually become China were fighting among themselves for territorial control. All the states, especially the weak ones, were constantly in danger of being attacked or annexed by their neighbouring states. People lacked means of livelihood; death and famine were part of their reality. Rulers struggled to protect their territories and hold onto their reign. Philosophers and scholars were busy advocating theories and policies that they believed would solve the urgent social problems of their time.

Mengzi believed that morality was the key to social transformation of his time, just as Confucius, his intellectual forebear, was adamant about its transformative power. Confucius and Mengzi both maintained that if proper morality was promoted and preserved, families, states, and even an entire Empire (*tianxia*, literally, "under the sky") could exist in peace. Both thinkers envisioned that, in a morally ideal world, all people—especially the rulers—should cultivate themselves, love their own families first, and then extend their love to others beyond their families.

As we have seen in the previous chapter, Confucius' conviction in the transformative power of morality was not grounded on an explicit doctrine of human nature. The style of his ethical instruction was generally straightforward, and he was reticent on abstract metaphysical issues. There is only one pithy remark from him on record concerning human nature—namely, that "human beings are similar in their natural tendencies,

---

3  The First Sage, of course, was Confucius.

but become varied through learning/habituation."[4] He did not seem to indicate clearly whether he thought human nature is good or evil. His remark merely shows that human beings are teachable and perfectible.

Mengzi came on the scene when there had been many rivals to Confucius. One such rival mentioned in the *Mengzi* was Yang Zhu (fourth century BCE), who reportedly claimed that humans are by nature egoistic,[5] and that he would not seek to benefit the world even if it only called for a single hair from his body.[6] Mengzi found this type of ethical egoism untenable, for it was premised on a rather dark and pessimistic view of human nature that, if true, would render moral perfection unattainable and ethical instruction futile. Another rival was Gaozi (fourth century BCE), who argued that human nature is neither good nor bad, and that morality is merely something that has been imposed upon human beings from the outside. Mengzi argued that this view of human nature was not any better than Yang Zhu's, for it would make morality psychologically unmotivated, and there would be nothing in the moral agent's inner life (such as any ethical predisposition) to ground her/his action. A third rival was Mozi (c. 400s–300s BCE), who advocated the doctrine of "impartial love" (*jian ai*), the view that one should love everyone to the same degree without partiality. For Mengzi, Mozi seems to share Gaozi's belief that human beings lack a moral nature, for it seems to negate the human predisposition to love first (in both temporal and logical priorities) those consanguineously related to them, then to love those who are not.

Facing these rival theories of human nature, Mengzi could no longer simply take for granted the transformative power of morality, as did Confucius some two centuries before; he had to ground it on a defensible theory of human nature. For this reason, he devoted much of the *Mengzi* to arguing for such a view against his rivals. Mengzi's view, in a nutshell, is that human nature is good.[7]

How does one demonstrate that human nature is good? One may simply point out that almost everyone does *some* good *sometimes*, or that a few *always* or *nearly always* do good. However, these observations, even if true, would at best be weak evidence, in that one can object that what the rest of the people do the rest of the time counts just as much towards a theory of human nature. These observations, even if true, do not conclusively support the view that human nature is good, but are compatible with the other alternative views mentioned above—namely, that human nature is bad (egoistic), or human nature is neither good nor bad.

Could we then simply equate human nature with human biological characteristics? All human beings need food and all healthy human beings have sexual desires once they have reached puberty. Could such desires for food and sex be regarded as human

---

4    The *Analects*, 17:2 (my translation); also see 5:12.
5    See section 3B9 in Bryan W. Van Norden's translation of selections from *Mengzi*, in *Readings in Classical Chinese Philosophy*, Philip J. Ivanhoe and Bryan W. Van Norden, eds. (New York: Seven Bridges Press, 2001). Further references to the *Mengzi* will, unless otherwise noted, refer to this translation.
6    7A26.
7    Mengzi said he was not fond of debate, but given the threat of rival theories to his moral convictions, he felt compelled to defend it. See 3B9.

nature?[8] One's answer to this question will depend upon one's understanding of what constitutes the *nature* of a human person. If by "nature" one means whatever biological properties humans have, then the desires for food and sex will at least constitute part of human nature. However, if by "nature" one means the characteristics that distinguish humans from other animals, then the desires for food and sex cannot be regarded as part of human nature, for they are not unique to human beings.[9]

To prove that human nature is good, Mengzi employs an ingenious argument based on a thought experiment, in which he has us imagine the following hypothetical situation:

> The reason why I say that humans all have hearts [*xin*] that are not unfeeling toward others is this. Suppose someone suddenly saw a child about to fall into a well: everyone in such a situation would have a feeling of alarm and compassion—not because one sought to get in good with the child's parents, not because one wanted fame among their neighbours and friends, and not because one would dislike the sound of the child's cries.[10]

In this thought experiment, Mengzi argues that the human heart (*xin*) is a heart of compassion (that is, not "being unfeeling toward others"), and a close reading of his description of it further suggests that he takes the human predisposition to compassion to be innate, generically endowed, and intrinsically motivated. It is innate because, as Mengzi sees it, anyone would immediately have a sympathetic or compassionate reaction to the child as soon as she/he perceives that the child's life is at risk; so this compassionate response is simply spontaneous and instinctive. It is generically endowed (i.e. to all normal human beings) because Mengzi has us imagine that "everyone" would feel the same way towards the child in such a situation.[11] Furthermore, it is intrinsically motivated, in that Mengzi visualizes that people would have sympathy towards the child not for any ulterior motive; they would feel sympathy for the child not because they want to win the favour of the child's parent or the praise of their friends and neighbours, or because they find the commotion created in the situation unbearable.

Mengzi goes on to extrapolate (perhaps somewhat dubiously) to other attributes of the human heart. He uses further metaphors to describe the human heart: the heart of disdain (i.e., having a sense of shame and disdain towards evil), the heart of deference (i.e., having a sense of deference or humility), and the heart of approval and disapproval (i.e., having a discerning sense of "right and wrong" or "good or bad"). He claims that these four hearts are the respective sprouts of humaneness or benevolence

---

8   See 6A4.
9   See 7B24.
10   2A6.
11   Also see 6A10 where Mengzi argued that all humans have the heart of desiring things more than life and hating things more than death.

(*ren*),[12] righteousness, propriety, and wisdom, and that they jointly constitute the essence of human nature. Without any of the four hearts, according to Mengzi, one would not be a human being.

> From this we can see that if one is without the heart of compassion, one is not a human. If one is without the heart of disdain, one is not a human. If one is without the heart of deference, one is not a human. If one is without the heart of approval and disapproval, one is not a human. The heart of compassion is the sprout of benevolence. The heart of disdain is the sprout of righteousness. The heart of deference is the sprout of propriety. The heart of approval and disapproval is the sprout of wisdom.[13]

Mengzi appears to be offering here a strictly moral definition of human nature. In asserting that without any of the four hearts one is not a human, he seems to be prescribing how we ought to act on the basis of the moral sentiments which he describes as essential to being human—that is, he seems to be relying on what he considers to be a human being's natural inclination to have certain moral sentiments as the basis of normative ethics.[14] This is not to say that Mengzi would deny that a morally evil person (who lacks any or all of the four hearts) is a member of the *Homo sapiens* species—that is, a person in the biological or physical sense.

In the Western tradition, rationality is generally regarded as a dominant characteristic of human nature, so that a Westerner would be surprised to see that Mengzi took the four hearts to be the constitutive elements of human nature without any reference to rationality or logical thinking. For Mengzi, "the sprout of wisdom" is moral wisdom, and our innate knowledge is moral knowledge.[15] Why does Mengzi put so much emphasis on moral wisdom or moral knowledge in defining human nature? The reasons seem to be that Mengzi believes first that the moral faculty is universal in humans, though they vary in physical features (height, gender, hair colour, beauty, etc.) and intellectual capacities (mathematics, language, arts, etc.), and second that this moral faculty puts everyone on the same footing.[16] This moral faculty is the key distinction between humans and other animals.

---

12  Our translation of *ren* in the *Analects* as "humanness" does not seem to fit Mengzi's use of the term, because unlike Confucius' general use of *ren* (as a moral demand and a practice), *ren* in the *Mengzi* focuses more on the psychological disposition to morality. Thus, *ren* in the *Mengzi* is better translated as "humaneness" or "benevolence."

13  2A6.

14  Even in contemporary China, the harshest oral condemnation of an immoral person states: "He (or she) is not a human" or "He (or she) is less than an animal."

15  7A15.

16  See 1A7. Confucius also believed that everyone has such a moral faculty (see *Analects* 4:6). The idea of the priority of moral awareness over physical strength also had its precursor in *Analects* 3:16 where Confucius said that in archery it is not piercing the hide (stretched as a target) that counts, since people have different physical strengths. It is hitting the target (i.e., doing the right thing) that counts.

## DOING PHILOSOPHY
*Human Beings: Rational or Moral?*

In the Western tradition, philosophers often have taken the defining, the most important, aspect of humans to be rationality. Aristotle (384–322 BCE), for example, is widely (and not entirely accurately) credited with defining humans as "rational animals"; René Descartes (1565–1650), in his *Meditations*, gives paramount status to his existence as a *thinking* being (*Meditations*, II). John Locke (1632–1704) holds that "it is the understanding that sets man above the rest of sensible beings, and give him all the advantage and dominion which he has over them" (*An Essay Concerning Human Understanding*, Introduction: 1). To be sure, not all philosophers in the West take rationality to be the most unique feature of being human. Nevertheless, it is the dominant view of human nature in the West.

By contrast, Mengzi apprehends human nature from a moral perspective, taking being moral or ethical as the most important and defining characteristic of being human. It must be noted, however, that the contrast between Mengzi and the above-mentioned Western philosophers is only a matter of emphasis, for Mengzi does not deny humans can think (6A15), nor do any of the above-mentioned Western philosophers deny that morality is essential to be human.

Question: What practical implications may the above different emphases on human nature lead to?

The following table gives a summary of Mengzi's conception of the human "heart" or human nature:

*Human Heart / Human Nature*

| THE MORAL "SPROUTS" | THE MATURE MORAL "PLANTS" |
|---|---|
| Compassion | Humaneness (or Benevolence) |
| Disdain (a sense of shame) | Righteousness |
| Deference (a sense of humility) | Propriety |
| Approval and disapproval (a sense of discernment) | Wisdom |

Mengzi believes that his thought experiment helps demonstrate that human nature is good. However, Mengzi does not see his view as implying that human beings always *act* morally in reality. Mengzi's analogy of the four hearts as sprouts suggests that the goodness inherent in human nature exists in an embryonic form and will continue to grow with proper cultivation and nourishment.

Mengzi's thought experiment has an intuitive appeal, but it can be criticized on several fronts. First, even if it is true that human beings have a natural predisposition to feel sympathy and compassion towards others, it is not evident how Mengzi may justifiably infer that the human heart must also include a sense of shame, humility, and discernment. The inference appears unwarranted. Mengzi did seem to try to explain why just these four hearts are so important when he likened them to the four limbs of a normal person,[17] but his explanation is not really convincing—to use the four limbs (rather than other parts of the human body) to explain the composition of human heart seems totally arbitrary. *not planned or chosen for a particular reason*

Secondly, it is not evident that other animals do not have sympathetic responses to their fellow creatures or that they do not have a heart of compassion. There are indeed true stories about dogs, cats, and other animals demonstrating behaviours that resemble what we call "behaviours of compassion."[18] Perhaps the heart of compassion, not to mention the other three hearts, is not unique to human beings.

Thirdly, Mengzi's thought experiment is based on an adult's response to an emergency, seeing a child in danger of falling into a well. This response does not seem to prove human nature is innately good. With adults, it is not clear whether such a response comes from nature or nurture.

Finally, in Mengzi's thought experiment, it seems that the interests of the adult witness were not threatened, and that that may be why he was inclined to help. But what if his interests (his life, for example) were threatened, would he still likely be inclined to help? Or would he be more likely to act selfishly and egoistically?

### DOING PHILOSOPHY
*A Thought Experiment that Is Different from Mengzi's:*
*Could Human Nature Be Evil?*

One way to challenge Mengzi's view of human nature is to construct a thought experiment in which human beings can be conceptualized as having a heart of greed, selfishness, and evil. Can you conceive of such a thought experiment? Can a thought experiment show that at least in some circumstances one is naturally inclined to do immoral things? An interesting example of this type of thought experiment is Plato's myth of Gyges,[19] which raises the question whether people would still act morally if they could get away with doing wrong. In what way is this myth relevant to a consideration of Mengzi's view of human nature?

---

17  See 2A6.
18  See Kristin Von Kreisler, *The Compassion of Animals: True Stories of Animal Courage and Kindness* (New York: Three Rivers Press, 1999).
19  Plato imagines that Gyges has a ring that makes him invisible, and thus can do whatever he wants without fear of the consequences. Plato asks whether Gyges would then act completely immorally (*Republic* 2.359c–2.360d).

In addition to his thought experiment, Mengzi also draws other evidence to buttress his conception of human nature. He argues that a starving beggar's refusal to accept food that is offered to him contemptuously is a sure sign that he has an innate sense of shame (i.e., a heart of disdain). Infants' love of their parents is a sign that they have innately a heart of benevolence. That younger brothers know to respect their elder brothers shows that they have innately a heart of propriety.[20] However, the evidence presented in these cases has less intuitive appeal than his thought experiment. For example, there is also a chance, though less likely, that a starving beggar *may* take the food that is offered contemptuously. While it is probably true that without exception all babies "know" to love their parents,[21] it is not evident that all younger brothers know to respect their elder brothers.

In establishing the claim that human nature is good, Mengzi not only argues for his position directly, he also defends it against counter examples and rival theories. Let's first examine his treatment of counter examples, and then turn to his debate with rival theories in the next section.

If, according to Mengzi, human nature is good, then why do people—at least some of them—act less morally or immorally at least some of the time? The fact that some people act immorally sometimes seems to be a genuine and powerful counterargument to Mengzi's view. To salvage his view, Mengzi must explain how the presence of less moral and immoral human activities can be compatible with his belief that human nature is good.[22]

First, Mengzi explicitly denied that a person's "becoming not good" is due to flawed human nature; he asserts, "As for what they are inherently, they can become good. This is what I mean by calling their natures good. As for their becoming not good, this is not the fault of their potential."[23] Here, Mengzi draws a distinction between what one inherently is and what one becomes. He argues that one can be inherently good, but become bad for reasons other than one's inherent nature. This point can be illustrated with an analogy. All watermelon seeds *by nature* have the potential to become (pro-duce) mature watermelons, provided that they are planted and grown in an appropriate environment including appropriate soil, water, sunshine, and cultivation. At the same time, watermelon seeds may fail to develop into watermelons if the appropriate conditions for their growth are not in place. But the fact that certain watermelon seeds fail to develop under certain circumstances does not negate the fact that the seeds are indeed watermelon seeds. By analogy, Mengzi argues, the fact that under some circumstances some humans do not do good does not prove that they are not inherently good.

---

20 See the *Mengzi*, 6A10, 7A15.

21 It is an interesting feature of ancient Chinese philosophy that philosophers often employed the same image to introduce different moral teachings. For example, both the *Mengzi* (7A15) and the *Daodejing* (Chapters 10, 20, 28, 55) appropriated the image of a baby in elucidating their respective thoughts. You may want to compare and contrast the disparate moral lessons that the *Mengzi* and the *Daodejing* have drawn from similar images.

22 Conversely, someone who advocates a theory that human nature is bad must explain why some people do act altruistically or unselfishly.

23 6A6; also see 6A7.

What then are the conditions that would cause inherently good people to fail to do good things? Mengzi identifies three such conditions. First, moral failure may result because of a lack of favourable external conditions or environment.[24] Mengzi holds that when people are placed in adverse conditions or environments, there is a good chance that they will behave out of step with their good nature. In a colourful analogy, Mengzi remarks that the trees in Ox Mountain, when besieged by hatchets, axes, oxen, and sheep, cannot flourish according to their nature.[25] For Mengzi, unfavourable external conditions seem to include situations where moral instructions are lacking.[26] Second, moral evil may result because of a lack of motivation.[27] If people do not concentrate on their good hearts (the hearts of compassion, disdain, respect, and approval and disapproval) or if they have become cynical about doing good, they are not likely to act morally. Third, failure to do good results because of a lack of proper cultivation. For example, if one follows one's "petty part" (presumably the senses) instead of one's "greater part" (presumably the moral hearts), then one is prone to do the immoral.[28]

## DOING PHILOSOPHY
### Evil: Mengzi versus Augustine

The way Mengzi tackled the question of how humans come to act immorally has some interesting parallels to the way St. Augustine (354–430 CE) dealt with the problem of evil in relation to Christian beliefs. In Christian theology, the existence of evil in the world poses a problem for the Christian idea of God, who is believed to be omni-benevolent and omnipotent. Given this idea of God, there should be no evil in the world, for God would and should eliminate all evil in the world. The existence of evil thus raises an issue about the nature and reality of God.

One of Augustine's solutions to this problem claims that evil has no independent reality and that it is a privation of that which is essentially good. According to Augustine, disease, for example, has no independent reality, but appears as an absence of health. And blindness is the privation of sight according to the exigencies of its nature in a being that ought to have sight. One

---

24 See 6A7, 6A8, also see 6A2. The point here bears relating to the famous but controversial Stanford Prison Experiment in 1971, a study of the psychological effects of becoming a prisoner or prison guard. In the experiment, some normal and decent undergraduate students were arbitrarily assigned to be guards and prisoners, and in the six-day period of experiment, the guards were found to have exhibited "genuine" sadistic tendencies towards the prisoners. The experiment seems to show that when good people are put in an "evil" place, they tend to become evil. (For more on this experiment, visit <http://www.prisonexp.org/>.)

25 6A8.

26 1A7, 3A4, 3B9.

27 Also see 6A7, 6A8.

28 See 6A15.

particular privation arises from human free will—a will *capable of* choosing moral actions but choosing to do evil instead. With regard to the problem of evil, therefore, it is humans rather than God who are to blame.[29]

For Mengzi, although humans by nature are capable of doing good or have the potential to do good, they sometimes still choose not to do good. But, in this case, their lack of good actions is not due to an evil human nature, but due to a lack of motivation and cultivation, or due to extremely unfavourable external conditions. Just as Augustine never questioned God's omni-benevolence and omnipotence, Mengzi never doubted the goodness in human nature.[30]

### DEBATES WITH RIVAL THEORIES

In opposition to Mengzi's view of human nature, his contemporaries proposed several different views. Let's now turn to how Mengzi debated with them.

1. *Human nature is neither good nor not good.* According to this view, human nature is morally neutral. Morality, if it exists, comes from external imposition. That is to say, when one acts morally (i.e., in a benevolent and righteous manner), it is not due to one's nature, but due to external factors which compel or coerce one to act that way, which is against one's will or nature. Gaozi illustrated this view with an analogy that likened human nature to a willow tree: "Human nature is like a willow tree; righteousness is like cups and bowls. To make human nature benevolent and righteous is like making a willow tree into cups and bowls."[31] To this view Mengzi was quick to point out that Gaozi's analogy does not work.

> Mengzi said, "Can you, sir, following the nature of the willow tree, make it into cups and bowls? You must violate and rob the willow tree, and only then can you make it into cups and bowls. If you must violate and rob the willow tree in order to make it into cups and bowls, must you also violate and rob people in order to make them benevolent and righteous? If there is something that leads people to regard benevolence and righteousness as misfortunes for them, it will surely be your doctrine, will it not?"[32]

---

29 One may further question why an all loving and all-powerful God could have created/caused or at least allowed people to do evil—a hot issue in philosophy of religion.

30 There is a piece of textual evidence in this regard suggested by Maurizio Scarpari: "It is significant that, in describing evil and having to indicate the concept opposite to *shan* 善 ('good,' 'goodness'), Mencius never used the term *e* 惡 ("evil," "wickedness"), as Xunzi did one century later; rather, he used *bushan* 不善—'not being good,' 'not becoming good.' Evil is therefore explained in terms of 'failure,' an inability to develop one's own potential and be in harmony with the *dao*, the Way" (Maurizio Scarpari, "The Debate on Human Nature in Early Confucian Literature," *Philosophy East and West* 53:3 [July 2003]: 328).

31 6A1.

32 6A1.

To better understand Gaozi's view and Mengzi's refutation of it, let's lay out Gaozi's argument and Mengzi's counter-argument in a clear logical format. Gaozi's argument can be outlined as follows:

> Premise 1: Human nature is like a willow tree (A is like B).
> Premise 2: Righteousness is like cups and bowls (C is like D).
> Premise 3: Making human nature benevolent and righteous is like making a willow tree into cups and bowls (Making A into C is like making B into D).
> Unstated conclusion: Human nature in itself is neither benevolent nor righteous. (Otherwise, there would be no need to make the former into the latter.)

Mengzi's counter argument can be outlined as follows:

> Premise 1: When the willow tree is made into cups and bowls, its *nature* (natural state) is being violated.
> Premise 2: Making human nature benevolent and righteous is like making a willow tree into cups and bowls (Gaozi's Premise 3).
> Sub-conclusion: Therefore, in order to make human beings benevolent and righteous, their nature must be violated.
> Unstated premise 3: It is wrong to violate a thing's (or a person's) true nature.
> Conclusion: Gaozi's understanding of human nature is untenable.

In the passage cited above, Mengzi appears to have gained an upper-hand in this first round of debate, as no counter-argument from Gaozi is included there. However, a closer reading of the argument and counterargument will reveal that the two thinkers have in fact exploited two different aspects of the analogy—Gaozi focuses on the (neutral) *shaping* of human nature, and Mengzi introduces a pejorative reading of the analogy and turns it into a *twisting* of human nature. Hence, Gaozi and Mengzi were actually talking at cross purposes. Although there is no rebuttal (from Gaozi) recorded in this round of debate, Gaozi did not simply concede. admit you're defeated

In a philosophy debate, one may (a) simply concede when confronted by an opponent's critique; alternatively, one may (b) revise one's argument to counter the critique; or, better yet, (c) devise an entirely new argument. The first option is fairly rare in philosophy. Gaozi adopted both the second and the third options. First, he revised his argument with a new analogy that likens human nature to the shape of water. According to this analogy, just as the shape of water is indefinite and can be formed differently by external forces, human nature is indefinite (neither good nor bad) and can be shaped differently by external imposition.[33] Then, he switched to an entirely new argument, in which he redefined human nature (*xing*, 性) as life (*sheng*, 生).[34] This redefinition of "nature" draws attention to the physical features shared by human beings and other animals, for example, eating and sex. This conception of human nature is what Irene

---

33  See 6A2.
34  See 6A3, 6A4.

Bloom dubbed "narrow biologism,"[35] which excludes any native moral endowment in humans, contrary to Mengzi who takes moral endowment to be part of what humans all share.[36] In short, for Mengzi, human nature (broadly construed) includes eating and sex as well as moral "sprouts," but the unique human nature (narrowly construed) is the moral "sprouts." By contrast, for Gaozi, human nature is only eating and sex, with no moral "sprouts."

---

**DOING PHILOSOPHY**
*The Mengzi-Gaozi Debate on Human Nature*

Mengzi rejected both options by Gaozi, and he employed the same strategy of counterargument, as in the first round of debate, of identifying points of disanalogy between the objects being compared. So, I will leave the unpacking of 6A2 and 6A3 to you as an exercise. Now carefully read 6A2 and 6A3 (bearing in mind Gaozi's opening sentence at 6A4) then tease out Gaozi's argument and Mengzi's counter argument in each passage and put them in clear logical format, and then evaluate them.

---

2. *Human nature can become either good or bad*. Like rival theory 1, this second rival theory assumes that human nature is morally neutral, except that the present position focuses on the malleability of human nature. According to this second rival theory, the malleability of human nature depends upon the moral character of a ruler. When the benevolent kings of Wen and Wu in the West Zhou Dynasty (1120–771 BCE) arose, the people were fond of goodness, and when corrupt rulers You and Li in the same dynasty arose, the people were fond of destructiveness.[37]

Mengzi disagrees with this theory. While he admits that humans sometimes fail to do good things, he denies that failing to do good stems from human nature.[38] As explained earlier, it is compatible to hold that human nature is good and at the same time that people do both good and bad things.

For Mengzi, the problem with the view that human nature can become either good or bad seems to be that it identifies human nature with whatever particular acts one happens to have learned or developed due to environmental or external factors. When people performed good actions, they were said to have a good nature. Conversely, if

---

35 Irene Bloom, "Human Nature and Biological Nature in Mencius," *Philosophy East and West* 47:1 (1997): 27.
36 Chung-Ying Cheng has interpreted Mengzi as seeing human nature both in broad and narrow senses: "Broadly, human nature included both rationality and animal desires such as food and sex; narrowly, however, 'human nature' distinguished the human being from animals in terms of moral feelings, moral choices, and moral actions" (Entry "Mencius," in *Encyclopedia of Chinese Philosophy*, Antonio S. Cua, ed. [New York and London: Routledge, 2003], 441). It is clear, however, that in his debate with Gaozi, Mengzi used human nature (*xing*) exclusively in its narrow sense.
37 See 6A6.
38 See 6A6.

they did something bad, they were regarded as having a bad nature. This view confuses the nature of human beings with their particular behaviours. A logical consequence of the view is that human beings would be deprived of a unified nature because human behaviour is subject to constant change and is thus volatile. Arguably, this view is still compatible with Confucius' observation that humans are similar in their natural inclinations. For Mengzi, however, it runs the risk of rendering morality baseless.

Students who read existentialism may find both rival theories 1 and 2 ("Human nature is neither good nor bad" and "Human nature can become either good or bad") attractive. They may question whether there is really anything wrong with these views. For both views seem to rightly presuppose free will and moral subjectivity; both views, depriving the idea of human nature of any real content, are close to the existentialists' denial of the existence of any substantial human nature. But this is reading modern existentialist themes into these ancient Chinese thoughts. Neither of Gaozi's metaphors for human nature (i.e., the willow tree and the water) presupposes free will or moral subjectivity. Indeed, they both assume that human nature is passive (rather than self-determining) and susceptible to external influences. Here is an example of how an apparently familiar idea may turn out to be quite alien when interpreted against a context that is radically different from its native cultural and intellectual contexts. Some of the joy of studying the ideas of a different tradition comes precisely from the discovery of a new cultural landscape.

3. *There is a good human nature, and there is also a bad human nature.* This view about human nature argues that since some people are good and some bad, human nature is likewise of two varieties: a good human nature and a bad human nature. In support of this view, its proponents cite the examples of Yao and Shun, who were model rulers, and they also point out that Shun's father and brother were perverse men,[39] so they reason that good people and bad people must be of different natures.

This view, according to Mengzi, conflates particular *kinds of person* (classified according to behavioural characteristics) with human nature, which is supposed to be generic, or irrelevant to, particular kinds of person; as Mengzi said, "the sage and we are the same in kind."[40] It also smacks of fatalism—the nature of people being prefixed or predetermined. And it would render moral cultivation unnecessary. If this view were true, good people would not need moral cultivation and bad people would not be able to better themselves even if they tried—all are destined to be the way they are.

One may argue that discussion of human nature is typically muddled when empirical discourse is mixed in with philosophical speculation. Philosophic speculation about human nature cannot be proved or disproved by empirical findings as a scientific hypothesis can. In other words, philosophic speculation is, in a sense, immune to or above empirical confirmation or disconfirmation. It serves certain (broadly construed) pragmatic purposes, which can be "harmonized" (with varying degrees of difficulty) with any facts. Therefore, instead of trying to *prove* scientifically that human nature is good, bad, or empty, it may be more profitable to explore what pragmatic benefits a

---

39  See 5A2.
40  6A7.

particular view of human nature may be able to offer. For example, we may benefit more by considering the ethical merits or detriments in maintaining that human nature is good, bad, or neutral. In particular, we may argue that education in Mengzi's conception of human nature seems more beneficial in terms of ethical practice than the other alternatives. The belief that humans have native moral endowment can empower and encourage all people to be ethical—it can foster a strong moral self-awareness and moral responsibility. By contrast, both rival view 1 (that human nature is neither good nor bad) and rival view 2 (that human nature can become either good or bad) have the potential to encourage people to dodge their moral responsibility and become resigned to being influenced by their external circumstances (since free will is out of the question in either view). Rival view 3 (that there is a good human nature and a bad human nature) is so deterministic and fatalistic that it renders moral choice, moral cultivation, and external moral influence impossible and thus deprives people of any motivation to act morally and to better themselves morally. Thus, Mengzi's view seems pragmatically superior to the rival views in that it provides incentive for social behaviours that contribute to the well-being of society.

## DOING PHILOSOPHY
### Moral Difficulties and Mengzi's Treatment

Many passages in the *Mengzi* deal with moral difficulties and how Mengzi resolves them (1B8, 4A17, 4B11, 4B28, 5A2). A moral difficulty is a case in which one apparently justifiably acts in violation of an established moral rule or moral practice.

In 5A2, for example, the Sage Shun was blamed for violating the rule that one must inform one's parents in taking a wife. To overcome this moral difficulty, Mengzi first calls on another rule: For a man and a woman to dwell together in one home is the greatest of human relations. He believes that this rule would override the first rule. Then he refers to the consequences that would result from applying the first rule (i.e., Shun would not be able to get married).

Now read these following passages: 1B8, 4A17, 4B11, 4B28, and see if you can spot the difficulties in them and understand how Mengzi manages to resolve them.

## LOVE WITH DEGREES VERSUS UNIVERSAL LOVE (IMPARTIAL CARE)

Imagine the following scenario. John's wife and mother are both drowning, and he is only able to rescue one of them. Whom would he save? Whom should he save? For John to choose one is to imply that the other is not as important. Thus, John seems to be caught in a moral dilemma with no easy escape. The crux of the dilemma is that our moral intuition seems to be that his wife and his mother are perhaps equally important to him, so he should treat them equally (that is, neither should be treated with priority). But, unfortunately, treating them equally—that is, saving them both—is not an option in this scenario.

Fortunately, it is extremely rare that a husband has to make such a tough choice in real life. Even if a husband did by chance get into such a predicament, he may not have the luxury of time to deliberate on the situation; he may simply jump into the water and try to save whomever he could reach first. Nonetheless, the moral questions posed by our hypothetical scenario are real and significant. Should we love everyone equally? Is it always possible to do so? If so, in what sense is it possible? If not, why not? Should love be gradated with respect to the beneficiary of that love? These questions can surely invite us to think more deeply about the essence of love and more generally about the nature of morality. Mengzi's debate with Mozi concerning universal love (or impartial care) deals with just these questions.[41] But before introducing their debate, a few words about Mozi are in order.

The exact dates of Mozi's life are not clear to us; yet we do know that his lifespan seems to cross the death of Confucius (479 BCE) and the birth of Mengzi (372 BCE). He was the first opponent of Confucius' teachings. Our main source of his thought is the book bearing his name, the Mozi, which contains fifty-three chapters. One of the chapters is even entitled "Anti-Confucianism" (Chapter 39), which contains Mozi's severe criticisms of the Confucians of his time. For example, he criticized Confucians for their advocacy and practice of partial love, instead of impartial care.[42]

Mozi believed that social chaos results not so much from people's lack of love as from their partial love. He argued that if people could love other families as much as their own, and if they could regard the cities and states of others as they regard their own, then they would not attack, overthrow, or injure one another.[43] Here are two passages where Mozi made his argument for impartial care.

> Suppose that here is a broad plain, a vast wilderness, and a man is buckling on his armour and donning his helmet to set out for the field of battle, where the fortunes of life and death are unknown; or he is setting out in his lord's name upon a distant mission to Pa or Yueh, Ch'i or Ching, and his return is uncertain. Now let us ask, to whom would he entrust the support of his parents and the care of his wife and children? Would it be to the universal-minded man, or to the partial man? It seems to me that, on the occasions like these, there are no fools in the world. Though one may disapprove of universality himself, he would surely think it best to entrust his family to the universal-minded man.[44]

41  See 3A5, 3B9, and 7A26.
42  Mozi also attacked Confucians for their lack of belief in the existence of ghosts and spirits and for their advocacy of elaborate and wasteful funerals and prodigal practice of music. See the Analects 6:20, 7:20, 11:11 for Confucius' view on ghosts and spirits.
43  Mo Tzu: Basic Writings, Burton Watson, trans. (New York: Columbia University Press, 1963), 40.
44  Mo Tzu, 42.

Let us examine for a moment the way in which a filial son plans for the welfare of his parents. When a filial son plans for his parents, does he wish others to love and benefit them, or does he wish others to hate and injure them? It stands to reason that he wishes others to love and benefit his parents. Now if I am a filial son, how do I go about accomplishing this? Do I first make it a point to love and benefit other men's parents, so that they in return will love and benefit my parents? Or do I first make it a point to hate and injure other men's parents, so that they in return will love and benefit my parents? Obviously, I must first make it a point to love and benefit other men's parents, so that they in return will love and benefit my parents.[45]

It is no accident that Mozi spoke about taking care of parents or filial piety, since Confucius' disciple Ziyou took filial piety and brotherly love to be "the trunk of humanness."[46] In the above passages, Mozi was critical of the Confucian practice of filial piety in his time, which embodied Confucius' doctrine of love with distinction. Mozi's argument in the cited passages can be rephrased as follows:

1. We have a moral obligation to love our parents.
2. Loving our parents implies that we want them to be loved by others as well (especially in case of war).
3. But in order to love one's parents, one has to take the initiative to love other people's parents first.
4. When one loves other people's parents, they will return that love by loving that person's parents.
5. Loving other people's parents first is a form of impartial love or love without distinction (unstated assumption).
6. Therefore, impartial love is prerequisite for filial piety.

To evaluate the argument, we find premises (1), (2), (3), and (4) are uncontroversial, but premise (5) can be contested. Premise (5) assumes that the love of one's own parents has the same *intensity* as the love of other people's parents. But this assumption is unwarranted. In other words, "wanting one's parents to be loved by others" does not necessarily imply that they are to be loved with the same intensity by others as they are loved by their own children.[47] Indeed, (5) seems to fall into the trap of a false dichotomy: to love (admitting of no degree) other people's parents or not to love other people's parents.[48] An important alternative has been ignored—one can love other people's parents, although with less intensity than one loves one's own parents. This important alternative is the

---

45  *Mo Tzu*, 46–47.
46  The *Analects*, 1:2.
47  At one point one disciple of Mozi admitted that the practice of love *temporally* begins with one's parents (see 3A5).
48  Mengzi imputed Mozi for going to an extreme and leaving aside other things. See 7A26.

idea of "love with distinction." It is precisely along this line of thought that Mengzi argued with Mozi.

While the idea of "universal love" sounds appealing, it is for Mengzi too impractical and can result in neglecting to respect one's parents. Mengzi argues that love admits of distinctions—love should start with one's parents and extend gradationally to others outside of the family. Mengzi's idea of love with distinction is best encapsulated in the following passage:

> Mengzi said, "Gentlemen, in relation to animals, are sparing of them, but are not benevolent toward them. In relation to the people, they are benevolent toward them, but do not treat them as kin. They treat their kin as kin, and then are benevolent toward people. They are benevolent toward the people, and then are sparing of animals."[49]

In the passage, love with distinction can be seen as involving three facets of distinction. First, it involves a distinction in *attitude*. The attitude of a gentleman (*junzi*, exemplary person) towards animals is different in kind from his attitude towards people: he is *sparing* of animals, but *benevolent* towards people.[50] Second, it involves a distinction in *intensity*. Although a gentleman is benevolent to those outside his family, he still does not consider them part of his family. This implies that he has greater regard for his own family than for those outside of his family. Finally, it involves a distinction in *priority*. A gentleman loves his kin first and then other people. It is only then that he is sparing of animals.[51]

It is important to note that the doctrine of love with distinction does not imply the acceptability of inhumane treatment of non-family members (including what the ancients call "barbarians"). As Neville has pointed out, "what was presupposed, though not acknowledged, in the 'love with differences' idea was a working ritual social system that clearly defined responsibilities in family, village, empire, and for the barbarians. When that system breaks down, *it is inhumane not to care for the barbarians*" (my emphasis).[52] It must be stressed that for Mengzi "priority regarding love" does not mean "exclusivity of love."

Based on his idea of love with distinction, Mengzi launched several criticisms against Mozi. First, he challenged Mozi's assumption that one has the natural capacity to truly love other people to the same degree or with the same intensity as one loves one's own kin.[53] Next, he argued that Mozi's doctrine of "universal love" completely abolishes the ethical priority defined on the basis of family structure, such that a father would no longer be recognized as a father, which, in Mengzi's dramatic way of putting it, amounts

---

49  7A45.
50  See 1A7.
51  See 7A46.
52  Robert Cummings Neville, *Ritual and Deference—Extending Chinese Philosophy in a Comparative Context* (Albany, NY: SUNY Press, 2008), 13.
53  See 3A5.

to not having a father.[54] Moreover, Mengzi also believed that it is impractical to insist on Mozi's "radical altruism" (as, according to Mengzi, Mozi would give of himself completely in order to benefit the whole world).[55]

## DOING PHILOSOPHY
### *Mengzi's Criticism of Mozi*

Read 3A5, 3B9, and 7A26 for Mengzi's criticisms of Mozi. Do you think Mengzi's criticisms of Mozi are fair? In real life, do we or should we apply love equally to everyone? How do we actually practice it if we choose to love everyone equally, without distinction? While it is commonly believed that the Bible preaches universal love, the idea of love with distinction is not entirely absent from it. Consider Galatians 6:10 "Therefore, *as we have opportunity*, let us do good to all people, *especially* to those who belong to the family of believers" (my emphasis; New International Version).

Peter Singer has famously argued that the "basic principle of equality [concerning humans and animals] does not require equal or identical *treatment*; it requires equal consideration. Equal consideration for different beings may lead to different treatment and different rights."[56] Does Mozi's "universal love" mean "equal treatment" or "equal consideration"?

## MORAL CULTIVATION

According to Mengzi, although we have innate moral dispositions, we do not have them in their mature forms at birth, and we do not become mature moral agents until we have cultivated ourselves morally and become exemplary persons, men of humanness, or sages. Thus, Mengzi argues that constant moral cultivation is indispensable to our moral development. For even though we innately have the four good "sprouts" (moral dispositions), unfortunately not everyone acts in accordance with these moral dispositions in all circumstances.[57] There is an important difference between "not acting" and "not being able to act."[58] While every normal person is *able to act* morally, because of weakness in the moral will, not everyone *actually acts* morally.

If, as Mengzi has claimed, our four good "sprouts" are analogous to our four limbs, then it would seem as easy to extend (cultivate) one's "sprouts" as to lift our arms. But Mengzi's analogy breaks down where he observes that it is not as easy to control one's

---

54  See 3B9.
55  See 7A26.
56  Peter Singer, *Animal Liberation*, second edition (New York: Ecco, 1990), 2.
57  Mengzi drew our attention to the difference between "acting out of" benevolence and righteousness and "acting out" benevolence and righteousness. See 4B19.
58  See 1A7, 2A6; also see a similar idea in the *Analects* 4:6, 6:12.

"sprouts" as it is to control one's limbs. For Mengzi, the cause of moral weakness is two-fold: one may have lost or neglected one's moral "sprouts"[59] and one may have given in to temptations (such as the distractions of the senses).[60] Correspondingly, then, moral cultivation consists in how to preserve and extend one's good "sprouts" as well as how to resist various temptations.

Mengzi first urged us to *preserve* our innate good moral "sprouts."[61] An important means to preserving the good "sprouts" involves moral self-reflection. Mengzi said, "Benevolence [*ren*] is like archery: an archer makes sure his stance is correct before letting fly the arrow, and if he fails to hit the mark, he does not hold it against his victor. He simply seeks the cause within himself."[62] To illustrate how moral self-reflection is put into practice, Mengzi used the example of a gentleman and explained how the gentleman will handle himself when he encounters someone who is harsh and disagreeable:

> Here is a person who is harsh to me. A gentleman in this situation will
> invariably examine himself, saying, "I must not be benevolent. I must be
> lacking in propriety. How else could this situation have come upon me?!"
> If he examines himself and *is* benevolent, and if he examines himself and
> *has* propriety, yet the other person is still harsh, a gentleman will invariably
> examine himself, saying, "I must not be loyal." If he examines himself and
> *is* loyal, yet the other person is still harsh, a gentleman says, "This person is
> simply incorrigible! What difference is there between a person like this and
> an animal?! What point is there in rebuking an animal?"[63]

In advocating moral self-examination, Mengzi did not suggest that one should introspect endlessly and even blame oneself blindly. He believed that self-examination should be balanced by practical wisdom, which enables one to know when to stop the introspection and when to suspend judgement on oneself.

Moral self-reflection requires one to pay special attention to the function of the heart. This is where Mengzi's view of moral psychology comes in, a view (as we will see) that is comparable to Plato's analysis of the structure of the soul.

> Kung-tu Tzu asked, "Though equally human, why are some men greater
> than others?"

59  See 6A10, 6A15.
60  See 6A10 and 6A15.
61  See 4B19.
62  2A7, D.C. Lau's translation; also see his translation of 4A4: "If others do not respond to your love with love look into your own benevolence; if others fail to respond to your attempts to govern them with order, look into your own wisdom; if others do not return your courtesy, look into your own respect. In other words, look into yourself whenever you fail to achieve your purpose. When you are correct in your person, the Empire will turn to you."
63  4B28; also see 7A4.

"He who is guided by the interests of the parts of his person that are of greater importance is a great man; he who is guided by the interests of the parts of his person that are of smaller importance is a small man."

"Though equally human, why are some men guided one way and others guided another way?"

"The organs of hearing and sight are unable to think and can be misled by external things. When one thing acts on another, all it does is attack it. The organ of the heart can think. But it will find the answer only if it does think; otherwise, it will not find the answer. This is what Heaven has given me. If one makes one's stand on what is of greater importance in the first instance, what is of smaller importance cannot displace it. In this way, one cannot but be a great man."[64]

In this passage, Mengzi responds to Kung-tu Tzu's inquiry into the origin of moral greatness. He advances the claim that what makes some people (morally) greater than others is their ability to attend to "interests of the parts of [them] that are of greater importance," and what makes them more disposed to moral guidance is their heart. Mengzi does not explicitly define what "things of smaller importance" and "things of greater importance" are. However, the textual context of the passage seems to suggest that by "things of smaller importance" he means physical desires (eating and sex, for example; also see 6A14), and by "things of greater importance" he means the four innate moral sprouts. According to Mengzi, the root of moral choice is "the organ of the heart" which can think (more in the sense of moral deliberation than in the sense of logical reasoning). This is similar to Plato's view that in the ideal structure of the soul, reason (the charioteer) is in control, or is the ruler, while physical appetite (dark winged horse) and spirit or passion (white winged horse) are the ruled.[65] However, if physical appetite and spirit are to control the soul, there will be no harmony in the person. In Mengzi's case, if "things of smaller importance" are given priority over "things of greater importance," then one will become a (morally) "smaller" person.

Another means to preserving one's heart, according to Mengzi, involves the technique of cultivating one's "floodlike *qi* (breath)" (*hao ran zhi qi*). Although there has been much scholarly interest in this idea, its interpretation remains controversial. This situation prompted Arthur Waley to conclude that the passage on "floodlike breath" is "hopelessly corrupt and obscure," and "it is impossible to say what exactly was the nature of his [Mengzi's] 'flood breath.'"[66] However, I am not as pessimistic as Waley. To see how we can make some sense of the material, let's look at the context where the idea of "floodlike breath" is discussed:

Gongsun Chou said, "I venture to ask what is meant by 'floodlike *qi*.'"

---

64  6A15 (D.C. Lau's translation).
65  Mentioned in Chapter 1 of this volume.
66  Authur Waley, *Three Ways of Thoughts in Ancient China* (London: George Allen & Unwin, 1939), 118.

Mengzi said, "It is difficult to put into words. It is a *qi* that is supremely great and supremely unyielding. If one cultivates it with uprightness and does not harm it, it will fill up the space between Heaven and earth. It is a *qi* that unites righteousness with the Way. Without these, it starves. It is produced by accumulated righteousness ..."[67]

Here Mengzi linked "floodlike *qi*" with "righteousness" and the "Way," which makes us speculate that in fact by "floodlike *qi*" Mengzi was talking about "*qi*" in a spiritual or moral sense. In other words, Mengzi may be making a comparison between exercising physical breath technique (*qi gong*) with cultivating moral virtues. Just as one's physical *qi*, through practice, can make one physically strong, one's moral *qi*, with persistent cultivation, will make one morally strong and upright.

Another important route to moral cultivation is to *extend* (*tui*) one's concern and care outward from oneself to members of one's family, then to people outside one's family but close to oneself, and then to members of society in general.[68] This process starts from self-examination and allows its effects to radiate outward to others through several concentric circles of care.

Given his emphasis on love with distinction, Mengzi recognizes that caring for our family remains our priority, but this is not to say that we will not care for those outside our family, only that we let our care spill over to them, as it were, so the intensity of our care will diminish gradually as we move from the innermost circle to the outer circles. Mengzi believes that society at large will be the ultimate beneficiary if one can learn to love one's own family as one should. When people do their part in this way, society as a whole will enjoy peace and harmony. As Mengzi puts it, "The Way lies in what is near, but people seek it in what is distant; one's task lies in what is easy, but people seek it in what is difficult. If everyone would treat their kin as kin, and their elders as elders, the world would be at peace."[69] This is precisely Mengzi's advice to King Xuan of Qi:

Treat your elders as elders [as they should be treated], and extend it to the elders of others; treat your young ones as young ones [as they should be treated], and extend it to the young ones of others; then you can turn the whole world in the palm of your hand.[70]

To extend care from one's immediate family to those outside one's family is not an easy task. What often happens in the application of care is that one's family is unduly stressed and one is inclined to stick with one's own family. When a conflict arises between loving one's family and loving people outside one's family or one's country,

---

67  2A2.
68  See 1A7, 4A11, 7B13, 7A15.
69  4A11; also see 4A5, 7B31, 7B32.
70  1A7.

one tends to favour one's family and to take serving people outside one's family or country less seriously and less willingly. One may even completely ignore people outside one's family.[71] According to Mengzi, had the old father of the emperor Shun killed a man, the emperor would have secretly carried his father on his back and fled away, never giving a thought to the Empire.[72] Therefore, when people care for their families there is no guarantee that they will actually care for others outside their families, even though they may be more likely to do so.

Ideally, though, no real conflict between serving one's family and serving one's country would arise. The Disney movie *Mulan* retells an old folktale about a young girl, Mulan, who managed to serve both her family and her country at the same time. She did this by joining the army in disguise, replacing her old and already injured father, thereby expressing not only filial piety, but also loyalty to the country.

## DOING PHILOSOPHY
### *Mengzi's Advice on Care beyond One's Family versus the Ethics of Care*

Nel Noddings (b. 1929) argues that morality is rooted in "natural caring," a primal emotional response to people close to you, parents, siblings, sons and daughters, friends, etc.[73] In this respect, Noddings's view is remarkably similar to Mengzi's view about the good moral "sprouts." However, contrary to Mengzi, Noddings does not consider acting on natural caring ethical: "In situations where we act on behalf of the other because we want to do so, we are acting in accord with natural caring. A mother's caretaking efforts in behalf of her child are not usually considered ethical but natural. Even maternal animals take care of their offspring, and we do not credit them with ethical behaviour" (p. 79). She believes that true ethical caring is based on natural caring, but requires a further effort to extend natural care to others that are usually not the recipients of natural care—strangers in need or the homeless, for example.

Which position do you find more convincing: distinguishing "natural caring" from "ethical caring" as proposed by Noddings, or viewing natural caring as a form of ethical caring (though not with the same intensity) as Mengzi would have us believe?

---

71 It has been argued that because Confucianism took filiality or more generally consanguineous affection to be the foundational and supreme principle of human life, it tended to subordinate sociality, individuality, and citizenship. See Qingping Liu, "Filiality versus Sociality and Individuality: On Confucianism as 'Consanguinitism,'" *Philosophy East and West* 53:2 (April 2003): 234–50.
72 See 7A35.
73 *Caring: A Feminine Approach to Ethics and Moral Education* (Berkeley, CA: University of California Press, 1984).

## DOING PHILOSOPHY
### *Is it possible to morally over-cultivate oneself?*

Mengzi portrays the cultivation process as natural,[74] gradual,[75] and motivated.[76] Try to detect the moral significance of the following story about a man who was trying to help his grain grow:

> One must work at it [moral cultivation], but do not assume success. One should not forget the heart, but neither should one "help" it grow. Do not be like the man from Song. Among the people of the state of Song there was a farmer who, concerned lest his sprouts not grow, pulled on them. Obliviously, he returned home and said to his family, "Today I am worn out. I helped the sprouts to grow." His son rushed out and looked at them. The sprouts were withered.[77]

Is the man trying too hard in his effort to cultivate his crops? Is it possible to over-cultivate oneself morally? If so, what would be the signs of such over-cultivation? If not, why not?

Mengzi insists that one must avoid unfavourable environments that may hinder one's effort of moral cultivation. He constantly compares moral cultivation with agriculture. For him, just as favourable environmental factors are crucial to the cultivation of crops, a morally healthy environment is indispensable to the cultivation of moral virtues. Citing the example of the trees in Ox Mountain, Mengzi argues that new shoots would not grow into big trees when they are besieged by hatchets, axes, oxen, and sheep. Although these environmental challenges would not destroy their nature, they would certainly hinder and suppress the natural expression or development of the trees' nature.[78] Recognizing the influence of external circumstances on moral development, Mengzi cautions people to choose their occupations carefully, because some occupations are not conducive to the expression and development of our ethical dispositions. For example, Mengzi despises the job of arrow-making, as it aims at harming people.[79]

A well-known legend about Mengzi and his mother also underscores the importance of favourable environmental conditions to one's moral growth. Mengzi's father died when Mengzi was a young child, so he was raised single-handedly by his mother, who is esteemed in the Chinese culture as a model mother. Once Mengzi's family lived near

---

74  See 2A2, 4A9, 6A1, 6A8, 7A16.
75  See 2A2.
76  See 1A7, 6A6, 7A3, 7B21.
77  2A2; Bryan W. Van Norden, *Mengzi: With Selections from Traditional Commentaries* (Indianapolis: Hackett, 2008); see also 7A27.
78  See 6A8.
79  See 2A7.

a cemetery, and his mother found him playing at grave digging. Worried about what her son might learn near a cemetery, Mengzi's mother decided to move to another place near the marketplace. She soon discovered him imitating the hawkers, and this prompted her to move again, this time near a school. When she saw her son now playing at studying sacred rites, she was satisfied.[80]

## POLITICAL PHILOSOPHY

With regard to moral cultivation, as we have seen above, Mengzi places great emphasis on empathy, with his idea that one should progressively extend care and consideration to those beyond one's own family. Mengzi insists that rulers or kings of states should follow the same path toward moral cultivation as ordinary people. He lobbied kings and exhorted them to extend their innate goodness to their people.[81] Thus, Mengzi's political philosophy can be seen as an extension of his moral philosophy, in which the practical and social ramifications of the latter are worked out.

In Mengzi's political philosophy, the state is an extension of the family. The relationship between the ruler and the subject is seen as analogous to the relationship between a father and his children. While children owe filial piety to their parents, subjects owe their rulers loyalty. Rulers, on the other hand, should treat their subjects with care as parents treat their children.[82]

Mengzi also proposes that, given the importance of his role, a ruler ought to practice moral cultivation more rigorously than the common people. First, the ruler is called upon to cultivate himself for the benefit of the people in the state, and even of all the people under heaven.[83] A ruler is urged to govern the people with benevolence rather than by force and compulsion, for only the former can make people sincerely and willingly submit to the governing.[84] Thus, a ruler must be a Sage (*sheng*) at heart first before he can successfully take on the task of being a ruler, or a king (*wang*). Mengzi calls this moral quality "inner sageliness and outer kingliness."[85] In addition, a ruler is called upon to be a good moral role model to those in subordinate positions. In fact, ideally, both the ruler and his ministers are to behave as moral exemplars for their subordinates and the common people. Mengzi believes that society as a whole will enjoy social harmony when the practice of moral suasion permeates the political system from the top down. Thus, according to Mengzi, when the prince (ruler) is benevolent, everyone else will be benevolent; when the prince is dutiful, others will be dutiful.[86]

---

80  See Appendix 2: "Early Tradition about Mencius," in Lao's *Mencius*, 215–16. A famous Chinese saying illustrates the same point: "One who mixes with vermilion will turn red, and one who touches pitch shall be defiled therewith" (*jin zhu zhe chi, jin mo zhe hei*). Also see a similar idea on the significance of environment in the *Analects* (4:1).

81  See 1A2, 1A7, 1B1, 1B2, 1B4, 1B5.

82  See 1A4, 1B7.

83  See 1A7.

84  See 2A3; also see the *Analects* 2:3.

85  3A4.

86  3A2, 4B5, 7A19, 7B4; also see the *Analects* 12:17, 12:19, 13:6.

According to Mengzi, in order to govern with benevolence, a ruler must put the welfare of his people first: "The people are of supreme importance; the altars to the gods of earth and grain come next; last comes the ruler."[87] This was a novel idea in Mengzi's time. While Confucius had much to say about governance,[88] he did not explicitly stress the importance of the people to the extent that Mengzi did. (One may question if this emphasis on the importance of the people is compatible with the social and political hierarchy implicit in the teachings of both Confucius and Mengzi.)

Mengzi also connects the will of the people with the will of heaven, arguing that the former is to reveal the latter. In essence, the will of heaven is simply the will of the people. Citing the authoritative historical text of his time, *The Classic of History* (the *Shangshu*), Mengzi declares, "Heaven sees with the eyes of its people, Heaven hears with the ears of its people."[89] The twofold metaphor here of heaven seeing and hearing the common people expresses with much rhetorical force the significance of the will of the people in Mengzi's political thinking.

In Mengzi's political thought, morality is seen as both a necessary and sufficient condition for a good government. That said, it is important not to misread him as putting morality, particularly benevolence and righteousness, against profit. At one point Mengzi refused to talk about profit when asked by a king.[90] But a more careful reading of Mengzi reveals that he is not questioning profit per se, only the viability of appealing to people's selfish gain as an instrument of governing. He reasons that if everyone operates from a selfish desire to seek profit, there will be conflict among people, within and between families and states. Mengzi does not oppose wealth per se, only selfish desire for and possession of it.[91] For him, morality has a priority over profit or material needs.[92]

For Mengzi, the practice of benevolence at the political level involves a set of concrete policies and measures that aim to reduce punishment and taxation.[93] He urges rulers not to be fond of killing,[94] and not to interfere with the busy seasons in the fields,[95] but to provide reliable livelihoods for the people,[96] and to conduct moral education by teaching people the virtues of filial piety, brotherly love, loyalty, and faithfulness.[97] Although most of these policies had already been advocated by Confucius in the *Analects*, Mengzi's policies provided additional concrete details and ways of implementation. For example, the *Analects* portrayed Confucius as one who displayed care for nature, for he fished with a line and not with a net and he did not aim at a roosting

---

87  7B14 (D.C. Lau's translation); also see 1A1, 1A5, 1A7, 2A1, 2A6, 3A4, 4A1.
88  See the *Analects* 1:5, 2:19, 5:16, 12:2, 13:4, etc.
89  5A5 (D.C. Lau's translation).
90  See 1A1; also see *Analects* 9:1.
91  See 1B5, 2B6, 7A25.
92  Confucius expressed similar views in the *Analects* (see 4:12, 4:16, 13:17, and 14:12).
93  See 1A5, 7A23, 7B27.
94  See 1A6.
95  See 1A3.
96  See 1A7, 7A22.
97  See 1A3, 1A5, 1A7, 3A4, 7A14.

bird.[98] Mengzi elaborates on such attitude of care for nature and develops it into a policy of sustainability. He states,

> If you do not allow nets with too fine a mesh to be used in large ponds, then there will be more fish and turtles than they can eat; if hatchets and axes are permitted in the forests on the hills only in the proper seasons, then there will be more timber than they can use. When the people have more grain, more fish and turtles than they can eat, and more timber than they can use, then in the support of their parents when alive and in the mourning of them when dead, they will be able to have no regrets over anything left undone. This is the first step along the Kingly way.[99]

In a hierarchical political system, if the king loses his original good "hearts" or fails to extend his care to his people, the consequences can be disastrous not only for the common people but also for the king himself. That was certainly the case in Mengzi's time. Mengzi believes that there is a chance that a new leader may rise up from the lower ranks to replace a bad ruler; that is, when a ruler disqualifies himself by not ruling properly, a new leader may win the support of society and the sanction of heaven. In actual practice, however, there is little that the common people in a hierarchical political system can do if their king is corrupt, especially if the king is skilful in manipulating the state-machine in the name of the mandate of heaven. Thus, for Mengzi, when the ruler is corrupt, there is a last resort to bring about a change of government, which is by means of a revolution, and Mengzi believes that the common people have the moral right to bring about a revolution. He holds that regicide would be justified in extreme cases of corruption and misrule, for in such cases it would no longer be regicide, because the king would have disqualified himself by forfeiting the mandate of heaven (which is to govern morally) and reduced himself to the position of a mere "fellow" or "loner."[100]

### THE UNITY OF HUMANITY AND HEAVEN

Mengzi believes that there is a comprehensive physical and spiritual correspondence between natural phenomena and the human realm. Human beings and human activities are seen as integral to the organic continuum of the world—which is expressed by such notions as *tiandi* (literally heaven and earth) or simply *tian* (heaven).[101]

Mengzi's view on heaven is a further development of Confucius' view on the same topic. In the *Analects*, Confucius uses the term *tian* with moral connotations. For example, he remarked that the legendary emperors Yao and Shun could learn from the

---

98  See the *Analects* 7:26.
99  1A3 (D.C. Lau's translation).
100  1B8.
101  During the Han Dynasty, the Confucian Dong Zhongshu (c. 195–c. 115 BCE) went so far as to deem a human body as a miniature of the world, arguing that human emotions like excitement, anger, sadness, and joy correspond respectively with spring, autumn, winter, and summer.

greatness of heaven (*tian*).[102] Following Confucius' idea on heaven, Mengzi further argues that our innate good hearts (humaneness, righteousness, propriety, and wisdom) are all heaven-endowed, and that to cultivate them is to "know" heaven. He also said, "A gentleman [*junzi*] transforms where he passes, and works wonders where he abides. He is in the same stream as Heaven above and Earth below."[103] As Fung Yu-lan has pointed out, for Mengzi, the universe (*tian*, heaven) is essentially moral:

> The moral principles of man are also metaphysical principles of the universe, and the nature of man is an exemplification of these principles. It is this moral universe that Mengzi and his school mean when they speak of Heaven, and an understanding of this moral universe is what Mengzi calls "knowing Heaven."[104]

Therefore, moral self-cultivation is not only the realization of self, but also a realization of the moral potential of the cosmos. As Mengzi puts it, "to fully apply one's heart is to understand one's nature. If one understands one's nature, then one understands Heaven. To preserve one's mind and nourish one's nature is the means to serve Heaven."[105] In this sense, ideally, human beings are "co-producers" of the cosmos.[106] Thus, Mengzi remarks: "The ten thousand things are all brought to completion by us,"[107] and "a gentleman is not ashamed to face Heaven above, nor is he ashamed to face persons below the Heaven."[108] These remarks make good sense when we interpret them in the light of Mengzi's belief that human beings and the cosmos together constitute a single moral continuum.

By relating human nature to heaven, Mengzi justifies his doctrine of human nature on metaphysical grounds. By connecting human nature to heaven, Mengzi explains why we should cultivate ourselves and why we should be moral in terms of a mandate we have as part of the cosmos. Mengzi's explanation here may appear to be providing an arbitrary seal to close off further debate regarding human nature. And this would be so if we accept his view of heaven. However, as we will see (in Chapters 6, 7, 8 of this book), neither the Confucian Xunzi nor the Taoists Laozi or Zhuangzi agreed with Mengzi's view of heaven. Indeed, these thinkers' distinctive views of heaven continued the debate on human nature in ancient China.

---

102 See the *Analects* 8:19.
103 7A13 (D.C. Lau's translation).
104 Fung Yu-lan, *A Short History of Chinese Philosophy*, Derk Bodde, ed. (New York: Macmillan Publishing, 1948), 77.
105 7A1.
106 For Mengzi, it is possible that people (especially the rulers) may lose their heaven-endowed nature and become corrupt, and when that happens, natural disasters, such as floods, earthquakes, and famine may be triggered.
107 7A4.
108 See 7A20.

Mengzi's view of the unity of humanity and heaven has been regarded by some as reflective of a mystical and religious side to his philosophy. Scholars are still debating just to what extent this aspect of Mengzi's philosophy is "religious." One thing is sure though: if religion has to do with transcendence, then this putative "religious" dimension of Mengzi's philosophy is about the experience of transcendence from within (as heaven is not considered by Mengzi to be external to human affairs), or transcendence from the immanent (because heaven and humans form a continuum), rather than transcendence into without. Such immanent transcendence is also characteristic of Chan/Zen Buddhism—a topic that we will examine in Chapter 9 (on the Platform Sutra) and Chapter 10 (the *Shobogenzo*) of this book.

## CONCLUDING REMARKS: THE INFLUENCE OF THE MENGZI

Mengzi's doctrine of human nature, together with Confucius' ideas on human nature, has had the most decisive influence on the Chinese understanding of human nature. Mengzi's view on human nature has been epitomized in the first line of a short Confucian catechism entitled *Three Character Classic* (*San Zi Jing*, compiled in the thirteenth century). It reads: "Men at their birth (*ren zhi chu*) are originally good (*xing ben shan*); their natures are similar (*xing xiang jin*), and their habits make [them] different (*xi xiang yuan*)." Despite being challenged by Gaozi, who argued that human nature is neither good nor bad, and by Xunzi (310–220 BCE), who held that human nature is bad, Mengzi's conception of human nature as good has been so embedded in the Chinese way of thinking that it can be considered part of the cultural DNA of the Chinese people. For this reason, many Chinese people find it difficult to accept the Christian doctrine of original sin.[109] Arguably, no theory concerning human nature other than Mengzi's has really taken root in the Chinese culture.

Moral cultivation, much emphasized in Mengzi's philosophy, has been an integral aspect of the Chinese tradition. Mengzi's political thought, especially his views on the importance of the populace and the practice of benevolence in governing, was hailed by later feudal dynasties as their guiding principles for political governance, even though they may have never completely implemented it in practice.

Mengzi's development and systematization of Confucius' ideas have been enshrined in the orthodoxy of Confucianism.[110] The *Mengzi*, together with the *Analects*, the *Great Learning*, and the *Mean*, have been revered as the four classics of Confucianism since the time of Zhu Xi (1130–1200 CE), who collected the four works as a single corpus and commented on them. It is not an exaggeration to say that Mengzi's philosophy has greatly moulded the Chinese mind.

---

109 The Chinese language uses the same word *zui* (罪) to refer to the notions of "sin" and "crime." This has made it even more difficult for many Chinese people to accept the idea of original sin.
110 Bryan W. Van Norden went as far as to see the *Mengzi* as "one of the treasures of world literature, easily in a class with Plato's *Republic*, the Qu'ran, and the Bhagavad Gita" (Preface, ix).

## WORK CITED AND RECOMMENDED READINGS

1. Bryan W. Van Norden's translation of selected passages from *Mengzi*, in *Readings in Classical Chinese Philosophy*, ed. Philip J. Ivanhoe and Bryan W. Van Norden (New York: Seven Bridges Press, 2001), 111–50.

2. Bryan W. Van Norden, *Mengzi: With Selections from Traditional Commentaries* (Indianapolis: Hackett, 2008).

3. D.C. Lao, trans., *Mencius* (New York: Penguin, 1970).

4. Kwong-loi Shun, *Mencius and Early Chinese Thought* (Stanford, CA: Stanford University Press, 1997).

5. Alan K.L. Chan, ed., *Mencius—Contexts and Interpretations* (Honolulu: University of Hawaii Press, 2002).

6. Philip J. Ivanhoe, "Interpreting the *Mengzi*," *Philosophy East and West* 54:2 (April 2004): 249–63.

7. Kim-Chong Chong et al., eds., *The Moral Circle and the Self—Chinese and Western Approaches* (La Salle: Open Court, 2003).

# CHAPTER 6

# The *Daodejing*

SUGGESTED PRIMARY READING

W.T. Chan's translation of the *Daodejing* (*Tao Te Ching*), in *A Source Book in Chinese Philosophy* (Princeton: Princeton University Press, 1969), or Chad Hansen's translation: *Tao Te Ching on the Art of Harmony: The New Illustrated Edition of the Chinese Philosophical Masterpiece* (London: Duncan Baird Publishers, 2009).

## LEARNING OBJECTIVES

By the time you have worked through this chapter, you should be able to

- Explain the indescribability of *dao*
- Describe Laozi's view of *sheng* (birth, live, grow, or produce)
- Explain Laozi's view that "the weak overcomes (or 'is better than') the strong"
- Describe Laozi's view of spontaneity or naturalness (*zi-ran*)
- Describe Laozi's view of non-action (*wu-wei*)

## KEY WORDS

*dao*, virtue (*de*), presence (*you*), absence (*wu*), non-action (*wu-wei*), spontaneity or naturalness (*zi-ran*), *sheng* (birth, live, grow, or produce), simplicity (*pu*, literally uncarved wood), reversion/returning (*fan*), *yin-yang*

## GUIDING QUESTIONS

Confucianism (in the *Analects* and the *Mengzi*, and the *Xunzi*—to be discussed in Chapter 8) advocates the practice of humanness and ritual propriety in order to restore social order and harmony. In this chapter, we will survey the ideas attributed to Laozi as presented in the *Daodejing* against the intellectual backdrop of Confucianism. In bringing the two traditions into a conversation, we will focus on the following guiding questions:

1. Does the practice of humanness and ritual propriety prescribed by Confucius and his followers (see Chapters 4, 5, and 8) really work? Might this practice lead to ethical and political coercion and thus destroy the naturalness and spontaneity of life?
2. In what way might the advocacy of social hierarchy (implied in both Confucianism and Moism/Mohism) lead to unnecessary, "puffed-up" desires?
3. What is Laozi's alternative way to restore social order and harmony?

## INTRODUCTION

The *Daodejing* (*Tao Te Ching*) is the first sourcebook of the school of Daoism (Taoism) or Daoist philosophy.[1] The received version of the *Daodejing* was edited by Wang Bi (226–49 CE), who organized the verses collected in the work into eighty-one chapters grouped as two parts (with part one containing Chapters 1–37 and part two Chapters 38–81). Another version of the text is the Ma-wang-dui (Ma-wang-tui) silk text, dated around 200 BCE, and unearthed in 1973 in Ma-wang-dui in central east China (present-day Hunan Province). The Ma-wang-dui text contains no chapter division markers and includes two manuscripts (A and B). The ordering of the chapters in this text is the reverse of that of the Wang Bi version (i.e., Chapter 1 of the Ma-wang-dui version is Chapter 38 of the received version). The most recently discovered version is preserved in a bundle of bamboo strips excavated in 1993 in Guodian in central east China (present-day Hubei Province). The text of this version was written by various hands on seventy-one strips of bamboo in three untitled bundles. These strips are dated approximately 350 BCE. A most notable feature of this edition is the absence of attack against Confucian values (e.g., Chapter 19 of the "received" version).[2] This suggests that originally the *Daodejing* may not have been as strongly opposed to the *Analects* as the dominant traditional account takes it to be.

---

1   The English translation "Daoism" is also used to refer to a native Chinese Daoist religion (*Dao-jiao*) that emerged in the East Han Dynasty (25–220 CE). A brief discussion of the relationship between Daoism as a philosophy (*Dao-jia*) and Daoism as a religion will be given in the concluding section of this chapter.

2   See Chapter 19 of the Guodian version, translated by Robert G. Henricks (*Lao Tzu's Tao Te Ching: A Translation of the Startling New Documents Found at Guodian* [New York: Columbia University Press, 2000]).

道 - dao 德 - de 经 - jing

The eighty-one chapters of the *Daodejing* consist of terse, aphoristic, and often cryptic verses. The Chinese character for *dao* (道) comprises two elements, one radical (辶) on the left meaning "to walk" or "to run" and the other on the right (首) denoting "a head." The character literally means (something alive is walking on) "a path" or "a road." But by metaphoric extension, it also means "a method" and "a principle."

"*Dao*" is the first word in Chapter 1 (Wang Bi's version: Part I), and "*de*" (德) the first word in Chapter 38 (Wang Bi's version: Part II), hence the first two words in the book's title: "*dao-de*." The word "*de*" means "virtue," but it is also a homonym of the word "*de*" *[another word w/ same spelling, but diff. meaning]* (得) which means "to obtain." Therefore, "*de*" is *dao* spoken of in terms of particular things or persons; it is "what is achieved when a person internalizes some *dao*, learns and practices it." The word "*jing*" (经) means "authoritative text" or "scripture." In short, the *Daodejing* is an authoritative text or scripture on the guiding principles in the world and in human affairs.

Tradition attributes the authorship of the work to Laozi (Lao Tzu, literally "The Old Master") and hence the work is so named. However, little is known about the historical Laozi; much of the popular lore about him is historically dubious.

According to one legendary account of Laozi's authorship, the wise sage had decided *[Speculated History (lacks evidence)]* to withdraw from Zhou society (770–476 BCE) in his later years to live in solitude. He rode an ox to Hangu Pass (in modern Henan Province) where the pass officer Guan Yi implored him to write down his doctrine. Thus, the *Daodejing* came to be written. It is a nice story but there is a lack of reliable historical evidence to support this legend. Additionally, the story seems to go against the political concerns expressed in the book,[4] which casts further doubt on its veracity.

According to another account in the earliest general history of China *Shi Ji* (*The Records of the Historian*) by Sima Qian (c. 145–90 BCE), the author of the *Daodejing* was *[Another account (Li Er - author)]* a person named Li Er, a native of the state of Chu (in modern Henan Province), a senior contemporary of Confucius, and an archivist for the Zhou government. According to this account, Confucius once went to Zhou to consult Li Er about issues of ritual and returned with great reverence for him. However, this account might have been fabricated by the followers of the *Daodejing* to bolster their claim that the *Daodejing* was superior to the *Analects*.

At any rate, there seems to have been a connection between Laozi and Confucius; the teachings contained in the *Analects* and the *Daodejing* have long been interpreted *[Humanness & ritual propriety would lead people away from dao.]* intertextually. According to the traditional account, the two works are diametrically opposed to each other, with the quest of the *Daodejing* being to transcend the social and political edifice built by the *Analects* based on humanness and ritual propriety—which Laozi believed would lead people astray from the genuine *dao* (see Chapters 3, 18, 19). Nonetheless, recent scholarship on the *Analects* and the *Daodejing* has underscored an

---

3  Chad Hansen, *Tao Te Ching on the Art of Harmony: The New Illustrated Edition of the Chinese Philosophical Masterpiece* (London: Duncan Baird Publishers, 2009), Introduction, 32.

4  The legend may have been imposed on the *Daodejing* by later religious Daoist practitioners in the East Han Dynasty. According to the Daoist religion, the highest human attainment is to become immortal, and the best place to practice for immortality is in the secluded setting of the mountains, away from the noise of secular life.

overlap between the two. One salient piece of evidence for this recent view is that the idea of wu-wei (literally "non-action," but contextually "not pushing," or "not forcing"), which figures centrally in the Daodejing, also appears explicitly and implicitly in the Analects (see 15:5, 2:1, 17:19).[5]

Many hands probably went into the authorship of the Daodejing. As Hansen points out, "[t]he traditional biographical information about Laozi is largely either fanciful (he lived to be 160 to 200 years old), historically dubious (he taught Confucius), or contradictory (his hometown, official posts, age). So in the sense that Laozi refers to the single author of the Daodejing, there may never have been one. There were more likely many."[6] However, for the sake of convenience, I will use the name "Laozi" to refer to the author(s) of the Daodejing, without assuming that the work was composed solely by a historical Laozi.

As we have noted in the Introduction to Chapter 4 of this volume, ancient China went through severe social upheavals during the Warring States period. The old social and political system in which a king ruled through vassal lords in multi-states had broken down. Inter-state wars were frequent and disastrous. During this time of social crisis, a host of questions took on a sense of urgency: What is the right Way (dao)? How can states (particularly the small and weak ones) and individuals survive? Many schools of thought arose during this period, each proposing its own solutions to social problems and its model for an ideal society. Philosophical schools were proliferating so rapidly that historians have called this period a time when "a hundred schools" were all competing to be heard. The most prominent schools of this time were Confucianism, Daoism, Legalism, and Moism (Mohism). Confucianism stressed moral cultivation and social order. Moism preached impartial love and no-war. The Daoism in the Daodejing advised people to live according to zi-ran (naturalness or spontaneity), that is, in harmony with the way or dao.

The Daodejing is not a neat philosophical treatise on one specific idea. Among the many passages on dao, some tend to be more descriptive and perhaps even metaphysical (Chapters 1, 4, 21, 25, 32, 34, 40, 42, 51), while others are more prescriptive (making political suggestions, for example), focusing on the patterns and functions of dao and what it means to us (Chapters 2, 8, 9, 14, 16, 18, 32, 37, 38, 46, 47, 48, 53, 55, 58, 59, 60, 62, 65), and still others deal with the teaching or language of dao (Chapters 35, 67). The temptation to assume that the term "dao" in its multiple occurrences must have the same meaning should be resisted. Additionally, the connection between chapters and sometimes even between verses within a chapter is often tenuous. The frequent occurrences of "so" or "therefore" (gu, or shi gu) in many of the chapters can appear

---

5   Edward Slingerland argues that wu-wei is "a common ideal for both Daoists and Confucians" (Effortless Action—Wuwei as Conceptual Metaphor and Spiritual Ideal in Early China [Oxford: Oxford University Press, 2003], Preface).

6   Chad Hansen, A Daoist Theory of Chinese Thought (New York: Oxford University Press, 2000), 210; also see D.C. Lau, Lao Tzu: Tao Te Ching (Harmondsworth, UK: Penguin Classics, 1963), Introduction, 12, 14–15.

surprising, since the content after "so" and "therefore" does not seem to follow logically from what comes before.

Also important to note is that, along with the untidiness of the text, there seem to be significant tensions, inconsistencies, or paradoxes. For instance, *dao* seems to be both describable (Laozi seems to be doing just this in writing the *Daodejing*!) and indescribable (Chapter 1); *dao* seems to be an independent existence before heaven and earth (Chapters 25, 42) and yet immanent in everything in the world (Chapter 51).

Given the above features of the text, it would be better to treat the *Daodejing* not as a neat philosophical treatise on one idea, but as a symphony with multiple, yet consistent, motifs.[7]

## DOING PHILOSOPHY
### Dao *versus Logos*

If you read ancient Greek philosophy, you may see an affinity between *dao* and logos. Logos is a very important concept in ancient Greek philosophy that carries a wide range of meanings and connotations, including thought, reason, order/pattern, and a principle of origination. Heraclitus (540–480/470 BCE), for example, was the first to formulate a theory of logos. He used the notion to describe the source that animates (akin to fire) and the principle that governs the cosmos. The Sophists used it to refer to forms or structures of argument that they could (for the purpose of persuasion) manipulate. Aristotle used it to refer to a reasoned argument that aims at truth. The Stoics took it to be the source and pattern of the cosmos.

*Dao* in the *Daodejing* can also mean the source, principle, origination, order/pattern, speech, and thought. But it is different from logos in at least three important senses. First, although *dao* is considered to be the source and the order of the universe, a material force, it is explained in terms of water (symbolizing the feminine) rather than fire (symbolizing the masculine). Second, the Sophists and Aristotle derived patterns of reasoning from the logos, but no ancient Chinese philosopher has ever sought to derive formal reasoning patterns from *dao*. In addition, "Logos" was later appropriated in Christianity as an equivalent term for God, as in John 1:1, "In the beginning was the Word [Logos], and the Word was with God, and the Word was God," whereas *dao* itself was never taken to be a personal God in ancient Chinese thought.

---

7   There is a general consensus among scholars on the *Daodejing* that it does have a consistent tone or consistent vision. See Chad Hansen, *A Daoist Theory*, 210; Philip J. Ivanhoe, trans., *The Daodejing of Laozi* (Indianapolis: Hackett, 2002), Introduction, xv; and Lau, Introduction, 15.

## IS *DAO* INDESCRIBABLE?

Readers of the *Daodejing* are very likely to be fascinated yet puzzled by a number of chapters that portray *dao* negatively or obscurely. For example, the text asserts variously that *dao* is "empty" and "bottomless" (Chapter 4); *dao* "has no name" (Chapters 32, 37); it is "hidden and nameless" (Chapter 41); it is "[i]nfinite and boundless" and "cannot be given any name" (Chapter 14); we "do not know its name" (Chapter 25); it is imperceptible to us (Chapters 14, 21). More confusing are the first four stanzas in Chapter 1, which seem to assert that the genuine *dao* cannot be talked about. Here are the first four stanzas in word-by-word translation:

| 1. | 道 | 可 | 道 | 非 | 常 | 道 |
|---|---|---|---|---|---|---|
| | *dao* (n. or v.) | *ke* | *dao* (v.) | *fei* | *chang* | *dao* (n. or v.) |
| | way; speak, walk, guide, lead | can | speak, walk, guide, lead | (is) not | constant | way; speak, walk, guide, lead |
| 2. | 名 | 可 | 名 | 非 | 常 | 名 |
| | *ming* (n. or v.) | *ke* | *ming* (v.) | *fei* | *chang* | *ming* (n. or v.) |
| | name/ naming | can | being named | (is) not | constant | name/ naming |
| 3. | 无 | 名 | 天 | 地 | 之 | 始 |
| | *wu* | *ming* (n. or v.) | *tian* | *di* | *zhi* | *shi* |
| | without/do not have | name (n.) or naming (v.) | heaven | earth | possessive apostrophe | beginning/ source |
| 4. | 有 | 名 | 万 | 物 | 之 | 母 |
| | *you* | *ming* (n. or v.) | *wan* | *wu* | *zhi* | *mu* |
| | with/have | name (n.) or naming (v.) | ten thousand | things | possessive apostrophe | mother |

These stanzas have been translated differently. Let's look at three examples:

1.

The Tao [Dao] that can be told of is not the eternal Tao;
The name that can be named is not the eternal name.
The Nameless is the origin of Heaven and Earth;
The Named is the mother of all things. (Chan)[8]

2.

A Way that can be followed is not a constant Way.
A name that can be named is not a constant name.
Nameless, it is the beginning of Heaven and Earth;
Named, it is the mother of the myriad creatures. (Ivanhoe)[9]

3.

The Tao [Dao] that can be trodden is not the enduring and unchanging Tao.
The name that can be named is not the enduring and unchanging name.
[Conceived of as] having no name, it is the Originator of heaven and earth.
[Conceived of as] having a name, it is the Mother of all things. (Legge)[10]

A popular interpretation of these opening stanzas of the *Daodejing* is that dao is "a mystic reality."[11] Chan's translation ("the eternal Dao," "the eternal name") and Legge's translation ("the enduring and unchanging Dao," "the enduring and unchanging name," and "the Originator") seem to support this interpretation of dao. Some even argue that "the ultimate Reality [Dao] is nameless; in other words it cannot be depicted by human language.... The opening passage of *Daodejing* tells us that *the world as we know it* is thus the result of the combined contribution of the reality-as-it-is and our human conception manifested in human language,"[12] and that "[n]ot only is *Dao* imperceptible to our senses, it is also unknowable by our limited cognition. We can even say that Dao is ineffable exactly because it is *cognitively closed* to us."[13] From a hermeneutical point of

---

8   Wing-tsit Chan, trans., *Daodejing* (*Tao Te Ching*), in *A Source Book in Chinese Philosophy* (Princeton: Princeton University Press, 1969).

9   Ivanhoe, trans. According to Chad Hansen, the traditional translation of Chapter 1 takes the term "dao" as a proper name, but it in fact functions as a general name (Hansen, *A Daoist Theory*, 215). Ivanhoe's translation of Chapter 1 shows some sensitivity to this understanding of the word "dao." His translation does not take the word "dao" to be a proper name: instead of translating "dao" as "the Way," he rendered it "A Way." However, since it is not always suitable to use "a way" to translate the word "dao" in all its occurrences in the *Daodejing*, I will keep the Chinese word "dao" untranslated.

10   James Legge, *The Texts of Taoism*, vol. 1 (Oxford: Oxford University Press, 1891; reissued New York: Dover, 1962).

11   Benjamin Schwartz, *The World of Thought in Ancient China* (Cambridge, MA: Harvard University Press, 1985), 194.

12   Jeeloo Liu, *An Introduction to Chinese Philosophy—From Ancient Philosophy to Chinese Buddhism* (Oxford: Blackwell Publishing, 2006), 133.

13   Liu, 137.

*(handwritten margin note: Dao similar to transcendentalism)*

view, such readings of *dao* in the *Daodejing* are understandable, because scholars often tend to see a similarity between the idea of *dao* and the idea of transcendental reality in Western philosophy (Plato's forms, God, Kant's noumenon, and so on).

But is *dao* really indescribable by "human language"? It seems not. The *Daodejing* does speak a lot about *dao*. The text not only uses terms and phrases like "*da*" (great) (Chapter 25), "the origin of heavens and the earth" and "the mother of all things" (Chapter 1) to describe *dao*, but also devotes considerable space to explaining the applications and functions of *dao* in social and personal contexts.[14]

*(handwritten margin note: Paradox)*

Hence, the paradox of *dao* is conspicuous: If *dao* is without name/description and not accessible to perception, how can one apply it or put it into practice? Conversely, if we do describe *dao* (in some way) and if we do practice it, why is it that the *Daodejing* stresses that *dao* is without name/description or cannot be named? It seems that the answers to these questions hinge largely on how we understand *dao*'s indescribability in the difficult chapters mentioned in the beginning of this section.

*(handwritten margin note: 2 senses of describability)*

Before getting to those chapters, let's first distinguish between two senses of indescribability—the relative and the absolute. Indescribability in its relative sense, I contend, means that something is indescribable in some qualified way, relative to a certain norm of description, or relative to someone's capacity. Thus, something can be indescribable in one sense (according to one norm of description, or due to one's limited capacity) but perfectly describable in a different sense (according to another form of description, or when one acquired a certain capacity). In this relative sense, indescribability does not imply that language itself is inadequate. In contrast, when something (a state or an experience) is claimed to be indescribable in its absolute sense, it is thought to be beyond *any* language description, as if language itself is intrinsically inadequate to the task. Absolute indescribability can be called (philosophical or religious) ineffability. To illustrate the proposed distinction, let's start with some examples of relative indescribability.

*(handwritten margin note: OF Relative indescribability)*

EXAMPLE 1: *X is not describable to a particular person due to that person's lack of some required (technical) capacity.* Something (e.g., Einstein's theory of relativity, quantum mechanics, or rocket science) may be beyond an individual's ability to comprehend and describe. For instance, rocket science is beyond the average elementary school student and the student may complain that rocket science is "not describable." But no doubt rocket scientists do understand rocket science and can describe how it works. Rocket scientists do exchange ideas about rocket science, and if they are good at translating complicated theories into simple language, they may very well help many laymen understand. In general, even those who do not

---

14  On people who follow *dao* (*you dao zhe*), see Chapters 24, 30, 31, 60; on people who practice *dao* skilfully (*shan wei dao zhe*), see Chapters 15, 23, 65, cf. Chapter 68; on saints who practice *dao*, see Chapters 2, 3, 7, 12, 22, 27, 28, 29, 39, 47, 49, 57, 58, 60, 63, 66, 70, 71, 72, 78, 79, 81.

understand rocket science and thus deem it "not describable" to them w
agree that rocket science is not "ineffable" or "mystical." Rocket science is
merely beyond some people's comprehension and ability to speak about it,
not beyond humanity altogether.

EXAMPLE 2: *X is not describable to a particular person due to that person's
lack of certain basic linguistic capacity.* A pre-linguistic child can *know*
through experience the danger of putting fingers to a fire, but the child does
not say "Fire is dangerous," or "Fire hurts." In this case, we may say that the
child is unable to speak of the danger of fire (even though the act of avoiding fire in the future shows that the child *understands* its danger). Upon
acquiring language, the child will be able to describe the danger of fire. The
child's not being able to articulate it verbally before learning the language
does not imply that the child did not have such and such experience. Also,
it is not because *language itself* is somehow lacking—it is due to the child's
lack of certain basic language ability.

EXAMPLE 3: *X is not describable at one time to all humanity but becomes
describable later (at least to some people).* An aspect of reality, once cognitively closed to us, may become cognitively accessible to us via instruments
and devices. Genes were once cognitively closed to scientists, but by using
sophisticated devices gene scientists can observe them. *In retrospect*, gene
scientists may say that gene codes were once closed to them. They realized
their sensory limitations because they (via the assistance of instruments)
have gone beyond previous limits—they have been there on "the other side"
of the limits. In this case, scientists (before the discovery of genes) ought
not to be blamed for their lack of capacity to describe genes, nor is language
itself to be accused of being inadequate.

EXAMPLE 4: *We sometimes say a situation (or a person) is indescribably (or
unspeakably) bad (good, or strange).* Here the indescribability of a situation
means that it is hard to find proper descriptions for the situation, or that
we want to stress the tremendous impact of the situation on us. The situation's being "indescribable" does not necessarily mean that the situation is
beyond *any* description. "The situation is extraordinarily bad," for example,
can count as a description.

The examples can go on, but I think you've got my point—relative indescribability is
conditioned to some norms of description, or to the describer's linguistic capacity. In
none of the above examples do we deem language itself to be inadequate.

The above examples seem too mundane to interest those philosophers who are particularly interested in a kind of indescribability that is *intrinsically* and *forever* beyond

*every* human's linguistic *capacity*—global, absolute indescribability, ineffability. God, for example, is sometimes understood as absoplutely ineffable.

Now let's return to the *Daodejing*. Is the *Daodejing* arguing that the *dao* is indescribable in a relative or absolute sense? Popular interpretations of the opening stanzas of Chapter 1 and other chapters mentioned in the beginning of this section tend to have us believe that *dao* is ineffable in the absolute sense. However, it seems more plausible and more fruitful to take *dao* as indescribable only in some restricted and qualified sense, relative to three possible contexts. *Dao* can be said to be not describable (a) relative to the norm for describing ordinary physical objects, (b) as a way of life commended by Laozi in contrast with other ways of life, and (c) due to the intuitive distinction between a direct experience of something and a linguistic description of it. Let's now look at each of these contexts in which *dao* can be understood as indescribable.

First, the passages that speak of *dao* as indescribable (Chapters 1, 4, 14, 21, 25, 52) can be read against the backdrop of Laozi's pre-scientific speculations on the nature of the cosmos in his time. In this reading, *dao* refers to a primordial and undifferentiated energy, symbolized in the image of uncarved wood, *pu* 朴 (Chapters 19, 28, 32, 37, 57). *Dao* is thus "described" as "empty," "bottomless," "hidden and nameless"; it does not refer to entities or objects with names. This field of primordial energy is regarded as the source or mother of everything. "It [*Dao*] seems to be the ancestor of the myriad creatures" (Chapter 4). It arose "before Heaven and Earth," and one can call it "the mother of Heaven and Earth" (Chapter 25; cf. Chapters 21, 52). Primordial though it is, *dao* is also "*in the universe*" rather than outside of it. (In this respect, it is rather unlike Plato's forms which lie beyond this world.[15]) *Dao's* being "before Heaven and earth," on this interpretation, is not after all "transcendentally before," but in the mundane sense that a mother is before her children.

This reading is plausible, in that it sheds light on some of the obscure passages in the *Daodejing*. The idea of primordial energy, for example, explains the intangibility of *dao*—that is, it is not to be perceived and felt in the way that ordinary objects are, and as such it cannot be named, cannot be heard, and is vague and elusive, even though it is real (Chapters 1, 4, 14, 21). *Dao* thus symbolizes a state or an image without objects (*wu wu zhi zhuang* 无 物 之 状, *wu wu zhi* xiang 无 物 之 象, Chapter 14).

Thus, *dao* is like the acupuncture points and meridians in the human body, which according to Traditional Chinese Medicine are real, despite the fact that we cannot see them directly. We can nevertheless feel their effects. *Dao* (as *qi*—energy) may thus be said to be indescribable relative to the way in which we describe ordinary objects (Chapter 21).

But why is *dao* often read to be absolutely indescribable? One reason for such a reading is that it is based on too narrow an understanding of what counts as description. It seems wrong to say that *dao* goes beyond *the limits of language* per se (understood as all kinds of linguistic activities), for after all Laozi does describe *dao* in many different ways. According to him, *dao* is the root of Heaven and Earth (Chapters 1, 4); it is the female/mother of the universe (Chapters 1, 6, 10, 20, 21, 25, 52, 59) with infinite

---

15  Cf. Charles Wei-hsun Fu, "Lao-tzu's Conception of Tao," *Inquiry* 16 (1973), 369 and A.C. Graham, *Disputers of the Tao: Philosophical Argument in Ancient China* (La Salle, IL: Open Court, 1989), 222–23.

potential; it is like water (Chapters 8, 68, 73, 78, 81) that is non-competing (Chapters 66, 68, 73, 81; cf. Chapters 3, 7–9, 22); it is like an infant (Chapters 10, 20, 28, 49, 55) that is resilient, focused, and pure; it is like uncarved wood (*pu*, 朴) (Chapters 19, 28, 32, 37, 57) that is simple and unfixed or unpolluted by human conventions. What's the justification for not taking these descriptions as description?

Second, *dao* as the way or teaching commended by Laozi can be said to be indescribable to those who do not subscribe to it. Throughout the *Daodejing* Laozi keeps warning his readers that he is advocating a *dao* that many may not understand. Perhaps only a few will be able to understand Laozi's *dao*; many others will actually laugh at it.

> My doctrines are very easy to understand and very easy to practice, / But none in the world can understand or practice them. / My doctrines have a source (Nature); my deeds have a mother (Tao). / It is because people do not understand this that they do not understand me. / Few people know me, and therefore I am highly valued. / Therefore the sage wears a coarse cloth on top and carries jade within his bosom. (Chapter 70)[16]

> When the highest type of men hear Tao, / They diligently practice it. / When the average type of men hear Tao, / They half believe in it. / When the lowest type of men hear Tao, / They laugh heartily at it. / If they did not laugh at it, it would not be Tao. (Chapter 41)[17]

There are at least two reasons why many do not understand Laozi's *dao*. One reason may be that some (perhaps especially the ruling class) are too much obsessed with material desires, so Laozi remarks that even though "broad ways" are extremely even, the ruling class are still fond of "by-paths" (Chapter 53). Another reason may be that the ruling class are too competitive (*zeng*) and aggressive (*you-wei*) to comprehend Laozi's message, which calls for non-obsessive, non-possessive acting (*wu/ bu wei*) (Chapters 2, 3, 10, 37, 38, 43, 48, 57, 63, 64) and non-competitiveness (*bu zeng*) (Chapters 3, 37). In short, many may be stuck in a way of life in which Laozi's *dao* is alien to their thinking or beyond their "horizon" (to borrow a word from Heidegger and Gadamer). Thus, for them, Laozi's *dao* appears to be ridiculous, incomprehensible, and indeed indescribable by means of their language (concerned with material desires, competing, acting aggressively, etc.). To someone whose sole concern in life is selfish physical pleasure, the value of sacrifice and altruism would defy articulation.[18] In

---

16  W.T. Chan's translation of the *Daodejing* (*Tao Te Ching*), in *A Source Book in Chinese Philosophy* (Princeton: Princeton University Press, 1969). Unless otherwise noted, quotations from the *Daodejing* are from this translation.

17  Chapter 20 gives a vivid description of how a *dao* practitioner is different from others who are strangers to *dao*.

18  Consider Wittgenstein's remark: "It is difficult to tell a short-sighted man how to get somewhere. Because you cannot say to him: 'Look at that church tower ten miles away and go in that direction'" (*Culture and Value*, G.H. Van Wright, ed., Peter Winch, trans. [Chicago: The University of Chicago Press, 1980], 1e). To the short-sighted man the instruction would not really count as an instruction.

this context, the indescribability of Laozi's *dao* (teaching) is ultimately linked to the limitations that exist in the minds of the listeners.

To those unsympathetic to Laozi's teaching, Lao's *dao* is indescribable because from their perspective it cannot be given a meaningful description. Very likely, Laozi's unsympathetic contemporaries simply *did not want to* listen to his *dao*, even though they may not necessarily have been incapable of understanding it. Otherwise, there would have been no point for Laozi to preach his *dao* to them at all. While Laozi regretted that his teachings had not been understood and implemented,[19] he continued to preach his *dao*. His persistence in this respect shows that he was confident that at least some would (at some point) understand his teachings, despite the fact that in reality "no one in the whole world *has been able to* understand or implement them" (Chapter 70).[20]

### DOING PHILOSOPHY
#### *Does Laozi Himself Know Dao?*

In Chapter 56 Laozi claims that "*zhi zhe bu yan, yan zhe bu zhi* (知 者 不 言, 言 者 不 知)," which is translated by Chan as "He who knows does not speak [about *dao*]. He who speaks does not know [*dao*]." (Compare with *Kena Upanishad* II: 4: "It is not understood by those who [say they] understand It. It is understood by those who [say they] understand It not.") According to this translation, if one knows *dao*, then one should not speak about it; if he speaks about it (as Laozi did in the *Daodejing*), then he does not know what *dao* is. Thus, by his own text Laozi suggests that he does not know what he is talking about!

But this is a situation created by interpretation. It also runs directly against Laozi's emphasis on honest attitude toward knowing things—"[t]o pretend to know when you do not know is a disease" (Chapter 71)—an attitude shared by both Confucius (see the *Analects* 2:17) and Socrates (*Apology* 21d).

Fortunately, we can translate and interpret the claim differently: "The wise (*zhi zhe* 知 /智 者, where *zhi* 知 and *zhi* 智 are sometimes interchangeable characters) do not promote government decrees (*yan* 言; cf. Chapters 2, 17, and 23), and those who promote government decrees are not wise." This translation coheres nicely with how the word "*yan*" is understood in Chapters 2, 17, and 23. On this translation, nowhere is there a trace of the puzzle of Laozi speaking about what he does not know.

---

19  Ivanhoe's translation of the second stanza of Chapter 70 ("no one in the whole world has been able to understand or implement them") seems better than Chan's ("none in the world can understand or practice them [my doctrines])." Chan's translation may give readers the impression that Laozi's doctrines cannot be understood.

20  Ivanhoe's translation, emphasis added.

Third, the indescribability of *dao* is related to the fundamental difference between directly experiencing something and understanding the thing through a description of it. The notion of indescribability comes into play when we, knowing this difference, insist that we be able to capture with words what is only accessible to us through direct experience. For example, if we smell the aroma of coffee, we know that words cannot capture the aroma of coffee in the same way that our noses can "understand." Suppose Peter, who had never smelt coffee, asked his friend John, a coffee lover, to tell him what the aroma of coffee is like. In response, John might say, "Let's go to have a coffee, and you can smell it yourself." Or John mighty say, "It simply smells like coffee!" or "It smells distinctively fragrant." The reply "It simply smells like coffee!" would not satisfy Peter at all. The reply "It smells distinctively fragrant" would not fare much better. How is Peter to understand without actually smelling coffee?

John and Peter can be likened respectively to the philosopher who has gone out of Plato's cave and a prisoner who is still stuck inside it. If the philosopher (John) describes what he has seen outside the cave to the prisoner (Peter), even assuming that John still speaks the same language as he did when he was inside the cave, Peter would still not understand John's description in the same way John understands it—Peter knows all the words John uses in the description, but no matter how meticulous John's description is, Peter still does not *experience* the world outside and so cannot be said to understand it in the same way John can.

By asking what coffee smells like, Peter seems to expect that a description of an experience can somehow substitute for the experience itself. But his expectation will fail, because it is based on a false assumption. Language cannot do what it is *not* equipped to do. When his expectation fails, Peter may invoke the notion of indescribability by which he blames language for not being capable of doing what it is *expected* to be capable of doing. But it is not reasonable to expect that language can do what it is not capable of doing. Why must we require that a verbal description of the aroma of coffee reveal to us what only our sense of smell can?[21] Why must words be able to capture that which only experience can?[22]

If the above distinction between experiencing something and understanding it through a description of it makes sense, then the first two verses of Chapter 1 may be plausibly translated as: "*Dao* can be talked about, [but it is] not the constant *dao-ing* (i.e., experiencing and practicing *dao*) / Name can be designated, [but it is] not the constant naming."

Thus, the gist in these two verses is that language (rules, regulations, and doctrines) does not act as a substitute for experience. In fact, only after one has directly experienced a thing (say, the aroma of coffee) can one truly understand a verbal description of it. Moreover, one should not expect language (rules, regulations, and doctrines) to be capable of fixing or always fitting the ever changing experiences. Language

---

21 Regarding the idea of indescribability of the aroma of coffee, see Wittgenstein, *Philosophical Investigations*, section 610.

22 What Peter really needs in the aroma of coffee scenario is not a *description* of the aroma of coffee, but an invitation to *smell* coffee. Similarly, what the prisoner in Plato's cave urgently needs is not a description of the "outside" world, but a command: "Get out of the cave and see for yourself!"

may be helpful and necessary to human transactions, but it does not replace direct, concrete experience. As Hansen explains, "*Daos* and names that guide require interpretation in each unique local situation. Guiding *daos* cannot be fixed because they rely on names (or a counterpart) that we have to interpret into concrete action in our own circumstances."[23] In other words, we should not demand language to capture or replace the fluid and ever changing experiences. Accordingly, what may be wrong with Confucianism, as Laozi sees it, is that rituals and names (language) are susceptible to ossification; they may be treated as if they can work independently, without people's responsive participation and interpretation in concrete situations. When rituals and names are ossified, people live in uniformity and conformity; they lose their spontaneous individual lives.

If the above analysis is reasonable, then *dao* is not indescribable in any absolute sense, and it does not designate any transcendental, mystical entity. It is indescribable only in some relative senses as I have explained above, and it is a metaphor of discourse which aims at teaching people (particularly rulers) pragmatic lessons (for example, "Do not confuse a direct experience of something with a linguistic description of it"). In short, the metaphysical reading of *dao* seems sterile, and a pragmatic reading seems more plausible.

### LAOZI'S PHILOSOPHY OF *SHENG* (生)

Just as the Dhammapada and the *Fundamental Verses on the Middle Way* are sensitive to impermanence or emptiness, the *Daodejing* is particularly attentive to how things change. The *Daodejing* sees the cosmos and all the things in it as a constant *sheng* process of *dao*.

The term "*sheng*" occurs thirty-five times (about half the number of occurrences of the word "*dao*") in seventeen chapters of the *Daodejing* (Chapters 2, 7, 15, 25, 30, 34, 39, 40, 42, 50, 51, 55, 59, 64, 75, 76). In these chapters, "*sheng*" is a term that means generally "happening" and implies an activity or process going on, but its specific meaning changes with circumstance. In the *Daodejing*, it means "to produce," "to give birth," "to grow," "to develop," "to emerge," "to occur," or "to live." The idea may originally come from observations of natural happenings, such as the "birth" or "giving birth" to a baby, or the "emerging" of a sprout. Laozi uses *sheng* as a technical term to signify the continuous process in which everything in the world participates. In order to better understand Laozi's views on the idea of *sheng*, let's divide our discussion into several subsections: (1) *Sheng* as a beginningless and endless process; (2) *Dao*'s *sheng* and God's creation; (3) *Sheng* versus human death.

#### 1. Sheng *as a Beginningless and Endless Process*

Some chapters of the *Daodejing* seem to suggest that the process of *sheng* has a metaphysical (absolute) starting point. For example, Chapter 42 may be read this way.

23  Hansen, *Tao Te Ching on the Art of Harmony*, 209.

Tao produced the One (*dao sheng yi* 道 生 一). / The One produced the
two (*yi sheng er* 一 生 二). / The two produced the three (*er sheng san* 二 生
三). / And the three produced the ten thousand things (*san sheng wan wu*
三 生 万 物). / The ten thousand things carry the yin and embrace the yang
and through the blending of the material force (*ch'i*) [*qi*, "vital energies"]
they achieve harmony. (Chapter 42)

This chapter has been traditionally read as holding the view that *dao* as the metaphysical
starting point created everything in the world, as Aristotle's First Cause or the God of
Genesis did. On this reading, *dao* is seen as temporally prior to everything else existing
as a unity (the One), and then somehow (mysteriously) it split up into *yin* and *yang*
energies (the two), which further evolved into *yin*, *yang* and the union of both (the
three), and finally produced all the ten thousand things.

The appropriateness of this reading of Chapter 42 may be reinforced by a common
interpretation of Chapter 25 and Chapter 4. This interpretation suggests that the process
of *sheng* has a metaphysical starting point, which existed before the existence of heaven
and earth and before *di* (帝), the Supreme Ancestral Spirit.

There was something undifferentiated and yet complete, / Which existed
before heaven and earth. / Soundless and formless, it depends on nothing
and does not change (*bu gai* 不 改). / It operates everywhere and is free
from danger (*bu dai* 不 殆; Hansen has "without limits"). / It may be considered the mother of the universe. / I do not know its name; I call it Tao. /
If forced to give it a name; I shall call it Great. / Now being great means
functioning everywhere, / Functioning everywhere means far-reaching. /
Being far-reaching means returning to [*fan*] the original point. (Chapter 25)

Tao is empty (like a bowl), / It may be used but its capacity is never
exhausted. / It is bottomless, perhaps the ancestor of all things. / It blunts
its sharpness, / It unties its tangles. / It softens its light. / It becomes one
with the dusty world. / Deep and still, it appears to exist forever. / I do not
know whose son it is. / It seems to have existed before the Lord [*di*, the
Supreme Ancestral Spirit]. (Chapter 4)

But this interpretation of Chapters 42, 25, and 4 may be challenged for several reasons. First, the traditional reading of Chapter 42 seems problematic. In the *Daodejing*,
*dao* is often used interchangeably with the "One" (Chapters 10, 14, 22, 39); thus, to say
"Tao [*Dao*] produced the One" (Chapter 42) is to say that *dao* produced itself, or that
*dao* is self-produced. In other words, *dao* did not produce another thing called the
One. And given the parallel structure of the first four verses of Chapter 42, it would
be legitimate to expect that "The One produced two" be read as saying "The One
produced itself, which is two." But "The One produced itself, which is two" does not
seem to make sense. How does *dao*, or the One, split into two (*yin* and *yang*) if *yin*
and *yang* are not already in *dao*?

## DOING PHILOSOPHY
### Yin-Yang Diagram

The Yin and Yang symbol is a distinctive symbol of Daoism, as the Cross is for Christianity. Yin and Yang represent the negative and the positive polarities.

| YIN | YANG |
| --- | --- |
| The moon | The sun |
| The shady side of the hill | The sunny side of the hill |
| Cold | Warm |
| Female | Male |
| Death (the underworld) | Life (this world) |
| Passive force | Active force |

The Yin-Yang diagram is also called the Yin-Yang (female-male) Fish Diagram. It represents a harmonious whole with balanced and symmetrical opposites. The black eye of the white fish and the white eye of the black fish stand for the mutual containment, complementarity, and transformation of yin and yang: a flower in full blossom portends its withering; a full moon its dying crescent.

Yin-Yang was an important component of the Traditional Chinese Medicine theory. It refers to various antitheses in anatomy, physiology, pathology, diagnosis, and treatment. According to this theory, an individual is in good health if the two opposing forces (yin and yang) are balanced, and in ill-health when they are out of balance.

Moreover, the traditional reading portrays *dao* as directly producing the One, which is *dao* itself, but only *indirectly* (through *yin, yang*, and the union of both) producing all the ten thousand things. This reading implies that the "mother" of all ten thousand things is the "three," not *dao*. But the *Daodejing* says explicitly that *dao*, not the three, is the "mother" of the ten thousand things (Chapters 1, 52).

The traditional reading of Chapter 42 is based on the traditional punctuation and translation of it, but Chapter 42 can be punctuated and translated differently as follows:

*Dao* produces (unfolds) itself (One) as itself (*dao sheng yi yi* 道 生 一 一), / produces the two as the two (*sheng er er* 生 二 二), / produces the three as the three (*sheng san san* 生 三 三), / produces the ten thousand things (as the ten thousand things) (*sheng wan wu* 生 万 物). (my translation)

On this translation, *dao* does not start at a metaphysical point and produce things in a temporal and hierarchical manner—from the One to the Many. Rather, it synchronically unfolds each particular thing as it is. It does not favour a particular thing so that it produces it first (cf. Chapters 5 and 79). The One, the two, the three, and the ten thousand things are all unfolding themselves simultaneously.

Second, the above interpretation of Chapters 25 and 4 (which suggests a metaphysical starting point) also seems problematic. It is true that Laozi claims in Chapter 25 that *dao* "does not change" (*bu gai* 不 改), but he also says that "It [*Dao*] operates everywhere," which suggests that *dao* is always in motion. The word "*dao*," construed this way, is a symbol for both particular changes of things and for the totality of all changes. But it is not something that underlies all the changes that exist independently of them (such as substance, entity, or Platonic Form).[24]

Laozi's claim that *dao* "does not change" does not imply that the *dao* does not move at all. *Dao*'s "not changing" may mean that the patterns of *dao*'s movement do not change, as, for example, in the case of the patterns of the movements of planets or the pattern of the shift of seasons. It may also mean that a thing's *sheng* is a constant process of returning to its source. For instance, an acorn, given proper conditions, will produce an oak tree, which in turn will bear more acorns. In other words, an acorn goes through the whole process of sprouting, trunk growing, branching, and leaves flourishing (the last three can happen simultaneously), and then returns to acorns again. All life forms seem to follow this pattern of returning to their sources. Thus, *dao*'s "not changing" may mean that *dao* is self-sufficient (for "it depends on nothing") and there is nothing external to it, and hence there is nothing that can alter it. Implied in this returning movement of *dao* is a cyclical conception of time and being. According to this conception, there is no need to search for the First Cause of Aristotle or the God of Genesis. In short, the universe is not caused but is in constant self-production (*sheng*); there is no metaphysical starting point.

If my interpretation of Chapters 42, 25, and 4 is reasonable, then *dao* is always in the process of *sheng*, always in motion; its generative process does not start with the One and then end with the ten thousand things. Rather, it constantly and endlessly produces all things in the cosmos. *Dao*'s process of *sheng* is "without limits" (*bu dai* 不 殆) since it is endlessly cyclical (Chapter 25); *Dao*'s generative power is "never exhausted" (Chapter 4). Laozi likens this infinite producing power of *dao* to the producing power of the female. He says,

The spirit of the valley never dies. / It is called the subtle and profound female. / The gate of the subtle and profound female / Is the root of the

---

24 Steve Coutinho characterizes *dao* as a "process" concept: "As a fundamental category, it [*dao*] places emphasis not so much on *what entities are* as *how processes occur*; it expresses the manner of changes, rather than the 'Being of entities'" (Steve Coutinho, "The Abduction of Vagueness: Interpreting the 'Laozi,'" *Philosophy East and West* 52:4 [October 2002]: 409).

Heaven and Earth. / It is continuous, and seems to be there. / Its use will never exhaust. (Chapter 6, Chan's translation modified)

*Dao*'s generative power "never dies" and "never exhaust[s]." Laozi would certainly admit that individual things (for example, a tree) die, but he does not seem to think individual things separate themselves from the whole *sheng* process of the cosmos. A tree, upon its death, returns to the natural environment and becomes a nurse log, which provides ecological facilitation to seedlings and nutrients to the insects on the ground. *Dao*'s process of *sheng* does not stop at the death of the nurse log. The cosmos is not a collection of isolated, independent entities which will sooner or later die, but a holistic and dynamic web of connections and functions in which everything in the cosmos participates. This holistic and dynamic view of the cosmos is very similar to the Buddha's view of interdependent-arising, or emptiness.

**DOING PHILOSOPHY**
*Laozi's* Sheng *and Pascal's Death:*
*How Would Laozi Respond to Pascal?*

Pascal in his *Pensées* portrays human life in the following way. "Let us imagine a number of men in chains," he says, "and all condemned to death, where some are killed each day in the sight of the others, and all those who remain see their own fate in that of their fellows, and wait their turn, looking at each other sorrowfully and without hope. It is an image of the condition of men."[25] Do you think this is a true depiction of human life? What implication does this depiction have? Given Laozi's view on *sheng* as a continuous process with no beginning or end, how do you think Laozi would respond to Pascal?

### 2. Dao's Sheng *and God's Creation*

The idea of the cosmos as *dao* unfolding itself offers a strong contrast to the idea of God creating the universe. There are several important differences between the two ideas.

First, although *dao*'s generative power is likened to a mother's reproductive power (Chapters 1, 5, 51, 52, 79), it is not seen as involving a conscious or rational process, as it is in the case of the father-God in the Book of Genesis.

Second, unlike the father-God who favours human beings (He created only Adam and Eve in His image), the mother-*dao* does not favour any particular thing she produces. "Heaven and Earth," following *dao* (Chapter 25), are not benevolent (*bu-ren* 不 仁) or partial (Chapter 5), but indifferent to all things. *Dao* "produces and fosters" everything (Chapter 51).[26]

25  Blaise Pascal, *Pensées*, W.F. Trotter, trans. (New York: Dover, 2003), §199.
26  Compare with Spinoza's God: "God is without passions, neither is he affected by any emotion of pleasure or pain ... strictly speaking, God does not love anyone" ("Ethics," in *The Chief Works of Benedict*

Third, *dao* is more primordial and primitive than *di* 帝 (Chapter 4), the Supreme Ancestral Spirit—a somewhat functional equivalent of God in Abrahamic religions, and the worship of *di* emerged as a later human practice. In this regard, the significance of the final verse in Chapter 4 ("It seems to have existed before *di*") must not be overlooked. The verse has been thought of as a pivotal move in the history of Chinese philosophy in which philosophy was liberated from mythology and religion. The idea that a transcendental God created the whole universe has never been an integral part of ancient Chinese philosophy.[27]

Finally, unlike the creator-God, the mother-*dao* produces things without possessing them or claiming credit for the production (Chapter 51). The sage, imitating the mother-*dao*, should do the same. Thus, "She produces them, but does not take possession of them. She acts, but does not rely on her own ability [does not expect any reward]. She accomplishes her task, but does not claim credit for it. It is precisely because she does not claim credit that her accomplishment remains with her" (Chapter 2).[28]

### 3. Sheng *versus Human Death*

Compared to what is said about *sheng* in the *Daodejing*, little is said about human death. But what it did say is significant.

While the *Daodejing* assumes that human death (the death of an individual) is inevitable (Chapter 76), it argues that in facing death one has to work on three things. First, one should try to avoid unnatural death by avoiding violence and fierceness,[29] because "[v]iolent and fierce people do not die a natural death" (Chapter 42; cf. Chapters 74, 76, 80). Second, one should know how to take care of one's body, not chasing after excessive desires (Chapter 12) (the word "body" is a translation of the Chinese word *shen* 身, which refers to physical body as well as personality and moral integrity). One should realize that "intensive striving after life" may lead to an unnatural death (Chapter 16). Third, one should get rid of egocentric thinking and follow the all-inclusive *dao*—a suggestion that is remarkably similar to the spiritual calling of "*Atman* is *Brahman*." To see this, let's examine Chapter 16:

> To know the eternal [*dao*] is called enlightenment. / Not to know the
> eternal is to act blindly to result in disaster. / He who knows the eternal
> is all-embracing. / Being all-embracing, he is impartial. / Being impartial,
> he is kingly (universal). / Being kingly, he is one with Nature. / Being one

---

*de Spinoza*, R.H. Elwes, trans. [London: G. Bell, 1901–12], V:17).

27 What comes close to the idea of Genesis is an ancient Chinese creation myth in which a mythic figure *Pan Gu* split the heaven and the earth with his magic axe. Then, as the myth goes, his bones turned into mountains, his veins and blood into rivers, his skin into earth, and his hair into vegetation. *Pan Gu*, however, is paradoxically considered to be one among many gods, not the God, and also it is obvious that he did not create the world *ex nihilo*.

28 Chan's translation modified; cf. Chapters 10, 77.

29 For Laozi's view on war, see Chapters 30, 31, and 46.

with Nature, he is in accord with Tao [*dao*]. / Being in accord with Tao
[*dao*], he is everlasting. / And is free from danger throughout his lifetime.

The suggestion in this chapter of the *Daodejing* is that, as in the case with the nurse
log discussed above, "[i]f one identifies with the *process* of change rather than with
individual substances, if one takes on an 'ontology of process' rather than an 'ontology
of substances,' then death loses its negativity."[30]

Another issue concerning Laozi's ideas on the death of an individual is whether he
believed in some kind of personal immortality. The answer to this question varies,
depending on how one translates and understands the last sentence in Chapter 33 (*si
er bu wang zhe shou* 死 而 不 亡 者 寿). Both Chan's and Legge's translations take
*bu wang* (不 亡) to mean "not perish." Their respective translations of the sentence
reads: "He who dies but does not really perish enjoys long life" and "he who dies and
yet does not perish, has longevity." Thus, Chan and Legge might lead to an interpretation according to which Laozi holds some kind of immortality. Chapter 50 may also
foster this interpretation:

> I have heard that those good at nurturing life, / On land do not meet with
> rhinoceroses or tigers, / And in battle do not encounter armoured war-
> riors. / Rhinoceroses find no place to thrust their horns; / Tigers find no
> place to sink their claws; / Soldiers find no place to drive in their blades. /
> Why is this? / Because such people have no place for death. (Chapter 50,
> Ivanhoe's translation)

In the last verse, "such people have no place for death," may suggest that these people
will never die. However, the textual evidence above (Chapters 16, 33, 50) suggests
an interpretation that does not warrant a belief in immortality. Most importantly,
Chapter 50 has to be taken metaphorically. First, the text does not imply that an individual's death does not happen, or those good at nurturing life literally do not die.
Second, the expression *bu wang* in Chapter 33 can be translated as "not forgotten," as
suggested by Henricks: "To die but not be forgotten, that's true long life." Henricks's
translation is based on the observation that the Chinese character *wang* ("to perish,"
"亡") and its homonym *wang* ("to be forgotten," "忘") are often used interchangeably
in ancient Chinese language. Thus, according to this translation, Laozi does not maintain any idea of literal immortality. Another plausible reading, perhaps a better one,
of *bu wang* has been suggested by Ivanhoe, who translates the verse as "Those who
die a natural death are long-lived." Ivanhoe's translation is based on thematic (rather
than linguistic) considerations. He notes that the message in the verse is reflected in
Chapter 42, which advocates the ideal of "dying a natural death."

---

30 Hans-Georg Moeller, *The Philosophy of the Daodejing* (New York: Columbia University Press,
2006), 125.

## DOING PHILOSOPHY
### Change: Laozi versus Aristotle

It is interesting to compare and contrast Laozi's and Aristotle's views on change.

1. Contrary to Aristotle, who is more like a mathematician in studying abstract (geometrical) spatial change, Laozi has no interest in any object's moving from point A to point B. Change for Laozi is almost always about particular states of affairs and concrete natural events (see Chapters 23, 25). Laozi focuses on the patterns of change and particularly what they mean to good living (Chapters 16, 59). In contrast, Aristotle has an objective, detached view on the changes of things; he has no interest in what moral lessons the changes of things can teach us. (There is a tendency in Chinese thought to moralize physical things. In Chinese painting and poetry, for example, pine and bamboo, among other things, are favourite subject matters, because the Chinese attribute to them positive qualities, which they consider human beings should have. Bamboo is tall and hollow, which is a symbol for modesty. It also has joints [*jie* 节] that allow them to withstand strong winds, so they are a symbol of inner strength that does not collapse in the face of an unfavourable force. Confucius, for example, speaks in the *Analects* [9:27] of the respectable character of pine and cypress: "when the year grows cold... we see that the pine and the cypress are the last to fade.")

2. Laozi provided no clear analysis of the cause(s) of change except for a cursory mention of *yin* and *yang* in Chapter 42. In contrast, Aristotle developed a formal theory of causation in terms of four causes: the material cause, the formal cause, efficient cause, and final (purposive) cause. For example, the material cause of a table is wood; its formal cause is the shape of the table; its efficient cause is the maker; the final cause is its purpose, namely, the table's use.

Based on the observations above, which view in your opinion is more likely to provide an impetus for the development of science—Laozi's or Aristotle's? Why?

## THE NATURE OF OPPOSITES

There is a cluster of ideas about opposites in the *Daodejing*, including the ideas of *yin* and *yang* (explained above), *you* and *wu* (translated by Chan as "being" and "non-being"), *rou ruo* and *gang qiang* (translated by Chan as "being weak" and "being strong") and good luck and bad luck. Since we have already explained the idea of *yin* and *yang* above, let's focus on the last three pairs of opposites, starting with the opposites of *you* and *wu*.

### 1. You versus wu

There seems to be an inconsistency regarding how the opposites of *you* and *wu* should be treated in the *Daodejing*, primarily involving Chapter 2 and Chapter 40. Using Chan's translation, the verses involving *you* and *wu* in the two chapters are as follows:

> "Being and non-being produce each other" (*you wu xiang sheng* 有 无 相 生). (Chapter 2)

> "All things in the world come from being. / And being comes from non-being" (*tian xia wan wu sheng yu you, you sheng yu wu* 天 下 万 物 生 于 有 / 有 生 于 无). (Chapter 40)

On this translation, *you* and *wu* in Chapter 2 are treated as ontologically equal, but in Chapter 40 *wu* is seen as ontologically more primordial than *you*. One may ask, why in Chapter 40 does Laozi only say "being comes from non-being"? Why didn't he say as he did in Chapter 2 that "being" also produces "non-being"? There seems to be an inconsistency here.

However, the inconsistency may be caused by Chan's translation; it may not be there in the text of the *Daodejing* itself. To show this, let us look at an alternative translation of the above two verses by Hansen. Hansen rendered the two verses respectively as

> Thus, "presence" [*you*] and "absence" [*wu*] mutually sprout. (Chapter 2)

> The social world's 10,000 natural kinds arise from presence [*you*]. / "Presence" [*you*] arises from "absence" [*wu*]. (Chapter 40)

On Hansen's translation, *you* and *wu* in Chapter 2 can be seen as referring to the distinction between "presence" and "absence." This interpretation of *you* and *wu* is also found in Chapter 11 (in Hansen's translation):

> Thirty spokes join one hub. / The cart's use lies where they are absent [*wu*]. / Throwing clay to make a vessel; / The vessel's use lies where the clay is absent [*wu*]. / Sculpting windows and doors to make a room; / The room's use lies where they are absent [*wu*, the empty space in the room]. / So we treat having something [*you*] as beneficial and treat lacking something [*wu*] as useable.

In both Chapters 2 and 11, the term "*you*" symbolizes the tangible aspect of a thing, for example, the spokes, the clay, the windows, and doors; the term "*wu*" signifies the intangible aspect of a thing, for example, the constructed space around the spokes, the

formed hollowness of the utensil, and the empty space in a room. On this interpretation, *you* and *wu* are complementary concepts, like *yin* and *yang*. Both are beneficial
and useable. Both exist simultaneously.

This interpretation aptly illustrates the idea of the mutual dependence of "presence"
(*you*) and "absence" (*wu*) in Chapters 2 and 11, but could it make sense of Chapter 40
where "presence" (*you*) is said to arise from "absence" (*wu*)? I think it can. According to
this interpretation of *wu* and *you*, Laozi is simply stressing the importance of "absence,"
as it is commonly ignored and neglected when people are dealing with things. He is
not suggesting that "absence" does *not* rely on "presence," nor is he suggesting that
"absence" is the ultimate First Cause of things in the world—a misunderstanding that
Chan's translation ("And being comes from non-being" 有 生 于 无) may lead us into.
Rather, he is suggesting that *you* and *wu* co-arise.

### 2. Rou ruo *versus* gang qiang (or jian qiang)

One well-known pair of opposites in the *Daodejing* is that of the *rou* 柔 and/or *ruo* 弱
on the one hand and the *gang* 刚, *qiang* 强, and *jian* 坚 on the other (Chapters 36, 43,
76, 78). These are commonly translated as "the weak" and "the strong" respectively. In
order to get a clear understanding of Laozi's view on this pair of opposites, let's examine
these *rou ruo* and *gang qiang* chapters one by one, starting with Chapter 36:

> In desiring to contract it, / You must basically have regarded it as
> "expanded." / In desiring to weaken (*ruo*) it, / You must basically have
> regarded it as "strong" (*qiang*). / In desiring to dissipate it, / You must
> basically have regarded it as "thriving." / In desiring to take it, / You must
> basically have regarded it as "given." / This is called subtle discerning. / Soft
> (*rou*) and pliant (*ruo*) win over hard (*gang*) and coercive (*qiang*). / Fish can-
> not leave watery depths. / The state's beneficial artefacts / Should [not] be
> displayed to humans. (Chapter 36)[31]

In this chapter, the soft-pliant and the hard-coercive, or *rou ruo* and *gang qiang*, is
seen as a pair of opposites. Laozi argues that the former, the soft-pliant is to be adopted,
and the hard-coercive is to be avoided. This view of Laozi seems to be in contradiction
with what he says in Chapter 2, where opposites are treated as equal:

> When all the social world regards beauty as "beauty," / Here already is
> "ugly." / If all treat mastery as "being good at" things, / Here already is "not
> being good at things." / Thus "presence" and "absence" mutually sprout. /
> "Hard" and "easy" mutually inform. / "Long" and "short" mutually gauged. /
> "High" and "low" mutually incline. / "Sound" and "tone" mutually blend. /
> "Before" and "after" mutually follow on. (Chapter 2, Hansen's translation)

---

31  Hansen's translation; the word "not" in the last verse is my addition.

If the soft-pliant and the hard-coercive are a pair of opposites, and if opposites, being equal, produce each other (Chapter 2), shouldn't Laozi also argue that the soft-pliant and the hard-coercive, being equal as opposites, are both to be avoided, or followed? Why did Laozi favour *rou ruo* in the opposites of *rou ruo* and *gang qiang*?

The reason seems to be that, in Chapters 2 and 36, Laozi was not talking about the same thing. In Chapter 2 he was focusing on the meanings (semantics) of opposites, that is, how opposite concepts ("presence" and "absence," "hard" and "easy," "long" and "short," "high" and "low," "sound" and "tone," and "before" and "after") get defined in opposing conceptual relationships. In that chapter, Laozi did not argue that an example of one side of the opposites (say, something that is "hard") will automatically transform into an example of the other side (say, something that is "easy"); he only argues that opposite concepts are defined together, in pairs.

In Chapter 36, however, Laozi was not addressing the semantics of opposites. Instead he was focusing on the pragmatics of various kinds of states of affairs and arguing that some are desirable, or worth achieving. According to Laozi, the state of being "soft and pliant" (*rou ruo*), for example, is more desirable than the state of being "hard and coercive" (*gang qiang*). Laozi's point is that *rou ruo* as a life coping strategy is better than *gang qiang*.[32]

*Rou ruo* and *gang qiang* are not descriptions of opposite states of affairs in brute nature. In nature, it is obvious that a rabbit (which is *rou ruo*, translated and interpreted as "the weak") is not likely to overcome a tiger (which is *gang qiang*, translated and interpreted as "the strong"). Nor are *gang qiang* and *rou ruo* about a person's physical strength and the lack of it (thus, Chan's translation of *rou ruo* as "the weak" and *gang qiang* as "the strong" is very misleading), because a physically weak person with a *rou ruo* (supple or flexible) mind may win over a physically strong man without such a

---

32  Laozi also uses other pairs of opposites to advocate life coping strategies. In Chapter 22, he claims,
> To yield is to be preserved whole (*qu ze quan* 曲 則 全). / To be bent is to become straight (*wang ze zhi* 枉 則 直). / To be empty is to be full (*wa ze yin* 窪 則 盈). / To be worn out is to be renewed (*bi ze xin* 敝 則 新). / To have little is to possess (*shao ze de* 少 則 得). / To have plenty is to be perplexed (*duo ze huo* 多 則 惑). (Chan's translation)

In this chapter Laozi argues that when one is in a certain state of being or when one acts in a certain way, he would (may) reach (or would hope to reach) another state of being. When one yielded in one aspect, he would (may) preserve his overall gain; when he made concessions, he would (may) straighten things out; if a place is concave, it will be filled (in a rain); when a tool is worn out, a new one would be requested to replace it; when one has little, he may be able to keep it; when one has too much, he may become confounded. Notice that Laozi is not addressing the mutually defining relationship between opposites, for clearly, "little" (*shao* 少) and "possess" (*de* 得) are not opposites, nor are "plenty" (*duo* 多) and "perplex" (*huo* 惑). If this interpretation makes sense, then Hansen's translation of the chapter must be taken cautiously. Hansen translates the first six verses of Chapter 22 as:
> "Crooked" implies "intact," / "Twisted" implies "straight," / "Vacuous" implies "filled," / "Worn out" implies "new," / "Less" implies "getting," / "Excess" implies "confounded."

On this translation, we must be careful not to read this chapter in the light of Chapter 2 (quoted earlier) where Laozi argues that opposites are mutually defined. When Laozi says "crooked" (*qu* 曲) implies "intact"(*quan* 全), he does not imply that "intact" also implies "crooked," even though in ancient and modern Chinese language *qu* 曲 and *quan* 全 can be said to be mutually defined. In Chapter 22, Laozi wants to argue that one can use the strategy of *qu* 曲 to achieve the aim of *quan* 全, not that one can use the strategy of *quan* 全 to achieve the aim of *qu* 曲. Similar analysis can be made regarding the other pairs of opposites in Chapter 58.

mind, and a physically strong man with a *gang qiang* (rigid or pushy) mind may often be defeated by a physically weak person without such a mind. Or, as in D.C. Lau's interpretation of the idea of *rou ruo*, a physically weak person with a *rou ruo* mind may at least avoid conflict and danger because he is not contending:

> The weak does not contend, so no one in the world can pick a quarrel with it. If one never contends, this at least ensures that one never suffers defeat. One may even wear down the resistance of one's stronger opponent by this passive weapon of non-contention, or at least wait for him to meet with defeat at the hands of someone stronger. It is in this sense that the submissive and the weak gain 'victory' over the hard and the strong.[33]

Lau explains that, as a coping strategy, *rou ruo*, understood as "not contending," may avoid contention and conflict. This idea can also be illustrated in a different context. In the practice of the martial art Tai Ji (Tai Chi), for example, if you are facing an opponent who is much stronger than you, a supple (*rou ruo*) and wise way to respond to an attack is not to venture aggressively, but to deflect your opponent's strike—a technique or strategy indicated by the saying, "A skilful parry of one pound can break a fisting of one ton" (*si liang bo qian jin*).

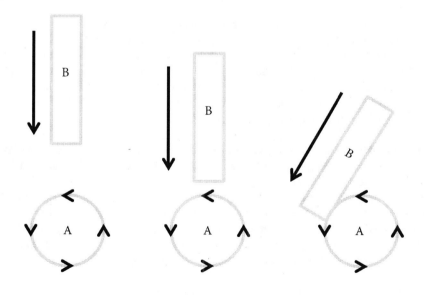

*When a forceful strike (B) comes to you (A), you can deflect it with minimal energy. In this limited sense "the physically weak can win over the physically strong."*

---

33  Lau, Introduction, 29.

However, the image of a physically weak person (in both Lau's example and the Tai Ji example) does not seem to do full justice to Laozi's view on *rou ruo* and *gang qiang*. Indeed, Laozi argues that, like water, what is *rou ruo* can be more powerful than what is *jian qiang*.

> Under the sky, nothing is softer [*rou*] or more yielding [*ruo*] than water. / And yet when it attacks firm [*jian*], rigid [*qiang*] things, / None of them can win against it. / Because they lack any means to move it. / That yielding [*ruo*] wins against force [*qiang*]; / That the soft [*rou*] wins over the hard [*gang*], / No one in the social world fails to understand. / No one can practice it. (Chapter 78, Hansen's translation)

According to Laozi, water is softer and more yielding than anything, but nothing can "win against" it. In other words, water, instead of being physically weak, can be most powerful! It can attack "firm, rigid things" and win over them. The power of water paradoxically comes from its inner quality of being "soft and yielding" (*rou ruo*)—flexible, accommodating, and resilient in whatever situation it is in. If water were hard and rigid (*gang qiang*), it would break itself when it attacked other things. As Laozi argues in Chapter 76, a thing's turning hard and rigid actually signifies death:

> Living humans are soft and limber [*rou ruo*]. / Dead they are hard and rigid [*jian qiang*]. / Living, the 10,000 grasses and wood species are soft and crisp [*ruo cui*]. / Dead, they are withered and tough. / So "hard" and "rigid" accompany death. / "Soft" and "limber" accompany life. / So if armies are coercive [*qiang*], they do not triumph. / When wood is strong, the axe comes out. / Strength and dominance reside below. / The soft and limber belong higher. (Chapter 76, Hansen's translation)

In Chapters 76 and 78, Laozi uses the examples of water, grasses, and wood species to teach a moral lesson about how humans should act. For example, he argues that "if armies are coercive, they do not triumph." The moral lesson is echoed in Chapter 43 when he urges that *rou ruo* ("soft and yielding") as an attitude or way of action is to be followed, and *gang qiang* ("firm and rigid") as an opposite attitude or way of action is to be avoided. In understanding *rou ruo* and *gang qiang* as attitudes or ways of action, *rou ruo* seems to mean "gentle, tender, and considerate," and *gang qiang* ("firm and rigid") seems to mean "pushy, aggressive, and coercive."

### 3. *Good Fortune* (fu 福 ) *versus Bad Disaster* (huo 禍 )

Another pair of opposites in the *Daodejing* that deserves special attention is good fortune and disaster (Chapter 58). This pair of opposites is neither like the pair of opposites in the *you wu* chapters (Chapters 2, 40) where the opposites are mutually

defined in the opposing conceptual relationship, nor like the pair of opposites in the
*rou ruo* and *gang qiang* chapters (Chapters 36, 43, 76, 78) where *rou ruo* is favoured as a
pragmatic coping strategy. Instead, Laozi claims that while good fortune and disaster
"rest on" each other, there is no way to figure out at any specific moment which one
will actually occur.

> Good fortune rests upon disaster; / Disaster lies hidden within good
> fortune. / Who knows the highest standards? / Perhaps there is noth-
> ing that is truly correct and regular! / What is correct and regular turns
> strange and perverse; / What is good turns monstrous. (Chapter 58,
> Ivanhoe's translation)

What is stressed here is that it is not possible to figure out when and how (under
what conditions) the opposites of good fortune and disaster transform into each other.
Unlike *rou ruo* as a way of acting or as an attitude which can be controlled by the doer,
disaster and good fortune depend on external and uncontrollable conditions. A good
way to illustrate this point is with an ancient Chinese story.

> An old man was living with his son on the frontier. One day, he lost a
> horse. The neighbours all came to express their sympathy at this bad luck,
> but the old man said, "How do you know this isn't good luck?"
> A little later the horse came back, and with it were some superior wild
> horses. The neighbours all congratulated the old man on his good fortune,
> but he said, "How do you know this isn't bad luck?"
> With so many horses, the son began riding, and one day he fell off and
> broke his leg. The injury left him with a bad limp. Again the neighbours
> came to sympathize, but the old man said, "You never know—this may be
> good luck."
> Another year passed, and a war came. All the able-bodied young men
> had to go to war, and many died. The son, because of his bad leg, was
> saved. (He was not enlisted in the army.)
> In this way, what seems to be good luck may really be bad, and what
> seems to be bad luck, good.[34]

The old man's attitude toward what happened to him and his son emphasizes calm
acceptance. This is not because he believes that God has a "big plan" for him, but
because he believes: a) the value judgment of a state of affairs is always relative to the
judgment maker in particular contexts, b) states of affairs are constantly changing,
and c) states of affairs are ultimately not under an individual's or even humanity's

---

34 This story comes from the *Huannanzi*, a second century BCE Chinese philosophical classic from the
Han dynasty that blends Daoist, Confucian, and Legalist concepts, including theories such as Yin-Yang
and the Five Elements—Gold, Wood, Water, Fire, Earth.

control.[35] Thus, a Daoist should adopt an open and non-obsessive attitude toward whatever happens to his life. This attitude is further developed by another Chinese Daoist philosopher, Zhuangzi, who argues that "to understand what you can do nothing about and to be content with it as with fate—this is the perfection of virtue"[36]

Laozi's teaching regarding our attitude towards good fortune and disaster may have two implications. First, it suggests that no one should take good fortune and disaster for granted—a warning indeed for the rulers, the fortunate, and the conceited. Second, it also seems to give less fortunate people hope that, even though they now lead desperate lives, their lives may change without notice—a spiritual antidote for those who are less fortunate. Thus, it suggests that one should be patient, waiting for good fortune to come in due course.

Our examination of the above three pairs of opposites in the *Daodejing* demonstrates that Laozi's treatment of opposites is case-by-case rather than abstract. His treatment focuses on offering real life coping strategies rather than on proposing a theory of opposites.

### THE IDEA OF *ZI-RAN* 自 然
### (SELF-SO-ING OR SPONTANEITY)

Another important concept in the *Daodejing* is the notion of *zi-ran*, which is often translated as "Nature" (Chapters 17, 23, 25, 51, 64). However, it seems better translated literally as "self-so-ing," "self-such-ness," "as-it-is-ness," or "spontaneity." To see why these are better translations, we need to read Chapter 25 carefully, which seems to foster the reading of *zi-ran* as "Nature" in the sense of the totality of natural happenings. Let's start with Chan's translation of Chapter 25:

> ... Therefore Tao [dao] is great. / Heaven is great. / Earth is great. / And the king is also great. / There are our great things in the universe, and the king is one of them. / Man models [*fa*] himself after Earth. / Earth models itself after Heaven. / Heaven models itself after Tao [*dao*]. / And Tao [*dao*] models itself after Nature [*zi-ran*].

On Chan's translation, the message of the chapter is that humans (should) directly model themselves after Earth, which in turn models itself after Heaven, which then models itself after *dao*, which finally models itself after Nature.

But this interpretation may lead to several problems. First, if humans (should) directly model themselves after Earth, should they model themselves indiscriminately after *all* natural happenings? The *Daodejing* never suggested that we model ourselves after fire, but advised us to model ourselves after water (Chapters 8, 68, 73, 78, 81). Hence it does not suggest that humans model themselves after all natural happenings. Second, it is difficult to make sense of the verse "Earth models itself after Heaven,"

---

35  See Hans Georg Moeller's nice analysis of Chapter 58 in his book *The Philosophy of the Daodejing* (New York: Columbia University Press, 2006), Chapter 7, 99–110.
36  The *Zhuangzi*, Section 4, Watson's translation, 56.

because Heaven and Earth (*tian di*) are used in the *Daodejing* as one unity (Chapters 1, 5, 7, 23, 25, 32). If Earth and Heaven are one unity, it does not seem to make sense to say "Earth models itself after Heaven."

Third, it is very odd that only Heaven *directly* models itself after *dao*. If *dao* (as "absence" *wu*) is the "beginning" of both Heaven and Earth (Chapter 1), then why didn't Earth also *directly* model itself after *dao*? Why does Earth *indirectly* model itself after *dao* via a detour through Heaven?

Finally, it makes no sense to say "*dao* models itself after Nature," for Nature (understood as Earth and Heaven) is regarded as having been produced by *dao* (Chapter 1). It would seem to make more sense to switch places between "Nature" and "*dao*" in the claim that "*dao* models itself after Nature," and to say this: "Nature models itself after *dao*."

Given the above problems with Chan's translation, many translators after Chan have decided that *zi-ran* (in the last verse) is better not translated as "Nature," but as "so of itself" (by Hansen) or "what is natural" (by Ivanhoe). But both Hansen's and Ivanhoe's translations still leave the parallel structure of the last four verses in Chapter 25 unaccounted for. Given the parallel structure of the four verses, if *dao* models itself after *zi-ran* (the last verse of the four), we may return to the other three verses and ask: Why didn't humans, Earth, or Heaven model themselves after *zi-ran*?

In order to avoid all the above interpretive problems, Qing Jie Wang has proposed a new translation and interpretation of Chapter 25, which I believe could make better sense of the message in the chapter.[37] Wang's translation is based on a different punctuation of the chapter made by a Daoist scholar, Li Yue, in the Tang dynasty (618–907 CE) and on a reading of the adjective *da* (大) as a verb. Wang's translation (modified) goes:

> Dao is great-ing (*dao da*).[38] / Heaven is great-ing (*tian da*). / Earth is great-ing (*di da*). / And the human being is also great-ing (*ren yi da*). / There are four great-ings in the universe (*guo zhong you si da*). / And the human being is one of them (*er ren ju qi yi yan*). / Human beings follow earth's being earth (*ren fa di di*),[39] / Follow heaven's being heaven (*fa tian tian*), / Follow the *dao*'s being the *dao* (*fa dao dao*), / Follow itself as it is naturally and spontaneously (*fa zi ran*).

This translation leads to a very interesting interpretation of Chapter 25. Contrary to the prevalent interpretation of the chapter, which maintains that Laozi is advising human beings to *model* after earth, the new interpretation suggests that he is only

---

37 Qing Jie (James) Wang. "'It-self-so-ing' and 'Other-ing' in Lao Zi's Concept of *Zi Ran*," in *Comparative Approaches to Chinese Philosophy*, Bo Mou, ed. (Burlington, VT: Ashgate, 2003), 225–44.
38 The word "*da*" (literally meaning "great") is read as a verb.
39 Chan, Ivanhoe, and Wang all translate "*fa* 法" as "model." On this translation, human beings are to model themselves after non-human beings, namely, earth, heaven. There seems to be a tension between humans' "modelling after" earth, heaven, the *dao*, and *zi-ran* (it-self-so-ing) and humans' letting them be themselves ("earth's being earth," "heaven's being heaven," and "the *dao*'s being the *dao*"—all in the sense of being themselves, *zi-ran*). Hansen's translation of "*fa* 法" as "follow" seems better.

advising human beings to *follow* ("observe") earth as it unfolds as earth, to *follow* heaven as it unfolds as heaven, to *follow dao* as it unfolds as *dao*, and in short, to follow everything as it-self-so-ing, or to self-so-ing just as the rest of the cosmos does.

The above interpretation of *zi-ran* seems to cohere well with Chapter 51. In this chapter *zi-ran* is portrayed as a natural, spontaneous process, not decreed or coerced. Here is my translation of Chapter 51:[40]

> *Daos* produce them (*dao sheng zhi*);[41] / Virtues rear them (*de chu zhi*); / Things shape them (*wu xing zhi*); / Circumstances complete them (*shi cheng zhi*). / For this reason, none among the ten thousand things failed to respect the *daos* and value virtues. / This respecting of *daos* / And valuing of virtues / Is not coerced, but always spontaneous (*zi-ran*, it-self-so-ing). / Hence *daos* produce them; / Virtues rear them; / Raise them and nurture them; / Bring them to maturity and security; / Nourish them and shelter (or return) them. / To produce without possessing; / To act with no expectation of reward; / To lead without lording over; / Such is Enigmatic Virtue!

In the first four verses of this chapter, four subjects (*daos*, virtues, things, and circumstances) are mentioned. If we follow the "subject (*dao, de, wu, shi*) + verb (*sheng, chu, xing, cheng*) + object (*zhi*)" grammatical structure of the four verses, then it is tempting to read the verses as saying that there are four *different* factors which *separately* contribute to four different processes of producing, rearing, taking shape, and completing the ten thousand things. In other words, it is tempting to objectify the four subjects and treat them as independent, entity-like forces.

But this reading of the four verses is wrong. According to Laozi, *daos* do not produce the ten thousand things and leave them alone for others (virtues, things, and circumstances) to rear, shape, and complete them. Rather, *daos* are always with the ten thousand things, always with their producing, rearing, taking-shape, and completing processes. These four processes *are* the unfolding processes of *daos*. To put it differently, the spontaneous, autonomous, and self-producing processes themselves are *daos*. If this interpretation is reasonable, then what Laozi really wants to say in the four verses is this: in addressing "the emerging/producing of the ten thousand things" the word "*daos*" can be used; in addressing "the sustaining of the ten thousand things" the word "*de*" can be used; in addressing "the taking-shape of the ten thousand things" the word "*xing*" can be used; and in addressing "the completing of the ten thousand things" the word "*shi*" can be used. But *dao, de, xing, shi* are about the one process which can be seen from different aspects.

Laozi believes that understanding *zi-ran* in this way (as natural and spontaneous unfoldings of the ten thousand things) can teach us important lessons about how to live a better human life and about how to govern a state. If the cosmos is a natural,

---

40  I have consulted the translations of this chapter by Chan, Ivanhoe, and Hansen.
41  Notice that the Chinese language does not distinguish singular and plural uses through a noun's morphology, so 道 can be translated as either *dao* or *daos*.

spontaneous, and self-producing process in which each species or thing follows its particular *dao* and *de* (virtue), then it is important that human beings also follow this process (see Chapter 25 explained above), and "support the ten thousand things in their self-so-ing processes (*zi-ran*) and never dare to act (against them)" (Chapter 64, my translation). On the political level, Laozi believes that the idea of *zi-ran* can teach rulers to be careful in taking their political measures and in keeping their promises. He explains in Chapter 17 and 23:

> The greatest of rulers is but a shadowy presence; / Next is the ruler who is loved and praised; / Next is the one who is feared; / Next is the one who is reviled. / Those lacking in trust are not trusted. / However, [the greatest rulers] are cautious and honour words [*gui yan*]. / When their task is done and work complete, / Their people all say, "This is just how we are" [*zi-ran*].[42] (Chapter 17, Ivanhoe's translation)

> To be sparing with words [*xi yan*] is what comes naturally [*zi-ran*]. / And so, / A blustery wind does not last all morning; / A heavy downpour does not last all day. / Who produces these? / Heaven and Earth! / If not even Heaven and Earth can keep things going for a long time, / How much less can human beings? / This is why one should follow the Way in all that one does. / One who follows the Way identifies with the Way. / One who follows Virtue identifies with Virtue. / One who follows loss identifies with loss. / The Way is pleased to have those who identify with the Way. / Virtue is pleased to have those who identify with Virtue. / Loss is pleased to have those who identify with loss. / Those lacking in trust are not trusted. (Chapter 23, Ivanhoe's translation)

In recommending rulers to follow the self-so-ing process of the cosmos, Laozi does not suggest that they leave everything alone, do nothing, and say nothing. He mentions that rulers get their "task done and work complete" (Chapter 17). Nor does Laozi believe that a *zi-ran* human life is one that is utterly absent of any artificiality, for he praises the artificial practice of "using knotted cords for counting" (Chapter 80), and he never urged people to go back to cave dwelling! His ideal *zi-ran* way of life is agrarian and innocent, but not without any artificiality (man-made-ness). He advises rulers to "honour words" and "to be sparing with words," not abandon words altogether.[43] In Chapter 17, by the idea of "honour words," Laozi suggests that rulers should be careful in keeping their promises to the people, for "[t]hose lacking in trust are not trusted." In Chapter 23, with the phrase "to be sparing with words," he argues that rulers should be careful about what they say or what policy they advocate. He seems to be warning Confucians and Mohists (who use discourses or policies as means

42  Also see Chapter 57 when a sage says "I eschew acting on constructs [or, 'doing nothing,' *wu-wei*] and subjects transform themselves" (*wo wu wei er min zi hua* 我 无 为 而 民 自化) (Hansen's translation).
43  The word "words" (*yan*) in ancient Chinese language can mean "discourse," "policy," and "what one promises."

to regulate social behaviour) not to use *yan* in a coercive way, for what appears to be coercive, like a blustery wind or a heavy downpour, does not last for long.

Laozi's *zi-ran* thus understood is radically different from Hobbes's idea of "natural conditions of mankind." In the idea of "natural condition of mankind," everyone is in conflict with everyone else. Using this idea, Hobbes argues for the necessity of a social contract. In contrast, in *zi-ran* state, humans live in innocence and harmony. Using the idea of *zi-ran* (in a social context) Laozi presents an ideal state in which human beings can live and flourish.

One may at this point want a clear criterion for what counts as *zi-ran* and what does not, but the *Daodejing* does not provide us with one. The *Daodejing* proposes a *philosophy* of *zi-ran*, not a rigid definition of it with a set of necessary and sufficient conditions. The text points to a general direction in the journey of an ideal life, not a detailed, specific itinerary, or fixed paths. The idea of *zi-ran*, like the ideas of tranquility (*jing*), softness (*rou*), acquiescence (*ruo*), and simplicity (*pu*), is a very elastic one; its application has to be negotiated case by case in concrete contexts. For example, Laozi explains that "to be sparing with words" is "what comes naturally (*zi-ran*)" (Chapter 23), but it is still up to the rulers to figure out what are natural uses of words and what are not.[44]

For Laozi and for other Chinese philosophers, it is not a problem at all to use a concept without being able to define it in terms of necessary and sufficient conditions—a concept can be illustrated by examples, images, stories, etc. Analogously, when Jesus was asked to explain who counts as a neighbour, he told the parable of the good Samaritan (Luke 10: 25–37). Does the story exhaust all the instances of a good neighbour? Definitely not. In real life situations, those who follow Jesus' teaching of "Love your neighbour" still have to figure out who counts as a neighbour and how to love him/her. But this does not in any way reduce the value of Jesus' teaching. We should adopt a similar attitude toward the teachings in the *Daodejing*.

## LAOZI'S PHILOSOPHY OF NON-ACTION (*WU-WEI*) 无为

Much of the *Daodejing* draws attention to political concerns, including how a ruler should govern a state and how he should discipline himself. In spite of what the legends say about Laozi's solitary life, his doctrine does not advocate a life of solitude. In fact, Laozi's engagement with political concerns is a feature that distinguishes him from his follower Zhuangzi (see Chapter 7 of this book), who sought to transcend such concerns.

Let's first locate Laozi's political philosophy against the backdrop of the then influential thoughts of Confucius and Mozi. According to Confucius, to restore social

---

44  Zhuangzi thinks that to pierce the nose of a cow and to put a headstall (halter) on the head of a horse is not natural (The *Zhuangzi*, Autumn Flood, Watson's translation, 104); the Daoist philosopher Guo Xiang (252–312 CE) however holds that it is natural to pierce the nose of a cow and to put a headstall on the head of a horse. For Guo Xiang, it is in the nature of cows and horses to work for human beings; and it is in the nature of human beings to employ these animals to work for them. The openness of the notion of *zi-ran* has left a huge space for different interpretations.

order, people (especially rulers) should act in accordance with Zhou morals and norms, most notably, humanness and rituals. For Mozi, the restoration of social order requires everyone to practice impartial love. Both Confucius and Mozi argue that rulers should adopt a policy that regulates the society into a hierarchy, which exalts the worthy (*shang xian*). They believe that exalting the worthy motivates people to strive for social advancement.

According to Laozi, the prescriptions by Confucius and by Mozi would not work, for they are all *you-wei* (有 为) politics (Chapters 2, 3, 20, 37, 38, 43, 48, 57, 63, 64). *You-wei* literally meaning "having doing," implies "doing things in possessive, coercive, and self-aggrandizing ways." To counter Confucius and Mozi who both focus on what rulers should do, Laozi warns rulers what they should not do—that is, they should not do certain things (not to interfere when things are spontaneously in order) or not do things in certain ways (e.g., in a coercive way). This philosophy of "not doing" is expressed primarily in the idea of *wu-wei*, or literally "non-action," or "not doing" (Chapters 2, 3, 10, 37, 38, 43, 48, 57, 63, 64).[45]

## DOING PHILOSOPHY
### Two Examples of You-Wei

*Zhuangzi* (a Daoist text that involves ideas similar to those in the *Daodejing*) illustrates the idea of *you-wei*, the opposite of *wu-wei*.

Once a sea bird alighted in the suburbs of the Lu capital. The Marquis of Lu escorted it to the ancestral temple, where he entertained it, performing the Nine Shao music for it to listen to and presenting it with the meat of the T'ai-lao sacrifice to feast on. But the bird only looked dazed and forlorn, refusing to eat a single slice of meat or drink a cup of wine, and in three days it was dead. This is to try to nourish a bird with what would nourish you instead of what would nourish a bird.[46]

---

45  The idea of *wu-wei*, however, should not be taken literally as "doing nothing." *Wu-wei* "has nothing to do with inactivity prompted by laziness, apathy, timidity, or neglect" (Forrest E. Baird and Raeburne S. Heimbeck, *Philosophy Classics, Vol.* vi: *Asian Philosophy* [Saddle River, NJ: Pearson Prentice Hall, 2006], 366). Nor does it mean simply being carried along by the course of events. Indeed, strictly speaking, no one can do nothing—sitting at home and "doing nothing," or lying on the beach "doing nothing," is paradoxically still *doing* something, namely, sitting at home or lying on a beach. Moreover, one's mind may still be doing a lot of things when one sits at home or lies on a beach. Hence, "doing nothing" is meaningful only in comparison with "doing something." For example, in relation to one's obligation to go to work, sitting at home may be regarded as "doing nothing." But in relation to sleeping, sitting at home can be seen as "doing something."

46  *Chuang Tzu: Basic Writings*, Burton Watson, trans. (New York: Columbia University Press, 1996), 116.

The emperor of the South Sea was called Shu [Brief], the emperor of the North Sea was called Hu [Sudden], and the emperor of the central region was called Hun-tun [Chaos]. Shu and Hu from time to time came together for a meeting in the territory of Hun-tun, and Hun-tun treated them very generously. Shu and Hu discussed how they could repay his kindness. "All men," they said, "have seven openings so they can see, hear, eat, and breathe. But Hun-tun alone doesn't have any. Let's trying boring him some!" Every day they bored another hole, and on the seventh day Hun-tun died.[47]

Now, let's change the scenario in the first story. Suppose this kind of bird is close to extinction because of its predation by another kind of bird. Should humans kill some of the predator birds in order to save the endangered kind? Would Laozi regard the killing as *you-wei*, an interference with what is sponta-neity or naturalness?

One thing that rulers should not do, according to Laozi, is to rouse people's desires that are beyond their natural or spontaneous needs. At first glance, this advice may sound very odd (if not totally ridiculous).

Not paying honour to the worthy [*shang xian*] leads the people to avoid contention. / Not showing reverence for hard-to-get goods leads them to not steal. / Not making a display of what is desirable leads their hearts away from chaos. / This is why sages bring things to order by emptying people's hearts / and filling their bellies. / They weaken the people's ambitions and strengthen their bones; / They make sure that the people are without knowl-edge or desires; / And that those with knowledge do not dare to act. / Sages enact nonaction [*wu-wei*] and everything becomes well ordered. (Chapter 3, Ivanhoe's translation modified)

Five colours stupefy human eyes. / Five tones desensitize human ears. / Five flavours numb human mouths. / Horse racing and hunting derange human minds. / Hard-to-get goods pervert human behaviour. / Using this: sages act for the belly, / Not the eye. / And so discard "that" and take up "this." (Chapter 12, Hansen's translation)

Order a state by doing right. / Use shock to deploy military force. / Use no dealing [*wu-shi*] to take up the social world. / How do I know these are so? / With this. / When the social world adds superstitious prohibitions, / It increases poverty of its subjects. / The more subjects have beneficial artefacts, / The more the state and society are befuddled. /

---

47  *Chuang Tzu*, Watson, trans., 95.

The more humans become skilled and clever, / The more strange things emerge. / The more standards and commands are promulgated, / The more thieves and robbers are present. / Hence sages say: / I eschew acting on constructs [*wu-wei*] and subjects transform themselves. / I incline towards calmness and subjects correct themselves. / I avoid dealings [*wu-shi*] and subjects enrich themselves. / I lack desires and subjects simplify themselves. (Chapter 57, Hansen's translation)

Many contemporary readers may find the above advice unrealistic. Wouldn't exalting "the worthy" and valuing "hard-to-get goods" motivate people to strive for self-improvement? What sort of policy is it to make the people "without knowledge or desires" (Chapter 3)? To answer these questions, we need to carefully examine Laozi's view on desires.

Laozi certainly did not urge people to abandon basic physical desires (such as the desire for food and water). He explicitly says in Chapter 3 that a sage ruler would "[fill the people's] bellies" and "strengthen their bones."[48] But it is also clear that he would like to keep people's desires down to a minimal level. He preferred the need of the "bellies" to the need of the "eyes" because he believes that the eyes tend to pursue what is unnecessary for simple and peaceful living, as in racing and hunting when the mind becomes "deranged" (Chapter 12).

Hence, Laozi has distinguished two kinds of desires, our natural or spontaneous ("the belly") desires and our desires beyond the natural ones, which can be called "puffed-up" desires. He believes that the "puffed-up" desires stem from mental projections as "ambitions" (Chapter 3). They are roused in or imposed upon people by their knowledge of the existence of "hard-to-get goods" and by the language that instigates the desire to have them. (Just think of how many of our desires nowadays are really necessary and how many are "puffed-up" by advertisements!) This role of language shapes people's taste and their discriminating attitudes;[49] it makes people obsessed with what they do not naturally need.

Laozi seems to have assumed that our natural desires are modest and limited, and that if people were left alone without desire-rousing and desire-imposing, they would survive well with the satisfaction of their natural needs and be happy. He even suggests that an ideal society is a small country with a small population, where people live a simple life (Chapter 80) and everyone gets his/her natural share (Chapters 32, 77).

Laozi's idea that human desires should be left un-agitated may sound too childish to some. Certainly it was criticized by Confucian philosopher Xunzi as being too naïve (see Chapter 8 of this book). An important objection to Laozi's view, as Xunzi would have us believe, is that people's desires would seem inevitably to evolve and expand, so it would be important to regulate them, rather than to reduce them.

---

48  Laozi did not say explicitly anything about sexual desire, but it would seem reasonable to believe that he would argue against sexual indulgence as it will harm one's body (health).

49  Cf. Hansen, *A Daoist Theory*, 213; cf. Lau, 34–37.

But Laozi believes that the Moist and the Confucian alternatives are socially dangerous. According to Laozi, "exalting the worthy," "valuing hard-to-get goods," and "displaying the desirable" would rouse desires, which in turn would not only cause social competition and theft, but would also severely disturb the mind. Even if those "puffed-up" desires could be satisfied, the satisfaction would not last. People would soon seek more, for their desires, when roused, are insatiable (Chapters 33, 34; cf. Chapter 32). If happiness required the satiation of "puffed-up" desires, then one would never be genuinely happy.

Another thing that rulers should not be doing, according to Laozi, is thinking or acting in possessive, coercive, and self-aggrandizing ways. *Wu-wei*, thus understood, deals with rulers' self-discipline in terms of not acting in the above ways, as well as (more importantly) of not mentally clinging to those actions.[50] Laozi explains this aspect of the idea of *wu-wei* in Chapter 38, which I translate below:[51]

> Those of superior virtue have no (clinging to) virtue and so they have it. /
> Those of inferior virtue never let go of (their clinging to) virtue and so they
> do not have it. / Those of superior virtue do not act (in possessive, coercive,
> or self-aggrandizing ways) nor do they have clinging to acting thus (*wu
> yi wei*). Those of inferior virtue do not act thus but have clinging to acting
> thus. / Those of superior benevolence (may have to) act thus but do not have
> clinging to having acted thus. / Those of superior righteousness act thus and
> have clinging to having acted thus. / Those who are ritually correct act, but if
> others do not respond, they roll up their sleeves and throw (them). / Hence
> when they lose the *dao*, they resort to virtue; / When they lose virtue, they
> resort to humanness; / When they lose humanness, they resort to righteous-
> ness; / When they lose righteousness, they resort to rites. / The rites are the
> wearing thin of loyalty and trust, and the beginning of disorder. / Those
> who first understood these, / Tried to embellish the *dao*, / But they initiated
> stupidity. / For this reason, men of greater maturity / Address the thick, /
> And do not dwell on the thin. / Address the substance, / And do not dwell in
> embellishment. / So they discard that and take up this.

This chapter argues that when rulers failed to discipline themselves against acting and thinking in possessive, coercive, and self-aggrandizing ways (for example, *display-ing* their virtues and *showing* their benevolence), there would be no true morality. The chapter suggests that the moral quality of rulers deteriorates gradually as they increas-ingly lose their rapport with *dao*. Finally they resort to rites and force to try to keep people in order. To restore their rapport with *dao*, Laozi argues, rulers have to practice "not act" (*wu-wei*) and "not cling to act" and "not cling to having acted" (*wu yi wei*). This means that rulers in their political role should abandon "benevolence" (*ren*, which Hansen translated below as "humanity") and "righteousness":

---

50  Both Hansen (*A Daoist Theory*, 212–13) and Slingerland (89) have noticed these two aspects of the idea of *wu-wei*.
51  I have consulted Hansen's, Chan's, and Ivanhoe's translations of this chapter.

Terminate "sageliness," junk "wisdom," / Your subjects will benefit a hun-
dredfold. / Terminate "humanity," junk "morality" [righteousness, *yi*] / Your
subjects will respond with filiality and affection. / Terminate "artistry," junk
"benefit," / There will be no thieves and robbers. / These three, / Treated as
slogans are not enough. / So now consider to what they belong: / Express
simplicity and embrace uncarved wood. / Lessen "self-focus" and diminish
"desires." (Chapter 19, Hansen's translation)

Chapter 38 does not elaborate on how rulers should actually practice *wu-wei* and
*wu-yi-wei*. Fortunately, some concrete advice on how to practice these two ideas is
presented elsewhere in the *Daodejing*. According to Laozi, the practice of *wu-wei*
and *wu-yi-wei* entails the practice of "not-contending" (*bu-zeng*, Chapters 3, 8, 22, 66,
68, 73, 81), not-possessing, not-expecting-reward, not-lingering-when-work-is-done,
not-lording-over (*fu/bu-you, fu/bu-shi, fu/bu-ju, bu-zhai*, Chapters 10, 51, 34, 77), not-
self-aggrandizing (*bu-wei-da*), not-manipulating (*wu-zhi*, Chapter 29), not-meddling
(*wu-shi*, Chapters 48, 57, 63), casting-off (selfish thinking) (*qu*, Chapters 12, 19, 29),
withdrawing-when-task-is-done (*tui*, Chapter 9), knowing-when-to-stop (*zhi-zi*,
Chapters 32, 44), knowing-contentment (*zhi-zu*, Chapters 33, 44), decreasing-"doing"
(*sun*, Chapter 48), and being-tranquil (*jing*, Chapters 6, 26, 37, 57). Given so many pieces
of advice on the practice of *wu-wei* and *wu-yi-wei* in the *Daodejing*, we may even regard
the text as a comprehensive manual of *wu-wei* and *wu-yi-wei*.

### DOING PHILOSOPHY
### Wu-Wei: *Does Laozi Suggest a Rejection of Intellectual Abilities?*

Ivanhoe argues that when Laozi advises us to follow the natural and spontaneous human needs and to reject puffed-up desires, he may be rejecting or
suppressing our most distinctive human characteristics. Ivanhoe says,

> In arguing that human beings by nature have few basic needs and a
> minimum set of desires, the *Daodejing* dramatically rejects what many
> have taken to be our most distinctive characteristics: our intellectual
> abilities, our creative capacities, and our strong sense of autonomy. It
> tells us that these in fact are the source of some of our worst troubles. It
> turns out that most of life's greatest difficulties are caused by our own
> propensity to make our lives more complicated than they need to be.
> Most of the wounds we suffer are self-inflicted, and only by unlearning
> what we know and hold most dear can we heal ourselves.[52]

Does Laozi suggest that we should reject our intellectual abilities? What do you
think?

---

52 Ivanhoe, Introduction, xxviii; cf. xxx.

DOING PHILOSOPHY
*From Self-Cultivation to the State Ruling:
Laozi and the Confucian*

Compare and contrast the following two quotations about self-cultivation
and ruling, one from the *Daodejing* and one from one of the Confucian classics, the *Great Learning*. Read them against the backdrop of the *Daodejing*
and Confucian philosophy. Explain the similarities and differences between
Laozi and the Confucian regarding self-cultivation and its relationship
with ruling.

*Laozi*

When one cultivates virtue in his person, it becomes genuine virtue. / When
one cultivates virtue in his family, it becomes overflowing virtue. / When one
cultivates virtue in his community, it becomes lasting virtue. / When one cultivates virtue in his country, it becomes abundant virtue. / When one cultivates
virtue in the world, it becomes universal. / Therefore the person should
be viewed as a person. / The family should be viewed as a family. / The
community should be viewed as a community. / The country should be
viewed as a country. / And the world should be viewed as a world. / How do I
know this to be the case in the world? / Through this (from the cultivation of
virtue in the person to that in the world) (Chapter 54).

*The Confucian*

The ancients who wished to manifest their clear character to the world
would first bring order to their states. Those who wished to bring order to
their states would first regulate their families. Those who wished to regulate
their families would first cultivate their personal lives. Those who wished
to cultivate their personal lives would first rectify their minds. Those who
wished to rectify their minds would first make their wills sincere. Those
who wished to make their wills sincere would first extend their knowledge. The extension of knowledge consists in the investigation of things.
When things are investigated, knowledge is extended; when knowledge is
extended, the will becomes sincere; when the will is sincere, the mind is
rectified; when the mind is rectified, the personal life is cultivated; when
the personal life is cultivated, the family will be regulated; when the family
is regulated, the state will be in order, there will be peace throughout
the world.[53]

---

53 *The Great Learning*, in Chan, 86–87.

## CONCLUDING REMARKS:
## THE INFLUENCE OF THE *DAODEJING*

The *Daodejing* has offered us a comprehensive philosophy about the cosmos and our place in it in terms of the notion of the *dao*. This seminal text has had a perennial influence on later Daoism (both as philosophy and as religion) and on Chinese culture in general. The text's interest in and respect for naturalness or spontaneity have profoundly shaped the Chinese way of seeing the cosmos and seeing an ideal human way of life.

The *Daodejing* is the first book of Daoist philosophy (*dao-jia* 道 家). Another Daoist book is the *Zhuangzi* (*Chuang Tzu*), which is attributed to a thinker by the same name, Zhuangzi (Chuang Tzu) (about 369–286 BCE). This latter work developed ideas that are quite similar to those in the *Daodejing*, albeit in spirit rather than in actual substance.[54] During the East Han Dynasty (25–221 CE), the names of Laozi and Zhuangzi were jointly used, and the ideas expressed in the two books (the *Daodejing* and the *Zhuangzi*) were fused together and dubbed "Lao-Zhuang thoughts." Lao-Zhuang thoughts also contributed to the native Chinese Daoist religion (*dao-jiao* 道 教) that emerged in the same period.[55]

The *Daodejing* is probably the most widely translated text among all Asian classics. Hundreds of translations have been published in many Western languages. Recent study on the *Daodejing* has witnessed an increasing interest in the ideas of *zi-ran* and *wu-wei* and their implications for environmental philosophy and for political philosophy and ethics. There is also an interesting ongoing comparative study of Laozi's *dao* and Heidegger's "Being," and of the possible influence of the *Daodejing* on Heidegger.[56] Both Laozi's *dao*-thinking and Heidegger's Being-thinking are seen as ways of thought that go beyond metaphysics and essentialism, and in this regard there seems to be a "fusion of horizons" between both thinkers which makes possible fruitful dialogue and mutual appreciation.

### WORK CITED AND RECOMMENDED READINGS

1. Herrlee G. Creel, "What Is Taoism?" in *What Is Taoism? And Other Studies in Chinese Cultural History* (Chicago: University of Chicago Press, 1970).

---

54 The traditional view about the dates of the *Daodejing* and the *Zhuangzi* puts the former before the latter. Also, due to their ideological affinity, thoughts in the *Zhuangzi* are regarded as a further development of those in the *Daodejing*. Some scholars, however, think that the *Daodejing* or at least some sections in it were written after the *Zhuangzi* (Schwartz, 186).
55 It is worth noting that there is a crucial difference between Daoism as a philosophy and Daoism as a religion. While Daoism as a religion preaches an ideal of physical immortality of the human body, Daoism as a philosophy does not. See Fung Yu-lan, *A Short History of Chinese Philosophy*, ed. Derk Bodde (New York: The Macmillian Company, 1948), 3. However, some passages in the *Daodejing* (particularly Chapter 10) can be read as instructions on physical practice for prolonging one's life.
56 See *Heidegger and Asian Thought*, Graham Parkes, ed. (Honolulu: University of Hawaii Press, 1987); Lin Ma, *Heidegger on East-West Dialogue: Anticipating the Event* (Oxford: Routledge, 2008); and Steven Burik, *The End of Comparative Philosophy and the Task of Comparative Thinking—Heidegger, Derrida, and Daoism* (Albany, NY: SUNY Press, 2009).

2. Robert G. Henricks, *Lao-tzu: Te-tao ching: A New Translation Based on the Recently Discovered Ma-wang-tui Texts* (New York: Ballantine Books, 1989).
3. Robert G. Henricks, *Lao Tzu's Tao Te Ching: A Translation of the Startling New Documents Found at Guodian* (New York: Columbia University Press, 2000).
4. D.C. Lau, *Lao Tzu: Tao Te Ching* (London: Penguin Books, 1963).
5. A.C. Graham, *Disputers of the Tao: Philosophical Argument in Ancient China* (Chicago and La Salle: Open Court, 1989).
6. Roger T. Ames and David L. Hall, *Daodejing: Making This Life Significant* (New York: Ballantine Books, 2002).
7. *Tao Te Ching on the Art of Harmony: The New Illustrated Edition of the Chinese Philosophical Masterpiece*, Chad Hansen, trans. (London: Duncan Baird Publishers, 2009).
8. Hans Georg Moeller, *The Philosophy of the Daodejing* (New York: Columbia University Press, 2006).

CHAPTER 7

# The *Zhuangzi*

## SUGGESTED PRIMARY READING

Chapters 1–7 from *Chuang-tzu: The Inner Chapters*, A.C. Graham, trans. (Indianapolis: Hackett, 2001), or Sections 1–7 from *Chuang Tzu—Basic Writings*, Burton Watson, trans. (New York: Columbia University Press, 1996).

## LEARNING OBJECTIVES

By the time you have worked through this chapter, you should be able to

> ➤ Describe the tale of *Peng* (Zhuangzi's imaginary big bird) and its philosophical significance
> ➤ Explain Zhuangzi's idea of "completed mind" (*cheng xin*)
> ➤ Understand Zhuangzi's view on life and death
> ➤ Explain Zhuangzi's understanding of freedom/wandering (*you*)
> ➤ Identify the differences and connections between Laozi and Zhuangzi

## KEY WORDS

completed mind (*cheng xin*), de-self (*sang wo/qu wo*), transformation of things (*wu-hua*), wandering (*you*)

## GUIDING QUESTIONS

The ancient Chinese philosophical texts we have discussed in previous chapters were all concerned about social, ethical, and political issues. The Daoist text in this chapter, the *Zhuangzi*, is rather different. Instead of advocating an alternative but normative morality and politics, the *Zhuangzi* launched an investigation into the very foundation of moral theories and political doctrines. Some of the questions raised by the text are as follows:

1. Are Confucian rituals and music (and other social conventions) means for self-realization, or are they actually barriers to an enlightened, *individual* spiritual life?
2. What is the authentic self? Is it one stripped of social conventions?
3. Is it possible to live a free/wandering life, like a fish in the river and a bird in the sky?
4. What is the true nature of birth/life and death from the perspective of *dao* (the natural and spontaneous way)?
5. How should we understand the relationship between humans and heaven (*tian*, naturalness or spontaneity)?

The *Zhuangzi* grapples with these questions and proposes a philosophy of life that emphasizes freedom, naturalness, and spontaneity.

## INTRODUCTION

Zhuangzi (Chuang Tzu) is traditionally known as the second great Daoist[1] and one of the most profound thinkers in Chinese history. Zhuangzi's esteemed status in the Daoist tradition as well as in Chinese culture is almost entirely due to the immensely influential Daoist text that bears his name, the *Zhuangzi*. In spite of the influence of the work, little is actually known about Zhuangzi himself, except what can be gleaned from Sima Qian's *Records of the Historian* (*Shi Ji*). According to this early historian, Zhuangzi was a native of the state of Song (now in Henan Province in central China), a relatively small and weak state compared to the other states during the Warring States Period (475–221 BCE). He might have once held a minor post (as an official in the Lacquer Garden) but abandoned it for private life. He is commonly believed to have been a contemporary of Mengzi, but it is difficult to determine exactly when he lived—scholars estimate 369–286 BCE. Our lack of knowledge about the historical Zhuangzi, however, should not prevent us from appreciating the greatness of his work. As remarked by Watson, "[w]hoever Chuang Chou [Zhuangzi] was, the writings attributed to him bear the stamp of a brilliant and original mind."[2]

---

1   The first great Daoist is Laozi (Lao Tzu) who allegedly wrote the *Daòdejing*.
2   Burton Watson, trans., *Chuang Tzu: Basic Writings* (New York: Columbia University Press, 1996), Introduction, 3.

The current version of the *Zhuangzi* was compiled by Daoist scholar Guo Xiang (Kuo Hsiang, d. 312 CE). The work contains thirty-three chapters, divided into three parts. Part one consists of the "Inner Chapters" (1–7) which are generally ascribed to Zhuangzi himself.[3] This part represents the core of Zhuangzi's Daoism. Part two, entitled the "Outer Chapters" (8–22), expounds and elaborates on the ideas presented in the "Inner Chapters." These chapters are probably the writings of Zhuangzi's followers. Part three, or the "Mixed Chapters" (23–33), consists of a collection of essays which, in some cases, do not seem to represent Zhuangzi's authentic teachings as reflected in the "Inner Chapters." We will focus on the seven "Inner Chapters," while occasionally drawing from some of the other chapters to help elucidate Zhuangzi's core teachings. The Inner Chapters include the following:

Chapter 1: "Free and Easy Wandering (*xiao yao you*)"[4]
Chapter 2: "Discussion on Making All Things Equal (*qi wu lun*)"
Chapter 3: "The Secret of Caring for Life (*yang sheng zhu*)"
Chapter 4: "In the World of Men (*ren jian shi*)"
Chapter 5: "The Sign of Virtue Complete (*de chong fu*)"
Chapter 6: "The Great and Venerable Teacher (*da zong shi*)"
Chapter 7: "Fit for Emperors and Kings (*ying di wang*)"

Contrary to Confucius, whose concerns were about harmony on the familial and the state levels in a time of great disorder, Zhuangzi was interested in individual spiritual freedom, not in state-ruling and social-political reform. According to Zhuangzi, we cannot experience personal freedom and live well not only because of human-produced social ills (such as war, poverty, and injustice) but also because of what we deem natural ills (such as disease and death). Watson summarizes Zhuangzi's project nicely:

Chuang Tzu [Zhuangzi] saw the same human sufferings that Confucius, Mo Tzu, and Mencius saw. He saw the man-made ills of war, poverty, and injustice. He saw the natural ills of disease and death. But he believed that they were ills only because man recognized them as such. If man would once forsake his habit of labelling things good or bad, desirable or undesirable, then the man-made ills, which are the product of man's purposeful and value-ridden actions, would disappear and the natural ills that remain would no longer be seen as ills, but as an inevitable part of the course of life. Thus, in Chuang Tzu's eyes, man is the author of his own suffering and bondage, and all his fears spring from the web of values created by himself alone.[5]

---

3  See A.C. Graham, trans., *Chuang-tzu: The Inner Chapters* (Indianapolis: Hackett, 2001), 3; and Watson 14. Most of the quotations from Zhuangzi in this chapter will be translations from this book of Graham's, or from Watson's book mentioned in the previous footnote. To distinguish these sources from each other, and from other books by these authors/translators, they will be noted parenthetically in the text or in footnotes by G or by W, respectively.
4  The translation of all the chapter titles is from W.
5  W, 4. The idea that "man is the author of his own suffering and bondage" reminds us of the opening verse in the Dhammapada: "Our life is shaped by our mind; we become what we think. Suffering follows

To release us from our own suffering and bondage, Zhuangzi advises (1) that we see the arbitrariness of human-centred (and self-centred) values, including the narrow-mindedness and the imposing nature of doctrines, such as Confucianism and Moism, and (2) that we should realize the inevitability of change, big or small, in human life and in the natural world. In proposing this outlook on life, Zhuangzi adopts as his frame of reference not humanity or society as construed by the Confucians, Moists, and others, but the natural and spontaneous *dao*.

Zhuangzi's advice posed a radical challenge in his time to the conventional think-ing about living and the meaning of human existence. It is no wonder that, for many of his contemporaries, Zhuangzi's philosophy appeared hopelessly impractical and wide of the mark. This was the opinion even of his good friend Huizi.[6] In a way, Zhuangzi's philosophy was addressed to "spiritual elites" rather than commoners in the society.[7] He seems to have assumed that the masses (perhaps particularly the Confucians and the Moists) were wallowing in the man-made "muddle," too trapped to be lifted out.[8]

Zhuangzi is a brilliant master of language whose literary talent was unparal-leled among the ancient Chinese philosophers. The style of the *Zhuangzi* is unique among the writings of ancient Chinese philosophers, in that it is imbued with novel metaphors, profound fables, and vivid imagery. In contrast to the verse style of the *Daodejing*, the *Zhuangzi* comprises short poetic prose essays and the ideas in them are more developed than those of the *Daodejing*. The *Zhuangzi* can be amusing as well as fascinating to read. However, readers may find it difficult to pin down what it conveys in a propositional form, for the allegorical nature of the text stubbornly resists any simple formulation. Intriguing as they may be, the ideas in the book often appear cryptic and elusive. It is therefore not uncommon for readers to experience a sense of disorientation when they first approach it.[9] Yet the ideas are also provocative and inspirational. General readers sometimes consider it merely a piece of colourful, imaginative literature, rather than a serious and profound philosophical text. But, interestingly, it is both art and philosophy.[10]

### THE TALE OF *PENG* AND ITS PHILOSOPHICAL SIGNIFICANCE

The first chapter of the *Zhuangzi*, entitled "Free and Easy Wandering," starts with a tale of a gigantic fish (*Kun*) and how it transforms into an enormous bird (*Peng*):

---

an evil thought as the wheels of a cart follow the oxen that draw it" (Easwaran trans.).

6   See below Zhuangzi and Hui Shi's discussion of "usefulness" and "uselessness" in Chapter 1 of the *Zhuangzi*.

7   W, 5.

8   See W, 33.

9   Some of my Western students in Chinese philosophy say that when they like the *Analects*, they know and can say why they like it, but even when they like the *Zhuangzi*, they find it very hard to explain why. This is a consequence of the interesting and at the same time elusive nature of the work.

10   The *Zhuangzi* has been a main source of inspiration in landscape painting, allegory, and poetry in China.

In the North Ocean there is a fish, its name is the K'un; the K'un's girth
measures who knows how many thousand miles. It changes into a bird, its
name is the P'eng; the P'eng's back measures who knows how many thousand miles. When it puffs out its chest and flies off, its wings are like clouds
hanging from the sky. This bird when the seas are heaving has a mind to
travel to the South Ocean. (The South Ocean is the Lake of Heaven.) In the
words of the *Tall stories*, 'When the P'eng travels to the South Ocean, the
wake it thrashes on the water is three thousand miles long, it mounts spiral-
ling on the whirlwind ninety thousand miles high, and is gone six months
before it is out of breath.' (The *Tall stories of Ch'i* is a record of marvels.) Is
that azure of the sky its true colour? Or is it that the distance into which
we are looking is infinite? It never stops flying higher till everything below
looks the same as above (heat-hazes, dust-storms, the breath which living
things blow at each other).[11]

What do we make of this huge imagined bird? What is the philosophical point of
the story? Why doesn't Zhuangzi state his point straightforwardly? While you may be
baffled by these questions, you may also find it amusing that the cicada and the little
dove could not make sense of what the giant bird is doing either.

*narrow mindedness*

The cicada and the little dove laugh at this, saying, "When we make an
effort and fly up, we can get as far as the elm or the sapanwood tree, but
sometimes we don't make it and just fall down on the ground. Now how
is anyone going to go ninety thousand li [distance unit, like the mile] to
the south!"
    If you go off to the green woods nearby, you can take along food for three
meals and come back with your stomach as full as ever. If you are going a
hundred li, you must grind your grain the night before; and if you are going
a thousand li, you must start getting the provisions together three months
in advance. What do these two creatures understand? Little understanding
cannot come up to great understanding; the short-lived cannot come up to
the long-lived.[12]

In this allegorical tale, the cicada and the little dove find it silly to fly "ninety thousand li to the south"; they do not understand the need to prepare the food ("getting the
provisions together three months in advance") before the flight. According to Zhuangzi,
the reason that the cicada and the little dove failed to understand *Peng*'s behaviour is
that they have very limited ("small") understanding.

*small understanding*

---

11  1, G, 43. Part II of G consists of seven chapters which are translations of the correspondingly num-
bered chapters of the *Zhuangzi* Inner Chapters. (G adds an eighth chapter on some related material.)
(The numeral preceding the "G" in this footnote and others is the chapter number in which the selection
is found. The number following the "G" is the page number in G.)
12  W, 24.

From the limitation (narrow-mindedness) of the cicada and the little dove, Zhuangzi moves to the cognitive limitation of the blind and the deaf, and then to the blindness and deafness of *human understanding*: "We cannot expect a blind man to appreciate beautiful patterns or a deaf man to listen to bells and drums. And blindness and deafness are not confined to the body alone—the understanding has them too."[13]

Zhuangzi is not laughing at the cognitive limitation of the physically blind and deaf, for these limitations are due to their bodily conditions rather than drawn arbitrarily by their minds. But he does want to laugh at those who are spiritually blind and deaf. He wants to open the "eyes" and "ears" of those with limited understanding so that they can realize their limitations in "seeing" and "hearing" the world. With open ears and eyes they would realize the arbitrariness of their habitual way of life and welcome alternative ways of life.

Now imagine you were the bird *Peng* up high in the sky. What do you see and how do you feel? Well, you would have a great vision (a bird's-eye view) and a tremendous sense of freedom. You would no longer be confined within the limited perspectives of the cicada or the little dove, etc. In this sense, the tale of *Peng* suggests that Zhuangzi wants to establish a transcendental perspective from which *Peng* can *judge* the perspectives of the cicada and the dove as limited, but not his own. On this reading, *Peng*'s perspective is like that of the philosopher outside Plato's cave, in that both perspectives are seen as criteria for judging those of others, but not to be judged by anything else.

However, I think this reading, interesting as it may be, does not capture the true message of the tale. In my opinion, in the tale of *Peng*, (1) Zhuangzi does not want to establish a transcendental perspective, and (2) he wants to illustrate a value-free *awareness*. Karyn Lai has argued for (1) in the following passage:

> The giant bird may be large and impressive, and the cicada and dove trivially small, in comparison. But Peng is capable only of a broad view and is unable to discern finer detail. It, too, has only a partial perspective. It likewise suffers from physical limitations: while the small creatures cannot fly far, the giant bird cannot take flight unless the wind conditions are sufficiently strong to carry it. There is neither a privileged observer nor an ideal adjudicator; Zhuangzi is sceptical about the ability of individuals to adopt value-free perspectives. Or, in other words, there are *no* value-free perspectives.[14]

I think Lai is right in arguing that for Zhuangzi "there are *no* value-free perspectives." But her interpretation of the tale does not entail that for Zhuangzi there is no value-free *awareness*—a spiritual awareness in which one realizes the limitedness and

---

13   1, W, 27. The numeral sometimes found to the left of "W" in these footnotes is the chapter of the *Zhuangzi* from which the selected passage is translated.

14   Karyn L. Lai, *An Introduction to Chinese Philosophy* (Cambridge: Cambridge University Press, 2008), 147.

arbitrariness of human conventions and doctrines, and in which one is not snared by man-made value distinctions.

First, contrary to Lai's interpretation, it is not plausible that Zhuangzi imagined the extraordinary big bird *Peng* merely to show that *Peng*'s own perspective (and any other perspective) is limited and "partial." He can show the limitedness of perspectives simply by pointing to the differences between the dove's perspective and the cicada's perspective: neither is able to see or feel what the other is able to see or feel. Indeed, the real problem with the cicada and the little dove is not their physical and cognitive limitations, but their *unwillingness* to recognize their limitations and their *unwillingness* to adopt an open mind towards other ways of life.

Second, Zhuangzi does not seem to be talking about the cognitive or physical limitations of *Peng*. In referring to the indefinite azure colour of the sky and the ever-changing wind conditions, Zhuangzi does *not* imply that *Peng* is "unable to discern finer detail." Rather, he suggests that *Peng does not care* about the differences on the ground or in the sky, and *Peng* is *not bothered* by how the little dove and the cicada laugh at him.

Thus, the message of the tale is that if one can lift oneself and "fly" above into the "spiritual sky" (awareness), one would not be bothered by man-made distinctions and differences. Accordingly, "the wind conditions" symbolize the conditions and circumstances for lifting oneself up to lofty spiritual awareness and freedom. In other words, the discussion of "the wind conditions" is not about physical limitations, but about knowing spiritual storing—namely knowing when circumstances are fit for action. In short, for Zhuangzi, although there is no value-free *perspective*, there is value-free *awareness*.

## DOING PHILOSOPHY
### The Cicada, the Well-Frog, and the Lord of the River

Two other fables about the ills of closed-mindedness are told in Chapter 17 ("Autumn Floods"), a very important Outer Chapter. One is the frog-in-the-well (W, 97, 107) and the other is the Lord of the Yellow River (W, 96ff.). The well-frog is very similar to the cicada and little dove in that he seeks to understand and judge the lives of others by his own way of life. By contrast, the Lord of the Yellow River is open to alternative ways of life. Read the following paragraphs about the spiritual journey of the Lord of the Yellow River.

The time of the autumn floods came and the hundred streams poured into the Yellow River. Its racing current swelled to such proportions that, looking from bank to bank or island to island, it was impossible to distinguish a horse from a cow. Then the Lord of the River was beside himself with joy, believing that all the beauty in the world belonged to him alone. Following the current, he journeyed east until at last he reached the North Sea. Looking east, he could see no end to the water.

The Lord of the River began to wag his head and roll his eyes. Peering far off in the direction of Jo [the god of the sea], he sighed and said, "The common saying has it, 'He has heard the Way a mere hundred times but he thinks he's better than anyone else.' It applies to me. In the past, I heard men belittling the learning of Confucius and making light of the righteousness of Po Yi, though I never believed them. Now, however, I have seen your unfathomable vastness. If I hadn't come to your gate, I should have been in danger. I should forever have been laughed at by the masters of the Great Method!" (W, 96)

In Zhuangzi's view, need a person be inherently confined to and limited by one's habitual understanding, like the cicada, the little dove, and the well-frog? Or can one, like the Lord of the River, be jolted into an awareness of one's limitations in understanding?

## ALTERNATIVE WAYS OF LIFE

Zhuangzi likens people involved in politics (perhaps the Confucians) to the cicada and the little dove, who are filled with both self-pride and closed-mindedness: "Those, then, who are clever enough to do well in one office or efficient enough to protect one district, whose powers suit one prince and are put to the test in one state, are seeing themselves as the little birds did."[15]

His examples of people whose alternative ways of life are closed to such people include one who is swayed neither by praise nor blame; one who is free from pedestrian entanglements in everyday life; and the "utmost man," the "daemonic man," and "the sage," who have no self-concerns at all.[16]

In addressing ways of life other than conventional political life, Zhuangzi went as far as to suggest that an individual's carefree life is superior to political life, which (he seems to assume) is not carefree. This point is clearly seen in the account of an exchange between two legendary people: the ruler Yao and a Daoist hermit, Hsu Yu. According to the account, when Yao wanted to cede the empire to Hsu Yu, the latter surprisingly declined.

"When the sun and moon have already come out," he [Yao] said, "it's a waste of light to go on burning the torches, isn't it? When the seasonal rains are falling, it's a waste of water to go on irrigating the fields. If you took the throne, the world would be well ordered. I go on occupying it, but all I can see are my failings. I beg to turn over the world to you."

15   1, G, 44.
16   See 1, G, 44–45.

Hsu Yu said, "You govern the world and [you think] the world is already well governed. Now if I take your place, will I be doing it for a name? But name is only the guest of reality—will I be doing it so I can play the part of a guest? When the tailorbird builds her nest in the deep wood, she uses no more than one branch. When the mole drinks at the river, he takes no more than a bellyful. Go home and forget the matter, my lord. I have no use for the rulership of the world! Though the cook may not run his kitchen properly, the priest and the impersonator of the dead at the sacrifice do not leap over the wine casks and sacrificial stands and go take his place."[17]

In this dialogue, Yao saw Hsu Yu as representing the natural lights of "the sun and the moon" and the natural resource of "the seasonal rains," which are superior to "the torches" and the "irrigating water" in his rulership—since the last two are man-made. But Hsu Yu was adamant that he had "no use for the rulership of the world." First, Hsu Yu did not want to take Yao's place because the taking-over might look like as if Hsu Yu was doing it for "name"—that is, for fame. (Hsu Yu may be implying that Yao was ruling for fame.) Second, and more importantly, Hsu Yu did not think it necessary to rule as Yao did, for if people lived naturally or spontaneously as the tailorbird and the mole did, then everything would be in its natural order and no ruling would be needed. According to Hsu Yu, since the cook on the one hand and the priest and the impersonator of the dead on the other has each his own way of life (role or duty to fulfill), there is no need to let one's role be played by another.

As Zhuangzi's Daoist exemplar, Hsu Yu is not the only one. Zhuangzi mentions Daoist master hermits who live a life similar to Hsu Yu's.

A man of Sung who sold ceremonial hats made a trip to Yueh, but the Yueh people cut their hair short and tattoo their bodies and had no use for such things. Yao brought order to the people of the world and directed the government of all within the seas. But he went to see the Four Masters of the far away Ku-she Mountain, [and when he got home] north of the Fen River, he was dazed and had forgotten his kingdom there.[18]

According to this passage, Yao must have been greatly impressed by the Daoist master hermits who were depicted as *shenren*. A *shenren* (Watson translates it as "Holy Man," and Graham as "daemonic man") was described as one whose skin and flesh are like ice and snow, and who is shy like a virgin, does not eat the five grains, but sucks the wind, drinks the dew, climbs up on the clouds and mist, rides a flying dragon, wanders beyond the four seas, and protects creatures from sickness and plague and makes the harvest plentiful by concentrating his spirit.[19] These metaphors suggest a way of life that is in harmony with everything and that allows everything to flourish through the

---

17  W, 26–27. The "you think" in the square brackets is my addition.
18  W, 28.
19  See W, 27; and 1, G, 46.

*shenren*'s own spiritual concentration. Yao's dazed state and his forgetfulness regarding his kingdom seem to suggest that being a ruler of a kingdom is not as desirable as being a *shenren*.

Given the radicalness of the *shenren* way of life, it is no wonder Zhuangzi's contemporaries (even his close friend Hui Shih) found him hard to understand and difficult to trust, so that they viewed him "talk[ing] big" with "no sense," as if he had left "the firm ground and never came back." They found his remarks like "wild extravagances" that have "nothing to do with man."[20] Indeed, to most people living in Zhuangzi's time, a period of social chaos, his ideas would have appeared ridiculously impractical.

However, Zhuangzi was convinced that his teachings were useful. According to him, whether something is useful depends on what we intend to accomplish through the use of it and the degree to which it is appropriate to the task. Zhuangzi told a story about a purveyor of a medicine for keeping hands from chapping who did not get rich from selling it to silk-bleachers, but when a stranger bought the secret medicine and introduced it to a king, the king's troops won a war in winter, and the stranger received a fief from the king.[21] The message of the story is that value depends on context. This point is explained further in Chapter 17 of the *Zhuangzi*:

> From the point of view of function, if we regard a thing as useful because there is a certain usefulness to it, then among all the ten thousand things there are none that are not useful. [On the other hand], [i]f we regard a thing as useless because there is a certain uselessness to it, then among the ten thousand things there are none that are not useless.[22]

Zhuangzi seems to be suggesting that a thing can be deemed useful in many ways, and that nothing is intrinsically useful or useless. The usefulness of a thing is what we make of it in particular contexts.

> Hui Tzu [Huizi] said to Chuang Tzu [Zhuangzi], "I have a big tree called a *shu*. Its trunk is too gnarled and bumpy to apply a measuring line to, its branches too bent and twisty to match up to a compass or square. You could stand it by the road and no carpenter would look at it twice. Your words, too, are big and useless, and so everyone alike spurns them!"
> Chuang Tzu said, "Maybe you've never seen a wildcat or a weasel. It crouches down and hides, watching for something to come along. It leaps and races east and west, not hesitating to go high or low—until it falls into the trap and dies in the net. Then again there's the yak, big as a cloud covering the sky. It certainly knows how to be big, though it doesn't know how to catch rats. Now you have this big tree and you're distressed because it's useless. Why don't you plant it in Not-Even-Anything Village, or the field of Broad-and-Boundless, relax and do nothing by its side, or lie down for

---

20  1, G, 46.
21  See 1, W, 28–29.
22  17, W, 101.

a free and easy sleep under it? Axes will never shorten its life, nothing can ever harm it. If there's no use for it, how can it come to grief or pain?"[23]

To Huizi, the tree is useless—it is too knobbly and bumpy—so that no carpenter can make use of it. To Zhuangzi, however, it can be very useful in its own way, that is, you can relax yourself by its side, or lie down for a free and easy sleep under it—a new use, and indeed (for him) a better use for carefree living![24]

Huizi, in the eyes of Zhuangzi, has a kind of aspect-blindness. His mind is not open to alternative ways of seeing things and doing things. Aspect-blindness is a cognitive reality that we cannot escape. For example, we are not able to see things that an owl can see at night, and we cannot smell things that a dog can. The sort of aspect-blindness that Zhuangzi addresses occurs in our intellectual and spiritual life. Aspect-blindness, for him, is a form of closed-mindedness. His allegories are intended to be jarring, jolting us into a fresh awareness through which we realize that we do not need to stick to the dogmatism of our limitations.

To borrow concepts from Martin Buber (1878–1965), Huizi's relationship with the tree is an "I-It" relationship, which is about possessing, using, and exploiting, whereas the alternative attitude Zhuangzi adopts is an "I-Thou" relationship: non-possessing, harmonious, and aesthetic. The message from Zhuangzi's reply to Huizi regarding the tree seems to be that humans are capable of being in harmonious union with nature (and other humans). And when they adopt such an "I-Thou" mode of existence, no strife and war are necessary; they are automatically attuned to *dao*—the natural ways of things.

Zhuangzi suggests that his teachings can help open people's minds to the ideal of a carefree life. In speaking about Huizi's great tree being spared the axe, he is also hinting that his teachings can help deliver people from the dangers of living in a chaotic time.[25]

---

**DOING PHILOSOPHY**
*On Politics: Zhuangzi versus Confucius*

The similarities and differences between Zhuangzi's view and Confucius' view on politics can be seen in the following passages:

Zhuangzi's view:

Chien Wu went to see the madman Chieh Yu. Chieh Yu said, "What was Chung Shih telling you the other day?" Chien Wu said, "He told me that the ruler of men should devise his own principles, standards,

---

23  W, 29–30. Compare this quote with Chapter 11 of the *Daodejing*.
24  Read more about Zhuangzi's view on uselessness on Professor Sam Crane's website "The Useless Tree" at <http://www.uselesstree.typepad.com/>.
25  The idea of protecting oneself by being useless also appears in Chapter 4 *Ren Jian Shi*. See W, 60 and 63.

ceremonies, and regulations, and then there will be no one who will fail to obey him and be transformed by them."

The madman Chieh Yu said, "This is bogus virtue! To try to govern the world like this is like trying to walk the ocean, to drill through a river, or to make a mosquito shoulder a mountain! When the sage governs, does he govern what is on the *outside*? He makes sure of himself first, and then he acts. He makes absolutely certain that things can do what they are supposed to do, that is all. The bird flies high in the sky where it can escape the danger of stringed arrows. The field mouse burrows deep down under the sacred hill where it won't have to worry about men digging and smoking it out. Have you got less sense than these two little creatures?"[26]

Confucius' view:

The Master said, Govern the people by regulations, keep order among them by chastisements, and they will flee from you, and lose all self-respect. Govern them by moral force, keep order among them by ritual and they will keep their self-respect and come to you of their own accord.[27]

The Master said, Once a man has contrived to put himself aright, he will find no difficulty at all in filling any government post. But if he cannot put himself aright, how can he hope to succeed in putting others right?[28]

Carefully examine the above passages and try to tease out the similarities and differences between Confucius' view and Zhuangzi's view on politics. Hint: Do they both stress the importance of putting oneself aright (*zheng*) in the first place? Do they understand "putting oneself aright" in the same way? How does Confucius' political strategy work? Does Zhuangzi agree with that strategy? Why? To answer this last question, you can consult Yan Hui's forgetting "benevolence, righteousness, ritual, and music" (W, 86–87), for they are regarded as destroying ("tattooing") the true nature of being human (W, 85), and Zhuangzi's view of neither praising Yao nor condemning Chieh [a legendary evil king] (W, 76). Moreover, what would be Confucius' response to Zhuangzi (see the *Analects* 18:6–7 and Chapter 6 of the *Zhuangzi*), about "wandering beyond or within the realm" of humanity (see W, 83)?

---

26  7, W, 89–90.
27  Waley's translation, *Analects* 2:2.
28  Waley's translation, *Analects* 13:13; also see 12:17, 13:6.

## FROM COMPLETED MIND (*CHENG XIN*) TO DE-SELF (*SANG WO*)

In Chapter 1, "Free and Easy Wandering," Zhuangzi points to a kind of awareness in which one realizes and transcends one's closed-mindedness, be it the cicada, the little dove, or Huizi. In Chapter 2, "Discussion on Making All Things Equal (*qi wu lun*),"[29] he starts to explore the root cause of closed-mindedness. He believes that once the root cause is identified, it can be removed, and once it is removed, closed-mindedness will disappear. Zhuangzi's exploration begins with a medley of mental states, which he describes as follows:

> In sleep, men's spirits go visiting; in waking hours, their bodies hustle. With everything they meet they become entangled. Day after day they use their minds in strife, sometimes grandiose, sometimes sly, sometimes petty. Their little fears are mean and trembly; their great fears are stunned and overwhelming. They bound off like an arrow or a crossbow pellet, certain that they are the arbiters of right and wrong. They cling to their position as though they had sworn before the gods, sure that they are holding on to victory. They fade like fall and winter—such is the way they dwindle day by day. They drown in what they do—you cannot make them turn back. They grow dark, as though sealed with seals—such are the excesses of their old age. And when their minds draw near to death, nothing can restore them to the light.[30]

In this passage, Zhuangzi offers a vivid description of what commonly goes on in people's minds. (1) They attach to things whether awake or sleeping; (2) their minds are used in all kinds of strife; (3) they have all sorts of fear; (4) they deem themselves as the arbiters of right and wrong; (5) they cling to their position (i.e., doctrine, belief, or theory). All these entanglements (strife, fear, and attachment) suffocate the spontaneous flow of energy so that their natural life decreases day by day until it is exhausted.

Zhuangzi argues that we have a diversity of emotional states, and if we let them be they happen naturally and spontaneously:

> Joy, anger, grief, delight, worry, regret, fickleness, inflexibility, modesty, wilfulness, candor, insolence—music from empty holes, mushrooms springing up in dampness, day and night replacing each other before us, and no one knows where they sprout from. Let it be! Let it be! [It is enough that]

---

29 There is a grammatical ambiguity in the title *qi wu lun*. As Thomas Michael has pointed out, "The Chinese terms are *qi* (equalization, parity), *wu* (being, things), and *lun* (explanation, essay, theory). The tenor of the title changes depending on whether one emphasizes *qi* or *lun*; if one gives emphasis to *lun*, then the title translates as 'A Discussion on the Equality of Beings' (*qiwu: lun*); if one emphasizes *qi*, the translation is 'Equalization of Things and Theories' (*qi: wulun*). Grammatically, nothing necessitates the reading of *qiwu: lun* to the exclusion of *qi: wulun*" (Thomas Michael, *The Pristine Dao—Metaphysics in Early Daoist Discourse* [Albany, NY: SUNY Press, 2005], 79).

30 2, W, 32.

morning and evening we have them and they are the means by which we live.[31]

Unfortunately, however, we are habitually entangled with things, and we pick and choose among these emotional states, clinging to some (e.g., joy, delight) and avoiding others (e.g., anger, grief). Zhuangzi argues that entanglements stem from a sense of self (*wo*). He claims that "*fei bi wu wo, fei wo wu suo qu* (非彼无我,非我无所取)," which I translate as "Without them [physical body and emotions] there would not be 'I'; without 'I' there would be no picking or choosing [or judging]."[32] On this translation, Zhuangzi's point is that on the one hand "my" life is based on my physical and psychological functions, and on the other hand "my" life (my sense of self) also forms the basis for my picking and choosing. While "my" life's reliance on my physical and psychological functions is natural and spontaneous, "my" life (my sense of self) as the basis of my picking and choosing [judging] is not. In fact, for Zhuangzi, all the troubles of human life arise from an obsessive sense of "I."

What is the nature of the sense of "I"? Where does it come from? Zhuangzi argues that it is vague and elusive and that it does not seem to arise from an organ in one's body:

The hundred joints, the nine openings, the six organs, all come together and exist here [as my body]. But which part should I feel closest to? I should delight in all parts, you say? But there must be one I ought to favour more. If not, are they all of them mere servants? But if they are all servants, then how can they keep order among themselves? Or do they take turns being lord and servant? It would seem as though there must be some True Lord among them. But whether I succeed in discovering his identity or not, it neither adds to nor detracts from his Truth.[33]

Zhuangzi seems to believe that the sense of self is elusive and formless, yet it is there in that it functions in all the mental states mentioned above. This formless self, I suspect, is what Zhuangzi calls *cheng xin* (成心) (translated as "completed mind" by Graham, and "a mind given" by Watson). *Cheng xin* is a self-centred stand from which one makes judgments of others, as in the cases with the cicada, the little dove, and Huizi.[34] For Zhuangzi, it is the root cause of all the problems in the complex of common human consciousness.

---

31  2, W, 32–33.

32  Watson translated Zhuangzi's claim as "Without them [the diverse emotions] we would not exist; without us they would have nothing to take hold of" (W, 33), and Graham translated it as "Without an Other there is no Self, without Self no choosing one thing rather than another" (2, G, 51).

33  2, W, 33.

34  *Cheng xin* is still a Chinese colloquial term, meaning someone does something on purpose or with a bias, or as a setup. A cognate of it is *chen jian* (completed or fixed view), which refers to a subjective, limited, and fixed view of someone or something.

If a man follows the mind given him (*cheng xin*) and makes it his teacher, then who can be without a teacher [*shi*, Graham has "authority"]? Why must you comprehend the process of change and form your mind on that basis before you can have a teacher? Even an idiot has his teacher. But to fail to abide by this mind and still insist upon your rights and wrongs—this is like saying that you set off for Yueh today and got there yesterday. This is to claim that what doesn't exist exists.[35]

Thus, a completed mind is one's self-centred, closed-minded perspective. When one is stuck in it, one uses one's own standard to judge the right and wrong of others, as with the debate between the Confucians and the Moists. "What one calls right the other calls wrong; what one calls wrong the other calls right."[36] Neither the Confucians nor the Moists realized that there exists no absolute standard of judgment and their respective standard is only arbitrary. For instance, Confucians believed that it is right to observe the convention-prescribed funeral and mourning rituals for one's parents (i.e., Confucians' three-year mourning ritual). Moists, by contrast, argued that Confucian funeral and mourning practice is wasteful and thus cannot be right. For Zhuangzi, both parties failed to realize that their perspectives were arbitrary at best, for whether or not one should observe these rituals is entirely based on man-made criteria.[37] To illustrate the non-absoluteness of any standard, Zhuangzi discusses a list of opposites in the following passage:

Everything has its "that" (*bi*), everything has its "this" (*shi*). From the point of view of "that" you cannot see it ["this"], but through understanding you can know it [alternative translation: "from the point of view of 'this' you can know it ('this')"]. So I say, "that" comes out of "this" and "this" depends on "that"—which is to say that "this" and "that" give birth to each other. But where there is birth there must be death; where there is death there must be birth. Where there is acceptability there must be unacceptability; where there is unacceptability there must be acceptability. Where there is recognition of right there must be recognition of wrong; where there is recognition of wrong there must be recognition of right.[38]

This passage tells us that "this" and "that," birth and death, acceptability and unacceptability, and right and wrong are all relative and arbitrary concepts. When a debate happens between two parties, both parties hold concepts such as these as absolute ones. They both hold ruthlessly to their own limited and fixed perspective. This makes their debate hopeless.

---

35  2, W, 34.
36  2, W, 34.
37  While Zhuangzi is hard on Confucians, he is not equally so with Confucius himself. In fact, he respects Confucius and uses Confucius as a spokesperson for his own Daoist view (see 4, 6, W, 42, 84–85).
38  W, 34–35; also see *Daodejing* Chapter 2.

Zhuangzi drives home this point in the fascinating passage below where he seeks to demonstrate the arbitrariness of trying to settle who is "right" in a dispute:

> Suppose you and I have had an argument. If you have beaten me instead of
> my beating you, then are you necessarily right and am I necessarily wrong?
> If I have beaten you instead of your beating me, then am I necessarily right
> and are you necessarily wrong? If you and I don't know the answer, then
> other people are bound to be even more in the dark. Whom shall we get to
> decide what is right? Shall we get someone who agrees with you to decide?
> But if he already agrees with you, how can he decide fairly? Shall we get
> someone who agrees with me? But if he already agrees with me, how can
> he decide? Shall we get someone who disagrees with both of us? But if he
> already disagrees with both of us, how can he decide? Shall we get someone
> who agrees with both of us? But if he already agrees with both of us, how
> can he decide? Obviously, then, neither you nor I nor anyone else can know
> the answer. Shall we wait for still another person?[39]

To help make clear the logic of Zhangzi's argument, let's illustrate how it works with two sets of scenarios as follows.

Disputants: John and Peter
Arbiter: Michael

POSSIBLE SCENARIOS

The first group of scenarios concerns John and Peter only:

1.  John wins. This does not mean John is necessarily right; it does not mean Peter is necessarily wrong either.
2.  Peter wins. This does not mean Peter is necessarily right; it does not mean John is necessarily wrong either.

The second group of scenarios brings in an arbiter Michael:

1.  If Michael is on John's side to begin with, then he will not be in a position to decide who (John or Peter) is right, for he is not an objective third party.
2.  If Michael is on Peter's side to begin with, then he will likewise not be in a position to render a fair decision on who (John or Peter) is right for precisely the same reason as in the previous scenario.
3.  If Michael is against both John's and Peter's positions to begin with, then he has (from the start) decided that neither of them is right and will therefore not be in a position to decide who (John or Peter) is right.

---

39  2, W, 43–44.

4. If Michael is for both John and Peter to begin with, then he has found (from the start) both agreeable. Thus, he will not be in a position to decide who (John or Peter) is right.

In this argument, Zhuangzi seeks to impress on us that there is an arbitrary element in the process of argumentation or justification. An argument must proceed from a certain background belief or assumption (i.e., a premise, an axiom, or a convention) that is simply taken for granted. Otherwise, there will be an infinite regress of justification. The acceptance of such background assumption is therefore a matter of choice or commitment, which is arbitrary.[40] In Zhuangzi's view, neither Confucianism nor Moism escapes the arbitrariness of argumentation.

Can one ever get out of the hopeless trap of a debate? How? According to Zhuangzi, it is possible to avoid the hopeless trap, but it is not easy. It may involve a radical change in one's mind-heart, that is, a change from the state of completed mind to that of de-self, a state that is vividly described in the dialogue between Ziqi and his pupil Yan Cheng Zi-you at the beginning of Chapter 2 of the *Zhuangzi*.

> Tzu-ch'i [Ziqi] of South Wall sat leaning on his armrest, staring up at the sky and breathing—vacant and far away, as though he'd lost his companion. Yen Ch'eng Tzu-yu [Yan Cheng Zi-you], who was standing by his side in attendance, said, "What is this? Can you really make the body like a withered tree and the mind like dead ashes? The man leaning on the armrest is not the one who leaned on it before!"
> Tzu-ch'i said, "You do well to ask the question, Yen. Now I have lost myself. Do you understand that?" (W, 31; see 2, G, 48)

The meaning of Ziqi's loss of self ("I") is not transparent to Yan Cheng Zi-you. While Yan Cheng Zi-you recognizes a drastic change in Ziqi's physical appearance upon his loss of self, he knows nothing about Ziqi's inner awareness, which appears to him as dead as "the dead ashes." Realizing that it is hard for Yan Cheng Zi-you to understand his active state of awareness merely from his physical appearance, Ziqi launches into an explanation of this selfless awareness, with a discussion of the functions of the pipings (sounds) of earth and of heaven.[41]

---

40  In Western philosophy, Wittgenstein remarked that justification cannot go on infinitely. In his view, justification comes to an end, not at some true propositions (for example, an axiom in Euclidian geometry), but at our accepting them in our acting (doing geometry, for instance). In Wittgenstein's own words, "Giving grounds, however, justifying the evidence, comes to an end;—but the end is not certain propositions' striking us immediately as true, i.e., it is not a kind of *seeing* on our part; it is our *acting* which lies at the bottom of the language-game" (*On Certainty*, G.E.M. Anscombe and G.H. von Wright, eds., D. Paul and G.E.M. Anscombe, trans. [Oxford: Basil Blackwell, 1969], §204; also see sections §164, §192). See also: "If I have exhausted the justification I have reached bedrock, and my spade is turned. Then I am inclined to say: 'This is simply what I do'" (*Philosophical Investigations*, §271; also see §485). For Wittgenstein, ultimately, justification comes to an end as we *in general* share a human form of life (see *Philosophical Investigations* §19, §23, §241).
41  2, W, 31–32.

Ziqi argues that the piping of the earth is diverse due to all kinds of hollows on earth, and the piping of heaven consists of all the natural happenings (the "sounds") in the cosmos: "Blowing on the ten thousand things in a different way, so that each can be itself—all take what they want for themselves, but who does the sounding?"[42] His question ("who does the sounding?") seems to suggest that, unlike the complex of habitual human mental states, there is no self-conscious agent behind all the soundings; they just spontaneously happen. There is no omniscient God who designs everything in the cosmos. In other words, for Ziqi, there are all these soundings, but there is no agent that picks or chooses among them, no value judgment of them. Ziqi seems to imply that his selfless awareness is like the piping of heaven which does no picking or choosing, makes no value judgment of whatever comes to his mind. In short, his mind is not as dead as "dead ashes," and presumably it will allow all "soundings" in his mind to arise as "they want for themselves."

Once one's completed mind is lost or dissolved,[43] one can best negotiate the disorienting disputes about right and wrong and bring *ming* (明)[44]—that is, illumination, clarity, or light—to the situation:

Therefore the sage does not proceed in such a way [i.e., holding dogmatically he is right and others are wrong], but illuminates all in the light of Heaven [*tian*, Nature or *dao*]. He too recognizes a "this," but a "this" which is also "that," a "that" which is also "this." His "that" has both a right and a wrong in it; his "this" too has both a right and a wrong in it. So, in fact, does he still have "this" and "that"? Or does he in fact no longer have a "this" and "that"? A state in which "this" and "that" no longer find their opposites is called the hinge of the Way. When the hinge is fitted into the socket, it can

---

42  2, W, 32. Also see *Kena Upanishad* I:1 regarding the question if there is an agent behind all natural happenings.

43  Zhuangzi's de-self (dismissing of completed mind) can be seen as a reaction to Mengzi, who holds that human mind-heart has inherent moral capacities, what he calls "four sprouts." For Zhuangzi, to see humans as having innate and inherent moral capacities (making distinctions and disputations) is to see one's mind-heart (*xin*) as fixed or completed (*cheng*). A fixed mind-heart would eclipse or block one's deeper spontaneity or the flow of the *dao* that is dynamic, flexible, illuminating (*ming*). This is why Zhuangzi advises the "fasting of the mind-heart" (*xin zhai*) (see the *Zhuangzi* Chapter 4), "sitting and forgetting" (*zuo wang*) (see the *Zhuangzi* Chapter 2 and Chapter 6) and to return to the primordial flow of *qi* (氣, energies), which all point to cleaning up the conventional "entanglements" (19, W, 197)—excessive, non-stop pursuit of fame, power, wealth, man-made value distinction and hierarchy, endless debate of right and wrong, and so on. Regarding mind-heart cultivation, Zhuangzi argues that the mind-heart should be emptied and be *nurtured* by the vital energy, contrary to Mengzi, who maintains that the mind-heart must *command* the vital energy. In sum, Zhuangzi's and Mengzi's cultivation procedures are exactly the reverse of each other. (See Bryan W. Van Norden, "Competing Interpretations of the Inner Chapters of the Zhuangzi," *Philosophy East and West* 46:2 [April 1996]: 257–58, and Scott Cook, "Zhuangzi and His Carving of the Confucian Ox," *Philosophy East and West* 47:4 [October 1997]: 534–35.)

44  The character *ming* juxtaposes the sun (日) and the moon (月) which means simply "light" or "brightness," and by extension means "make manifest" or "to understand." Compare with the idea of *ming* in *Daodejing* (see Chapters 16, 27, 36, 47, 52).

respond endlessly. Its right then is a single endlessness and its wrong too is a single endlessness. So I say, the best thing to use is clarity (*ming*).[45]

Let's use an example to illustrate Zhuangzi's point. When two parties are involved in a debate, each side sticks to their position and denies the other's. For example, one party insists that the process of a-bean-turning-into-a-sprout is the "birth" of the beansprout, and the other contends that the same process is actually the "death" of the bean. One party recognizes its "this" ("birth") but denies "that" ("death") while the other recognizes its "this" ("death") but denies "that" ("birth"). Each party is one-sided and fixed. By contrast, the sage recognizes both "this" and "that." That is, if he recognizes "this" ("birth"), he also recognizes "that" ("death"), or if he recognizes "this" ("death"), he will also recognize "that" ("birth"). For both "this" and "that" describe precisely the same process; the categorization of "this" ("birth"/"death") and "that" ("death"/"birth") is totally arbitrary! Once the sage realizes that neither "this" nor "that" is substantial (he may still accept "this" and "that" as conventional opposites), he is able to respond endlessly (that is, open-endedly and fluidly) to whatever happens to him. This open-ended and fluid response Zhuangzi calls clarity (*ming*).

Clarity can also be seen as disclosing. In a debate between two parties, due to closed-mindedness neither party wants to see what the other party sees, so there is always a side that is concealed. However, if one can dissolve one's completed mind, one will be able to see and accept the world as-it-is. The world (all the concrete circumstances) then manifests itself in its authentic form. Zhuangzi's remark on illuminating all "in the light of Heaven" (*zhao zi yu tian*) suggests a mirror image of Nature in which every particular thing is disclosed in its own authentic being, not distorted by any category or conceptualization.

## DOING PHILOSOPHY
### *Is Zhuangzi's Idea of Completed Mind Analogous to Gadamer's Notion of "Prejudice"?*

Is Zhuangzi suggesting that we should eliminate all preconceptions and prejudices? Or is he merely recommending that we cultivate an open mind? Our lives are confined by location, community, class, and the like. We know only slices of reality even though we are equipped with the most advanced communication technology that history has witnessed. Heidegger argued that preconception or pre-understanding is an indispensable condition for any understanding. Following the footsteps of Heidegger, Hans-Georg Gadamer (1900–2002) has also elaborated on the inevitability of "prejudice" (used in

---

45   2, W, 35.

a neutral sense) in the act of interpreting and understanding. By "prejudice," Gadamer means the judgment we render about a text or a situation before we have in fact examined it in detail. For both Heidegger and Gadamer, while we can become aware of our preconceptions and "prejudices," and adjust our interpretative judgments accordingly, we cannot completely get rid of them.

Is Zhuangzi suggesting that we eliminate all preconceptions or prejudices, contrary to Heidegger's and Gadamer's analysis of what goes into the process of interpretation? How do you think Zhuangzi would respond to the view that "prejudices" are inevitable? Can we equate Zhuangzi's idea of completed mind-heart with Gadamer's notion of "prejudice"?

Zhuangzi uses the analogy of a mirror to talk about the nature of the exemplary Daoist (the Perfect Man's) mind. The Perfect Man's mind does not block the reflections of things when they "come"; and he lets the reflections "go," with no trace (attachment) of them left on the mirror. In other words, the mind of a Perfect Man sees things as they are without value judgment, without attachment to notions of how things ought to be.

> Do not be an embodier of fame; do not be a storehouse of schemes; do not be an undertaker of projects; do not be a proprietor of wisdom. Embody to the fullest what has no end and wander where there is no trail. Hold on to all that you have received from Heaven but do not think you have gotten anything. Be empty, that is all. The Perfect Man uses his mind like a mirror—going after nothing, welcoming nothing, responding but not storing. Therefore he can win out over things and not hurt himself.[46]

Zhuangzi's idea of the mind-heart as a mirror is different from Francis Bacon's (1561–1626) conception of mind—as an objective mirror (having been rid of all "idols of the tribe"),[47] and from John Locke's "tabula rasa" (blank slate) idea of mind.[48] Zhuangzi's teaching about the mirror-like "mind-heart" is not an abstract theory of how the mind represents objects and events, but a practical teaching on how to accept things as they are without clinging to any preconceived value judgment of how things ought to be. It enables us to free ourselves from the desire always to make the world conform to our expectation.

Given Zhuangzi's view about the mirror-like mind-heart, what is wrong with the cicada or the little dove in the first chapter "Free and Easy Wandering" is not that they

---

46  7, W, 94–95; also see 5, W, 65.
47  *Novum Organum* (Orig. 1620), Book I, §41 (London: William Pickering, 1844), 18.
48  *An Essay Concerning Human Understanding* (Orig. 1690), Book II, Chapter 1, §2. Locke's phrase here is actually "white paper" (Peter H. Nidditch, ed. [Oxford: Oxford University Press, 1975], 104).

*[handwritten: Open mindedness important in forms notice diversity in of life]*

have a limited perspective, but that they do not grasp that there are other natural forms
of life. Zhuangzi seems to have assumed that animals are innocently confined to their
habitual ways of thinking and understanding, and their own perspectives. However,
this is not so with the dogmatism of Confucians and Mohists, for they sought to impose
their views (i.e., benevolence, righteousness, right and wrong) on others ("tattoo" one's
natural body and "cutting off" one's nose[49]), such that others are denied the opportunity
to live authentically or spontaneously.

The sage can accept the world-as-it-is (all the concrete circumstances), according to
Zhuangzi, because he can recognize the uses or functions of things as equivalent. This
is the point of the following passage:

*[handwritten: Sage accept the world as is]*

> A road is made by people walking on it; things are so because they are called
> so. What makes them so? Making them so makes them so. What makes them
> not so? Making them not so makes them not so. Things all must have
> that which is so; things all must have that which is acceptable. There is
> nothing that is not so, nothing that is not acceptable.
>
> For this reason, whether you point to a little stalk or a great pillar, a leper
> or the beautiful Hsi-shih,[50] things ribald and shady or things grotesque
> and strange, the Way makes them all into one. Their dividedness is their
> completeness; their completeness is their impairment. No thing is either
> complete or impaired, but all are made into one again. Only the man of
> far-reaching vision knows how to make them into one. So he has no use
> [for categories], but relegates all to the constant. The constant is the useful;
> the useful is the passable; the passable is the successful; and with success, all
> is accomplished. He relies upon this alone, relies upon it and does not know
> he is doing so. This is called the Way.[51]

According to this passage, it is people's practice ("walking," "calling," and "pointing
to") that makes all things different; it is people who attribute values ("acceptable or
not," "beautiful or not," "complete or impaired") to things. In other words, no thing
is *intrinsically or essentially* so (or not so), acceptable (or not acceptable), beautiful
(or not beautiful), complete (or impaired). Thus, the sage would not impose closed
subjective views or rigid categories on the diverse and constantly changing world. For
Zhuangzi, everything as it is is perfectly in place in *dao*. The fish has its place in the
water, and the bird has its place in the sky. When the fish lives its own natural form
of life in the water and when the bird lives its own natural form of life, there is no
"debate" between them.

*[handwritten: every creature has its place]*

However, it seems wrong to think that for Zhuangzi there is simply no distinction
among things whatsoever. Nor does it make sense to think that he is suggesting that all

---

49  6, W, 85.
50  Xi Shi, a woman who was one of the renowned Four Beauties of ancient China.
51  W, 36.

things are identical and that we should treat everything identically.[52] Zhuangzi would agree that, on a practical level, we do have to make cognitive differentiation between things, for example, between a poisonous mushroom and an edible one. But he suggests that while we observe and recognize differences between things, we do not judge them to be intrinsically good or bad according to our completed mind. A mushroom poisonous to a human being may be good food to other species, or it may be important to eco-diversity. In Zhuangzi's words, "great wisdom observes both far and near, and for that reason recognizes small without considering it paltry, recognizes large without considering it unwieldy, for it knows that there is no end to the weighing of things."[53] And one in accordance with *dao* knows how to "deal with circumstances" and he still "distinguishes between safety and danger, [but he] contents himself with fortune or misfortune, and is cautious in his comings and goings. Therefore nothing can harm him."[54]

Zhuangzi argues that it is natural that we leave things as they are—every particular thing has its unique role in the world. If we do not stand on a human (or individual)-centred position, then we would see that a dragonfly is no better than a mosquito, a rat is no worse than a cat, and a cockroach is as interesting as a butterfly. These things are indeed different from each other, but their differences do not elicit value judgments. Since without the imposition of valuation everything is equivalent, we should not favour or cling to any one thing or state of affairs over another. To put it differently, the Daoist sage, based upon a profound understanding of the pluralistic nature of things, simply accepts whatever happens in life without being attached to any value judgment. *It is in this sense that things even out.* As paradoxical as it may seem, this evening out of things comes about because of the uniqueness and particularity of each individual thing. The sage can even out things precisely because he pays special attention to specific "times" and "circumstances,"[55] and to "what is suitable" in concrete situations:[56] "Fish live in water and thrive, but if men tried to live in water they would die. Creatures differ because they have different likes and dislikes. Therefore the former sages never required the same ability from all creatures or made them all do the same thing."[57]

For Zhuangzi, the world is neither a conglomerate of uniform objects nor a melting-pot that dissolves the uniqueness of particular things and events. The world is rather like an ecosystem in which biodiversity is critical to the flourishing of all the different species. Moreover, for Zhuangzi, to say that it is *right* for the fish to live in water is simply to say: fish live in water. And to say it is *wrong* for the fish to live in the sky is no

---

52 Things could be treated equally yet not identically. For example, according to Peter Singer, to argue that all animals are equal is not to argue that they all should be treated identically or in exactly the same way. It would be absurd, in striving to treat everyone equally to grant a man the right of abortion, just as it would be ridiculous if we granted the same political right, the right to vote to a nonhuman animal, say a dog (see Chapter 1: "All Animals Are Equal" in Peter Singer's *Animal Liberation* [New York: Avon Books], 1990).
53 17, W, 98.
54 17, W, 104.
55 17, W, 106.
56 18, W, 116.
57 18, W, 116.

more than to say that fish do not live in the sky. In this light, value judgment attempted here becomes totally redundant. Consequently, there is no need for any disputation.

## DOING PHILOSOPHY
### *Does Zhuangzi's View on Valuation Open the Door to Immoral Behaviour?*

If from a non-self-centred point of view, no real value distinction exists, and no choosing (value judgment) is made, do we have to face the consequence of "anything goes"? Does this open the door to immoral behaviour?

If the concept of immorality comes from self-centredness (or a completed mind) then removing self-centredness would remove any notion of immorality. But the question is: "Does the idea of immorality stem from a completed mind?"

## LIFE AND DEATH

From Zhuangzi's Daoist point of view, all differences and opposites are essentially human constructions and conceptualizations. A tree is not in itself short or tall, ugly or beautiful, useless or useful, if *we* do not compare it with other trees and if we do not judge its value to *us*. From the view of *dao*, these differences and opposites vanish, in the way that differences down on the ground diminish and then vanish when you look through a window of an airplane. Compare this to the bird *Peng*'s vision or awareness.

The problem is that human beings are normally obsessed with differences and opposites. One pair of opposites that we normally hold to most firmly is birth/life and death. This pair is investigated closely in Chapters 2, 3, and 18 of the *Zhuangzi*.

Most of us are inclined to take birth/life on the one hand and death on the other as completely different. While it seems natural that we cherish life and fear death, in the eyes of Zhuangzi, our love and fear are actually forms of intense attachment to this life. In history, many philosophers have seen such attachment as unnecessary, but they provide different reasons. Socrates, for example, urges people (especially those who live a virtuous life) to welcome death, because death for him meant the separation of the soul from the body, or more significantly, the freeing of the soul from the body that contaminates it. In Christianity, death is regarded as a consequence of sin, and salvation involves the hope of resurrection. In contrast, Confucius suggests that we focus on good living in this life instead of worrying about our death (while observing rituals concerning our parents' death), for death is a natural and inevitable process.[58] To Zhuangzi, all these views of death would still seem to entail a value judgment on birth/life over death (à la Confucius) or on death over birth/life (à la Socrates and Christianity). Zhuangzi's view on birth/life and death is radically different from all the above.

---

58 See the *Analects* 12:5, 12:7.

**DOING PHILOSOPHY**
*Pascal versus Zhuangzi: On the Finitude of Human Beings*

Zhuangzi argues that one's place "between heaven and earth" is like "a little stone or a little tree [sitting] on a huge mountain" (17, W, 97); one's "life has a limit" (3, W, 46). The French philosopher Blaise Pascal (1623–62) also seriously ponders the finitude of human beings—we are so tiny in the vast universe, our knowledge is limited, and we are mortal, etc. But unlike Zhuangzi who accepts the finitude of human beings as it is, Pascal feels frightened when he contemplates our limits. The following remarks from his *Pensées* reflect Pascal's view:

> Let us imagine a number of men in chains, and all condemned to death, where some are killed each day in the sight of the others, and those who remain see their own fate in that of their fellows, and wait their turn, looking at each other sorrowfully and without hope. It is an image of the condition of men.[59]
>
> When I consider the short duration of my life, swallowed up in the eternity before and after, the little space which I fill, and even can see, engulfed in the infinite immensity of spaces of which I am ignorant, and which know me not, I am frightened and am astonished at being here rather than there; for there is no reason why here rather than there, why now rather than then. Who has put me here? By whose order and direction have this place and time been allotted to me?[60]

Regarding the finitude of being human, do you feel the same way as Pascal or as Zhuangzi? What consequences would Pascal's way lead to? What consequence would Zhuangzi's way lead to? Or, you may be sympathetic to another philosopher, Frank Ramsey (1903–30) who says:

> Where I seem to differ from some of my friends is in attaching little importance to physical size. I don't feel the least humble before the vastness of the heavens. The stars may be large, but they cannot think or love; and these are qualities which impress me far more than size does. I take no credit for weighing nearly seventeen stone.
>
> My picture of the world is drawn in perspective, and not like a model to scale. The foreground is occupied by human beings, and the stars are all as small as three penny bits.[61]

59 Blaise Pascal, *Pensées*, W.F. Trotter, trans. (New York: Dutton, 1958), 199.
60 Pascal, 205.
61 *The Foundations of Mathematics and Other Logical Essays* (Oxford: Routledge, 2001), 291.

Zhuangzi's view of life and death is that these opposites, like all others, will even out in the larger scheme of things. Life and death to Zhuangzi are natural and inevitable processes, just like the shift of day into night and vice versa, or the change of seasons. From the view of *dao*, no priority should be given to day, nor should any preference be given to any season. In other words, day and night, as well as the four seasons, are all "on equal footing"—equal in importance and value. Zhuangzi asks, "How do I know that to take pleasure in life is not a delusion? How do I know that we who hate death are not exiles since childhood who have forgotten the way home?"[62] Instead of fearing, hating, or feeling sad about the end of life, Zhuangzi urges us to welcome and accept it, just as we accept birth/life, not in the hope of some kind of afterlife, but in the calm awareness that this is how things transform. Here are two passages that clearly reflect Zhuangzi's view on death.

> When Lao Tan [Lao Tzu, or Laozi, the reputed author of the *Daodejing*] died, Ch'in Shih went to mourn for him; but after giving three cries, he left the room.
>
> "Weren't you a friend of the Master?" asked Lao Tzu's [Laozi's] disciples.
> "Yes."
> "And you think it's all right to mourn him this way?"
> "Yes....Your master happened to come because it was his time, and he happened to leave because things follow along. If you are content with the time and willing to follow along, then grief and joy have no way to enter in....
> "Though the grease burns out of the torch, the fire passes on, and no one knows where it ends."[63]
> Chuang Tzu's wife died. When Hui Tzu went to convey his condolences, he found Chuang Tzu sitting with his legs sprawled out, pounding on a tub and singing. "You lived with her, she brought up your children and grew old," said Hui Tzu. "It should be enough simply not to weep at her death. But pounding on a tub and singing—this is going too far, isn't it?"
> Chuang Tzu said, "You're wrong. When she first died, do you think I didn't grieve like anyone else? But I looked back to her beginning and the time before she was born. Not only the time before she was born, but the time before she had a body. Not only the time before she had a spirit. In the midst of the jumble of wonder and mystery a change took place and she had a spirit. Another change and she had a body. Another change and she was born. Now there's been another change and she's dead. It's just like the progression of the four seasons, spring, summer, fall, winter.
> "Now she's going to lie down peacefully in a vast room. If I were to follow after her bawling and sobbing, it would show that I don't understand anything about fate. So I stopped."[64]

---

62   2, G, 59.
63   3, W, 48–49.
64   18, W, 113.

If anyone nowadays were to do what Zhuangzi did when he learned of his wife's death ("sitting with his legs sprawled out, pounding on a tub and singing"), he would certainly stun his relatives and friends. To many, Zhuangzi's attitude toward death seems rather unsettling. Can we say, for instance, to a mother who has just lost her son in a car accident that "Look at it this way: birth/life and death are just like day and night. They happen." It may be more comforting to say to the mother, "I am sorry for your loss. May your son rest in God's hands." But these words of comfort, if taken literally, are based on presuppositions (God and personal identity) which Zhuangzi does not seem to accept.[65]

Whatever we may think of his view of death, Zhuangzi's attitude is serious, sincere, and true to his philosophy;[66] he is as sincere as Socrates who believed that his soul would live with gods after its separation from his body. Notice that Zhuangzi did feel "grief" when his wife died, albeit only for a brief moment, like Ch'in Shih's giving of "three cries" (brief cry). This seems to indicate that Zhuangzi's way of treating death is not entirely callous, only that his "grief" was moderated by his belief that however shocking it may be, the experience of loss need not "injure" one's still mind,[67] for ultimately death (just like birth/life) is merely part of the endless process of change or transformation inherent in nature:[68] "Though the grease burns out of the torch, the fire passes on, and no one knows where it ends."[69] Interpreting this view of death as part of endless change, Graham remarks, "'[i]n losing selfhood I shall remain what at bottom I always was, identical with everything conscious or unconscious in the universe' ... extinction of self does not matter since at bottom I am everything and have neither beginning nor end."[70]

To rectify our common illusionary attachment to birth/life, Zhuangzi even goes as far as to suggest, through an imagined dialogue with a skull, that the state of death is "better" than that of life, and that even the skull would not want to "take on the troubles of a human being again."[71]

---

65  Is comfort more important than truth in this instance?

66  Regarding death (and anything else), "he [Zhuangzi] is someone with an absolutely fearless eye" (G, Introduction, 3).

67  Using Confucius as a spokesperson, Zhuangzi praises Meng-sun Ts'ai in his handling of his mother's death: "But in his case, though something may startle his body, it won't injure his mind; though something may alarm the house [his spirit lives in] his emotions will suffer no death" (6, W, 85).

68  See the idea of self-transformation (zi-hua) in Daodejing Chapter 37.

69  Zhuangzi's Daoism in general does not try to explain further the "mechanism" of the change and transformation of things, and this is where Buddhism departs from Zhuangzi's Daoism. Buddhism, while also underscoring the change (impermanence) of things, worked out sophisticated structures and "mechanisms" of change, for example, the idea of interdependent-arising and its general acceptance of karma theory from Hinduism. Zhuangzi's view "to live is to borrow" (18, W, 114) expresses a similar idea to that of "interdependent-arising," but lacks the details of the Buddhist idea of "the wheel of becoming." Laozi's "Heaven's net" (Daodejing, Chapter 73) points to an organic system of the world, yet provides little analytical structure of its working except that opposites transform into each other.

70  G, Introduction, 23.

71  18, W, 115.

One of the "Mixed Chapters" contains an account of Zhuangzi's own death. What Zhuangzi is reported to have said about his own burial aptly illustrates his ideal of seeing things as "standing on equal footing."

> When Chuang Tzu [Zhuangzi] was about to die, his disciples expressed a desire to give him a sumptuous burial. Chuang Tzu said, "I will have heaven and earth for my coffin and coffin shell, the sun and moon for my pair of jade discs, the stars and constellations for my pearls and beads, and the ten thousand things for my parting gifts. The furnishings for my funeral are already prepared—what is there to add?"
>
> "But we're afraid the crows and kites will eat you, Master!" said his disciples.
>
> Chuang Tzu said, "Above ground I'll be eaten by crows and kites, below ground I'll be eaten by mole crickets and ants. Wouldn't it be rather bigoted to deprive one group in order to supply the other?"[72]

So what is the value of survival at all if birth/life and death are ultimately equal? Should we then treat any death (death in war, death in a car accident, and death due to aging) as all equal? Zhuangzi's answer seems to be "No." For instance, he argues that it is better to "live out [one's] years,"[73] or to "live out the years that Heaven gave [one] without being cut off midway."[74] For Zhuangzi, then, a natural death is to be welcomed and celebrated, but an unnatural death is unfortunate. The Hun-tun story quoted in the previous chapter on the *Daodejing* aptly illustrates the point. Hun-tun's death is unfortunate because harm was imposed upon him, and he was not able to live his natural course of life. The symbolic meaning of Hun-tun's death is clear: unnaturalness can lead to death.

*[handwritten margin note: unnaturalness can lead to Death Unfortunate]*

## WANDERING (*YOU*) (INDIVIDUAL SPIRITUAL FREEDOM)— A POSSIBLE WAY OF LIVING

At the end of Chapter 17 of the *Zhuangzi*, there is an amusing conversation between Zhuangzi and Hui Shi who were discussing whether the fish they saw swimming in the Hao River were happy. Zhuangzi said that the fish were happy. Hui Shi quickly replied, asking Zhuangzi on what basis he knew they were happy—since he was not a fish and could not possibly know how the fish felt. Here is my translation of the conversation:

---

72 Burton Watson, *The Complete Works of Chuang Tzu* (New York: Columbia University Press, 1968), 361.
73 3, W, 46.
74 6, W, 73.

Zhuangzi and Hui Shi were strolling across (*you* 游) the bridge over the Hao River. Zhuangzi said, "The minnows are out swimming around (*chu you* 出 游) at ease—That is what happiness is for a fish."[75]

Hui Shi replied, "You are not a fish—how (*an* 安) can you know that they are happy?"[76]

Zhuangzi replied, "You are not me—how can you know that I don't know that the fish are happy?"

Hui Shi said, "I am not you, so I certainly cannot know what you know. But you are not a fish, so you certainly cannot know whether the fish are happy either."

Zhuangzi said, "Let's get back to your initial question. When you asked 'Whence (*an* 安) do you draw the knowledge that the fish are happy?'[77] you already knew that I knew about the fish's happiness, but you still asked me this question. I knew it (from here) above the Hao River."

Some interpreters of the *Zhuangzi* treat this exchange between Zhuangzi and Hui Shi as a piece about epistemology. For instance, Allinson reads Zhuangzi as proposing "a form of naïve, perceptual realism,"[78] and Goodman takes it to be "the clearest case of antiscepticism."[79] Both Allinson and Goodman interpret Zhuangzi as defending a knowledge claim.

However, I do not think that Zhuangzi is defending an epistemological view in this story. Instead, I think he is presenting his ideal of a carefree life. Now, let's see how we can arrive at this reading. First, at the beginning of the exchange Zhuangzi does not set scepticism as a target. He does not initially *claim* that he *knows* anything, as G.E. Moore does (by claiming that "I know I have two hands") in his famous paper, "A Defence of Common Sense."[80] So, the conversation does not start off as a discussion on knowledge versus scepticism. Zhuangzi simply says "This is the way in which they [fish] are happy." It is only due to Hui Shi's questioning that Zhuangzi finally ends up saying he *knows* that the fish are happy.

---

75  This passage is playing with the double meanings of the word *you* 游, which can be translated as "swimming" or "wandering."

76  Hui Shi's initial question "*an zhi yu zhi le?*" may be translated in two ways: "How can you know that the fish are happy?" and "How do you know that the fish are happy?" The question, translated in either way, may presuppose the possibility of knowing that the fish are happy, or it may not presuppose that possibility at all. Here Hui Shi does not presuppose that Zhuangzi knows that the fish are happy; he is questioning the very possibility of that knowledge.

77  Zhuangzi intentionally misread Hui Shi's initial question. He plays with the ambiguity of the word *an*, which can mean either "how" or "whence."

78  Robert Allinson, *Chuang Tzu for Spiritual Transformation: An Analysis of the Inner Chapters* (Albany, NY: SUNY Press, 1989), 140.

79  Russell Goodman, "Skepticism and realism in the *Chuang Tzu,*" *Philosophy East and West* 35:3 (1985): 233.

80  In *Contemporary British Philosophy* (2nd series), J.H. Muirhead, ed. (London: George Allen and Unwin, 1925), 193–223.

Second, Zhuangzi's final answer to Hui Shi, "I knew it (from here) above the Hao River," should not be understood as a knowledge-claim "I know that *p*" (*p* being that the fish are happy). Zhuangzi was not offering a logical justification for what he had claimed, for he did not intend to say "I knew it on the grounds that...." His reference is spatial—"(from here) above the Hao River." Thus, it is more plausible to read it as a reaffirmation of Zhuangzi's vision that the fish's swimming at ease is an expression of their happiness.

Zhuangzi's utterance ("The minnows are out swimming around at ease—That's what happiness is for a fish!") is an interpretive, rather than descriptive, statement.[81] The utterance expresses the freedom Zhuangzi saw in the fish. They were just swimming around, having no worries. For him, that's what happiness is all about for a fish. On this occasion, he was not engaging Hui Shi in a philosophical argument; he was just admiring the fish's way of life. He makes no claim about being able to read the fish's mind or experience their joy as if he himself were a fish.

This conversation between Zhuangzi and Hui Shi nicely reveals the ideal way of living that Zhuangzi envisions.[82] Zhuangzi's observation of the fish strikes a sympathetic chord in his heart that vibrates with a way of living that is free, natural, and spontaneous. This way of life is more than a way of seeing the world; it is a way of actually living in it. But why does Zhuangzi see the fish's swimming (*you* 游) freely and his own wandering (*you* 游) about as *happy* experiences?

To answer this question, we have to explore how the ideas of wandering (*you*), non-action (*wu-wei*), and happiness (*le*) interrelate. In Zhuangzi's usage, the three notions exist in a symbiotic relationship. First, the wandering way of living is the way of non-action—those who follow the *dao* "wander free and easy in the service of inaction [non-action]."[83] Non-action, as we have seen it in the *Daodejing*, does not mean doing nothing, but rather letting things be what they are. In the *Zhuangzi*, the notion of *wu-wei* has been further developed and has a richer meaning. It includes at least three aspects:

1. Paradoxically it can mean skilfully and spontaneously doing something, as in the case of Cook Ting (Chapter 3 of the *Zhuangzi*; the story quoted below), that may involve good training and serious practice.
2. It also means not imposing on things whatever is unnatural and unfitting. This can be seen in the stories of two deaths: of the emperor of the central region, who gets holes bored in him and of the bird fed with human food

---

81  In English when we say "happy as a clam (at high tide)" we *interpret* a clam's being at high tide as its happiness. Do we need a proof of this interpretation?

82  For other interpretations that do not treat the exchange as an epistemology piece, see Roger Ames, "Knowing in the Zhuangzi: 'From Here, on the Bridge, Over the River Hao,'" in Ames, ed. *Wandering at Ease in the Zhuangzi* (Albany, NY: SUNY Press, 1998); Steven Shankman and Stephen Durrant, *The Siren and the Sage: Knowledge and Wisdom in Ancient Greece and China* (London: Cassell Academic, 2000); Michael Crandell, "On Walking without Touching the Ground: 'Play' in the Inner Chapters," in Victor H. Mair, ed. *Experimental Essays on Chuang-tzu*, (Honolulu: University of Hawaii Press, 1983).

83  6, W, 83.

(both stories have been quoted in our previous chapter on the *Daodejing*). In this sense, non-action implies an attitude of openness and sensitivity to concrete particulars in the world.

3. It further means living a life transcending worldly conventions (of, for example, ethics, politics, economics, society, family), as shown here in Zhuangzi's free wandering along the river. This way of living is also vividly depicted by the tale of the free wandering of the giant bird *Peng* in the first chapter of the *Zhuangzi*.

Second, for Zhuangzi, non-action is also linked to the idea of happiness (*le*). As he puts it, "I take inaction [non-action] to be true happiness" and "The highest happiness, keeping alive—only inaction gets you close to this!"[84] Now it must be noted that keeping alive is not merely surviving in a state of indolence. It is about accepting the natural transformation of things and staying in tune with it. It is staying-away from political entanglements. To Zhuangzi, only the one who "goes along with things" can "let his mind move freely,"[85] like a good swimmer who can stay afloat because he goes under with the swirls and comes out with the eddies, and follows along the way the water goes, never thinking about himself.[86] In other words, the one who understands *dao* flows with natural happenings and transforms himself with the *dao*; he welcomes change and is happy with any circumstances that arise naturally, including death. An ideal person, for Zhuangzi, is a kind of existential and spiritual wanderer, who roams about freely in the way of *dao*. The wanderer in the way of *dao* need not be moving around physically, for to wander about existentially and spiritually is to be at one with all the things around you—like getting completely absorbed in a piece of music—and in this case the music of the cosmos—*dao*.

It has to be noted that, for Zhuangzi, a wandering (*you*) Daoist may not be exactly a fish that is swimming (*you*) about freely. As Eske Mollgaard has explained, for Zhuangzi, the fish's *you* is a matter of instinctive animal spontaneity, or a kind of unity with nature that stems from animal instinct, but the story with human beings is different:

> "[H]uman beings can become *aware* that they are moved by the Way, and this awareness *is* their freedom. In this freedom, which Zhuangzi calls wandering (*you*), human beings are no longer mere things (*wu*) but companions of the Way that things things [that is, that things transform themselves as they are, naturally and spontaneously], and as such they experience the ceaseless self-emergence of life. Animals, on the other hand, do not experience transcendental life and therefore animals cannot wander (*you*)."[87]

---

84  18, W, 112.
85  4, W, 57.
86  See 19, W, 126.
87  Eske Møllgaard, *An Introduction to Daoist Thought: Action, Language, and Ethics in Zhuangzi* (Oxford: Routledge, 2007), 124.

In other words, for Zhuangzi, only human beings can be off the track (*dao*), and also return to it. In contrast, animals (fish, for example) are primordially in tune with *dao*; they neither deviate from *dao* nor return to it.

The Daoist wanderer is free from human conventions and value distinctions. While he may not appear to be taking life seriously, he is by no means simply muddling along. A loser in a competitive game may say, "Who cares?!" or "There isn't any real difference between a winner and a loser." This utterance is really just a form of rationalization that aims to provide one with some consolation. It smacks of the proverbial sour grapes. Indeed, the loser *cares* about the game as much as the fox cares about the grapes. However, with Zhuangzi's wanderer, the situation is totally different: he presupposes no value difference among things, so he could claim that he simply does not care, and that he is simply here to enjoy the journey itself, whatever he may embark on. For Zhuangzi, both winners and losers, whenever they are fixated on their winning or losing, are just like the frog-in-the-well, that desperately needs to broaden its horizon and wake up from its narcissistic illusion.

Zhuangzi is not advocating that people should become hedonists and let loose their desires, for a hedonistic life is for him not a carefree life. In his view, a hedonist is enslaved by his desires, which can only be satisfied temporarily in ways that are contingent upon external conditions. According to Zhuangzi, the world honours "wealth, eminence, long life, a good name," it finds happiness in "a life of ease, rich food, fine clothes, beautiful sights, sweet sounds," it looks down on "poverty, meanness, early death, a bad name," and it finds bitter "a life that knows no rest, a mouth that gets no rich food, no fine clothes for the body, no beautiful sights for the eye, no sweet sounds for the ear."[88] When people cannot get these things they "fret a great deal and are afraid," and when they can get riches and eminence, they "wear themselves out rushing around on business, piling up more wealth than they could ever use," and "spend night and day scheming and wondering if they are doing right":[89] at no time are they free from worry! Zhuangzi's wanderer, on the other hand, is at ease with himself wherever he dwells. Since he has transcended all conventional distinctions, external changes do not bother him anymore.

Nor is Zhuangzi encouraging us to flee the world in order to live like a hermit in the mountains, although throughout history some people have understood this as his message. According to Zhuangzi, "It is easy to keep from walking; the hard thing is to walk without touching the ground."[90] His idea seems to be that it is easy to avoid the world and to hide in the mountain ("stopping footprints" in this world), but it is much harder to live in the world while remaining free of its contamination or entanglement ("walking without touching the ground").[91] Several places in the *Zhuangzi* suggest that Zhuangzi sought to avoid politics and political office.[92]

---

88  18, W, 111.
89  18, W, 111.
90  4, W, 54.
91  Compare with the following in *Daodejing* Chapter 27: "Those good at traveling leave no tracks or traces."
92  See Hsu Yu's conversation with Yao, in 1, W, 26–27, and Zhuangzi's rejection of an offer of political office, in 17, W, 109.

Finally, is Zhuangzi an advocate of anarchism? The answer, I think, is no. It seems more plausible to interpret him as arguing that social problems are ultimately traceable to people's departure from *dao*, and if they return to *dao*, politics will become redundant. It is perhaps for this reason that Zhuangzi has much to say about how to open one's mind and become in tune with *dao*, but has very little to say about politics and governance.

## THE NURTURING OF LIFE

While the extraordinary vision depicted so vividly in the first chapter of the *Zhuangzi* may appeal to people who worry about survival and long for freedom in a precarious time, it does not seem to give them much practical guidance to help them negotiate the concrete challenges of life. They cannot fly up in the sky like *Peng*, the imaginary giant bird. Roaming away in "the realm of Nothing whatever"[93] may not be very instructive either, not so at least to the majority of the general populace. While the second chapter of the *Zhuangzi* is successful in making a thorough philosophical presentation of his understanding of the cause of closed-mindedness and the arbitrariness of values, readers understandably may want something more instructive and more specific about the general way of life recommended by Zhuangzi, which is not just a theory but a matter of practice. This is probably why in chapter three Zhuangzi comes down from the high clouds to the ground to offer people practical life skills.

The first piece of advice Zhuangzi offers is to warn us of the perils of our inquisitiveness. Our life is limited, but our desire for knowing is limitless, so we will never be fully satisfied. This, according to Zhuangzi, poses a severe danger: "Your life has a limit but knowledge [the desire to know] has none. If you use what is limited to pursue what has no limit, you will be in danger. If you understand this and still strive for knowledge, you will be in danger for certain!"[94]

The advice here seems ridiculous, in that it seems to suggest that we have to simply give up the pursuit of knowledge and knowing. This may be so, but we must first admit that there is some truth to what he says. Let's visualize a circle to represent the domain of knowledge we have obtained. Let's think of what is beyond the periphery as the domain of the unknown. As the circle gets bigger, the periphery gets bigger as well. By analogy, as the domain of knowledge enlarges, the domain of the unknown increases in proportion as well. Many more questions will be asked, because some things that previously lay in the domain of the unknown now have become potential questions. Paradoxically, the more we know, the less we know—since we have more unanswered questions.[95]

---

93  1, G, 47.

94  3, W, 46.

95  In a way, what Zhuangzi is saying here may be comparable to Kant's view of transcendental paradoxes, although Zhuangzi is not so interested in epistemology in Kant's sense. According to Kant, because we are merely equipped with limited human experience and limited categories of understanding, to seek unlimited knowledge by the limited faculty is to try to jump out of our skin, as it were. Our

*Acert limits*

The above reading is possible. However, a more plausible reading is to take Zhuangzi as suggesting that we should accept the limits of life and be content with the vicissitudes of life. Our cravings for wealth, fortune, fame, social status, and so on are insatiable, so we will always feel dissatisfied in life if we make the pursuit of these things our ultimate aim. The pursuit of gratification is a Faustian drive. It can be maddening, like the project of trying to ascertain the largest natural number—a vain pursuit of what Hegel called an "evil infinity." The chief peril of inquisitiveness, if we follow Zhuangzi's logic, is precisely that it is a pursuit for gratification, which can leave us caught in the endless cycle of dissatisfaction. Perhaps, this is what Zhuangzi is referring to in the second chapter: "Is it not sad how we and other things go on stroking or jostling each other, in a race ahead like a gallop which nothing can stop?"[96] And it is also why Zhuangzi thinks "knowledge" in this sense of endless pursuit "is an offshoot."[97]      *thought / close minded ness to the side to acquire*

*Poison of inquisition = Pursuit for gratification*

The author(s) of Ecclesiastes presents remarkably similar ideas: "For with much wisdom comes much sorrow; the more knowledge, the more grief" (1:18); "Be warned my son ... Of making many books there is no end, and much study wearies the body" (12:12). To be sure, neither Zhuangzi nor the author(s) of the Ecclesiastes suggest that one should not study or read books; they are only warning us that we do well to know the limits of human capacities, and that ignoring those limits will bring about disastrous consequences. Zhuangzi tells us that it is futile for an angry mantis to frantically wave its arms in an attempt to stop an approaching carriage, and it is equally so with people who do not know their limits.[98]

Zhuangzi's warning on knowing one's limits is echoed at several places in the *Zhuangzi*: "to understand what you can do nothing about and to be content with it as with fate—this is the perfection of virtue."[99] "He who has mastered the true nature of life does not labour over what life cannot do. He who has mastered the true nature of fate does not labour over what knowledge cannot change."[100] What are the things we have to accept in life? Zhuangzi specifies: "life, death, preservation, loss, failure, success, riches, worthiness, unworthiness, slander, and fame, hunger, thirsty, cold, heat"—pretty much everything in life.[101] This accepting attitude is clearly exemplified in the case of "The Commander of the Right" who, though single-footed, accepts his physical situation as it is, with contentment and happiness.[102]

---

metaphysical tendency to apply the categories of understanding beyond the sphere of their legitimate employment will result in a tangle of paradoxes and illusions. In that sense, it is indeed dangerous since one is prone to treat paradoxes and illusions as true knowledge. Consider, for example, simultaneously believing that the world is both infinite and limited.

96  2, G, 51.
97  5, W,71; Graham translates the sentence as "knowledge is a curse" (5, G, 82).
98  See 4, W, 59.
99  4, W, 56; for similar expressions see and 5, W, 66; 6, W, 76.
100  19, W, 197.
101  5, W, 70.
102  See 3, G, 64.

**DOING PHILOSOPHY**
*The Story of Cook Ting*

The tale of Cook Ting is one of the most popular of Zhuangzi's stories. It provides an object lesson on how to nurture one's life.[103] (The tale is so much a part of Chinese culture and so well written that it has long been adopted in China as a sample essay in literature textbooks.)

> Cook Ting was cutting up an ox for Lord Wen-hui. At every touch of his hand, every heave of his shoulder, every move of his feet, every thrust of his knee—zip! Zoop! He slithered the knife along with a zing, and all was in perfect rhythm, as though he were performing the dance of the Mulberry Grove or keeping time to the Ching-shou music.
>
> "Ah, this is marvellous!" said Lord Wen-hui. "Imagine skill reaching such heights!"
>
> Cook Ting laid down his knife and replied, "What I care about is the Way, which goes beyond skill. When I first began cutting up oxen, all I could see was the ox itself. After three years I no longer saw the whole ox. And now—now I go at it by spirit and don't look with my eyes. Perception and understanding have come to a stop and spirit moves where it wants. I go along with the natural makeup, strike in the big hollows, guide the knife through the big openings, and follow things as they are. So I never touch the smallest ligament or tendon, much less a main joint.... That's why after nineteen years the blade of my knife is still as good as when it first came from the grindstone.
>
> "However, whenever I come to a complicated place, I size up the difficulties, tell myself to watch out and be careful, keep my eyes on what I'm doing, work very slowly, and move the knife with the greatest subtlety, until—flop! The whole thing comes apart like a clod of earth crumbling to the ground ..."
>
> "Excellent!" said Lord Wen-hui. "I have heard the words of Cook Ting and learned how to care for life!" (3, W, 46–47)

In what way is Cook Ting's ability to carve up the ox "beyond skill"? How does one get to this level of competence? In his last remark to Cook Ting, Lord Wen-hui says, "I have ... learned how to care for life!" In what way does Cook Ting's story contribute to our understanding of how to care for or nurture life?

---

103 Other stories with a similar moral to the Cook Ting in the *Zhuangzi* include: the wheelwright with his unsayable skill (W, 152–53), the skilful hunchback cicada catcher, the ferryman, and the wood carver (W, 198–200).

A further point: Cook Ting knows what he is doing (knowing-how), and this is a perfect example of Zhuangzi's Daoist way of living. To a Daoist, abstract philosophical questions, such as whether the external world exists or not (realism), whether one's perspective is only relative to oneself (relativism), or whether one knows the truth of the external world (epistemology) do not arise at all. For Zhuangzi, one should not seek after a *dao* that is allegedly outside or independent of concrete everyday activities. *Dao* only exists as concrete *daos*—the *dao* of cooking, the *dao* of planting, the *dao* of weaving, the *dao* of driving, and so on. Zhuangzi never assumed in the first place that there is *the* truth of the external world, nor did he subsequently claim that because each species is subject to the limits of its perspective, no one can get access to *the* truth. His discussion of the relativity of perspectives (in Chapter 1 of the *Zhuangzi*) is intended to shatter the human impulse to impose one's standard on others (cf. central-region emperor in Chapter 7, the marquis of Lu and the sea bird in Chapter 18), and not to prove that there is *the* truth beyond all the relative perspectives. The uniqueness of human beings is not that they are the only species who can know *the* truth, but that they may often fall into the trap of imposing their own perspectives on others. Fortunately, however, they can be enlightened to *allow* all other species to live as they do.

Another aspect that matters in the nurture of life is revealed in the example of the pheasant. "The swamp pheasant has to walk ten paces for one peck and a hundred paces for one drink, but it doesn't want to be kept in a cage. Though you treat it like a king, its spirit won't be content."[104] The message is pretty straightforward: freedom, both physically and spiritually, is paramount in the nurture of life. The pheasant, if confined physically in a cage, would not have the same free spirit. To nurture life, then, is to live in freedom—physical and spiritual. The opposite of the pheasant is the sea bird in Chapter 18 who was unnaturally nourished with human music and food, a practice that leads to its death.[105]

## LAOZI AND ZHUANGZI IN COMPARISON

As Daoists, Laozi and Zhuangzi share basic common ground. For example, they both frame their philosophy in reference to *dao*, and they both stress the idea of *wu-wei*, non-action. This is why the Chinese tradition has branded them together as "Lao-Zhuang" since early in the Han Dynasty. Yet, their thoughts are not identical. The *Zhuangzi*

---

104 3, W, 48.
105 Contrary to Graham's interpretation, that this passage looks like a misplaced fragment (see 3, G, 64n.), I think the passage nicely epitomizes another aspect of Zhuangzi's thought on the nurture of life.

was not a mere appendage to the *Daodejing*, nor was Zhuangzi just a clone of Laozi.[106] To think otherwise would detract from the originality of Zhuangzi and his unique contribution to Daoism.

One conspicuous difference between Zhuangzi and Laozi can be found in their attitude toward politics. While Laozi has an obvious political concern and advises political strategies (e.g., winning by yielding), Zhuangzi is completely politics-free. The art of rulership or statecraft, which was stressed in the *Daodejing*, occupies no place in Zhuangzi's thinking. As he makes clear in the story of Hsu Yu (who was offered an Empire): "I have no use for the rulership of the world."[107] Indeed, for Zhuangzi, political achievements, no matter how great, are inferior in comparison to the Daoist way of life.

The appeal of the Daoist way of life is dramatically illustrated by the story of King Yao, who was so taken by a group of Daoist hermits (the Four) in the Mountain of far-off Ku-she that he became dazed and forgot his kingdom.[108] In this regard, an even more startling story is told in one of the Outer Chapters (Chapter 17, "Autumn Floods") in which Zhuangzi is reported to have rejected outright an offer of a political office. According to this account, Zhuangzi told the two officials who came to deliver him the offer that he would rather be alive and dragging his tail in the mud like a tortoise than serve in the government![109]

From the Confucian perspective, Zhuangzi's attitude toward politics is very impractical and irresponsible. For Confucians, the teachings of rituals and humanness are necessary in order to maintain social order, and to be sure, rituals may be abused and humanness may be used as a pretext for ethical and political imposition, but the rituals themselves cannot be thus discarded. While Zhuangzi rightly stresses the importance of individual (spiritual) freedom, spontaneity, and intuitiveness, he seems to be rather apathetic toward social concerns and responsibilities. It is perhaps for this reason that Confucius (in Zhuangzi's imaginary account) regarded Zhuangzi's philosophy as full of "wild and flippant words"[110] and anyone who followed these words as a "wander[er] beyond the [human] realm."[111] This is also why the Confucian, Xunzi, criticized Zhuangzi for being "obsessed with Heaven but [failing to] understand humans."[112] For the Confucians, in a time of social chaos individuals' spiritual freedom was perhaps not as urgent as social order (even if restoring social order might in some cases come with a price of suppressing individual freedom in Zhuangzi's sense).

106 According to A.C. Graham, "since the 'Inner Chapters' show no clear evidence of acquaintance with Lao Tzu the book is conveniently treated after Chuang-tzu, although there is no positive proof that it is later" (A.C. Graham, *Disputers of the Dao: Philosophical Argument in Ancient China*, [La Salle, IL: Open Court, 1989], 217–18).
107 W, 27.
108 See W, 28.
109 See W, 109.
110 6, W, 42.
111 6, W, 83; also see 2, W, 42.
112 See note 14 in Chapter 8 of this book.

A significant lesson we can learn from this comparison of Zhuangzi and Laozi is that there is often diversity within any given "school" of philosophy. Philosophers (whether Eastern or Western) are often grouped together into schools of thought for pedagogical purposes. While this practice may be helpful for teaching, it tends to ignore subtle, but important, differences among philosophers. This is analogous to the experience of learning a new language where initially we group synonyms together and often use them interchangeably, only to discover later that these words have subtle differences and may not be used interchangeably in all cases. It is only after much experience with the language that we really know how to use the words as they are intended to be used. In a similar fashion, Zhuangzi and Laozi are both unique. Thus, to appreciate their respective thoughts, we need to pay special attention to their particularity and uniqueness.

## CONCLUDING REMARKS: THE *ZHUANGZI*'S HISTORICAL STATUS AND INFLUENCE

Among many things that the Chinese have learned from the *Zhuangzi*, two philosophical points are most salient. The first point is that a good life is characterized by a spirit of freedom, unfettered by any conventions, social and political concerns, and attachments. Zhuangzi considered himself as a member of the world. This makes him a Chinese counterpart of the ancient Greek cynic Diogenes (404–323 BCE) who claimed "I am a citizen of the world—a cosmopolitan," and who asked Alexander the Great to step aside because he was blocking the sunlight. The *Zhuangzi* has also inspired generations, especially young people, from the East and the West to defy conventions and traditions in an effort to pursue a carefree, wandering way of life. Zhuangzi's ideal has also served as a spiritual refuge for those who have failed in social and political arenas.

The second point is that a good life is also characterized by a respect for differences as the basis of ethics. This is seen in the spirit of equality manifested in the *Zhuangzi* (particularly in the second chapter) that has fostered keen awareness of the uniqueness and the right to life of those who may appear ugly, inferior, and deformed. As Hyun Hochsmann and Yang Guorong have noted, "Zhuangzi's conception of an ethical life of harmony, freedom and equality presents a view of morality that is completely independent of hierarchy and social and political status, and even of natural ability."[113] It is also worth mentioning that this spirit of equality, among other things, was later appropriated by Buddhism in the interpretation of universal compassion. Furthermore, ideas like *wu-wei*, meditation, and sitting-forgetfulness in the *Zhuangzi* have all been fused into Buddhism to form a uniquely Chinese Buddhism—Chan.

---

113 Hyun Hochsmann and Yang Guorong, *Zhuangzi: Translation and Introduction* (New York: Pearson Longman, 2007), Preface, xvi.

## WORKS CITED AND RECOMMENDED READINGS

1. Ⴎ.ᵤᵤang Tzu: Basic Writings, Burton Watson, trans. (New York: Columbia University Press, 1996).

2. Chuang-tzu: Inner Chapters, A.C. Graham, trans. (Indianapolis: Hackett, 2001).

3. The Complete Works of Chuang Tzu, Burton Watson, trans. (New York: Columbia University Press, 1968).

4. Victor H. Mair, ed., Experimental Essays on Chuang-tzu (Honolulu: University of Hawaii Press, 1983).

5. Ames, Roger, ed. Wandering at Ease in the Zhuangzi (Albany, NY: State University of New York Press, 1998).

6. P.J. Ivanhoe and Paul Kjellberg, eds. Essays on Skepticism, Relativism, and Ethics in the Zhuangzi (Albany, NY: State University of New York Press, 1996).

7. Bryan W. Van Norden, "Competing Interpretations of the Inner Chapters of the Zhuangzi," Philosophy East and West 46:2 (April 1996): 247–68.

CHAPTER 8

# The *Xunzi*

## SUGGESTED PRIMARY READING

*Hsun Tzu: Basic Writings*, Burton Watson, trans. (New York: Columbia University Press, 1963).

## LEARNING OBJECTIVES

By the time you have worked through this chapter, you should be able to

- Explain Xunzi's demarcation of heaven and the human
- Understand Xunzi's practical attitudes towards "desire" (*yu*) and "emotion" (*qing*)
- Explain Xunzi's criticism of Mengzi's conception of human nature
- Understand Xunzi's view on the regulative use of rite and music
- Understand the role Xunzi played in synthesizing ancient Chinese philosophies

## KEY TERMS

(human) nature-is-bad (*xing e*), deliberate effort (*wei*), desire (*yu*), emotion/disposition (*qing*), rectifying names (*zhengming*), rite (*li*)

## GUIDING QUESTIONS

Both Confucius and Mengzi argued that in order to restore social order it is necessary and essential to rely on the transformative power of morality. Xunzi, however, suggested that Confucius and Mengzi might have been too naïve in underestimating the need for social regulation (including the use of punishment). In particular, Xunzi asked the following questions:

1. Has Mengzi not been too optimistic in arguing that human nature is good?
2. Should one think of heaven (*tian*) in completely naturalistic terms? Or should one follow Confucius and Mengzi in treating heaven as, instead, moralistic, and even quasi-personal?

In answering these questions, Xunzi seeks to incorporate insights from Confucius' rivals into the sage's general vision. He famously argues that heaven is totally naturalistic, human nature is bad, and a harmonious human society is not possible without deliberate social regulation and individual effort.

## INTRODUCTION

The book *Xunzi* was written mostly by the last pre-Qin[1] Confucian philosopher Xunzi (c. 340–245 BCE), with only a small portion of it by his students. Xunzi, a native of the State of Zhao (whose territory included areas in modern Inner Mongolia, Hebei, Shanxi and Sanxi Provinces), lived in the late Warring States Period (475–221 BCE). He travelled to the State of Qi (now in Shangdong Province) during his teen years and studied at the Jixia Academy (now near Zibo city)—a centre of philosophical discourse at the time. He later taught at the same academy and quickly rose to prominence. He also visited the State of Qin (now in Shanxi Province), which later, in 221 BCE, became the power that unified China. Xunzi was greatly impressed by Qin's military and economic power and efficiency, even though he had doubts about its harsh legal practices.

Like Mengzi, Xunzi claimed to be a firm believer in Confucius' vision. However, unlike Mengzi, whose development of Confucius' philosophy took merely a defensive posture in relation to rival theories (particularly Yang Zhu and Moism), Xunzi actively sought to appropriate elements from rival schools of thought (Moism, Daoism, and early Legalism) while maintaining an unyielding Confucian stance. This feature of Xunzi's thought has been generally acknowledged by commentators and translators of the *Xunzi*. For example, Schwartz has noted, Xunzi "is keenly responsive to other currents of thought and certainly does not hesitate to learn from them."[2] Watson is even more specific: Xunzi's thought "is thus marked by eclecticism, embracing a strain of Taoist quietism, a hard-headed realism reminiscent of the Legalist writers, a concern

---

1   The Qin Dynasty was the first imperial dynasty in China, 221–207 BCE.
2   Benjamin Schwartz, *The World of Thought in Ancient China* (Cambridge, MA: Belknap Press of Harvard University Press, 1985), 290.

for the correct use of terminology which he had learned from the philosophers of the school of Logic."[3] In this light, Xunzi's philosophy can be seen as more sophisticated and well-rounded than Mengzi's. It would seem that his line of Confucianism should have been more popular than Mengzi's. But what in fact transpired was quite another story: Confucius' ideas were substantially developed by his followers after the Han Dynasty (206 BCE-220 CE). In the Song Dynasty (960–1279 CE), in particular, Confucian thought was completely re-interpreted and indeed reinvented as Neo-Confucianism. By this time, Mengzi came to be regarded as the legitimate heir of Confucianism, while Xunzi became marginalized, in the shadow of the former.[4] The marginalization of Xunzi may have been due to the notoriety of two of his students, Han Feizi (281–233 BCE) and Li Si (c. 280–208 BCE), who were known as tough-minded legalists and whose ideas were implemented by the State of Qin in its effort to bring about the unification of China, during what is commonly believed to be a brutal period of China's history. Thus, Xunzi's reputation was tarnished by association with his two infamous students.

Despite its importance in the history of Chinese philosophy, traditionally the *Xunzi* has never enjoyed a status equal to that of the *Analects*, the *Mengzi*, the *Daodejing*, or the *Zhuangzi*. So why, contrary to the Confucian tradition, do we include the *Xunzi* as a classic to study here? Our choice is justifiable on several grounds. First, as noted above, the *Xunzi* is philosophically rich: it synthesizes the pre-Qin philosophies. A study of the *Xunzi* helps elucidate the contrast among different schools of thought in pre-Qin China as well as the fusion of previously competing ideas. It gives us a clearer picture of the intellectual landscape of this period. Second, the style of the book is commendable. While the *Xunzi* lacks the concrete conversational contexts of the *Analects* and the *Mengzi* and the colourful metaphors, images, and allegories of the *Zhuangzi*, it contains well-reasoned, self-contained essays that are thematically organized. As A.C. Graham has pointed out, "no other pre-Han thinker has organized the full range of his basic ideas in such coherently reasoned essays."[5] This feature of the text recommends Xunzi "as a more accessible conversation partner for Western philosophers."[6] A further reason for including the *Xunzi* here is that there has been a burgeoning interest in this book in the past two decades.

The *Xunzi* was first collated by the Han librarian Liu Xiang (77–6 BCE) as a collection of 32 essays. A Tang Dynasty scholar Yang Liang wrote a commentary on it around the beginning of the ninth century CE and put these essays in their now-standard

---

3   Burton Watson, trans., *Hsun Tzu* [Xunzi]: *Basic Writings* (New York: Columbia University Press, 1963), Introduction, 4.

4   Xunzi's influence may have been greater than Mengzi's up to the Han period. According to Wing-tsit Chan: "Hsun Tzu exerted far greater influence up through the Han period (206 BCE–220 CE) than did Mencius ... His influence was extensive in the Han. However, since then he was largely neglected until the nineteenth century.... His work was not elevated to the position of a Confucian classic" (Chan, *Sourcebook in Chinese Philosophy*, 115).

5   A.C. Graham, *Disputers of the Tao: Philosophical Argument in Ancient China* (La Salle, IL: Open Court, 1989), 237.

6   T.C. Kline III and Philip J. Ivanhoe, eds., *Virtue, Nature, and Moral Agency in the* Xunzi (Indianapolis: Hackett, 2000), Introduction, xiv.

order.[7] The more philosophical and thus more studied essays include: "The Regulations of a King" (essay 9), "A Discussion of Heaven" (17), "A Discussion of Rites" (19), "A Discussion of Music" (20), "Dispelling Obsession" (21), "Rectifying Names" (22), and "Man's Nature Is Evil" (23). We shall focus on these essays.

---

### DOING PHILOSOPHY
*General Life Attitudes: Confucius, Zhuangzi, Mengzi, Laozi, and Xunzi*

Confucius: He said of himself that he was "the one who knows a thing [good governing or moral perfection] cannot be done and still wants to do it" (*Analects* 14:41, Chan's translation).

Zhuangzi: "To understand what you can do nothing about and to be content with it as with fate—this is the perfection of virtue" (*Chuang Tzu—Basic Writings*, Watson's translation, 56).

Mengzi: "Though nothing happens that is not due to destiny, one accepts willingly only what is one's proper destiny" (*Mencius*, 7A2, D.C. Lau's translation).

Laozi: "Doing nothing [*wu-wei*] and nothing is undone" (*Daodejing*, W.T. Chan's translation; see Chapters 3, 37, 48).

Xunzi: "Understand what is to be done and what is not to be done" ("A Discussion of Heaven," 81).[8]

To what extent do the life-attitudes reflected in these remarks differ from one another? Are these differences a matter of substantive contrast or a matter of emphasis?

---

### HEAVEN VERSUS HUMAN: THE DEMARCATION

As noted in earlier chapters, one of the key philosophical issues discussed by ancient Chinese philosophers is the relationship between heaven and humanity. In Confucius' *Analects*, heaven is variously taken as nature which runs its course without speaking, or as a quasi-personal god, or as the source of virtues.[9] For Mengzi, heaven is the ultimate

---

7   See *Stanford Encyclopedia of Philosophy*, entry "Xunzi," by Dan Robins, at <http://plato.stanford.edu/entries/xunzi/>.
8   Here and elsewhere in this chapter, quotations from Xunzi will be identified (inside double-quotes) by the name of the source essay. Unless otherwise indicated, the translation will be taken from Watson's book, *Hsun Tzu: Basic Writing*, with the page number in that book given.
9   See *Analects* 17:19, 3:13, and 7:23.

source of morality, but it is no longer associated with a quasi-personal god.[10] Both Confucius and Mengzi emphasize the connection, as well as the continuity, between heaven and humanity. Mozi, in particular, stresses this continuity: he thinks that there is a continuum of existence between heaven and humanity that includes ghosts and spirits, and that the non-human elements, including heaven, all have wills that mete out rewards and punishments to human beings.[11]

The *Daodejing* in general does not stress the continuity between heaven and humanity, nor does it moralize the relationship between them. Instead, it argues that heaven operates on its own principles, and it is neither purposive nor moral. Heaven and earth are neither humane nor impartial.[12] At the same time, however, the *Daodejing* says that humans should follow/model after (*fa*) Earth, and the Earth should follow/model after Heaven.[13] Thus, there appears to be an attempt in the *Daodejing* to decouple heaven and humanity, but the attempt remains clouded by the book's assumption that earth, heaven, and humanity share the same model.

Nor, according to Xunzi, does Zhuangzi correctly understand the relationship between heaven and humanity. Zhuangzi focused so much on heaven that he was "obsessed by thoughts of Heaven [what is given in nature] and did not understand the importance of man [what is established through human efforts]."[14]

Hence, Xunzi rejects the conception of the heaven/humanity relationship held by all these philosophers—Confucius, Mengzi, Mozi, Laozi, and Zhuangzi. He maintains that they all failed to see the sharp distinction between heaven and humanity: heaven signifies the non-purposive, amoral, and purely objective processes in nature. According to him, the work of heaven is "to bring to completion without acting, to obtain without seeking."[15] This view is ambiguous about "who" is not acting and not seeking, in that it could be construed as "to bring to completion without [heaven's] acting, to obtain without [heaven's] seeking." This reading echoes the familiar message of the *Daodejing*: heaven is not a conscious, intentional being.[16] It could also be construed as "to bring to completion without [human] acting, to obtain without [human] seeking." Perhaps

---

10 See *Mengzi*, 7A1.

11 See Mozi [Mo Tzu], "The Will of Heaven," in *Basic Writings of Mo Tzu, Hsun Tzu, and Han Fei Tzu*, Burton Watson, trans. (New York: Columbia University Press, 1963), part I, 78–83. With Mozi the Chinese had a glimpse of a vision that sees the world as ultimately controlled by gods, but thanks to Laozi's and Xunzi's naturalistic (non-divine) understanding of the world, that vision was quickly eclipsed.

12 See the *Daodejing*, Chapter 5.

13 See the *Daodejing*, Chapter 25.

14 "Dispelling Obsession," 125. It must be pointed out that Zhuangzi also wants to draw a line between heaven and man: "He who knows what it is that Heaven does, and knows what it is that man does, has reached the peak. Knowing what it is that Heaven does, he lives with Heaven. Knowing what it is that man does, he uses the knowledge of what he knows to help out the knowledge of what he doesn't know, and lives out the years that Heaven gave him without being cut off midway—this is the perfection of knowledge. However, there is a difficulty. Knowledge must wait for something before it can be applicable, and that which it waits for is never certain. How, then, can I know that what I call Heaven is not really man, and what I call man is not really Heaven?" (Watson's translation, *The Complete Works of Chuang Tzu*, 77). But in the eyes of Xunzi, Zhuangzi still did not value human effort sufficiently.

15 "A Discussion of Heaven," 80.

16 See *Daodejing*, Chapter 5.

Xunzi meant his words to have both meanings. Both meanings serve to separate human existence (which requires conscious efforts and has a moral dimension) from heaven (which consists in mere natural processes).

Xunzi argues that what it means to be human and what it means to live a human life cannot be read off the mere operation of natural processes. Heaven follows its own course objectively, without regard to human preferences or the moral status of human individuals, particularly the rulers.

> Heaven's ways are constant. It does not prevail because of a sage like Yao; it does not cease to prevail because of a tyrant like Chieh.[17]
> Heaven does not suspend the winter because men dislike cold; earth does not cease being wide because men dislike great distances.[18]
> The ranks of stars move in progression, the sun and moon shine in turn, the four seasons succeed each other in good order, the yin and yang go through their great transformations, and the wind and rain pass over the whole land. All things obtain what is congenial to them and come to life, receive what is nourishing to them and grow to completion.[19]

Since the processes of nature are simply that which humans must accept or that which constrains human action, Xunzi argues that we cannot simply read a set of moral values and principles off nature itself. The ways of humanity are not the way of heaven.[20] Values—moral and non-moral—are invented by human beings just as weights and measures have been invented.[21]

With the line clearly drawn between humanity and heaven, Xunzi proceeds to argue that it is pointless to overstep the line and to try to do what only heaven can do. "Thus, although the sage has deep understanding, he does not attempt to exercise it upon the work of Heaven; though he has great talent, he does not attempt to apply it to the work of Heaven; though he has keen perception, he does not attempt to use it on the work of Heaven. Hence it is said that he does not compete with Heaven's work."[22] Nor is there any point in cursing heaven when times are bad, for social disorder is solely the result of human actions, especially those of the rulers.[23] In short, human affairs are largely shaped by the wills, desires, and actions of human agents.

Therefore, Xunzi suggests that, on the individual level, one has to rely on one's own effort to effect a change in life, instead of passively waiting for good things to come fortuitously.[24] It is significant to note that, for Xunzi, what distinguishes a "gentleman

---

17 "A Discussion of Heaven," 79.
18 "A Discussion of Heaven," 79.
19 "A Discussion of Heaven," 80.
20 Contrast with the *Daodejing*, Chapter 25.
21 "Rectifying Names," 140.
22 "A Discussion of Heaven," 80.
23 See "A Discussion of Heaven," 79.
24 This should remind us of Confucius' following remark: "A man can enlarge his Way; but there is no Way that can enlarge a man" (*Analects* 15:28).

(*junzi*), or exemplary person, from a petty person (*xiaoren*) is precisely this knowledge of the demarcation between heaven and humanity":

> The gentleman cherishes what is within his power and does not long for what is within the power of Heaven alone. The petty man, however, puts aside what is within his power and longs for what is within the power of Heaven. Because the gentleman cherishes what is within his power and does not long for what is within Heaven's power, he goes forward day by day. Because the petty man sets aside what is within his power and longs for what is within Heaven's power, he goes backward day by day.[25]

In other words, an exemplary person knows his station in life and exerts himself accordingly whereas a petty person has no inkling about his duties and roles in life and makes no efforts to live up to his potentials and responsibilities, but merely relies on luck to get through life.

On the social and political levels, Xunzi urges governing and managing efforts: the ruler should "encourage agriculture and [be] frugal in expenditures," "provide the people with the goods they need and demand their labour only at the proper time,"[26] and he also should "honour rites and promote worthy men" and "rely upon laws and love the people."[27]

On the basis of this sharp demarcation between heaven and humanity, Xunzi severely criticizes various superstitions that take rare and abnormal natural phenomena to be signs of purposive supernatural gods, advocating a purely naturalistic explanation. When stars fall or sacred trees around the altar make strange sounds, people are terrified, Xunzi argues, but these things happen because of changes that take place in heaven and earth (i.e., the natural world) and because of the mutations of Yin and Yang. To wonder at them is fine, but to fear them as if they were caused by gods is to fail to understand the nature of things.[28] Xunzi explains that one may mistakenly describe things as caused by the gods when one "does not see the process taking place, but sees only the results."[29]

To illustrate this point, imagine showing a cigarette lighter to some primitive tribal people who have never encountered such a device and thus have no knowledge of its working. They might feel shock, awe, or disbelief when they see a fire just "magically" appear at a simple click of the device. They might call the device "godlike," because they literally cannot see the mechanism that brings the fire into being. If they could see and understand the mechanism by which the fire is produced, they probably would not consider it "godlike."

---

25  See "A Discussion of Heaven," 83.
26  "A Discussion of Heaven," 79.
27  "A Discussion of Heaven," 86.
28  See "A Discussion of Heaven," 83–84.
29  "A Discussion of Heaven," 80.

Xunzi explains that the belief in the existence of gods, ghosts, and spirits is caused by cognitive confusions.

> There was a man named Chuan Shu-laing who lived south of Hsia-shou. He was stupid and easily frightened. One night he was walking in the moon-light when, glancing down and seeing his shadow, he took it for a crouching ghost. Looking up, he caught sight of his own hair and took it for a devil standing over him. He whirled around and started running, and when he reached his home he fell unconscious and died. Is this not sad? Always when people see ghosts, it is at times when they are aroused and excited, and they make their judgments in moments when their faculties are confused and blinded. At such times they affirm that what exists does not exist, or that what does not exist exists, and then they consider the matter settled.[30]

Xunzi's naturalistic and rational attitude toward what appears to be mystical can be seen as an extension of Confucius' pragmatic attitude towards the paranormal, includ-ing the existence of ghosts and spirits,[31] and it has had a great impact on how the Chinese have come to regard "supernatural" phenomena in subsequent generations. It is worth noting, however, that Xunzi did not argue for a complete abandonment of rites related to the arts of divination and to praying for rain. He accepted their values as psychologically comforting ornaments, yet warned people not to take them as signs of purposive gods.[32] Xunzi's subtle rejection of the existence of purposive gods may reflect his concern that such beliefs may encourage people passively and stubbornly to rely on fortuitous forces (i.e., heaven), rather than effecting change by their own effort.

### DOING PHILOSOPHY
#### Xunzi versus Epicurus (341–270 BCE) on Gods

It is interesting to compare Xunzi and Epicurus on the idea of gods. Epicurus applies his view of atomism to the realm of the gods: he believes that the gods are composed of exceedingly fine atoms, and they are simply not concerned about the human world or human affairs because they dwell in unchangeable blessedness. He argues that:

> There is no reason ... to fear the gods ... The heavenly bodies, moreover, are not demons and divinities that rule our destinies. Sun and moon, planets and stars are composed of atoms and the void just like every-thing else. Their behavior can be explained in exactly the same kinds of ways we explain familiar phenomena on earth. So it is inappropriate—

---

30  See "Dispelling Obssession," 134–35.
31  See the *Analects* 6:22, 7:21.
32  See "A Discussion of Heaven," 85.

ignorant—to look to the heavens for signs and portents, to go to astrologers for predications, and try to read the riddle of the future in the stars.[33]

Epicurus' ideas on gods are analogous to Xunzi's view on gods in three aspects: (1) that the events that are supposedly caused by the gods in fact arise from the mutation of Yin and Yang (namely, natural forces), (2) that the ways of heaven are constant and do not change for the sake of human beings, and (3) that "godlike" happenings are not to be feared (except that Xunzi still accepted the ornamental value of some rites, e.g., praying for rain). Notice also that Epicurus and Xunzi come from different ontological assumptions: Epicurus believes in atomism, Xunzi holds Yin and Yang theory.

## TO ESTABLISH A PROPER PLACE FOR "DESIRE" (*YU* 欲)

Laozi was quick to trace the social chaos of his time to the contaminating nature of desires that go beyond basic physical needs. Thus, he argued:

The five colours cause one's eyes to be blind. / The five tones cause one's ears to be deaf. / The five flavours cause one's palate to be spoiled. / Racing and hunting cause one's mind to be mad. / Goods that are hard to get injure one's activities. / For this reason the sage is concerned with the belly [basic physical need] and not the eyes. / Therefore he rejects the one but accepts the other.[34]

Laozi's solution to the problem of rampant desires is to eliminate them through the intervention of a sage-ruler by the paradoxical means of "non-intervention."

Do not exalt the worthy, so that the people shall not compete. / Do not value rare treasure, so that the people shall not steal. / Do not display objects of desire, so that the people's hearts shall not be disturbed. / Therefore in the government of the sage, / He keeps their hearts vacuous, / Fills their bellies, / Weakens their ambitions, / And strengthens their bones, / *He always causes his people to be without knowledge (cunning) or desire, / And the crafty to be afraid to act.* / By acting without action, all things will be in order.[35]

---

33  Norman Melchert, *The Great Conversation—A Historical Introduction to Philosophy*, fifth edition (Oxford: Oxford University Press, 2007), 202.
34  The *Daodejing*, Chapter 12, Chan's translation. Does this sound like Laozi is firing at the wrong target? Are the colours, tones, and flavours morally wrong in themselves? Is this similar to what the workers in the early industrial revolution were trying to do, namely, destroy machines, in order to save their jobs?
35  The *Daodejing*, Chapter 3, Chan's translation; emphasis added.

Some may find Laozi's solution attractive, but Xunzi considers it naïve and over-simplistic. If people are to be satisfied with simply having their basic physical needs met (i.e., the needs of the "belly" and "bones"), then human beings would not be any different from other animals, whose desires are also the mere satisfaction of their basic physical needs. But we are human beings, and we are different from animals, so Laozi's solution simply would not be viable, as it fails to acknowledge the place of other desires in human existence. Thus, for Xunzi, the solution to the wildness of human desires is to *regulate*, and not to *reduce*, human desires. We should not give up eating—as it were—for the fear of getting hiccups or choking on our food.

Laozi claims that when people are satisfied that their basic needs are being met, even "the crafty" will be "afraid to act." This notion is simply too naïve for Xunzi, who contends that common people remain content when it is not possible to have more than their basic needs met. But this solution may not work with "the crafty," who are "crafty" precisely because they are not satisfied with merely getting their basic needs met. They want more and will try to get more by whatever means available to them. Laozi suggests that the government can conceal the truth that there is more to be had. However, would this suggestion, if adopted, lead people to stand still, never striving for more and thus never making any progress? Therefore, for Xunzi, the urgent issue is not to conceal that there is more in order to reduce human desires, but to regulate these desires.

For Xunzi, Mengzi does not fare any better, for he is in the same camp with Sung Tzu who is "obsessed by the need to lessen desires."[36] Mengzi says, "There is nothing better for the nurturing of the heart than to reduce the number of one's desires. When a man has but few desires, even if there is anything he fails to retain in himself, it cannot be much; but when he has a great many desires, then even if there is anything he manages to retain in himself, it cannot be much."[37] The difference between Mengzi and Sung Tzu is that while Mengzi, in arguing for fewer desires, was focusing on "nurturing the [moral] heart," Sung Tzu was making the inference that with fewer desires people are more likely to be satisfied, and thus happy. Xunzi notes that both of them have taken a negative approach to human desires in not considering the possibility of guiding or channelling them. Arguing against Sung Tzu, Xunzi maintains that living well, for humans, is not merely "a matter of physical satisfaction."[38]

Therefore, contrary to Laozi, Mengzi, and Sung Tzu, Xunzi argues that a better way to live is to channel or regulate desires instead of reducing or even eliminating them.

> All those who maintain that desires must be gotten rid of before there can be orderly government fail to consider whether desires can be guided, but merely deplore the fact that they exist at all. All those who maintain that desires must be lessened before there can be orderly government fail to consider whether desires can be controlled, but merely deplore the fact that they are so numerous.[39]

---

36  "Dispelling Obsession," 125.
37  The *Mengzi*, Van Norden's translation, 7B35.
38  "Dispelling Obsession," 125.
39  "Rectifying Names," 150.

According to Xunzi, then, in order to create a good society, it is important to avoid the extremes of suppressing desires on the one hand and leaving them unchecked on the other. The former turns life into a sub-human existence; the latter leads to social chaos—like the Hobbesian "State of Nature" where human life is "solitary, poor, nasty, brutish, and short."[40] He remarks: "man is born with desires. If his desires are not satisfied for him, he cannot but seek some means to satisfy them himself. If there are no limits and degrees to his seeking, then he will inevitably fall to wrangling with other men. From wrangling comes disorder and from disorder comes exhaustion."[41]

To put human desires in perspective, Xunzi argues that desires are inborn, natural, and legitimate, but at the same time must be controlled. A harmonious society is possible only if desires are given a rightful place in life.

> Even a lowly gatekeeper cannot keep from having desires, for they are the inseparable attributes of the basic nature. On the other hand, even the Son of Heaven cannot completely satisfy all his desires. But although one cannot completely satisfy all his desires, he can come close to satisfying them, and although one cannot do away with all desires, he can control the search for satisfaction....The Way in its positive aspect can lead one close to the satisfaction of all desires and in its negative aspect can serve to control the search for satisfaction. In this respect, there is nothing in the world to compare to it.[42]

For Xunzi, proper social rituals, as well as a legal system, are fundamental to human existence; without them human beings would not even be able to have their physical needs satisfied.[43] Like Hobbes, Xunzi assumes that while other animals live according to their instincts and form a natural balance of co-existence, such a natural balance is not possible for humans. Yet unlike Hobbes, who argues that the (imagined) "State of Nature" should lead to a powerful sovereign on the basis of a social contract, Xunzi does not appeal to the notion of a social contract. Instead, he argues that social rituals and laws have all been pre-established for everyone by kings and sages through their deliberate exertion,[44] and that peace and harmony in society are guaranteed as long as they are followed.

The relationship between desires and social regulation can be illustrated with the analogy of the channelling of water by means of man-made structures such as aqueducts, dams, and dikes, which allow water to flow within bounds. Human desires, for Xunzi, need to be directed or guided like water, so that they can be expressed and gratified within bounds. Social order ensures that human desires are thus channelled. Rites

---

40  *Leviathan*, Chapter xii.
41  "A Discussion of Rites," 89.
42  "Rectifying Names," 152.
43  See "Rectifying Names," 154–55. Also compare the *Analects* 12:11: "For indeed when the prince is not a prince, the minister not a minister, the father not a father, the son not a son, one may have a dish of millet in front of one and yet not know if one will live to eat it" (Waley's translation).
44  One may question Xunzi how it is possible for the sages and kings to figure out the ritual and legal systems when they themselves have "bad" nature and when they have no prior ritual and legal systems to learn from.

and the associated standards of propriety, argues Xunzi, are the bounds within which human desires may find satisfaction:

> The former kings hated such chaos, and so they established rituals and the standards of righteousness in order to allot things to people, to nurture their desires, and to satisfy their seeking. They caused desires never to exhaust material goods, and material goods never to be depleted by desires, so that the two support each other and prosper. This is how ritual arose.[45]

However, human desires are insatiable and human beings are prone to excess, so how can human desires be tamed? Xunzi's answer is that human beings are fortunate enough to have minds, which allow them to be masters, rather than slaves, of their desires. "Although a man's desires are excessive," says Xunzi, "his actions need not be so, because the mind will stop them short. If the dictates of the mind are in accord with just principles, then, although the desires are manifold, what harm will this be to good government? Conversely, even though there is a deficiency of desire, one's actions can still come up to the proper standard because the mind directs them. But if the dictates of the mind violate just principles, then, although the desires are few, the result will be far worse than merely bad government. Therefore, good or bad government depends upon the dictates of the mind, not upon the desires of the emotional nature."[46]

Xunzi's discussion of human desires, along with the need to properly nurture (*yang*) as well as limit them, must be understood against the background of the feudal hierarchical social structure of his time and the role of division of labour in society.[47] The limits of desires, as well as their gradation, are not merely a function of biological constraints, such as how much food, alcohol, or sex one can physically tolerate, though they have a role to play. More importantly, the proper "limits and degrees" of desires are

---

45 "Discourse on Ritual," Eric Hutton, trans., in *Readings in Classical Chinese Philosophy*, Philip J. Ivanhoe and Bryan W. Van Norden, eds., 265. Compare with Watson's translation of the passage: "The ancient kings hated ... disorder, and therefore they established ritual principles in order to *curb* it, to *train men's desires* and to provide for their satisfaction. They saw to it that desires did not overextend the means for their satisfaction, and material goods did not fall short of what was desired. Thus both desires and goods were looked after and satisfied. This is the origin of rites" ("A Discussion of Rites," 89, emphasis added). Watson's translation makes Xunzi seem tougher on man's desires than he actually is.
46 "Rectifying Names," 151. Here Xunzi is close to Mengzi in stressing the importance of the mind in (ethical) decision-making. For Mengzi's view on *si* 思 (thinking), see *Mengzi*, 6A15.
47 In contrast with Xunzi's understanding of desires as conditioned by social factors (such as social roles and social status), Epicurus classified desires according to certain features internal to an individual's biological make-up. According to Epicurus, some desires are natural (sexual desire, food, drink, and shelter), some are vain (luxuries of all kinds), and the natural kind includes necessary ones (food, drink, shelter) and not necessary ones (sexual desire). Moreover, of the necessary desires, some are necessary for happiness (friendship), and some for the ease of the body (a bed), and some for life itself (food, drink, shelter). The aim of such classification of desires, for Epicurus, is not to satisfy them all in equal proportion, but to weigh them and make a prudent, moderate, balanced satisfaction so that a happy life is ensured (see Melchert, 203).

constructed socially on the basis of one's station in life—namely, one's social roles in the feudal hierarchy and one's duties in the overall regime of division of labour in society.

> The gentleman, having provided a means for the satisfaction of desires, is also careful about the distinctions to be observed. What do I mean by distinctions? Eminent and humble have their respective stations, elder and younger their degrees, and rich and poor, important and unimportant, their different places in society. Thus the Son of Heaven has his great carriage spread with soft mats to satisfy his body. By his side are placed fragrant herbs to satisfy his eye.... [As for the king's officials] let them understand clearly that to advance in the face of death and to value honour is the way to satisfy their desire for life; to spend and to supply what goods are needed is to satisfy their desire for wealth....[48]

Xunzi does not think that the constraints imposed on human desires are the same for everyone, because "where ranks are all equal, there will not be enough goods to go around; where power is equally distributed, there will be a lack of unity."[49] Xunzi argues, contrary to Mengzi, that to govern properly does not simply entail reducing people's desires universally, regardless of their roles in the society; instead, it calls for satisfying people's needs and distributing rank and power on the basis of people's social positions.

In practice, the distribution of "rank and power" entails the policy of "name-rectifying." Here Xunzi appears to have picked up the idea mentioned in the *Analects* of Confucius.[50] As you may recall, the "rectification of names" aims to define the various social roles and their behavioural norms in an ideal society. Confucius believed that this process is fundamental to social order. Accepting this doctrine, Xunzi explains:

> [T]he wise man is careful to set up the proper distinctions and to regulate names so that they will apply correctly to the realities they designate. In this way he makes clear the distinction between things that are eminent and humble and discriminates properly between things that are the same and those that are different. If this is done, there will be no danger that the ruler's intentions will not be improperly communicated and understood, and his undertakings will suffer no difficulties or failure. This is the reason why correct names are needed.[51]

Thus, according to Xunzi, if men and women fulfill their roles in society as defined by their government and go about satisfying their desires within the bounds of social regulation, then there is social order. To enforce these norms, Xunzi advocates that

---

48 "A Discussion of Rites," 89–90.
49 "The Regulations of a King," 36.
50 See the *Analects* 12:11, 13:3.
51 "Rectifying Names," 142.

transgressors, those who tamper with the rectified norms, "should be punished in the same way that one punishes those who tamper with tallies or weights and measures."[52] While we may not agree with Xunzi's view in linking the feudal hierarchical system with needs, the need for social regulation (and hence the socially sanctioned curbing of desires) exists in all societies, including democratic societies. Even libertarians subscribe to a minimalist view of the role of government intervention or regulation.

## TO ESTABLISH A PROPER PLACE
### FOR EMOTIONS OR DISPOSITIONS (QING 情)

Xunzi recognizes that human beings do not merely have physical desires (such as the desires for food, drink, and shelter); they also have emotions, especially those of joy and sorrow. "In people's lives originally there are the beginnings of these two dispositions [joy and sorrow]."[53] Xunzi argues that these emotional dispositions need to be properly nurtured through rituals as do physical desires: "ritual, the standards of righteousness, good form and proper order are the way to nurture one's dispositions (qing)."[54]

Xunzi argues that without proper sacrificial rites people would not have the means to fully express their relevant emotions—of which filial affection is the strongest—which need the external guidance of rituals for proper release.[55] In particular, the strong emotions one feels towards one's dying or dead parents find their proper expression through mourning or burial rituals. Thus, Xunzi remarks: "In every case, ritual begins in that which must be released, reaches full development in giving it proper form, and finishes in providing it satisfaction."[56] The "proper form" of a ritual is midway between emotional indulgence and emotional denial. In general,

> the way ritual makes use of fine ornaments is such as not to lead to exorbitance and indulgence. The way it makes use of coarse mourning garments is such as not to lead to infirmity or despondency. The way it makes use of music and happiness is such as not to lead to perversity or laziness. The way it makes use of weeping and sorrow is such as not to lead to dejection or self-harm. This is the mid-way course of ritual.[57]

Xunzi's mid-way attitude towards emotion also involves a mediating understanding of one's duties towards the dead and the living: "To deprive the dead for the sake of the living is niggardly; to deprive the living for the sake of the dead is delusion; and to

---

52  "Rectifying Names," 40.
53  Hutton, 270.
54  Hutton, 266.
55  See the *Analects* (3:17): "Tzu-kung wanted to do away with the presentation of a sacrificial sheep at the Announcement of each New Moon. The Master said, Ssu! You grudge sheep, but I grudge ritual" (Waley's translation).
56  Hutton, 266.
57  Hutton, 269; cf. Watson's translation, 100–01.

kill the living and force them to accompany the dead is hideous."[58] In maintaining a balanced approach to both the dead and the living, Xunzi never fails to emphasize the proper treatment of the dead:

> To be generous in the treatment of the living but skimpy in the treatment of the dead is to show reverence for a being who has consciousness and contempt for one who has lost it. This is the way of an evil man and an offence against the heart. The gentleman would be ashamed to treat even a lowly slave in a way that offends the heart; how much more ashamed would he be to treat those whom he honours and loves in such a way! The rites of the dead can be performed only once for each individual, and never again. They are the last occasion upon which the subject may fully express respect for his ruler, the son express respect for his parents.[59]

In this remark, Xunzi brings up another important function of rituals—that of moral purification. When people attend to the dead through rituals, they are paying them respect for the last time, thereby purifying the heart (i.e., the seat of human emotions and dispositions). This observance of ritual has the overall effect of enhancing society's morals. Xunzi's approach on rituals is completely consistent with that of Confucius, who similarly stresses the beneficial function of sacrificial rites.[60]

In addition to rituals, for Xunzi, music also plays an important role in the regulation of human emotions. On this point, Xunzi also follows Confucius closely.[61] He notes that music is highly expressive of human emotions, so when properly guided, it can be a powerful vehicle for directing human desires and emotions. He explains:

> Man must have his joy, and joy must have its expression, but if that expression is not guided by the principles of the Way, then it will inevitably become disordered. The former kings hated such disorder, and therefore they created the musical forms of the odes and hymns in order to guide it. In this way they made certain that the voice would fully express the feelings of joy without becoming wild and abandoned, that the form would be well ordered but not unduly restrictive, that the directness, complexity, intensity, and tempo of the musical performance would be of the proper degree to arouse the best in man's nature, and that evil and improper sentiments would find no opening to enter by.[62]

---

58 "A Discussion of Rites," 105; cf. the *Mengzi* 1A4.
59 "A Discussion of Rites," 97.
60 See the *Analects* 1:9.
61 See the *Analects* 8:8, 11:1, 13:3, 14:2, 17:18.
62 "A Discussion of Music," 112.

## IS HUMAN NATURE BAD?

Confucius says "By nature [people] are alike; through habituation-learning [they] become apart."[63] He evaded (intentionally or unintentionally) the metaphysical question of whether human nature is good or bad. Mengzi, by contrast, argues that human nature is good, in order to set an inner foundation for morality. For Mengzi, while humans share certain similarities with other animals (e.g., the desires for food, sex, etc.), they differ from other animals in that they have the innate "sprouts" of moral goodness. A practical implication of Mengzi's conception of human nature is that, since human nature is innately good, to live ethically requires an awareness of humanity's innate potential for moral goodness and an ongoing effort to cultivate it. Moral cultivation in this view is a natural and spontaneous process.

Xunzi, however, departs substantially from these two thinkers. He thinks that neither innate moral goodness nor innate moral badness is part of human nature.

In order to appreciate what Xunzi says about human nature, we need to first gain an understanding of what he means by human nature. Xunzi defines human nature as that which is endowed by Heaven at birth: "The nature is that which is given by Heaven; you cannot learn it, you cannot acquire it by effort."[64] "That which is as it is from the time of birth is called the nature of man. That which is harmonious from birth, which is capable of perceiving through the senses and of responding to stimulus spontaneously and without effort, is also called the nature."[65] In this view, human nature is composed merely of capacities, such as sensation. There is no mention of any such notion as sprouts of goodness or badness. This view is in fact similar to Gaozi's view that likens human nature to water, which is subject to the shaping of external factors. As far as human being's inherent nature is concerned, Xunzi seems to think that it is morally neutral.[66]

Xunzi characterizes human beings with the phrase *xing e*, which is commonly translated as "human nature is base, or bad." This translation gives the impression that Xunzi believes that human beings are innately or inherently bad, and that his position is diametrically opposed to Mengzi's. However, this reading of Xunzi is not accurate. In characterizing human nature this way, Xunzi is drawing attention to human beings' tendency to do things that lead to bad consequences if their heaven-endowed nature is

---

63  The *Analects* 17:2 (my translation).
64  "Man's Nature Is Evil," 158.
65  "Rectifying Names," 139.
66  Bryan Van Norden has proposed a different interpretation of why Xunzi did not call human nature neutral as Gaozi did. According to Van Norden, Gaozi was perhaps too much of a "voluntarist" to say this—holding, that is, that all that is required in order to become moral is a simple act of choice on one's part, while Xunzi stressed that ethics needs accumulative efforts. So Xunzi, in calling human nature bad, was trying to distance himself from Gaozi. (See Bryan Van Norden, "Mengzi and Xunzi: Two Views of Human Agency," in Kline and Ivanhoe, eds., 126–27.) However, I think Gaozi's water and wood analogies do not seem to support a "voluntarist" view of ethics, as water and wood do not "choose" to be this or that; rather, external factors make them into this or that.

not properly guided or shaped.[67] Thus, it is misleading to construe Xunzi's position as one about humanity's inherent nature in the same order as Mengzi's position.

What are the innate features in people's heaven-endowed nature that can lead to destructive consequences when left unchecked? Xunzi believes that there are three such features: a fondness for profit, innate feelings of envy and hate, and innate desires of the eyes and ears. When a person indulges in his fondness for profit, he is likely to get entangled in interpersonal wrangling and strife. As a result, all sense of courtesy and humility will quickly disappear. When a person indulges in his feelings of envy and hate, these will lead him into violence and crime, so that his sense of loyalty and good faith will be gone. When he is obsessed with his fondness for beautiful sights and sounds, he is likely to give into a lifestyle of licentiousness and wantonness, and all ritual principles and correct forms will be lost.[68]

Xunzi further explains that it is the nature of man that when he is hungry he will desire satisfaction, when he is cold he will desire warmth, and when he is weary he will desire rest. This is his emotional nature.[69]

In other words, for Xunzi, only the human actions themselves are driven by innate tendencies and desires, and these tendencies and desires lead to bad actions only if they are not checked, or properly regulated.[70] Thus, human nature can be regarded as *xing e* in virtue of these tendencies and desires that have the potential of wreaking moral havoc in life.[71]

---

67 "The term Xunzi uses to describe man's inborn nature is *e*—'evil.' Translating *e* as 'evil' often overstates its meaning since the Chinese does not carry the sinister and baleful overtones of the English word…. the inborn nature of man must be judged evil not because its inborn qualities are sinister or baleful, but because they lead to evil results" (John Knoblock, *Xunzi—A Translation and Study of the Complete Works*, Vol. 1 [Stanford, CA: Stanford University Press, 1988], Introduction, 99). To translate *e* as "badness" seems better than to translate it as "evil."

68 See "Man's Nature Is Evil," 157.

69 See "Man's Nature Is Evil," 159.

70 "A Discussion of Rites," 89.

71 This reminds us of Socrates' even harsher and more pessimistic view on the body. According to Socrates, "as long as we have a body and our soul is fused with such an evil we shall never adequately attain what we desire [intellectually or spiritually], which we affirm to be the truth. The body keeps us busy in a thousand ways because of its need for nurture. Moreover, if certain diseases befall it, they impede our search for the truth. It fills us with wants, desires, fears, all sorts of illusions and much nonsense, so that, as it is said, in truth and in fact no thought of any kind ever comes to us from the body. Only the body and its desires cause war, civil discord and battles, for all wars are due to the desire to acquire wealth, and it is the body and the care of it, to which we are enslaved, which compel us to acquire wealth, and all this makes us too busy to practice philosophy" (*Phaedo*, 66b–d, G.M.A. Grube, trans. [Indianapolis: Hackett, 1977]). Xunzi would think it crazy to "escape from the body and observe things in themselves with the soul by itself" as well as to believe that only "when we are dead, [can we] attain that which we desire and of which we claim to be lovers, namely, wisdom" (*Phaedo* 66d–e). But he would *in a way* agree with Socrates that "we [should] refrain as much as possible from association with the body and do not join with it more than we *must*" (*Phaedo*, 67a, emphasis added). Unlike Socrates who discusses desires in a generic way, Xunzi links them to social hierarchy to determine which desires count as necessary and which not.

Some critics have questioned whether Xunzi is justified in characterizing human nature as a function of the potential consequences it may unleash. For example, Janghee Lee has argued,

> However, even though human *xing*, particularly emotions and desires, tends to be destructive, this does not confirm that these incipient tendencies are themselves bad. Take the example of a wild horse. Without a bridle it is likely to destroy fences and injure people, yet if it is well trained and controlled with a bridle, it could be a good horse. In this case we do not say the horse is bad; we just say that the horse has a tendency to be wild that can be controlled with proper training and a bridle.[72]

Lee's objection here is that Xunzi is not justified in calling something "bad" simply because of its tendencies. Lee's point is well-taken if we can only be talking about the inherent nature of something every time we describe something as good or bad. But there are other contexts in which we can justifiably call something—a wild horse included—good or bad based on the consequences it tends to produce. For example, if we are comparing the suitability of a tamed horse versus a wild horse for the purpose of riding, we can justifiably call a wild horse "bad." Likewise, if we are talking about human nature in the context of how it may or may not contribute to social order, we may justifiably judge human nature as good or bad in light of the type of society it tends to produce without external constraints. Xunzi's assessment that human nature is bad can be simply understood in this way: "All men in the world, past and present, agree in defining goodness as that which is upright, reasonable, and orderly, and evil as that which is prejudiced, irresponsible, and chaotic. This is the distinction between good and evil."[73] It is clear for Xunzi that the standard of goodness and badness is external to human nature rather than innate in it.

If Xunzi's claim that human nature is bad is located as part of a larger discussion of what it takes to create social order, then it should not be read simply as a straightforward contradictory thesis to that of Mengzi about humanity's inherent nature.[74] Instead, a more cautious and nuanced reading is required, which takes into account three issues: (1) how the term *e* should be translated, (2) what a denial of Mengzi's claim entails, and (3) what sorts of claims Mengzi and Xunzi each actually make.

First, according to Xunzi, human beings are neither humane nor inhumane originally or primordially. In Ivanhoe's words, human beings for Xunzi are by nature in "a state of utter moral blindness" (in the sense that they are *amoral*, rather than

---

72 Janghee Lee, *Xunzi and Early Chinese Naturalism* (Albany, NY: State University of New York Press, 2005), 28–29.

73 "Man's Nature Is Evil," 162.

74 See Watson's comment on Xunzi: "But it [Xunzi's view that human nature is evil] flatly contradicts the view of Mencius, who taught that man is naturally inclined to goodness" ("Introduction," 5).

*immoral*).[75] For Xunzi, human nature in its original state does not know what is good and what is not. Therefore, it is misleading to translate the world "*e*" as "evil." Second, it is important to bear in mind, as pointed out by Chad Hansen, that denying Mengzi's claim that human nature is inherently good covers a wide range of possibilities, including the views that human nature is inherently devoid of essence, neutral, bad, or a mixture of good and bad.[76] Xunzi denies Mengzi's claim by asserting that human nature is *amoral* rather than bad. Third, Mengzi and Xunzi have each located their statements about human nature in different domains of discourse. Mengzi locates it against a discussion of the intrinsic nature of humanity and Xunzi against the role of human dispositions in the making of social order. Mengzi offers a statement of human nature that encompasses at once a descriptive claim about humanity's innate potential for moral goodness and a prescriptive claim about what action *ought to* take place in order for that potential to be fully realized. Xunzi, in contrast, offers a value judgment about the degree to which unchecked human dispositions are conducive to social order. For Mengzi, humaneness—see Chapter 5, note 12—is that which makes a person human. A creature that is not inherently humane is not human. For Xunzi, a person need not be inherently humane to be human, for that feature is not a part of a person's naturally endowed make-up. When a person acts inhumanely, he is still a person, though a bad one. In short, while it is true that Mengzi and Xunzi disagree on human nature, the disagreement must not be simplistically construed as a clash of views about innate moral goodness versus innate moral badness.

In advancing his view on humanity as *xing e*, Xunzi has also criticized Mengzi, but his critique of Mengzi is less compelling than his positive argument for his own view. He finds Mengzi's view of inherent moral goodness wanting on the grounds that it would render redundant such social institutions as rites and laws: "Now suppose that man's nature was in fact intrinsically upright, reasonable, and orderly—then what need would there be for sage kings and ritual principles?"[77] Xunzi's criticism is premised on the assumption that inherent moral goodness and moral cultivation are mutually exclusive, but this is an assumption to which Mengzi has never subscribed. Mengzi's sprouts of moral goodness still require cultivation in order to grow and flourish. For Mengzi, it is completely consistent to maintain the truth of inherent moral goodness and the need for moral cultivation. Xunzi has in fact imposed onto Mengzi a false dichotomy of inherent moral goodness versus the need for moral cultivation. Indeed, for Mengzi, there is no dichotomy between the two: human nature is good AND moral goodness requires cultivation.

Now, let's return to Xunzi's view that human beings do not have any innate moral inclinations and that unchecked human desires tend to lead to social chaos. How does Xunzi account for the fact that human beings do not simply go around creating chaos,

---

75  Philip J. Ivanhoe, "Human Nature and Moral Understanding in the *Xunzi*," in Kline and Ivanhoe, eds., 243–44.
76  See Chad Hansen, *A Daoist Theory of Chinese Thought: A Philosophical Interpretation* (New York: Oxford University Press, 1992), 336.
77  "Man's Nature Is Evil," 162.

and that human beings are able to constrain themselves at least some of the time? Xunzi's answer is that all human beings, including the common person in the street, are also endowed with the essential intelligence to understand benevolence, righteousness, and proper standards, and they also have the potential capacity to put these virtues and rules into practice:[78] "Any man in the street *can* understand the duties required of a father or a son and *can* comprehend the correct relationship between ruler and subject. Therefore, it is obvious that the essential faculties needed to understand such ethical principles and the potential ability to put them into practice must be a part of his make-up."[79]

Xunzi further believes that human beings have a sense of duty that uniquely distinguishes them from other creatures. He remarks: "Fire and water possess energy but are without life. Grass and trees have life but no intelligence. Birds and beasts have intelligence but no sense of duty. Man possesses energy, life, intelligence, and in addition, a sense of duty. Therefore, he is the noblest being on earth."[80]

Xunzi seems to believe that this "sense of duty" is innate. However, he has not elaborated on the notion of innateness as Mengzi has. Instead, he focuses on the social consequences that are issued from such sense of duty.

> He is not as strong as the ox, nor as swift as the horse, and yet he makes the ox and the horse work for him. Why? Because he is able to organize himself in society and they are not. Why is he able to organize himself in society? Because he sets up hierarchical divisions. And how is he able to set up hierarchical divisions? Because he has a sense of duty. If he employs this sense of duty to set up hierarchical division, then there will be harmony.[81]

### DOING PHILOSOPHY
#### Xunzi's View of Humanity as Xing e versus the Notion of "Original Sin" in Christian Theology

The doctrine of "Original sin" in Christian theology assumes that Adam and Eve surrendered to external (the snake's) temptation, acting against God's will. Thus they were sinful; and only God's grace can bring them back to the state before they had sinned.

For Xunzi, the tendency of satisfying one's desires without limits is intrinsic to humans. Don't blame the snake! Neither Heaven nor gods will save us from the mess that stems from leaving our desires unchecked. Release from the mess is possible only through *human* "deliberate exertion," including particularly the

---

78  See "Man's Nature Is Evil," 166.
79  "Man's Nature Is Evil," 166–67.
80  "The Regulations of a King," 45.
81  "The Regulations of a King," 45–46.

ritual and legal systems that sages (not gods or God) had established. While the Original Sin doctrine may cultivate a sense of humbleness and elicit a realistic attitude toward human nature, it *might* also downgrade or even destroy self-esteem and human worth. Might Xunzi's view on human nature result in a decrease of self-esteem and human worth as well?

Several key points have emerged in our comparison of how Xunzi and Mengzi viewed human nature and its implications for moral education and governance. (1) Xunzi and Mengzi start with different assumptions. The latter believes that human nature is good (i.e., endowed with "sprouts" of moral goodness) whereas the former does not. This difference leads to an array of other differences. (2) Mengzi holds that the source of morality is internal or intrinsic to humans, so moral education entails extending and nurturing humanity's innate moral capacities; Xunzi, on the other hand, argues that unchecked human desires can cause social chaos and thus need to be reshaped and reformed, and this effort constitutes the central task of moral education. (3) Mengzi believes in human spontaneity whereas Xunzi does not. (4) Mengzi believes that moral education or cultivation should be essentially enjoyable, for it is consistent with one's innate aspiration, which is to let the sprouts of moral goodness grow. Xunzi, in contrast, believes that moral education—the taming of human desires—requires arduous effort and may eventually become enjoyable only at a later stage.

In spite of these differences, both thinkers are directed by the same underlying assumption that everyone can become a sage, and it is possible to build a harmonious society. It seems that they are really aiming at the same destination, though through different routes. Given their common goals, it is more fruitful to explore the practical implications of their theories rather than trying to settle whose theory is right.

Let's take the example of how the two theories may shape a parent's approach to encouraging her child to take piano lessons. Following Mengzi's ideas, a mother may encourage her eight-year-old son to take piano lessons by explaining that (1) everyone can learn to play piano (loving piano/music is part of his innate potential), and that (2) taking piano lessons helps him realize his potential, so it should not be a chore, but fun (as realizing one's potential is supposed to be fun!). The son may follow his mother's wishes, eventually becoming a good pianist, and feel grateful to his mother for having encouraged him to take piano lessons. The son may also be reluctant to take up the instrument, complaining that it is too hard, and his fingers hurt from the practice. In this case, the mother might not abandon the idea of encouraging her son to take piano lessons. She may still believe in her son's innate potential and continue to encourage and persuade him to persist in the lessons.

A parent that follows Xunzi's ideas may approach the matter very differently. The parent may insist that (1) everyone can learn to play the piano (regardless of whether one has any innate musical aptitude), and that (2) learning to play the piano is difficult and may even be painful, especially in the beginning. The parent may also insist that the son must persist in the lessons if he ever wants to become a good pianist. If the son is obedient, he may gradually come to exert himself and master the instrument. But the son may also defy his parent's wishes. In this case, the parent might not relent, but may continue to insist that her son should keep taking lessons and keep practicing. To encourage him to do so, she may even resort to the use of punishment. For this Xunzian parent, a child is not naturally motivated by the right desire, even though he may eventually be so motivated.

The hypothetical scenarios above suggest that Mengzi's approach works best when the child is cooperative, but it may not be very effective when the child is resistant. (Many children do not tend to practice piano without their parents' supervision—a fact that the Xunzian parent is much more aware of than the Mengzian parent.) In contrast, Xunzi's approach works whether the child is obedient or not, albeit at the risk of causing discomfort or pain to the child emotionally or even physically. In real life, an experienced parent may use an eclectic approach that draws from the ideas of both thinkers.

## DOING PHILOSOPHY
### Regarding Rites and Laws: Is Xunzi a Constructionist or a Realist?

A dominant interpretation of Xunzi's view on good government and rituals maintains that Xunzi believes that there is only one correct Way to govern the world, and that rites and laws, as well as social hierarchy, are all fixed.[82] This interpretation is based on the following remarks from the *Xunzi*:

There are no two Ways in the world; the sage is never of two minds ("Dispelling Obsessions," 121).

The Way is the proper standard for past and present ("Rectifying Names," 153).

Music is unalterable harmonies. The rites are unchangeable patterns ("A Discussion of Music," 117).

He who tries to travel two roads at once will arrive nowhere; he who serves two masters will please neither ("Encouraging Learning," 18).

According to this interpretation, Xunzi appears to be unaware that rites and laws can change with time. (It might be that he considers the ways of Heaven,

---

82  See, for example, Chad Hansen, *Language and Logic in Ancient China* (Ann Arbor: University of Michigan Press, 1983), 182; Chad Hansen, *A Daoist Theory*, 342; Paul Goldin, *Rituals of the Way: The Philosophy of Xunzi* (Chicago: Open Court, 1999), 99; David Nivison, *Introduction to the Ways of Confucianism: Investigations in Chinese Philosophy*, Bryan Van Norden, ed. (Chicago: Open Court, 1996), 3.

as well as the ways of humanity, as constant.) This aspect of Xunzi's philosophy is difficult for many to accept. Is it not possible that some rituals may have worked well for certain times in the past, but have become obsolete? Are there not cases in which a ritual is in fact unjust right from the start—see Xunzi's remark "To kill the living and force them to accompany the dead is hideous"?[83] Is it really the case that an orderly society cannot be maintained or preserved without immutable and timeless rites and laws?

Following Lee H. Yearley's interpretation of Xunzi,[84] Kurtis Hagen argues that it is more plausible to see Xunzi as a constructionist than as a realist regarding rites. Hagen remarks that according to Xunzi, "[t]he sages over time and through trial and error developed a workable set of social institutions. This does not entail that it is the only, or even absolutely best, set of institutions, or that it is final, complete, universal, or timeless. Rather, institutions are social constructs designed to facilitate peace and social harmony. As circumstances change, the institutions may also change."[85] How do you think Hagen's interpretation would reconcile with the four above quotes from the *Xunzi*?

## XUNZI'S CRITICISM OF OTHER SCHOOLS OF THOUGHT

The flourishing of "the hundred schools" in and before Xunzi's time is generally recognized by historians as an important development in China's intellectual history. However, Xunzi takes a rather dim view of this development. He thinks that the various schools were all proposing one-sided doctrines, with the pernicious effect of confusing the minds of the rulers and leading them astray. According to Xunzi, "[t]here are not two Ways in the world,"[86] and "[t]he beginning of good government lies in understanding the Way."[87] It was crucial for him to reject all other schools and defend his version of Confucianism,[88] so he launched a wholesale attack against all the other schools:

> Mo Tzu was obsessed by utilitarian considerations and did not understand the beauties of form. Sung Tzu was obsessed by the need to lessen desires, for he did not understand how they could be satisfied. Shen Tzu

---

83  He is talking about a ritual of human sacrifice. See "A Discussion of Rites," 105, and the *Mengzi* 1A4.
84  See Lee H. Yearley, "Hsun Tzu on the Mind: His Attempted Synthesis of Confucianism and Taoism" *Journal of Asian Studies* 39:3 (May 1980): 465–80.
85  Kurtis Hagen, *The Philosophy of Xunzi—A Reconstruction* (Chicago: Open Court, 2007), 3; see also 39.
86  "Dispelling Obsession," 121.
87  "Dispelling Obsession," 127.
88  Fung Yu-lan [FengYoulan] has considered Xunzi "the most skilled of all the ancient Chinese philosophers in criticizing other philosophical schools" (*A History of Chinese Philosophy*, Vol. 1, Derk Bodde, trans. [Princeton: Princeton University Press, 1952], 280).

was obsessed with the concept of law and did not understand the part to be played by worthy men. Shen pu-hai was obsessed by the power of circumstance and did not understand the role of the human intelligence. Hui Tzu was obsessed by words and did not understand the truth that lies behind them. Chuang Tzu was obsessed by thoughts of Heaven [i.e., Nature] and did not understand the importance of man.[89]

Since we have explained Xunzi's criticism of Chuang Tzu (Zhuangzi) and Sung Tzu (Songzi) in previous pages of this chapter, let's now focus on his criticism of Mozi, the legalists Shenzi (Shen Tzu) and Shen Bu-hai (Shen pu-hai), and the logician Hui Shi.

Xunzi's criticism of Mozi focuses on two of the latter's attacks on Confucianism—on the Confucian practice of extravagant sacrificial rites and its embrace of luxurious music. Mozi criticizes both on the grounds that they lack practical utility. According to Mozi, the three great worries of the people are "that when they are hungry they will have no food, when they are cold they will have no clothing, and when they are weary they will have no rest."[90] Although music can be pleasing and entertaining, Mozi argues, it cannot alleviate the three great worries of the common person. In fact, luxurious musical performances exist for the ruling class and are supported by heavy taxes imposed on the common people, which in turn interfere with their efforts to produce food and clothing.[91]

In a similar fashion, Mozi also argues against expensive sacrificial rites on the ground that it is a waste of limited resources. He thinks that when a benevolent man plans for the welfare of the world, he focuses on three things: "enrich the poor," "increase the population," and "bring [people] to order,"[92] but the expensive sacrificial rites do nothing to contribute to these three tasks.[93] Mozi's criticisms did not come out of a vacuum. In his time, it was not uncommon that Confucian rites and music were performed merely as empty forms. Confucius himself had even acknowledged the problem of empty performance of rituals in his time.[94] Thus Mozi says, "the Confucians corrupt men with their elaborate and showy rites and music and deceive their parents with lengthy mournings and hypocritical grief."[95] Instead of blaming the "petty Confucians" (or false Confucians) for such meaningless performance of rites and music, he locates the problem in the Confucian rites and music themselves. One example of Mozi's criticism that targets the Confucian sacrificial rites is the following:

When a parent dies, the Confucians lay out the corpse for a long time
before dressing it for burial while they climb up onto the roof, peer down

89  "Dispelling Obsession," 125.
90  Mozi, "Against Music," part I, Mo Tzu: Basic Writings, Burton Watson, trans. (New York: Columbia University Press, 1963), 111.
91  Mozi, "Against Music" (Watson, Mo Tzu), 112–13.
92  Mozi, "Moderation in Funerals" (Watson, Mo Tzu), 64.
93  "Moderation in Funerals" (Watson, Mo Tzu), 64–77.
94  See the Analects 3:3, 3:10, 3:26, and 4:13.
95  Mozi, "Against Confucians" (Watson, Mo Tzu), 127.

the well, poke in the ratholes, and search in the washbasins, looking for the dead man. If they suppose that they will really find the dead man there, then they must be stupid indeed, while if they know that he is not there but still search for him, then they are guilty of the greatest hypocrisy.[96]

Xunzi could have argued logically that even if there are "petty Confucians," their empty performance of rites and music has nothing to do with the real beauty and function of rites and music per se. But he did not. Rather, he targets the "utility" grounds on which Mozi made the criticisms. He argues that practicing the Way is not simply or totally "a matter of material profit," or of "utilitarian concerns."[97] Thus, he criticizes Mozi for his obsession with material profit and his lack of understanding that music and sacrificial rites, *when preformed properly*, are beautiful and beneficial: they can, for example, "arouse the best in man's nature"[98] and contribute to social order and better governance.

Xunzi criticizes Mozi for taking the rituals too literally (e.g., in assuming that they presuppose some form of afterlife that the deceased continue to enjoy) and failing to appreciate the symbolic meanings of the acts and gestures used in the rituals. As observed by Antonio Cua, ritual acts and gestures can be seen as "objects of our emotions or thought, expressive of our moral attitudes."[99] They signify our inner attitude, so they are fitting expressions of love for the deceased. Thus, Xunzi seems to have adopted Confucius' view that in performing the rituals (on behalf of the deceased), people are really enacting their respect for the deceased as if they lived on after death. In this respect, Xunzi, like Confucius, stresses the moral function of sacrificial rites.

Xunzi also took issue with the Legalists, primarily Shen Tzu and Shen Bu-hai. Contrary to Shen Tzu, Xunzi does not think that to govern properly is simply a matter of drafting better laws and policies. Instead, he stresses the role of incentive—that is, reward and punishment: "[e]ncourage them [people] with rewards, discipline them with punishments, and if they settle down to their work, then look after them as subjects; but if not, cast them out."[100] In addition, Xunzi believes that to govern well requires entrusting important roles to worthy men. "Order is born from the gentleman, disorder from the petty man."[101]

Xunzi's view on government is solidly rooted in the Confucian tradition. Although two of his students Han Feizi and Li Si infamously became Legalists of substantial influence, Xunzi himself always remained nothing but a firm Confucian.[102] In spite of

---

96 "Against Confucians" (Watson, *Mo Tzu*), 125. It is not likely that Chinese people nowadays perform sacrificial rites in exactly the way described by Mozi here.
97 "Dispelling Obsession," 125.
98 "A Discussion of Music," 112.
99 Antonio S. Cua, "The Ethical and the Religious Dimensions of Li (propriety)," in his book, *Human Nature, Ritual, and History—Studies in Xunzi and Chinese Philosophy* (Washington, DC: The Catholic University of America Press, 2005), 189.
100 "The Regulations of a King," 34.
101 "The Regulations of a King," 36.
102 Chad Hansen seems to take Xunzi as a downright utilitarian. See Chad Hansen, *A Daoist Theory*, 307: Xunzi often "slipped into calculating utility only from the point of view of the rulers or high

his emphasis on reward and punishment, he does not believe that social order requires nothing more than the mechanical application of the principles of positive and negative reinforcement. Instead, he emphasizes that rites exist to help people internalize social virtue, so he continues to uphold the values held dear by the worthy and the wise sages, including the importance of voluntary participation in virtue-generating practice. Given Xunzi's Confucian stand on internalization of social virtues, he would have very likely seen the negative, legalist turn of Han Feizi's and Li Si's thinking as the unintended consequence of his own views.

Lastly, Xunzi is also a stern critic of those who advocate the pursuit of abstract, theoretical knowledge. The "Way" in the *Xunzi* and in Chinese philosophy in general is not to be equated with the Platonic "Truth" that is beyond sense experience, universal, and necessary. The Way refers to the right Way of governing, which is rooted in history and experience. Thus, learning the Way does not primarily entail learning about external objects in a scientific manner, but learning about, or indeed embracing, the correct "moral principles" and "regulations" that are constitutive of an orderly society (which he thought were created by the sage and kings). For this reason, Xunzi criticizes the attitude of "knowing for knowing's sake" as endless and futile: "[t]he gentleman despises those who consider perception to consist merely in the analysis of words, or discrimination to consist merely in the description of objects. The gentleman despises men of broad learning and powerful memory who yet do not conform to the regulations of the king."[103] This criticism applies fittingly to Huizi (Hui Shi), who (according to Xunzi) was "fixated on words" and turned the Way into a matter of "discourse," without knowing the true reality (*shi* 实)—what is the case and what ought to be the case.

## CONCLUDING REMARKS: THE INFLUENCE OF THE *XUNZI*

Mengzi and Xunzi can be regarded as two horses (one tender-minded and the other tough-minded) that are pulling along the chariot of Confucianism. They can also be seen as two architects who sought to consolidate the moral and social teachings of Confucius into a grand edifice. Mengzi preserves Confucius' view on "Inner Sageliness" whereas Xunzi extends Confucius' view on "Outer Kingliness (kingly-ruling)." The evolution from Confucius to Mengzi and Xunzi illustrates how a single living tradition can develop different branches, each with its own strengths and beauty.[104]

While Mengzi has been more influential, especially since the Song Dynasty, Xunzi's contribution to Confucianism must not be overlooked. (1) He brought sophisticated argumentation strategies into Confucianism. (2) He stressed "Outer Kingliness" more than Confucius and Mengzi. Confucius and Mengzi believed that a virtuous ruler gives rise to a virtuous government, which in turn gives rise to a harmonious society,

officials." For a view of Xunzi not as a downright utilitarian, see Schwartz, 300 and Lee, 77.
103 "Dispelling Obsession," 137; cf. the opening passage of "The Secret of Caring for Life" in the *Zhuangzi*.
104 Similar cases can be found in the traditions/schools that evolved from the historic Buddha himself, or in the various "petals" of Chinese Chan Buddhist schools from allegedly one single flower of Bodhidharma Chan.

and a virtuous ruler would not need to use reward and punishment to create social order. Xunzi, on the other hand, advocated the use of reward and punishment on the grounds that human beings require external incentives to keep their desires in check. On this point, Xunzi also significantly influenced two later Legalists, Han Feizi and Li Si. Through the influence of the Legalists, Xunzi's view on the need for strong social regulation has become China's implicit (though not official) ideology for governing since the Han dynasty. As this chapter has argued, the legacy of Xunzi can be found both in the development of Chinese intellectual history and in the practice of government throughout much of Chinese history.

## WORKS CITED AND RECOMMENDED READINGS

1. Kurtis Hagen, *The Philosophy of Xunzi—A Reconstruction* (Chicago: Open Court, 2007).
2. Eric Hutton, trans., *Xunzi* (excerpt), Chapter 6 in *Readings in Classical Chinese Philosophy*, Philip J. Ivanhoe and Bryan W. Van Norden, eds. (New York: Seven Bridges Press, 2001).
3. *Xunzi: A Translation and Study of the Complete Works*, John Knoblock, trans., vols, 1–3. Vol. 1 (1988) books 1–6; vol. 2 (1990) books 7–16; vol. 3 (1994) books 17–23 (Stanford, CA: Stanford University Press).
4. Antonio S. Cua, *Human Nature, Ritual, and History: Studies in Xunzi and Chinese Philosophy* (Washington, DC: Catholic University of America Press, 2005).
5. T.C. Kline III and Philip J. Ivanhoe, *Virtue, Nature, and Moral Agency in the Xunzi* (Indianapolis: Hackett, 2000).
6. Janghee Lee, *Xunzi and Early Chinese Naturalism* (Albany, NY: State University of New York Press, 2005).
7. Masayaki Sato, *The Confucian Quest for Order—The Origin and Formation of the Political Thought of Xunzi* (Leiden: Brill, 2003).
8. Paul Rakita Goldin, *Rituals of the Way: The Philosophy of Xunzi* (Chicago: Open Court, 1999).

CHAPTER 9

# The Platform Sutra

SUGGESTED PRIMARY READING

*The Platform Sutra of the Sixth Patriarch*, Philip B. Yampolsky, trans. (New York: Columbia University Press, 1967), 125–83.

LEARNING OBJECTIVES

By the time you have worked through this chapter, you should be able to

> ‣ Describe the general features of Chinese Chan Buddhism
> ‣ Describe Hui Neng's understanding of "seeing into self-nature/ Buddha-nature"
> ‣ Compare and evaluate Shen Xiu's "gradual awakening" and Hui Neng's "sudden awakening"
> ‣ Compare and evaluate Mengzi's moral psychology ("Human nature is good") and Hui Neng's meta-psychology ("Human nature is empty")

KEY WORDS

self-nature/Buddha-nature, no-thought (*wu-nian*), no-abiding (*wu-zhu*), no-form (*wu-xiang*), chan (*dhyana*), gradual enlightenment, sudden enlightenment

## GUIDING QUESTIONS

Buddhism spread beyond the borders of India and arrived in China in the first century CE, and since then it has gone through a long process of transformation and integration with the Chinese tradition. In understanding this process, we can focus on the following questions:

1.  How did Indian Buddhism fuse with the indigenous Chinese Confucianism and Daoism?
2.  How did Chan Buddhism, the most distinctive Chinese version of Buddhism, transform Indian Buddhism as well as revive Gautama Buddha's teachings?
3.  Did Chan Buddhism advocate a gradual practice (relying strictly on sitting meditation) or did it argue for a sudden awakening (not merely relying on sitting meditation)?

This chapter tries to answer these questions through a focused examination of the Platform Sutra.

## INTRODUCTION

Buddhism was introduced into China in the transitional period from the West Han Dynasty (206 BCE-25 CE) to the East Han Dynasty (25-220 CE). Both Mahayana and Theravada (Hinayana) schools had been introduced to China, but the Chinese were particularly interested in the Mahayana school.[1] During the next few hundred years, Buddhism continued to interact with Chinese thought in a variety of ways, including collision, accommodation, and fusion.

The vital presence of Buddhism in China is evidenced by the translation of Buddhist sutras into Chinese, the spread of temples, the arrival of Indian monks, and the increasing number of Chinese monks and nuns. Mahayana Buddhism began to develop from the Wei-jin Dynasty (220-589 CE) on, though not without resistance and criticism from Confucianism and religious Daoism.[2] By the Sui Dynasty (581-618 CE) and Tang

---

1    The Theravada (Hinayana) school stresses strict discipline, and liberation for a limited select number. Theravada was and still is chiefly popular in Sri Lanka, Myanmar, Thailand, Laos, and Cambodia. Mahayana has prevailed in China, Tibet, Japan, and Korea. "Maha" means "great," (and "hina" means "small") and "yana" means "vehicle," so "Mahayana" means a teaching that is like a great vehicle that helps *all sentient beings* to get from "this shore" (suffering) to the "other shore" (enlightenment), whereas "Hinayana" refers to a school that focuses on individuals' self-liberation.
2    A famous Confucian, Han Yu (768-824 CE), for example, criticized Buddhism for its alleged advocacy that one renounce one's family responsibility and one's loyalty to the state (see *A Treatise on Dao* [*Yuan Dao*]). During the North Wei Tai Wu Emperor ruling period (423-52 CE), the North Zhou Wu Emperor ruling period, (560-578 CE), and the Tang Wu Emperor ruling period, (841-46 CE), the central feudal government decided to crack down on Buddhism, due to the Buddhists' increasing encroachment on the government's political and economic powers. Religious Daoists had fostered the crackdown for their own interests. Ideas and terms in philosophical Daoism (and particularly in its new-Daoist

Dynasty (618–907 CE), Mahayana thought was flourishing in China and had become fully integrated into Chinese thought. Chinese Buddhist schools, such as Sanlun, Faxiang, Huayan, Tiantai, Jingtu (Pure Land), and Chan, all blossomed.[3]

The most domesticated and influential of these schools was Chan. Its name is a phonetic translation of *dhyana*[4] in Sanskrit; much more commonly it is known in English by the Japanese equivalent name, "Zen." Unlike other schools of Chinese Buddhism (such as Tiantai and Huayan) that tend to be scholastic and theoretical, Chan had made Buddhism a practical, direct, and non-scholastic way of life. While the Chinese mind had long been fascinated with Buddhist thought (particularly Mahayana Buddhism), it finally managed to put forth an interpretation of Buddhism—in the form of Chan—that is distinctively Chinese.

According to the Chan tradition, Bodhidharma (470–543 CE) travelled to China from India in 526 CE to preach *dhyana* as a way of practicing Buddhism. He first sought to make converts (though unsuccessfully) in Jian Kang (now Nanjing) during the reign of Emperor Wu of the South Dynasty. Then he travelled to the North Wei (386–534 CE) capital of Luoyang. (According to one legend, he crossed the Yangtze River on a single reed.) Finally, he settled down at Shaolin Temple in Mount Song.[5]

Although *dhyana* techniques had been introduced into China as early as the second century, Bodhidharma has always been venerated as the First Chan Patriarch in the Chinese Chan lineage.[6] This is no accident; it was he who took the initiative to promote Chan, which in turn received from Hui Neng (the sixth Chinese Chan Patriarch [638–713 CE]) a fresh reinterpretation catered to the Chinese mind. It is largely due to the efforts of these two foundational figures of Chinese Buddhism that Chan flourished into a national movement in China.

---

form of *Xuan Xue*, "Esoteric Daoism"), by contrast, were appropriated by the Buddhists in translating and interpreting Buddhist sutras.

3   The Sanlun (Three-Treatise) school is the Chinese counterpart of the Indian Madhyamika school. It focuses on these three treatises: Nagarjuna's *Fundamental Verses on the Middle Way*, *Dvādashanikāya-Shāstra*, and Nagarjuna's disciple Aryadeva's (third century BCE) *Catusataka* (400 verses). Its founder was Ji Zang (Chi-tsang, 549–623 CE). The Chinese version of Yogachara is Faxiang (fa-hsiang, the Dharma-Character School, or the Consciously-Only School) whose founder was Xuan Zang (Hsuan-tsang, 596–664 CE). The Tiantai (T'ien-t'ai) School is named after a sacred mountain where its founder Zhi Yi (Chih-I, 538–97 CE) preached. Huayan (Hua-yen, or the Flower Garland) School received its name from a sutra with the same title, and its founder was Fa Zang (fa-tsang, 643–712 CE). Finally, Jingtu (Ching-t'u, the Pure Land) school was based on Pure Land Sutras, and its founder was Hui Yuan (334–416 CE).

4   *Dhyana* technique seems to have derived from ancient Indian Yoga; its methods include breathing adjustment for better concentration and equanimity of mind, and the cultivation of compassion for all sentient beings.

5   According to one legend, Bodhidharma had practiced sitting meditation in a cave for nine years near the Shaolin Temple in Northern China. The Shaolin Temple was established in 495 CE by an allegedly Indian *dhyana* master, Buddhabhadra; it is where the famous martial arts movie *The Shaolin Temple* was shot.

6   Hui Ke (487–593 CE), Seng Can (dates unknown), Dao Xin (580–636 CE), and Hong Ren (601–74 CE) are the second, third, fourth, and fifth Patriarchs respectively, and Hui Neng, whose preaching is the basis of the Platform Sutra, is regarded as the sixth Patriarch.

Hui Neng's Chan practice was central to the success of Chan in China, and instrumental to the transformation of the Indian religion into its current Chinese expression. The book reputed to record his teachings, the *Platform Sutra of the Sixth Patriarch* (PS for short hereafter), is regarded as a monumental text in Chinese Chan.

The PS contains an autobiography of the sixth Chinese Chan Patriarch Hui Neng (638–713 CE), plus lectures and sermons.[7] The word "platform" refers to the pulpit, or a raised structure, from which a sermon is delivered. The text is unique in that it is the only Chinese Buddhist text to have been honoured as a "sutra"—a term that is traditionally reserved for the teachings of Buddha or a Buddha. There are several extant versions of the text, but the basic teachings in them are the same.[8] The minute distinctions among these versions of the sutra may be of interest to scholars of Chinese Chan, but for our purposes, it suffices to follow the Dun-huang version that is translated by Philip B. Yampolsky.[9]

The Dun-huang version, like other versions, is probably not the work of one single author, nor does it necessarily reflect a verbatim record of the teachings of Hui Neng.[10] In fact, the main elements of Chan Buddhism in eighth century China are all gathered together in the sutra. This explains why the PS is the largest, and considered the most authoritative, text of Chinese Chan. A careful study of this sutra appears a must for a genuine understanding of Chinese Chan.

The PS consists of three parts: Hui Neng's autobiography (Sections 2–11), sermons (Sections 12–33), and further expositions of his teachings (Sections 34–57). Most of the technical terms and key ideas appear in sections that contain Hui Neng's sermons (Sections 12–33), and we'll focus on them.

The PS tells us that Hui Neng was a man of humble origins. His father died when he was small, and his mother suffered from extreme poverty—barely surviving by selling

---

7   Whether the teachings recorded in the Platform Sutra were Hui Neng's verbatim speech or even largely his teachings is a controversial issue in Chan scholarship. Hu Shi (1891–1962) argues that the teachings largely belong to Shen Hui (670–762), a disciple of Hui Neng, citing the similarities between works by Shen Hui and the Platform Sutra. Others disagree with Hu Shi. For example, Guo Peng and Yang Zengwen maintain that Shen Hui may have just quoted from the Platform Sutra (see Red Pine, *The Platform Sutra—The Zen Teaching of Hui-Neng* [Emeryville, CA: Shoemaker & Hoard, 2006], 59).

8   The Zongbao version (1291) is the most popular version of the Platform Sutra. The earliest extant version, probably dating from the Tang Dynasty (seventh to tenth century CE) is the Dun-huang (Dun-huang) version, discovered in 1900 at Dun-huang. There are also two Japanese versions: the *Koshoji* text, written in 967, and discovered in the 1930s, and the *Daijoji* text kept by Dogen (1200–53). The scholarly English translations of the sutra include Wing-tsit Chan's *The Platform Scripture* (New York: St. John's University Press, 1963), based on the Dun-huang version, and Philip B. Yampolsky's *The Platform Sutra of the Sixth Patriarch* (New York: Columbia University Press, 1967), also based on the Dun-huang version. Furthermore, according to Red Pine, there was a second version of the Dun-huang text, now kept in Dun-huang Museum (thus called the "Dun-huang Museum Version"). This second version has fewer mistakes and omissions than the first version; it was discovered in 1943 in China, and published in 1986 by Zhou Shaoliang, and in 1993 by Yang Zengwen. (See Pine, 56–57.) For more about the history of the sutra, see Carl Bielefeldt and Lewis Lancaster, "T'an Ching (Platform Scripture)," *Philosophy East and West* 25:2 (1975): 197–212.

9   Yampolsky, 125–83.

10   See Heinrich Dumoulin, *Zen Buddhism: A History*, Vol. 1: *India and China*, James W. Heisig and Paul Knitter, trans. (New York: Macmillan, 1988), 123–29.

firewood in the market. Though he was supposed to be unlettered, one day when delivering firewood to a customer's house he heard a person chanting the *Diamond Sutra* and was instantaneously awakened! Eager to know more about the *Diamond Sutra* and its teaching, Hui Neng asked about the source of the sutra and was directed to the place of Huang Mei where the Fifth Patriarch of Chan, Hong Ren, was preaching.

Upon his first interview with the Fifth Patriarch Hong Ren, Hui Neng was tested with this question: "Since you are from an uncivilized part of China, and you are a barbarian, how can you become a Buddha?" Hui Neng confidently replied that all people (regardless of their place of birth) are capable of attaining Buddhahood: "Although people from the south and people from the north differ, there is no north and south in Buddha-nature" (Section 3).[11]

Hui Neng was then kept around working as a rice pounder. After eight months, Hong Ren, considering passing on the robe of Bodhidharma (a symbol for patriarchship) and the Dharma (the authentic Buddhist teachings) to the would-be Sixth Patriarch, asked the monks to write a verse on a wall to show their understanding of Chan. The head monk Shen Xiu wrote one verse but Hong Ren did not think that he had shown a true understanding of Chan, for he was merely "at the gate," without "entering it" yet. Hui Neng also conceived one verse, and with the help of another monk, wrote it on the wall. Hong Ren saw it and realized that Hui Neng had arrived at a real understanding of Chan, but did not announce it publicly for fear of jealousy from other monks.

Several months later, after giving further instruction to Hui Neng on the *Diamond Sutra* privately late at night, Hong Ren secretly passed the robe and the Dharma to Hui Neng and sent him to south China, but advised him not to preach the Dharma until three years later.

Although grounded on Indian Mahayana Buddhism, the PS advocates a way of life or a way of liberation that has been adapted for the Chinese. The doctrine of "'seeing' one's nature and becoming a Buddha" (*jian xing cheng fo*), for example, stands in contrast to other schools of Buddhism and presents a way of liberation that is direct, practical, non-scholastic, and open to all. As we will see, the sutra also reflects an evident fusion of Indian Buddhism with Confucianism and Daoism—two major systems of indigenous Chinese thought.

Generally speaking, the PS draws upon two important teachings from the two schools of Mahayana Buddhism: the Yogacara teaching of Mind-only (or Consciousness-only) and the Madhyamika (Middle Way) teaching of emptiness. The PS appropriates these ideas from several Indian *Prajnaparamita* (Perfect Wisdom) Sutras, such as the *Diamond Sutra* (see PS Sections 2, 7, 9, 28), *Lankavatara Sutra* (see PS Section 5), *Vimalakirti Sutra* (see PS Sections 14, 17, 19), and *Nirvana Sutra* (not mentioned by name in the Dun-huang version of the PS). *Lankavatara Sutra* is scholastic and contains the notions of the Tathagata (the one who is beyond coming and going or who sees reality as such, that is, reality as-it-is) and the triple-fold body of the Buddha. It focuses on the psychological aspects of the process of enlightenment. The sutra

11  Unless otherwise noted, translations will be Yampolsky's, from *The Platform Sutra of the Sixth Patriarch*, identified by section number.

teaches that enlightenment comes from a conversion of the deepest and highest level of consciousness, which is expressed in the doctrine of the "storehouse-consciousness" (*alayavijnana*). This is also the main sutra upon which the Northern school of Chan, led by Shen Xiu, relied.

The *Diamond Sutra* emphasizes the importance of realizing the illusory nature of all phenomena. According to this sutra, when one penetrates the emptiness of all things and grasps their suchness, one becomes free from attachment and thus enlightened. In the *Diamond Sutra*, enlightenment or realization comes through many means, not necessarily or exclusively by means of sitting meditation. This is the sutra that Hui Neng primarily based his teaching on.

Hui Neng also seems to have drawn from the *Vimalakirti Sutra* and the *Nirvana Sutra*. The *Vimalakirti Sutra* contains a series of dharma talks by the layman bodhisattva Vimalakirti, who explicated important Mahayana ideas, such as non-duality, sudden awakening, straightforward mind, and Buddhist practice in everyday life. Finally, Hui Neng may also have been influenced by the *Nirvana Sutra* which contains some well-known narratives about the final months of the Buddha's life. It teaches that all sentient beings have Buddha-nature—the foundation or potentiality for enlightenment.

In short, the teachings of Hui Neng are firmly rooted in the fundamental ideas of Buddhism, drawing on the Wisdom Sutras in the Mahayana tradition. That there is a close connection between Indian Buddhism and Chinese Chan is evident. However, as we shall see below, Chinese Chan also developed in its own direction, departing from Indian Mahayana practice. In the process, Chan integrated the authentic spirit of Gautama Buddha's teaching into China's indigenous intellectual traditions, namely, Confucianism and Daoism.

## "SEEING" INTO SELF-NATURE (OR BUDDHA-NATURE)

A fundamental presupposition in Hui Neng's teaching is that all humans have innate Buddha-nature—the nature to be enlightened or awakened, regardless of their place of birth, or anything else for that matter. This is clearly seen in his initial dialogue with the Fifth patriarch Hong Ren [Hung-jen]. When Hui Neng told Master Hong Ren that he came all the way from Ling-nan in southern China to learn Buddhadharma,

> The Master then reproved me, saying: "If you're from Ling-nan then you're a barbarian [northern Han Chinese in ancient times had a prejudice against the inhabitants of southern China, regarding them as barbarians, close to wild animals]. How can you become a Buddha?"
>
> I replied: "Although people from the south and people from the north differ, there is no north and south in Buddha-nature. Although my barbarian's body and your body are not the same, what difference is there in our Buddha-nature?"[12] (Section 3)

---

12  In general, the PS prefers to use the terms "self-nature," "original nature," or simply "nature" rather than "Buddha-nature," which appears only in 5 sections (3, 8, 12, 32, 34). This may not be accidental. The

According to Hui Neng, while people can be different in many other ways, they are similar to each other in sharing the same Buddha-nature. This notion of a universal Buddha-nature is crucial to Hui Neng's soteriology, in that it implies that everyone is able to be enlightened. Indeed, it is a concept that empowers, as do such ideas as *Atman*-is-*Brahman* and human-nature-is-good, for it enables people to trust in their own capacities and endeavours. Thus, it makes Hui Neng's teaching appealing to people from diverse backgrounds, regardless of their birth place, social status, and so on.

Hui Neng is careful to maintain that although everyone is endowed with Buddha-nature or self-nature, not everyone can "*see' into self-nature*" (see Sections 14, 20, 23, 24, 25, 29, 30, 35, 41, 42, 48, 52).[13] Sections on Buddha-nature or self-nature can be rather puzzling at first glance, for the terms "seeing" and "self-nature" can be rather misleading if they are understood based on everyday usage. In this case, "seeing" may suggest a dualism of a subject (the seer) and an object (the seen),[14] on the basis of which one may construe Hui Neng's "'seeing' into self-nature" as some kind of "introspection into the inner essence of the self," which is something like the Cartesian cogito, the Socratic soul, or the hidden kernel of a walnut. However, as a Buddhist, Hui Neng must have subscribed to the teaching of interdependent-arising, which lies at the heart of Buddhism. Thus, he would have regarded everything as empty—a view that Nagarjuna had potently defended. Following the logic of interdependent-arising, Hui Neng would have maintained that self-nature, as everything else, is empty or non-substantive.

Self-nature, or Buddha-nature, though empty, is called Bodhi, the supreme wisdom or enlightenment the Buddha Gautama achieved under a Bodhi tree. In this sense, the Buddha-nature assumes a capacity for enlightenment in *all sentient beings*. This is a crucial idea in Mahayana Buddhism. The PS followed this idea (Section 12) but supposes a narrow interpretation of "sentient beings" that refers exclusively to human beings (Sections 48 and 30). This is perhaps why the idea of Buddha-nature is also expressed variously as "human nature," "self-nature" (Sections 20, 24, 25, 41), and "heart-mind" (Sections 14, 30, 35, 41, 42). In this respect, Hui Neng's "self-nature" seems close to Mengzi's "human nature." In both cases, it is a very encouraging and reassuring concept that all individuals have the self-sufficient capacity for transcendence—liberation (for Hui Neng) and moral perfection (for Mengzi). We will see in the next chapter that Dogen, by contrast, broadly interprets Buddha-nature as "beings" rather than some property possessed by sentient beings or even by human beings alone. For Dogen, any being—the sun, the moon, the trees, the birds, etc.—all *are* Buddha-nature, in the sense of impermanence. In the light of impermanence, as Dogen argues, not just all human beings are equal, *all beings are equal.*

---

terms "original nature," "nature," and especially "self-nature" emphasize the immanent and subjective basis for enlightenment.

13 The word "heart-mind" (*xin*) in the PS is used in two senses: (1) the original heart-mind, the heart-mind ground, the One Heart-mind, the Buddha Heart-mind, and the heart-mind of thusness, (2) the false heart-mind, or the ordinary heart-mind dominated by conditioning, desire, aversion, ignorance, false sense of self, or the heart-mind of delusion. In the first sense, "heart-mind" is used in the same sense as "Buddha-nature" or "self-nature."

14 And the object, in this case, is the self-nature, or the Buddha-nature (Sections 20, 24, 25, 41).

**DOING PHILOSOPHY**
*The Circle Symbol of Chan versus the Yin-Yang Symbol of Daoism*

A Symbol of Chan

A common symbol for Chan is a circle, and it can be interpreted as symbolizing several things: (1) Reality (and one's original mind) is empty (no entity or object in the circle); (2) Reality (and the original mind) is perfect-as-it-is, lacking nothing. The roundness of the circle reflects the perfection of the world-as-it-is (or the original mind as-it-is). (3) The circle is like a mirror, reflecting everything yet being contaminated by nothing. (4) The circle symbolizes the clear and bright moon, silently illuminating all beings without discrimination. (See Sections 14, 24, 25, 31 about what emptiness/no attachment is or is not.) Now compare the circle symbol of Chan with the Yin-yang symbol of Daoism (below). What are the similarities and differences between the two symbols?

The Yin-yang Symbol of Daoism

As you may recall, Mengzi has to explain why the sprouts of goodness inherent in human nature sometimes fail to produce good deeds. Hui Neng faces a similar problem: he has to explain why many remain deluded, or unenlightened, in spite of the universality of Buddha-nature. In order to explain the interrelationship between self-nature, delusion and enlightenment, Hui Neng likens the co-existence of illusions and Buddha-nature, or self-nature, to the co-existence of clouds and a blue sky.

> ... although the nature of people in this world is from the outset pure in itself, the ten thousand things are all within their own natures. If people think of all the evil things, then they will practice evil; if they think of all the good things, then they will practice good. Thus it is clear that in this way all the dharmas are within your own natures, yet your own natures are always pure. The sun and the moon are always bright, yet if they are covered by clouds, although above they are bright, below they are darkened, and the

sun, moon, the stars, and planets cannot be seen clearly. But if suddenly the
wind of wisdom should blow and roll away the clouds and mists, all forms
in the universe appear at once. The purity of the nature of man in this world
is like the blue sky; wisdom is like the sun, knowledge like the moon ...
(Section 20)

If human nature is originally pure (Sections 12, 20), how is it that many people
are deluded? Hui Neng's answer is: because their egoistic passions are "deep-rooted"
and they follow "heterodox views"[15] (Section 29). That is, they do not "see" their true
nature—just as when the clouds cover the sun and the moon, the true nature of their
brightness is not seen (Sections 20, 29). How can the deluded be awakened then? Hui
Neng's answer is: "They must seek a good teacher to show them how to see into their
own natures" (Section 12), and they must think of all the good things. This last point
is clearly in line with the opening verses of the Dhammapada.

In the above quote, "the ten thousand things are all within their own natures," and
"all the dharmas are within your own natures" must not be taken literally or superficially as to mean that one's nature "contains" (in a spatial sense) the "ten thousand
things" and "all the dharmas." These words are to be taken figuratively: the goodness
or badness of one's act is "determined" by one's free nature of choosing.

Hui Neng's view on the pure mind, delusion, and awakening naturally reminds
us of Mengzi's view about cultivating the original good heart. Recall that for Mengzi
the reason why some become morally "great" and some morally "small" is that they
choose to act differently: the former choose to follow the innately good heart-mind,
and the latter choose to pursue physical and egoist desires (see *Mengzi*, 6A15).

While Hui Neng and Mengzi stress the importance of thinking (choosing) and
both underscore the significance of distinguishing good and evil, it is important to
note their differences. First, for Hui Neng, the purity of human nature does not point
to any substantial characteristics; the purity of human nature itself is neither good
nor bad; it is not like Mengzi's four "sprouts" of moral goodness that he argues are
inherent in all humans. The purity of human nature for Hui Neng is *free* or *empty* of
substantive nature.[16] Therefore, Hui Neng's view of human nature seems to be much
closer to the existentialist dictum of "existence precedes essence"—what a person
does is primary, not some (pre-existent) nature of that person or of all persons—than
to Mengzi's notion of innate sprouts of moral goodness. Second, notice that unlike
Mengzi, Hui Neng did not argue for his claim on human nature as did Mengzi, for he
merely illustrated his view with an analogy (that of clouds against the blue sky), rather
than supporting it with an argument.

Hui Neng argues for the importance of "seeing" into one's nature. But if one's nature
is empty, non-objectified or non-reified, then how can one "see" into it? The key here

---

15  Presumably the views assume a substantive understanding of self and things.
16  The unsubstantive feature of human nature is characterized by Hui Neng variously as pure (Sections
17, 18), empty (Section 24), and no-abiding (Section 17).

is how to understand the word "see" (*jian*, 見). In the PS, a crucial distinction is pre-supposed between the word "*jian*" and another word "*kan*" ("look," 看). *Kan* ("look") tends to objectify what is being looked at. As Dumoulin has pointed out, the Chinese character *kan* (看) is composed of two elements: an eye (目) and a hand (手). Together they serve to objectivize the act of seeing.[17] Thus, *kan* is a static process that suggests a distinction between the seer and the seen (see Section 14 on "sitting in meditation without moving" and "sit viewing the mind and viewing purity").

Contrary to *kan*, the word *jian* (見) is composed of an eye (目) and two legs (儿), thus signifying a dynamic, ongoing awareness that erases any trace of separation of the seer and the seen. To *jian* is to experience or realize a state of being, with no dualism, discursive thinking, analysis, or evaluation. It is an awareness of the undif-ferentiated unity of all existence. One might call such seeing "meta-seeing" (beyond ordinary seeing), "transcendental seeing," or "primordial seeing" for it posits no sub-ject and object dualism that is presupposed in ordinary seeing and experiencing.

We can illustrate Hui Neng's view on "seeing" (one's nature) by comparing it with Aristotle's view on seeing. The latter is epistemic or cognitive, based on a subject/object dualism and the assumption that things are differentiated: we prefer seeing—the sense of sight—to other senses, because seeing, "most of all the senses, makes us know and brings to light many differences between things" (Aristotle, *Metaphysics*, Book 1, part 1). Seeing, for Aristotle, is to form a mental picture (representation) of what there is or what is the case.

Hui Neng's "seeing," by contrast, is not epistemic or cognitive, but existential, in that it is about "experiencing," "actualizing," and "doing." Thus, to say that you "see" your Buddha-nature is the same as saying that you are practicing Buddha's way. To practice the Buddha's way is therefore to see one's Buddha-nature. This view dissolves various forms of dualism, including knowing/acting, being/doing, seer/seen, subject/object, and so on. For Hui Neng, there is simply no gap between seeing and acting.[18]

Seeing (experiencing or actualizing) self-nature is a personal issue, and nobody else and nothing else can see for you. As Chan masters often state, "It [the experience of 'seeing'] is just like the fish swimming in the water; they alone know whether the water is cold or warm." Chan emphasizes not only the privacy of "seeing," but also the human being's innate capacity to "see" (Sections 12, 19, 24, 29, 31, 35, 36, 41, 42, 52, 53). Here we can notice a close affinity between Hui Neng and Mengzi. While Mengzi and Hui Neng understand human nature differently, they both see human nature as

---

17  Dumoulin, *Zen Buddhism*, 140.
18  Cf. D.T. Suzuki's comment on the idea of "seeing" in the PS: "For in spite of the fact that seeing is an act just as much as moving a hand or a foot, or as the uttering of words, there is not so much of perceptible muscular movement in seeing as in the shaking of hands, or in ejecting sounds out of the throat and the mouth; and this anatomical peculiarity tends to make us regard the act of seeing from the quietistic point of view. The more intellectual type of mind may remain contented with this tendency, but the case is otherwise with strongly practical people" (*Zen Doctrine of No-mind—The Significance of the Sutra of Hui-neng (Wei-lang)* [London: Rider and Company, 1969], 84–85).

self-sufficient for moral perfection in this life.[19] For Mengzi, all human beings can become sages; for Hui Neng, all human beings can become Buddhas. Both advocate self-reliance in spiritual liberation, thus dispensing with any need for an external power, such as God, that effects moral perfection. Hui Neng says: "Good friends, each of you must observe well for himself. Do not mistakenly use your minds. The sutras say to take refuge in the Buddha within yourselves; they do not say to rely on other Buddhas. If you do not rely upon your own natures, there is nothing else on which to rely" (Section 23; see also Sections 19, 24, 29, 31, 35, 36, 41, 42, 52, 53). From the point of view of Chan, to place one's hope in the hands of God for a future life is to postpone the problem of life rather than to deal with it right now and right here.[20]

The following *koan* (*gong an* in Chinese, meaning "public case" or "story") nicely demonstrates Chan's emphasis on independence and self-reliance.

> The student Doken was told to go on a long journey to another monastery. He was much upset, because he felt that this trip would interrupt his studies for many months. So he said to his friend the advanced student Sogen: "Please ask permission to come with me on the trip. There are so many things I do not know; but if you come along we can discuss them—in this way I can learn as we travel." "All right," said Sogen, "But let me ask you a question: If you are hungry, what satisfaction to you if I eat rice? If your feet are lame, what comfort to you if I go on merrily? If your bladder is full, what relief to you if I piss?"[21]

The spirit of independence in Chan, however, does not imply that practitioners can simply or automatically "see" (understand or realize) their Buddha-nature without instruction and thus become enlightened. In most cases, Chan maintains, practitioners must seek good teachers who can show them how to "see" into their own natures (Sections 12, 20, 31).[22] Often, they also need to rely on heuristic devices.

---

19 The character of not relying on external force in Chan was later radicalized in Linji's (Rinchi's) (?–866) iconoclastic temperament: "When you see ('encounter,' or 'be bound by') a Buddha, kill him; when you see a Patriarch, kill him."

20 If your present life is problematic, an (infinite) extension of it will be no less problematic. The assumption of an infinite life will not automatically solve your life problem. As Wittgenstein puts it: "Not only is there no guarantee of the temporal immortality of the human soul, that is to say of its eternal survival after death; but, in any case, this assumption completely fails to accomplish the purpose for which it has always been intended. Or is some riddle solved by my surviving forever? Is not this eternal life as much of a riddle as our present life?" (*Tractatus Logico-Philosophicus*, 6.4312).

21 [Anon.], *Zen Buddhism—An Introduction to Zen With Stories, Parables and Koan Riddles Told by the Zen Masters, with Cuts from Old Chinese Ink Paintings* (Mount Vernon, NY: The Peter Pauper Press, 1959), 15.

22 Compare this with Mengzi's seeking for one's lost original heart, see the *Mengzi* 6A10.

## DOING PHILOSOPHY
*Chan: With or Without Language?*

According to the traditional Chan accounts, Chan/*dhyana* allegedly began
with Gautama the Buddha. It was said that one day on the Mount Vulture
Peak, the Buddha was preaching in front of an assembly of monks. Instead of
talking, he stayed silent for a long period of time while holding a bouquet of
flowers. Nobody knew what the Buddha's gesture meant, except Mahakasyapa,
who contently smiled at the Buddha, as if he had completely understood the
Buddha's body language or object lesson. Only then did the Buddha open his
mouth and speak to Mahakasyapa, "I have the most precious treasure which I
am now handing over to you."

This account may have well been fabricated by Chan followers, but it reveals
two important points about Chan. First, Chan purports to be following the
teachings of Gautama the Buddha. Chan practitioners understood Chan as
authentic Buddhist practice whose lineage is traceable to the Buddha himself.
Second, the practice of Chan is beyond conceptual language, or to put it differently, Chan is about acting rather than about mere speaking. This skeptical
attitude towards language also shows a clear affinity to Daoism (see especially
the *Daodejing*, Chapter 1).

The PS held the same attitude towards language. In the beginning of the sutra,
we are told that Hui Neng was uneducated and hence could neither read nor
write (Sections 8 and 42); nevertheless he was awakened upon hearing the
*Diamond Sutra*. This account may seem a bit exaggerated, for it is hard to see
how an illiterate person could comprehend the highly literary language of the
Buddhist sutra. The account, however, makes it clear that discursive thinking,
including its verbal expression, is not essential in the practice of Chan. Hui
Neng says: "in the original nature itself the wisdom of *prajna* exists, and that by
using this wisdom yourself and illuminating with it, there is no need to depend
on written words" (Section 28). Indeed, even though the PS was influenced
by many sutras, it proclaimed to be beyond sutras. This explains why Chan
tradition later describes itself as transcending language: "No dependence upon
words and letters; a special transmission outside sutras. Direct pointing to the
human mind; seeing into [Buddha] nature to attain Buddhahood."

This skeptical attitude toward language in Chan, however, does not imply
that the sutras are useless. Hui Neng himself was enlightened because of
the *Diamond Sutra*. The point emphasized by Chan is that one must not
become so fixated in the finger (i.e., language) that points to the moon that
one loses sight of the moon itself (i.e., reality). The finger that points to the

moon, nevertheless, has a rightful place too, and all the sermons given by Hui Neng—indeed the whole PS—are performing precisely this function. They are all "expedient means," or "skillful means" (*upaya* in Sanskrit, or *fang-bian* in Chinese) that guide the practitioners to Truth; yet, they are not Truth themselves. In this respect, Hui Neng follows closely Nagarjuna's teaching about convention or dependent designation.

The PS highlights several heuristic devices in their practice. A heuristic device is analogous to a conceptual model that helps elucidate and guide actual practice and that is not meant to be taken literally. Two such devices are the idea of the threefold body (*Trikaya*) of Buddha and the discourse of Heaven (the Pure Land of the West) and Hell. Practitioners are cautioned not to "look" (*kan*) at them (that is, treating them literally, spatially, or in a reified way), but to "see" them (that is, enacting the practice they point to).

The notion of the threefold body of the Buddha is used to help practitioners realize three important aspects of capabilities of a Buddha (Section 53) in their practice. The threefold body of the Buddha consists of the Law-body (or dharma-body), the Reward-body (or Enjoyment-body), and the Transformation-body (or Body of Incarnation).[23]

Taken literally, the threefold body would refer to three spatially separate entities, but the PS warns us not to misconstrue it this way. Instead, the threefold body is a kind of conceptual map and a mnemonic that summarizes the dynamics of Buddhist psychology. It is not about three gods that float in Heaven with which Chan practitioners should strive to unite;[24] neither does it concern the stages of a physically morphing Buddha. This doctrine is an extended metaphor, rather than a physical description of reality. It provides a tool for practitioners to observe and understand their own practice.

The Law-body is the self-nature or Buddha-nature, the body of the truth or principle. It signifies the Buddha-nature and the awareness of it. So when one is reminded to "take refuge in the Dharma- (Law-) body," this is a metaphorical reminder to practice the Buddhist way and be awakened (Section 20). The Reward-body is the person embodied with his enlightenment. It symbolizes the consequences of intentions and deeds to oneself and others. The Transformation-body is the body appearing variously to save people. It represents various ways one adopts in Buddhist practice or preaching.

By the same token, Hui Neng thinks it is wrong-headed to take heaven and hell as external to our lives at present; he regards them as close and intimate: "If you think of evil things then you [will] change and enter hell; if you think of good things then you [will] change and enter heaven"[25] (Section 20). In other words, heaven and hell are immanent in what one does right now and right here; they are more about one's state of being than the location or space one occupies. Heaven is the state of happiness and

---

23 They are read in Sanskrit as *Dharmakaya*, *Sambhogakaya*, and *Nirmanakaya* respectively.
24 The threefold body of the Buddha naturally reminds us of the Trinity Doctrine in Christian theology.
25 There is no future tense intended in the original Chinese text, so the "will" would be better deleted.

hell is the state of suffering; neither of them is simply a place or location. Even if you are in a preferable location (say Hawaii), if your being is not happy, your being in that location would not assure your happiness. This is precisely Hui Neng's point when he talks about the Pure West Land: "people of the East, just by making the mind pure, are without crime; people of the West, if their minds are not pure, are guilty of a crime. The deluded person wishes to be born in the East or West, [for the enlightened person] any land is just the same. If only the mind has no impurity, the Western Land is not far" (Section 35).

### SITTING MEDITATION AND SUDDEN AWAKENING

As noted above, Master Hong Ren initiated a spirit verse "contest" to see who among his disciples would be qualified to be the Sixth Chan Patriarch. Both Shen Xiu (c. 606–706), the well-learned, best reputed pupil at Hong Ren's monastery, and Hui Neng, an illiterate new monk, wrote verses to express their understanding of Chan. Their respective verses epitomize two different approaches to the practice of Chan.[26] The verse by Shen Xiu advocates the practice of sitting meditation whereas the verse by Hui Neng emphasizes sudden awakening.[27] The PS appears to favour the latter (see Sections 2, 8, 9, 29, 31, 33). Let's first examine Shen Xiu's verse:

> The body is the Bodhi tree,[28] / The mind [i.e., Buddha-nature] is like [the stand of] a clear mirror. / At all times we must strive to polish it; / And must not let the dust collect. (Section 6)

The first two lines express, in a symbolic way, that everyone has a primordial, pure Buddha-nature/heart-mind ("a clear mirror") that contains perfect wisdom. The last two lines stress the importance of constant practice ("polishing"), that is, sitting meditation. The gist of the verse is that constant practice helps keep one's original mind pure. Keeping one's original mind pure (i.e., clear of delusion) is awakening. Letting the mind collect dust (a metaphor for external attachments to objects, sound, smell, taste, touch and ideas), on the other hand, is to become deluded.

This approach to enlightenment is reminiscent of Mengzi's view of moral cultivation. Just as Mengzi argues that our heart-mind is innately good, Shen Xiu suggests that

---

26  It is a significant fact that the Fifth patriarch Hong Ren did not ask the monks to write a (theoretical) treatise, but a verse. Chan (and Chinese culture in general) prefers everyday yet poetic expressions to theoretical argumentation.

27  The first Chinese Buddhist who underscored sudden awakening can be traced back to Dao-sheng (355–434 CE); Dao-sheng argues unprecedentedly in China that sudden awakening is open to everyone, even those who claim not to believe in Buddhism are endowed with Buddha-nature—a potential for Buddhist awakening. See Fung Yu-lan, *A History of Chinese Philosophy*, Vol. 2, Derk Bodde, trans. (Princeton: Princeton University Press, 1952), 388.

28  Recall that the Buddha obtained awakening under a Bodhi tree. "Bodhi tree" thus symbolizes "the basis of awakening."

the mind is originally pure. Both Shen Xiu and Mengzi emphasize the importance of preserving (and returning to) the original state of heart-mind. Both underscore the centrality of constant practice as a path to their respective spiritual goals. Nevertheless, they differ in two respects. First, Shen Xiu's original pure mind is neither good nor bad, for it transcends such dualistic description. Second, Mengzi's notion of moral cultivation involves a linear process in which the sprouts of goodness grow into maturity, whereas Shen Xiu's practice does not *require* a linear process of maturation, although it may very well involve such a process. It simply emphasizes the constant clearing of an originally "clear mirror" (Buddha-nature).

Shen Xiu's approach to the practice of Chan, in Hui Neng's assessment, involves a cluster of problems: if the mind is originally pure, why is it necessary to constantly polish it? If the mind could be somehow contaminated by "dust," would there not be a dualistic assumption that the pure heart-mind and the dust are distinct entities? Shouldn't Buddha-nature still be pure even if it were not polished—because both polishing and not polishing come from Buddha-nature itself? Is the pure heart-mind substantively pure and the dust substantively contaminating? Do they both have substantive nature? Hui Neng's Verse II appears to target these problems.

The mind is the Bodhi tree, / The body is the [clear] mirror stand. / The mirror is originally clean and pure; / Where can it be stained by dust? (Section 8)

For Hui Neng, if self-nature or heart-mind is primordially pure (beyond duality), then it cannot be "stained" by anything. It is rather like the sun whose brightness can be "covered" by the clouds but not "stained" by them (Sections 20, 29). In other words, it seems to Hui Neng that Shen Xiu's "dust-staining-mirror" image implies that the dust in fact changes the nature of the mirror whereas Hui Neng's "the sun-being-covered-by-clouds" image does not entail a change of the sun's bright nature. The meteorological analogy offered by Hui Neng seems to have some intuitive appeal here. But how far can one take the analogy before it breaks down and turns into a form of dualism that flatly contradicts Mahayana Buddhism (including Chan)? For example, the clouds and the sun are two separate "things." The former does not come from the latter and vice versa. If we press this point of comparison, we might be tempted to say that delusions do not come from a person's pure nature, but from some external causes. In this case, the analogy just might have forced us into a dualistic way of thinking. Thus, however useful Hui Neng's analogy may be as a teaching tool, we will do well to note that, like any analogy, it will break down at some point when pressed too far.

According to Hui Neng, Shen Xiu's method of practice tends to objectify the so-called original pure state of heart-mind. It may be like a static and passive "looking" at some kind of reified mental state (see Section 18). To objectify the so-called original pure state of heart-mind is to assume two forms of duality: the *I* (the heart-mind, the inner) versus dust (the outer) on the one hand, and practicing ("polishing" as the means) versus awakening (clearing the heart-mind as the goal), on the other. This dualistic approach to practice also distinguishes sitting meditation from other everyday activities. It suggests that when practicing Chan, one should stay away from any possible external contamination in everyday life, that is, one should live a secluded way of life— more in the traditional Indian way of meditation. Hui Neng's Verse 1 addresses this specific flaw in Shen Xiu's approach.

> Bodhi originally has no tree, / The mirror [i.e., mind] also has no stand. / Buddha-nature is always clean and pure; [other versions of the *Sutra* have: "From the beginning not a thing is"] / Where is there room for dust? (Section 8)

According to Hui Neng, Chan meditation is not "looking at" nor seeking to restore some kind of pure mental state, because neither Bodhi (wisdom) nor the mind has any fixed form (no "tree" nor "mirror stand"). As a matter of fact, "from the beginning not a thing is [fixed, or with self-essence]," and therefore, nothing (no inherent "dust") can contaminate anything else. The claim "from the beginning not a thing is" expresses the same idea as the claim that "the world is empty (interdependent-arising)." Therefore, contrary to Shen Xiu, Hui Neng sees awakening not as some special mental state, but as a way of being or a way of living. He criticizes Shen Xiu's metaphor of "polishing" ("sitting meditation") for its tendency to degrade awakening as a mere inner mental state. Hui Neng explains that the notions of "look at" the mind and "purity" are great obstructions to the Way:

> Good and learned friends, in this [Hui Neng's] teaching, sitting in meditation has never involved viewing [*kan*, 看, "look at"] the mind or viewing purity, nor should one remain motionless. Suppose one advocates viewing the mind. [Such a] mind is, from the very start, a delusion. And since delusions are illusory, there is really nothing to view. Suppose one advocates viewing purity. [But] one's nature, in itself, is pure. Only because of deluded thoughts is Thusness covered over and obscured. Apart from deluded thoughts, one's nature is pure. If one does not see [*jian*, "见"] the fundamental purity of one's own nature and instead stirs up one's mind to view purity, this will only generate delusions of purity. This delusion is without a basis [in reality]; therefore, we know that those who view it are viewing a delusion ... (Section 18, Ivanhoe's translation;[29] Chinese words added by me)

As Hui Neng sees it, the practice of Chan does not entail living a secluded life, "looking at" some ideal state of mind, or sitting there motionlessly (which would be a distorted understanding of meditation), nor is it a theoretical business that focuses on reasoning, logic, and abstraction (which would be a false view of wisdom). Rather, it is about engaging everyday life, or better, it *is* everyday life. Even though the deluded

---

29   Philip J. Ivanhoe, trans., *Readings from the Lu Wang School of Neo Confucianism* (Indianapolis: Hackett, 2009).

individuals "keep their physical bodies motionless," "as soon as they open their mouths, they speak of the right and wrong others have done" (Section 18, Ivanhoe translation). In other words, for Hui Neng, the practice of Chan is not merely a matter of imitating the external form of meditation practice, but a matter of enacting the teachings of the Buddha in everyday life, the most important of which is the elimination of an egocentric way of being in the world. In Hui Neng's Chan, "sitting meditation" is not spiritually superior to other everyday activities, such as walking, sitting, and lying. In short, Chan is to be practiced in every activity in life (Section 14). The very practice of Chan itself is surprisingly, yet ultimately, awakening (Sections 17, 20, 22, 26, 29). When sitting meditation is viewed literally as merely involving sitting passively "without moving and casting aside delusions without things [arising] in the mind," the vitality of Chan as a life-transforming practice is completely eclipsed, and human life becomes equated with the insentient (Section 14).

Awakening, then, for Hui Neng, is right here and right now with every choice we make and every action we take. Meditation (*ding*) and prajna (*hui*) (or practice and enlightenment) are one:

> Never under any circumstances say mistakenly that meditation and wisdom are different; they are a unity, not two things. Meditation itself is the substance [body] of wisdom; wisdom itself is the function of meditation. At the very moment when there is wisdom, then meditation exists in wisdom; at the very moment when there is meditation, then wisdom exists in meditation. (Section 13)

Hui Neng emphasizes the oneness of "meditation" (*dhayna, ding*) and "wisdom" (*prajna, hui*) in order to address the potential problems he sees in keeping them apart. When meditation and wisdom are kept apart, one would be tempted to think of one (either meditation or wisdom) as occurring here and now, and the other there and then. This way of separating meditation and wisdom is analogous to separating an action from its intention and regarding the intention as preceding the action. If you believe in this way of thinking, you may find it perfectly coherent to say that for the present you are only working on your intention, and you won't worry about your action until sometime in the future. Following this way of thinking, you may also be inclined to believe that one can *say* good things without any good intention. For Hui Neng, this sort of dualistic talk must be dismissed in Chan practice, for the practice of Chan emphasizes the unity of intention and action. The unity between the two can be likened to the oneness of birth and death in a sprouting acorn: the "birth" of the sprout and the "death" of the acorn seed refer to exactly the same happening. By the same token, intention and action are two different names for the same event.[30]

---

30  Hui Neng uses a lamp-light metaphor to explain the unity of intention (mind) and action. "Good friends, how then are meditation and wisdom alike? They are like the lamp and the light it gives forth. If there is a lamp there is light; if there is no lamp there is no light. The lamp is the substance of light; the light is the function of the lamp. Thus, although they have two names, in substance they are not two. Meditation and wisdom are also like this" (Section 15). This analogy is helpful in some sense. As Whalen Lai has explained, unlike the passive image of seeing the mind as a mirror, "The mind as lamp is active,

In drawing attention to the unity of meditation-and-wisdom, and intention-and-action, Hui Neng emphasizes that the practice of Chan takes place at each and every moment. This idea of unity differs from Mengzi's notion of moral cultivation, which implies that maturity comes in the future after a period of cultivation. It also differs from Shen Xiu's path to enlightenment, in which one slips into a static mental state, by means of sitting meditation. Hui Neng remarks, "The very practice of Buddha, this is Buddha" (Section 42).[31] Therefore, there is no need to wait for a future maturity or for a static mental state that one may reach in the future. Both heaven and hell are found here and now—as it were—for an instant of evil thought can make life into hell, and an instant of good thought can reveal heaven (Sections 20, 22, 26).

Given Hui Neng's focus on everyday life as the site in which practice-and-enlightenment takes place, the role of past training and past experience becomes less necessary. Ultimately, it is your present, immediate choice or conduct that determines the current state of your mind-heart. Even if you have had good moral education in the past, you may still do evil things in the present or in the future (though it is less likely). On the other hand, even if you received little moral training in the past, you may still do good things at this very moment. The only real moment (relevant to the practice of Chan) is right now, the immediate present. You do not experience your life as a whole nor have a god's eye view of your whole life. To regard your life from such a point of view is to become bogged down in abstract or theoretical thinking, and it is to reify yourself as a subject or agent and your life as another object or a continuous process with a personal identity. But the only real moment is now, so that you are what you do now. From this point of view, you cannot blame the past for who you are, nor can you retroject the future into the present to excuse your behaviour now. Neither the past nor the future determines the moral exertions of the present (your doings at every present moment). For Hui Neng, the urgency of present practice couldn't be stronger!

The experience of awakening in Hui Neng's Chan can be compared to that of sudden scientific discovery. As the (probably apocryphal) story goes, when Archimedes discovered a method for determining the purity of gold, he cried "Eureka!" (literally, "I have found [it]"). A "eureka" experience is a moment of sudden discovery. It is also descriptive of the moment of Chan awakening, in which one suddenly realizes one's self-nature (Buddha-nature). But unlike the scientific "eureka" experience, which is a realization at one single moment, awakening in Chan is a continuous, moment by moment, process—an ongoing process of practicing and acting in the Buddhist way. As Hui Neng puts it, "When *at all times* successive thoughts contain no ignorance, and you always

---

the source of light that reveals external realities. As fire, it is also self- and other-purifying, burning off any dust or defilements and chasing away of the gloom of ignorance, *wu-ming* (the absence of light, illumination)" (Whalen Lai, "Ch'an Metaphors: Wave, Water, Mirror, Lamp," *Philosophy East and West* 29:3 [1979]: 250). But as with any metaphor it is not perfect. As Red Pine has noted, "[m]etaphors are never as good as what they represent ... After all, we can have a lamp but not light, and we can have light but no lamp. But if we cultivate One Practice Samadhi, we can't have meditation without wisdom, nor can we have wisdom without meditation. Meditation without wisdom is Dead Tree Zen. Wisdom without meditation is Pie in the Sky Zen" (Pine, 137).

31  Compare with Confucius' claim: "Is humanness far away? If I (really) want it, it arrives right away" (the *Analects* 7:30, my translation).

practice wisdom, this is known as the practice of *prajna*. If but *one instant* of thought contains ignorance, then *prajna* is cut off; but if *one instant* of thought contains wisdom, then *prajna* is produced.... Those who awaken to this Dharma have awakened to the Dharma of *prajna* and are practicing the *prajna* practice. If you do not practice it you are an ordinary person; if you practice for *one instant* of thought, your Dharma body will be the same as the Buddha's" (Section 26, emphasis added; also see Sections 36, 43).

Hui Neng's characterization of awakening as an ongoing experience finds interesting parallels in how the experience of conversion is characterized in other faiths, including Christianity. Conversion sometimes involves a decisive moment in which one takes a drastic turn from one's previous way of life. This type of sudden conversion experience occurs like a flash of lightning. However, conversion for many involves a continuous, moment by moment process in which one takes mini-steps towards reorienting one's life on an ongoing basis. This is probably what Søren Kierkegaard (1813–55) means when he says it is not even correct to say one *is* a Christian, only that one is *becoming* a Christian.

Hui Neng has surely noted potential problems in Shen Xiu's method of Chan practice. But is Shen Xiu's Chan method completely unsuited for the practice? I think the answer is no. First of all, Hong Ren, the Fifth Patriarch, did not consider what Shen Xiu expressed in his verse completely mistaken, but only incomplete. He, in fact, regarded it as having "great benefit": "It would be best to leave this verse here and to have the deluded ones recite it. If they practice in accordance with it they will not fall into the three evil ways.[32] Those who practice by it will gain great benefit ... If common people practice according to your [Shen Xiu's] verse they will not fall" (Section 7). However, Hong Ren did not think that the verse represented the deepest understanding of Chan.

Second, Hui Neng himself did not negate the value of gradual wakening (alluding to Shen Xiu's "sitting meditation"). As Hui Neng remarks: "Good and learned friends, in the *dharma* there is no such thing as sudden or gradual. (However,) among people there are those with sharp and those with dull spiritual capacity. Deluded individuals pursue the gradual [method]. Enlightened individuals follow sudden cultivation. To realize one's original mind is to see one's original nature. Those who are enlightened realize that from the very start there is not the slightest difference" (Section 16, Ivanhoe's translation; also see Sections 36, 39). For beginners who practice Chan and for those who are with "shallow capacities" (Section 41), sitting meditation may be a great tool that helps them concentrate. In this sense, the gradual awakening method may very well be complementary to the sudden awakening method; the difference between these two methods is a matter of emphasis. What Hui Neng emphasizes, though, is that Chan

---

32  Red Pine translated "the three evil ways" (*san e dao*) as "three unfortunate states of existence." He explains: "Buddhists liken the varieties of existence to a wheel with six spokes, and thus six sections through which we pass from one life to the next. The three fortunate states of existence include celestial beings (*devas*), malevolent beings (*asuras*), and human beings (*manus*). The three unfortunate states include sinners in one of the hells (*narakas*), hungry ghosts (*pretas*), and plants and animals (*tiryagyoni*). Their existence is the result of the Three Poisons: delusion (sinners), greed (hungry ghosts), and anger (plants and animals). The reason these are called 'unfortunate states of existence' is because there is no access to the Dharma in such a state" (Pine, 100–01).

meditation (or practice) is objectless, non-attaching, non-clinging, and at the same time immanent in all facets of everyday life. "Sudden" awakening does not single out certain moments (and activities) as being of higher spiritual significance relative to other moments (i.e., what is commonly seen as the mundane). Thus, awakening is about becoming fully engaged in everyday life; this is far from the common misconception that it is about escaping from this life.

## NO-THOUGHT, NO-FORM, AND NO-ABIDING

No-thought, no-form, and no-abiding are the cardinal ideas of Hui Neng's approach to Chan. They illustrate what the idea of emptiness, which is a fundamental teaching in Mahayana Buddhism, is in concrete psychological and ethical terms. Hui Neng stresses that no-thought (*wu-nian*) is the main doctrine of Chan, no-form (*wu-xiang*) is its substance/body, and no-abiding (*wu-zhu*) is its basis (Section 17). A good grasp of these three notions is crucial to our understanding of Hui Neng's Chan practice.

It must be noted, from the start, that no-thought does not mean "sitting without moving and casting aside delusions without letting things arise in the mind," which is dubbed by Hui Neng as a practice for "insentiency and the cause of an obstruction to the Tao" (Section 14). Nor does it mean "make one's mind empty and do not think" (Section 25; see Sections 24, 31). Following the *Diamond Sutra*, Hui Neng insists that though one must not attach to things, one must "produce a mind which stays in no place" (see Section 9 and note 41). Thus, Chan for Hui Neng is not equivalent to quietism or a state of unconsciousness. In this sense, "no-thought" has a close affinity with the important Daoist idea of non-action (*wu-wei*) which, you may recall from the *Daodejing* and the *Zhuangzi*, does not mean "doing nothing." Under this consideration, it may be more felicitous to translate *wu-nian* (non-thought) as "a-thinking" or "de-thinking."

At Section 31 "no-thought" is further explained to mean, "even though you see all things, you do not attach to them." Chan masters sometimes explain the idea with the image of a lotus that grows out of mire yet in no way is contaminated by the mud. Therefore, the practice of "no-thought" does not mean hiding from the world, retreating from worldly involvement and literally thinking nothing. Instead, it means staying engaged in this life without being entangled in or "bothered" by whatever happens (see Section 25 on not being bothered by good and evil). To elucidate this point, let's consider the following scenario:

You live in a city where winter is very long (six months) and cold (with frequent heavy snow), yet its summer is very mild and beautiful. You strongly dislike the winter, but you dearly love its summer. During the winter, you feel bad, complaining about the weather all the time, even trying to escape from the city. During the summer, you enjoy yourself very much, but at the back of your mind you fear that its summer is too short and fleeting.

From a Chan perspective, your love of the city's summer and your dislike of its winter are both attachments. For your love of the summer, you hold on to it, unwilling to accept its impermanence (emptiness). For your dislike of its winter, you hold on to it negatively in not accepting its inevitable presence. In either case, you have trouble accepting the world-as-it-is (suchness). To put it differently, in both cases, you are being "pushed" or "agitated" by self-centred desires. In both cases, you refuse to become fully present to the world or to fully embrace your being-in-the-world. The attachments are based upon two forms of duality—summer-winter duality and weather-I (environment-I) duality—that lead to a value judgment or attachment: winter is bad and summer is good *to me*. This value attachment is sustained by these dualistic distinctions. However, in reality, the world-as-it-is entails no such distinctions.

If we take our analysis one step further with the above scenario, "no-abiding" means that you accept the weather as it is, "unstained in all environments" (Section 17). It is a state that is not "bothered" by any changing conditions. When you practice non-attachment in any concrete situation, you experience oneness with the situation. Being at one with your situation is not merely a psychological state of acceptance, but a profoundly existential awareness of non-duality. When it is winter, everything is winter; when it is summer, everything is summer. When you realize this oneness of being, you experience not only clarity and serenity, but also aliveness in each and every moment.

To further explain the idea of no-abiding, let me borrow an example from a popular spirituality writer, Eckhart Tolle. Tolle observes that "after two ducks get into a fight, which never lasts long, they will separate and float in opposite directions. Then each duck will flap its wings vigorously a few times, thus releasing the surplus energy that built up during the fight. After they flap their wings, they float on peacefully, as if nothing had ever happened."[33] The ducks do not cling to the fight; their behaviours after a fight are in sharp contrast with that of humans. If two persons (groups, or countries, etc.) are in a fight, their minds will most likely become entangled: their fight gets replayed again and again in their minds like a movie, generating strong anger and hatred, for days, months, years and even ages. It seems that we humans have to learn from the ducks to not cling to what has happened.

Finally, no-form (or de-form, *wu-xiang*) does not mean no things exist. Rather, it means one must not become attached to the forms (i.e., concepts) of things. The word "form" is a translation of the Chinese word "*xiang*" (相), which means concept, convention, or image, in contrast with Reality (or Thusness). To return to the weather example, the weather-as-it-is is the true reality-as-it-is, and "winter" and "summer" are our human concepts (forms, *xiang*). If you cling to the concepts (and distinctions), you do not see the world-as-it-is, and you do not live in the world-as-it-is, or in other words, you do not live authentically. To hold no-thought, to overcome or transcend *xiang*, and to practice no-abiding amounts to the same thing, that is, to transcend all forms of dualism (Sections 44, 45, 46). In other words, the ideas of no-thought, no-abiding, and no-form all point us in the same direction: that liberation is possible when we transcend dualistic attachment or clinging. A life thus free of attachment is a joyous life—one free from suffering.

---

33 Eckhart Tolle, *A New Earth: Awakening to Your Life's Purpose* (New York: Penguin Plume, 2006), 137–38.

Does this discourse of non-duality mean that in Chan, ethically, "anything goes"? It has certainly been construed this way by some in the counterculture of the 1960s. Yet, nothing can be further away from Chan (especially Chan in the PS) than to think that it promotes ethical anarchism or nihilism.

First, the foundation of Chan is Buddhism, and the pillar of Buddhism is the doctrine of no-self, which calls for an unselfish and compassionate way of life. To realize no-self means to transcend dualism, which is different from doing evil. Evil is in turn rooted in the very idea of an ego and selfishness. Acting compassionately is a natural flowering of realizing no-self.

Second, Hui Neng does not argue that we abandon good and evil altogether. As he remarks, "[i]f people think of all the evil things, then they will practice evil; if they think of all the good things, then they will practice good" (Section 20). Instead, he argues that we should adopt an open attitude toward good and evil, for good and evil, like mere space, do not have fixed nature: "To see...both the good and the bad, good dharma and bad dharmas, without rejecting them and without being corrupted by them, this is to be like space. This is what we mean by 'great'" (Section 25).[34] Adopting this attitude, we should view good and bad dharmas with no repulsion ("rejecting them") or involvement ("being corrupted by them").

### DOING PHILOSOPHY
#### Emperor Wu and the Unconditional Good

During one interesting encounter between Bodhidharma and Emperor Wu of Liang, the emperor asked Bodhidharma if he found any merit in his building temples, giving alms, and making offerings, and Bodhidharma answered, bluntly, that the emperor had no merit whatsoever. But why? To this question, Hui Neng explains:

Building temples, giving alms, and making offerings are merely the practice of seeking after blessings. One cannot mistake merit with blessings. Merit is in the *Dharmakaya* [dharma-body], not in the field of blessings. In Dharma nature itself there is merit (*kung-te*). [Seeing into your own nature is *kung*]; straightforward mind is *te*. Inwardly, see the Buddha-nature; outwardly, practice reverence. If you make light of all men and do not cut off the ego, then you yourself will be without merit. If in successive thoughts there is virtuous practice and there is straightforward mind, merit will not be held lightly and practice will always be reverent.

---

34 The translation of this verse is by Red Pine, 20–21. In Philip B. Yampolsky's translation of verse 25—"Although you see ... evil and good ... you must not throw them aside, nor must you cling to them, nor must you be stained by them, but you must regard them as being just like the empty sky", the phrase "nor must you cling to them" does not exist in the original Chinese text of the verse.

Your own practice with the body is *kung*; your own practice with the mind is *te*. Merit is created from the mind; blessings and merit are different. The Emperor Wu did not understand the true principle; hence the Patriarch was not in the wrong. (Section 34)

What do you think is the difference between "blessings" and "merit"? Could we say that behaviours that seek "blessings" are still tainted with an idea of ego ... ions without an idea of ego are ... ui Neng said: "Merit is created ... aightforward mind" similar to ... t is unconditionally good?

DEBIT
d#:  XXXXXXXXXXXX0062
2.83
lication Label: US DEBIT
: a0000000980340
Verified
: 8080048000
: 6800

Connect with us on Social

ock-   @BNOremUT
gram-  @bn_orem
er-    @BN_Orem

12A          12/12/2016   02:47PM

CUSTOMER COPY

MARKS:
LATFORM SUTRA

ation of Indian Buddhism into the
velopment of Zen thought in China
the Indian pattern, but after him its
hinese channel. The intellectual see-
dian mind, now exhibits what may
nese Zen."[35]
solated from everyday life, Chan in
The Chan way of life distinguishes
utes it, rather than by the location
. It can be practiced anywhere while
g, eating, lying down, and so on. Thus,
the practice of Chan is straightforward and inclusive, instead of being restricted to the learned classes. That Chan is integrated into everyday life is evidenced by the fact that monks in China have been growing their own food since the time of the Fifth Patriarch, Hong Ren, whereas monks in India do not work and rely on alms.

For Hui Neng, the practice of sitting meditation (understood literally as silent sitting) is neither a necessary nor a sufficient condition for awakening (see Section 14). As we have noted, Hui Neng was not against meditation itself. However, he reinterpreted "sitting" figuratively as meaning "without any obstruction anywhere, outwardly and under all circumstances, not to activate thoughts [attachments]." Accordingly, he also offered a figurative understanding of "meditation" as seeing internally one's original nature without becoming confused (see Section 19). Hui Neng's reinterpretation of "sitting meditation" exhibits a shift from the Indian practice of *dhyana* meditation to the Chinese practice of Chan meditation. As W.T. Chan has explained, "[i]n Indian meditation, the mind tries to avoid the external world, ignores outside influence, aims

---

35 Suzuki, 85.

at intellectual understanding, and seeks to unite with the Infinite. Instead, Chinese meditation works with the aid of external influence, operates in this world, emphasizes quick wit and insight, and aims at self-realization."[36]

Because Chan is embodied in everyday life, the practice serves to strengthen the Mahayana Bodhisattva ideals. Hui Neng's Chan practice exemplifies Mahayana's social concerns and converges with the humanistic concerns of Confucianism. In line with his emphasis on Chan's intimate connection with everyday life, Hui Neng also stresses that all sutras are ultimately the works of men: "All the sutras and written words, Hinayana, Mahayana, the twelve divisions of the canon, all have been postulated by men. Because of the nature of wisdom [within man] it has been possible, therefore, to postulate them. If we were without this wisdom, all things would, from the outset, have no existence in themselves. Therefore it is clear that all things were originally given rise to by man, and that all the sutras exist because they are spoken by man" (Section 30). The humanistic concerns here can also be seen as a revival of Gautama Buddha's humanistic teachings expressed in the Dhammapada.

We can also see many affinities between Hui Neng's Chan and Daoism. (1) Dao is everywhere immanent (particular see the *Zhuangzi*) in all of reality, so it is with Buddha-nature. (2) As dao is beyond language, reasoning and argumentation, so it is with Buddha-nature. (3) Just as Daoism stresses individual *wu-wei* (non-action, or effortless action) and *zi-ran* (naturalness and spontaneity), Chan underscores *wu-nian* (no-thought, or de-attaching), *wu-zhu* (no-abiding, or de-abiding), and *wu-xiang* (no-form, or de-differentiating)—all point towards a spontaneous, non-artificial mind, or state of being. (4) Hui Neng's non-dualism also echoes the attitude of regarding all things as equal (*qi wu*) in the *Zhuangzi*. Given the parallels noted above, it is no wonder that Dumoulin has remarked, "[t]he complex structure of Mahayana, which is the genuine form of Chinese Buddhism [we may add, particularly Hui Neng's Chan], also absorbed the ancient Chinese wisdom of the Tao. Without the Tao, the many expressions that the Mahayana Buddhists used for ultimate reality could never have touched the hearts of the Chinese."[37]

Chan was the dominant form of Buddhism in China from the ninth to the fourteenth century. During this period, Chan exerted a strong influence on Chinese philosophy, art, and even everyday life. For example, it shaped the development of the Neo-Confucian views of human nature (or heart-mind nature) and moral cultivation, which flourished in the Song Dynasty (960–1279) and the Ming Dynasty (1368–1644).[38] Artistically superb Chan poems also appeared during the Tang and Song periods. The verses by Hui Neng and Shen Xiu marked the beginning of a movement in which simple poetic language becomes the vehicle through which the experience of Chan is given expression. Furthermore, Hui Neng's ideas—particularly his idea of sudden awakening—also shaped the development of the Chinese language, in that many stock expressions and proverbs have their origins in these ideas. The proverb *fangxia tudao*

---

36  W.T. Chan, 429.
37  Dumoulin, *Zen Buddhism*, 147–48.
38  Ivanhoe, 3–13.

*lidi chengfo* (meaning "A butcher becomes a Buddha the moment he drops h.. .
is a good case in point. In sum, the Chinese intellectual and spiritual landscape would
look very different today without the historical influence of Chan.

After the time of Hui Neng, Chan flourished in several schools, among which were
the Linji (Rinzai) and Caodong (Soto) schools. The two schools rose to prominence and
were later introduced to Japan. There they continued to develop, becoming the important sources of influence on Dogen, which takes us to the subject of our next chapter.

### WORKS CITED AND RECOMMENDED READINGS

1. D.T. Suzuki, *The Zen Doctrine of No Mind—The Significance of the Sutra of Hui-
   neng (Wei-lang)* (London: Rider & Company, 1969).
2. W.T. Chan, *The Platform Scripture* (New York: St. John's University Press, 1963).
3. Peter N. Gregory, ed., *Sudden and Gradual: Approaches to Enlightenment in
   Chinese Thought*, Studies in East Asian Buddhism, no. 5 (Honolulu: University of
   Hawaii Press, 1987).
4. Heinrich Dumoulin, *A History of Zen Buddhism*, Paul Peachey, trans. (Boston:
   Beacon Press, 1963).
5. Heinrich Dumoulin, *Zen Buddhism: A History*. Vol. 1: *India and China*, James W.
   Heisig and Paul Knitter, trans. (New York: Macmillan Publishing, 1988).
6. Philip J. Ivanhoe, trans. and intro., *The Platform Sutra (Tan Jing)*, in *Readings
   from the Lu-Wang School of Neo-Confucianism*, Part One (Indianapolis:
   Hackett, 2009).
7. Red Pine, *The Platform Sutra—The Zen Teaching of Hui-Neng* (Emeryville, CA:
   Shoemaker & Hoard, 2006).

# CHAPTER 10

# The *Shobogenzo*

## SUGGESTED PRIMARY READING

Norman Waddell and Masao Abe, trans. *The Heart of Dogen's Shobogenzo* (Albany, NY: State University of New York Press, 2002), Chapters 4, 5, pages 59–65 of Chapter 6, and Chapter 8.

## LEARNING OBJECTIVES

By the time you have worked through this chapter, you should be able to

> - Describe Dogen's unique understanding of being-time (*uji*)
> - Explain Dogen's view on life/birth-death (*shoji*)
> - Describe the connection between Hui Neng's Chan and Dogen's Zen as well as the differences between the two
> - Identify the similarities and differences between the Upanishads' notion that "*Atman* is *Brahman*" and Dogen's view that "Entire being is Buddha-nature"

## KEY WORDS

Buddha-nature (*bussho*), sitting meditation (*zazen*), birth/life-death (*shoji*), being-time (*uji*)

## GUIDING QUESTIONS

Buddhism was introduced to Japan from China and Korea early in the sixth century CE. Among the many schools of Buddhism that were introduced to Japan, Chan/Zen[1] became the most influential. And among Zen practices and teachings, Dogen's is the most prominent. In order to understand Dogen's Zen, we shall ask the following questions:

1.  What are the similarities and differences between Dogen's Zen and Hui Neng's Chan?
2.  How does Dogen understand sitting meditation, birth/life-death, being-time, and Buddha-nature?
3.  How can Dogen's Zen teaching be related to thoughts in the Upanishads, the Dhammapada, the *Fundamental Verses on the Middle Way*, and the *Mengzi*?

## INTRODUCTION

The *Shobogenzo* (Treasury of the True Dharma Eye) was written by Dogen (1200–53), perhaps the most gifted philosopher in Japanese history, certainly of Japanese Zen. This text, both a religious text and philosophical masterpiece, is Dogen's *magnum opus*. It contains ninety-five particular fascicles—sections, discrete "bundles" of text—on Zen teaching and practice, each of which is complete in itself. For centuries, it has primarily been the core religious text of the Japanese Soto sect, which was founded by Dogen himself. However, early in the twentieth century, philosophers began to take an interest in the philosophical ideas in the text.[2] Scholarly attention to the text has continued to grow over the past few decades.

Dogen's thought broadly follows the spirit of Chinese Chan, which is based on Mahayana Buddhism (specifically Nagarjuna's *Middle Way*). However, compared to the Chinese Chan masters (e.g., Hui Neng), Dogen is much more radical in his understanding and expressing of Mahayana thought. He deliberately and creatively (mis)read Mahayana and Chan expressions, in an effort to dissolve the various forms of duality that he thought were implicit in them. Thus, one can hardly find in Dogen's thought any trace of duality—including such common dichotomies as life/birth and death, being and time, practice and enlightenment, and sentient beings and Buddha. Dogen's treatment of these expressions demonstrates his unparalleled sensitivity to the philosophical implications of Zen language.

Compared to Hui Neng's Platform Sutra, Dogen's *Shobogenzo* exhibits a style that is more elaborate, more carefully reasoned and philosophically sophisticated, particularly

---

1    "Zen" is the conventional romanization of the rendition into Japanese of the Chinese "Chan."
2    According to T.P. Kasulis, Dogen was "the first writer to use the Japanese language in a truly philosophical way, [and] was looked upon as a forefather of Japanese 'philosophy' (*tetsugaku*) in its modern sense" (T.P. Kasulis, "The Zen Philosopher: A Review Article on Dogen Scholarship in English," *Philosophy East and West* 28:3 [July 1978]: 357).

in its fascicles on Buddha-nature (*bussho*), being-time (*uji*), life-death (*shoji*), and man-ifesting suchness (*genjokoan*). It is these fascicles that we will focus on in this chapter.

Dogen uses a wide range of literary genres—stories (*koans*), images, analogies, and metaphors—to explain his understanding of Zen Buddhism. It is clear that in con-trast with Nagarjuna's style in the *Fundamental Verses on the Middle Way*, Dogen's *Shobogenzo* is more illustrative than argumentative, more concrete than abstract, and more vivid than obscure. Dogen followed a stylistic trend that first appeared in Hui Neng's Platform Sutra—that is, employing concrete language to show how the Buddhist path is in fact immanent in the details of everyday life.

In a broader context, Dogen's philosophy can be read as a synthesis of various thoughts that have been introduced in this volume. In the *Shobogenzo*, we encounter the idea of identity of "entire being" with "Buddha-nature"—an idea that resembles the identity of *Atman* with *Brahman* in the Upanishads. We also find a more vivid and colourful expression of Nagarjuna's "Middle Way," as well as elements of Zhuangzi's Daoism, such as "sitting forgetfulness" (*zuo wang*) and "everything is equal" (*qi wu*). Dogen's criticism of the view that likens Buddha-nature to a seed waiting to be cul-tivated also can be read as an indirect criticism of Mengzi's view of innate sprouts of moral goodness. Thus, Dogen can be seen as interacting widely with various ancient Asian philosophers. For this reason, this chapter is particularly important, in that it weaves together various threads of thought that we have explored in the preceding chapters.[3]

One must read selected chapters from the *Shobogenzo* extremely slowly. Dogen's ideas are profound and radical; his writing style is pithy, poetic, but often notoriously difficult. Waddell and Abe's translator's footnotes[4] often clarify and unpack ideas that are otherwise obscure and dense. This will inevitably slow down the reading process, but it is worthwhile, for it will allow us to serious grapple with the text.

### DOGEN'S LIFE

Buddhism was introduced to Japan from China and Korea as early as 522 CE. During China's Sui Dynasty (581–618), Japan began to send students to China to be trained in Buddhism and Confucianism. More students were sent to China during Japan's Nara and Heian Periods (710–1185), and subsequently different sects of Buddhism were intro-duced to Japan. The sects of Tendai (Tian-tai) and Shingon (Zhen-yan) attracted many followers due to their emphasis on the universality of salvation or of attainment of Buddhahood. But Tendai was basically a scholastic sect and Shingon more of a mystical and occultist sect. The popularization of Buddhism continued in the Kamakura period

---

3   I am not claiming that Dogen is *consciously* making a synthesis of the thoughts in the mentioned classics; rather, I am only claiming that he can be read that way, and reading thus can help us draw con-nections among Asian philosophy classics. Nor would I imply that the *Shobogenzo* occupies the ultimate peak of Asian philosophical thought, while other classics rank lower on a value hierarchy. I would rather see all Asian philosophy classics introduced in this book as distinctive thoughts of equal beauty.

4   Norman Waddell and Masao Abe, trans. *The Heart of Dogen's Shobogenzo* (Albany, NY: State University of New York Press, 2002).

(1192–1333) when three other Buddhist sects emerged: Jodo (Pure Land), Nichiren, and Zen, all of which emphasized personal experience, intuition, and simple spiritual exercises over dogmas and rituals.[5] The Rinzai (Lin-ji) sect, a prominent Zen sect in China following the teachings of Hui Neng, was introduced to Japan in 1191 by Myōan Eisai (1141–1215). This sect found a large number of followers among the samurai warriors, which were then the leading social class. It was against this historical background that Dogen came on stage.

More details concerning Dogen's life are available to us than for any other philosopher we have discussed in this book. Dogen was born into an aristocratic family in Kyoto in 1200. His childhood was not a happy one, for his father died when he was only two and his mother passed away when he was seven. Losing both at a young age had a profound effect on him, and he started to seriously ponder the meaning of life and its transient nature at an early age.

At the age of thirteen, Dogen became a monk at Mount Hiei near Kyoto, then the centre of the Tendai sect. Soon he was puzzled by a question: "If, as the sutras say, all human beings are endowed with the Buddha-nature, why is it that one must train oneself so strenuously to realize that Buddha-nature, that is, to attain enlightenment?"[6] As we shall see below, all the major aspects of Dogen's thought revolve around this baffling question. Haunted by this question, Dogen was unable to get a clear and satisfactory answer from his Tendai teachers, so he switched to the Rinzai Zen sect for help. He studied with Eisai, the founder of Japanese Rinzai Zen, but only briefly due to his master's death in 1215. He then studied with Eisai's disciple Myozen (1184–1225) for about eight years. Dogen acknowledged that he had learned a lot during his long years of training in Rinzai Zen, but still found that his question was not fully answered.

In 1223, at the age of twenty-three, Dogen made a hazardous journey to China, in the hope of studying authentic Buddhism there in search of an answer to his persistent question. He visited numerous monasteries and consulted many Chan masters in China before he met Ru-Jing (Ju-Ching, 1163–1228), a Cao-Dong Chan (Soto Zen, in Japanese) master at Mount Tiantong (in modern Zhejiang province). Cao-Dong Chan was founded in the second half of the ninth century by Caoshan Benji (840–901) and his teacher Dongshan Liangjie (807–69). This school emphasizes the practice of *da-zuo* (*zazen*, in Japanese), or sitting meditation, as a way of gaining enlightenment. *Da-zuo* is also called *mo-zhao. Mo* means "silent concentrated sitting," *zhao* refers to "meditating on original pure mind and nature." Following the example of his master Ru-Jing, Dogen devoted himself to the practice of *zazen* day and night.

Early one morning, as Master Ru-Jing was making his usual round of inspection at the beginning of the formal *zazen* period, he discovered one of the monks was dozing. Scolding the monk, Master Ru-Jing said, "To practice *zazen* is to drop off the

---

5    For example, both Jodo and Nichiren sects stressed the continual chanting of short formulas as a means for salvation.

6    "Fukanzazengi" in Waddell and Abe, 2. All translations of the *Shobogenzo* are from Waddell and Abe, identified by the chapter name and page number in that book. These chapter names are also Dogen's original fascicle names.

body-mind. What do you expect to accomplish by dozing?" Upon hearing these words, Dogen suddenly realized enlightenment. Dogen immediately followed the master to his room to have his enlightenment confirmed; he burned some incense and prostrated himself before the master. When Ru-Jing asked him why he was doing this, Dogen replied, "I have experienced the dropping off of body-mind." Ru-Jing, realizing that Dogen was indeed enlightened, confirmed it by saying: "You have indeed dropped off the body-mind!"[7]

Dogen continued his training under Ru-Jing for about two more years even after his enlightenment. As explained in his *Genjokoan* and *Bussho* in the *Shobogenzo*, there is no gap between practice and enlightenment, and enlightenment is not a once-and-for-all experience. Instead, the process of practice *is* the process of enlightenment. By this time, Dogen may have figured out an answer to his original question—that is, even though all humans "have" Buddha-nature, their Buddha-nature does not have a manifestation that is independent of practice. In 1227 Dogen went back to Japan "empty-handed,"[8] and he started to preach passionately what he believed to be genuine Buddhism to the Japanese, until his death in 1253.

Dogen opened his monastic community to everyone, regardless of social status, profession, and gender. (For him there was no caste or class discrimination!) Unlike those scholastic and ritualistic schools of Buddhism in Japan of his time, Dogen's zen practice, *zazen*, is simple and accessible to most people. Moreover, Dogen's zen distinguishes itself from Rinzai Zen in his approach to *koans* (zen tales) as something that is present in everyday life. Rinchi Zen had a tendency to overemphasize the restrictive use of *koans* in zen training, at the risk of slipping into formalism. Dogen, on the other hand, emphasized that the use of *koans* as a vehicle for Zen training is not merely a matter of verbal expression, but a way of engaging the practice of *zazen* as well as the practice of everyday life. Reality, or suchness, is present to us in the here and now at each present moment. Let's now begin our exploration of Dogen's thoughts in *Genjokoan*— Manifesting Suchness.

## DROPPING OFF BODY-MIND

As we have seen in the previous chapter on Hui Neng, Chan inherited the doctrines of Mahayana Buddhism, adapted for the Chinese ethos and social contexts. An essential doctrine of Mahayana Buddhism is that human suffering stems from the illusion that things in the world, both mental constructs (such as ideas and conventions) and physical objects (including human beings), have self-essence (i.e., exist as independent entities with stable, intrinsic properties). Attachment to this view of reality causes

---

7   See Yuho Yokoi, with Daizen Victoria, *Zen Master Dogen—An Introduction with Selected Writings* (New York: Weatherhill, 1976), 32.

8   By "empty-handed" Dogen might have meant that he came back from China without icons, relics, and regalia, but in Steven Heine's words, he was certainly not "empty-headed (although he may have a head full of emptiness [impermanence])," because his whole being was liberated and transformed (Steven Heine, "Koans in the Dogen Tradition: How and Why Dogen Does What He Does with Koans," *Philosophy East and West* 54:1 [January 2004]: 1).

suffering because the entire world is in fact impermanent and arises interdependently. For Buddhists, the solution to human suffering consists in accepting the truth that everything, including every human person, is impermanent or empty of self-essence.[9] To live by this truth is enlightenment.

All Chan sects agree with the doctrine of interdependent-arising, but they differ in their approaches to practice and training due to their disparate interpretations of how the doctrine informs practice. The First Patriarch of Chinese Chan Lineage, Bodhidharma, for example, emphasized two ways of penetrating this teaching of the Buddha: studying Buddhist scriptures, and, more importantly, practicing wall-facing sitting meditation. The Sixth Patriarch, Hui Neng, however, stressed seeing into one's Buddha-nature, specifically by means of the practice of no-thought, no-form, and no-abiding. For Hui Neng, neither the study of scripture nor the practice of wall-facing sitting meditation is indispensable.[10]

Dogen not only argues against the idea of a permanent self, but also stresses the importance of the practice of no-self. Let's first look at his argument against the idea of a permanent self. Dogen's critique is presented in the form of two analogies: one is that of firewood turning to ash—(an issue that was examined by Nagarjuna in Chapter 10 of his *Fundamental Verses on the Middle Way*), and the other is that of winter "passing into" spring or spring "passing into" summer.

> Once firewood turns to ash, the ash cannot revert to being firewood.
> But you should not take the view that it is ashes afterward and firewood
> before.... Buddhists do not speak of life becoming death. They speak of
> being "unborn." Since it is a confirmed Buddhist teaching that death does
> not become life, Buddhists speak of being "undying." Life is a stage of
> time, and death is a stage of time. It is like winter and spring. Buddhists do
> not suppose that winter passes into spring or speak of spring passing into
> summer.[11]

According to Dogen, although we ordinarily speak of winter passing into spring, there is in fact no underlying winter-state in the process of winter changing into spring. When it is winter we see all signs manifesting winter; when it is spring we see all scenes showing spring. In neither case does "*it*" refer to a changeless, self-identical, and self-substantive state. It is not the case that winter itself, as a state with immutable properties and independent self-existence, paradoxically changes into spring, or that something—the "*it*" in question—is at one time winter, at another, spring. The transition from winter to spring, in Dogen's understanding, is similar to the passing of the flame from one candle to another, in which case the flame is not actually transposed at all (see Chapter 2 of this book).

---

9    "Fukanzazengi," 5.
10   See Platform Sutra, Sections 14, 18, and others.
11   "Genjokoan," 42.

Now, let's turn to Dogen's firewood-turning-into-ash image. Can we equally apply the above understanding of change (with the image of winter-changing-into-spring) to the firewood-turning-into-ash image? We may find it is hard to do so. Why? Our habitual thinking tends to treat the two images differently. In the "winter-turning-into-spring" image, when it is winter, we are not likely to say that "winter" (as a state) somehow persists and is hidden in "spring." But the story with the "firewood-turning-into-ash" image is different. We tend to believe that some constant substance can still be found in the ashes despite the perceptible changes that the firewood undergoes during the burning process. This tendency to believe in object persistence is not accidental. Modern psychology reveals that human beings, as well as some animals, display a tendency of "perceptual constancy"—that is, the tendency to see familiar objects as remaining constant across time. To illustrate this tendency, consider the following experiment: show a short and wide glass beaker with water to a child. Then, transfer the water from the beaker to a taller and thinner glass beaker, and ask the child if the amount of water has changed, she would answer "no." This experiment demonstrates that beginning in childhood, humans have the tendency to perceive physical quantities as unchanging, in spite of variations in appearance. Perceptual constancy also holds with regard to the size and colour of an object regardless of changes in the angle of perspective, distance, or lighting.

These perceptual-conservation tendencies are part of our innate capacity, and they are crucial to such common tasks as identification of physical objects, coordination of bodily movements, physical navigation, and so on. Unfortunately, these abilities also tend to mislead us into believing that things (physical objects, human beings, and even ideas!) are permanent substances or entities when in fact everything is impermanent. These tendencies thus give rise to all forms of attachment—to things, including ideas, and the sense of the self or ego. In the words of Japanese philosopher Toshihiko Izutsu, perceptual constancy and conservation contribute to the mental habit of "essentialization":

> Each one of the things of the world, whether internal or external, is seen to have its own solidly fixed essence because the mind so sees it, because the mind "essentializes." Essences are perceived everywhere by the mind, not because they are objectively there, but simply because the mind is by nature productive of essences. It is the mind that furnishes a thing with this or that particular essence.[12]

This tendency of the mind to essentialize creates all forms of attachment, and it is this attachment that Dogen criticizes. His analogies of winter-turning-into-spring-turning-into-summer and of firewood-turning-into-ashes are meant to help us to see that firewood does not "pass into" ashes, nor ashes "pass into" firewood, just as winter does not "pass into" spring, and spring does not "pass into" summer. Like the seasons, the firewood and the ashes are not permanent entities; humans are not permanent entities either.

---

12   Toshihiko Izutsu, *Toward a Philosophy of Zen Buddhism* (Boulder, CO: Prajna Press, 1982), 13.

Dogen further explains that people tend to see themselves as having a certain immu-table essence because they almost always see themselves as the unmoving centre-point of reference against which to judge all things external to them. This posture of the mind is analogous to a man sitting in a boat at sea looking back at the shoreline, who believes that the shore is moving but he himself is not. The belief comes from an optical illusion. To disperse the illusion, suggests Dogen, the man in the boat should "[fix] his gaze closely on the boat" so that he will realize that it is the boat that is moving.[13] By analogy, Dogen argues that when practicing zen a person has to "fix his gaze closely" on himself.[14] Only then will he realize that the permanent self is just a mental construc-tion. As Rein Raud has explained, "[a]n 'objective subject,' an independent observer who analyzes reality from a timeless and extra spatial 'absolute' standpoint, is for him [Dogen] an illusory construction."[15] But what does it mean by "fixing one's gaze closely" on oneself? Dogen explains:

> To learn the Buddha Way is to learn one's self [true self]. To learn one's self is to forget one's self [false self]. To forget one's self is to be confirmed by all dharmas. To be confirmed by all dharmas is to cast off one's body and mind and the bodies and minds of others as well.[16]

This leads us to Dogen's zen practice. Dogen refers to the practice of no-self or the emptying of the self as "dropping off body-mind"—that is, to cast off or completely for-get that the self is there at all. He insists that the most effective way to practice "dropping off body-mind" is by doing *zazen*, sitting meditation—a practice, if taken literally, that seems contradictory to what Hui Neng preaches in the Platform Sutra. Dogen claims that this kind of practice has been handed down by the Patriarchs and is suitable for all people, whether they are of superior, mediocre, or inferior capacities.[17]

In zazen, you are to sit upright in a relaxed manner in a lotus posture, typically against a wall (as Bodhidharma did when he preached Chan in China), while you maintain a focus on your whole body. From this steady and relaxed position, you are to breathe steadily. The steady breathing is done along with a concentration on what you see, hear, smell, and feel, as they are, without mental "spinning" or mental attachments—that is, without comparison, association, and judgment. The point of this exercise is to keep your body-mind (bodily senses and mental states) undivided, or in complete union, in the present moment. You are not sitting there with your mind wan-dering to your next party, meeting, or project. You dissolve your whole body-mind into the environment, such that the environment becomes your body-mind—you are the

---

13  "Genjokoan," 41.
14  "Genjokoan," 41.
15  Rein Raud, "'Place' and 'Being-Time': Spatiotemporal Concepts in the Thought of Nishida Kitaro and Dogen Kigen," *Philosophy East and West* 54:1 (January 2004): 47.
16  "Genjokoan," 41. Also see Dhammapada, Chapter 12 on self-effort.
17  See "Fukanzazengi," 3 and 5; also see *A Primer of Soto Zen—A translation of Dogen's Shobogenzo Zuimonki*, Reiho Masunaga, trans. (Honolulu: University of Hawaii Press, 1971), 16.

world and the world is you.[18] (Does this fusion of an individual with the world sound familiar? Is it not reminiscent of the Upanishadic teaching that "*Atman* is *Brahman*"?)

It is important to note that Dogen's dropping off body-mind should not be confused with self-denial or asceticism. Dropping off body-mind is not dropping-dead, or becoming inert or torpid; it is not spiritual suicide. In Dogen's words, the practice is not intended to "destroy man."[19] Rather, its purpose is to get you to get rid of or to "forget" your misconceptions of yourself or anything else as permanent, independent entities.[20] In other words, Dogen's message is: Don't essentialize anything, your self or anything else. Don't attach to bodily desires or mental conceptions, including the duality of mind and body, and that of I and Others. How does *zazen* actually help? Contemporary Zen master Norman Fischer provides the following helpful explanation:

> Zazen is a physical practice. We don't usually think of spiritual practice as physical, and yet, life, soul, spirit, mind don't exist in the sky, they exist in association with a body. In Dogen's way of practice, body and mind (or spirit, soul) are one thing, and so to sit—to actually and literally sit down— paying close attention to the body as process, unifying consciousness and breathing with that process until you can enter it wholeheartedly—is to return naturally to what you most truly are. You have been this all along, whether you sit or not. But when you sit in zazen, you return to it and embrace it completely.[21]

We have to be cautious here with Dogen's exhortation to "forget your self." He does not mean to imply that you are essentially a permanent entity and that somehow you have to forget this fact. Dogen is, in fact, making the point that the permanent ego is an illusion, and it is this illusion that you are to dispel by forgetting that there is such a thing to begin with. This is a change of view, but not merely this: it is a total change of your way of being. When you have dropped off your "mind-body," you drop off selfishness, and feel compassion towards everything around you. In other words, the primary aim of *zazen*, for Dogen, is religious: it can help people to realize their Buddha-nature, its impermanence or emptiness, and thus become enlightened.

While Dogen emphasizes *zazen*, he does not neglect other aspects of life. For him, anything done with total concentration can be seen as a practice like *zazen*. Dogen stresses that all walking, standing still, sitting, and lying down are to be conducted in the spirit of *zazen*. In the *Shobogenzo*, there is one fascicle on washing the face and another on cleaning the body. In this sense, Dogen is following Hui Neng in maintain-

---

18 Interested readers may read Dogen's prescription and description of zazen in "Fukanzazengi," 3–4, and "Zazengi," 109–10.

19 "Genjokoan," 42.

20 Here we see clear parallels between Dogen and Laozi and Zhuangzi in underscoring the importance of "forgetting oneself." See the *Daodejing* (especially Chapters 7, 13, 22) and the *Zhuangzi* (especially the beginning of Chapter 2).

21 Norman Fischer, *Beyond Thinking—A Guide to Zen Meditation*, Kazuaki Tanahashi, ed. (Boston: Shambhala Publications, 2004), Introduction, xxvii.

ing that practice is what matters, whether it is in a temple or not (though compared with Hui Neng, Dogen seems to place more emphasis on monastic life).

This fusion with the world or dropping off body-mind cannot be completely grasped by intellectual means alone. Dogen remarks, "Do not think that in attaining this place [enlightenment] it will ever become your own perception, and be knowable by means of intellection."[22] To know it, or to realize it, one has to devote oneself to the serious practice of *zazen*. Consider how one knows the taste of a pear. I cannot know the taste of a pear by studying it intellectually and theoretically. Unless I actually take a bite of a pear, its taste is forever a mystery to me. By the same token, zen stresses direct experience. Practicing zen or living a zen life is often likened to a fish's experience of water's warmth or coldness. The emphasis on direct experience and the downplaying of mere intellectual understanding has become an integral aspect of the Japanese mentality.[23]

## DOING PHILOSOPHY
### *Dropping Off Others' Bodies and Minds?*

What strikes us as puzzling is that Dogen says that when a person casts off his or her body and mind, she or he at the same time is dropping off "the bodies and minds of others as well" (*The Heart of Dogen's Shobogenzo*, p. 41). How is it ever possible for *me* to cast off *others'* bodies and minds?

Review what is explained above about "dropping off body and mind" and offer your interpretation of what Dogen might be driving at. Bear in mind that the *I* that is dropping off the body-mind of others is not the ego-self, but the egoless self, the self that has dropped off any attachment to conceptions and senses. The action/being of an egoless self will both define the self and its environment, as a conversation defines both parties participating in it. In this sense, by the expression of "dropping off one's and other's minds and bodies," does Dogen simply mean "to remove the barriers between one's self and others" (as Yuho Yokoi has translated Dogen's words[24])?

## BEING-TIME (*UJI*)

According to Dogen, to see the world as it is (as suchness, or impermanence), not as what we (mistakenly) think it is, we need to understand temporality in a way that is radically different from our habitual understanding. According to our habitual conception,

---

22 "Genjokoan," 44.
23 See Charles A. Moore, "Editor's Supplement: The Enigmatic Japanese Mind," in *The Japanese Mind—Essentials of Japanese Philosophy and Culture*, Charles A. Moore, ed. (Honolulu: University of Hawaii Press, 1967), 289.
24 Yokoi, 39.

time is distinct from being, and can be divided up into past, present, and future, such that practice (means) and enlightenment (end) are likewise kept distinct in our mind. According to Dogen, a person who holds the habitual conception of time "imagines it [enlightenment] is like crossing a river or a mountain: the river and mountain may still exist, but *I* have now left them behind, and at the present time *I* reside in a splendid vermilion palace. To him, the mountain or river and I are as distant from one another as heaven and earth."[25]

Dogen intends to reveal four interrelated dualities through this analogy. (1) The duality of subject and object/environment—*I*, conceived as an independent entity, or a bystander, is separated from the river and the mountain. (2) The duality of being and time—the *I* keeps constant (has no temporality) in the process of crossing a river or mountain, whereas the river or mountain has been left behind (has temporality). (3) The duality of past and present—the river and the mountain were in the past, and *I* at the present time reside in a splendid vermilion palace. (4) The duality of means and end—crossing a river or a mountain serves as a means to the end of reaching the splendid vermilion palace. In the *Uji* fascicle, Dogen tries to dissolve all these interrelated dualities. Because these dualities are interrelated and interpenetrating, the debunking of one is intrinsically linked to the debunking of the others. But to keep our interpretation of Dogen's thoughts simple and manageable, we will focus on four topics that underlie these dualities: being-time, immediate now, ranging, and practice-enlightenment.

### BEING-TIME (RATHER THAN "BEING *AND* TIME")

Dogen starts the *Uji* fascicle with multiple examples of being-time:

> An old Buddha said: / For the time being, I stand astride the highest mountain peaks. / For the time being, I move on the deepest depths of the ocean floor. / For the time being, I'm three heads and eight arms [the figure of the ashura or fighting demon, unenlightened existence in general]. / For the time being, I'm eight feet or sixteen feet [a Buddha, Shakyamuni, in seated and standing attitudes respectively] / For the time being, I'm a staff or a whisk. / For the time being, I'm a pillar or a lantern. / For the time being, I'm Mr. Chang or Mr. Li [a particular person: Tom, Dick, or Harry]. / For the time being, I'm the great earth and heavens above.[26]

According to Dogen, time is not to be understood as detached from being. The "*I*" in the multiple cases listed here is not constant; it is rather the multiple beings or acts themselves, so there is no separation between "*I*" and what "*I*" is or does. Moreover, what "*I*" is or does (being, or, to-be) *is* time, not what "*I*" is or does is *in* time. In this understanding, being and time is one, rather than divided.

---

25 "Uji," 50.
26 "Uji," 48.

To show the oneness of being-time, Dogen deliberately and creatively reads *uji* (literally "being-time" but is ordinarily taken to mean "sometimes," "at a certain time," or "once") not as two separated entities—*u* (being) and *ji* (time), but as the oneness of being-time. For him, time *is* being and being *is* time. Without "time," "being" does not exist either:

> Mountains are time, and seas are time. If they were not time, there would
> be no mountains and seas. So you must not say there is no time in the
> immediate now of mountains and seas. If time is destroyed, mountains
> and seas are destroyed. If time is indestructible, mountains and seas are
> indestructible.[27]

In other words, whatever happens—and everything is a happening—is time (temporal), and time is whatever happens. Thus, pine trees, bamboos, rats, tigers, mountains, and seas are all times, not *in* time, which suggests that time is a container and that whatever happens in it is independent from it. As Stambaugh has explained, for Dogen, "[t]ime is simply the way these beings take place or presence; they are nothing over and above and beyond this taking place and presencing."[28] Christian Steineck concurs with an interesting analogy of "boats on the river": "[t]o Dogen, the temporal is not an order externally projected onto things, but an intrinsic property of any mode of being. Real entities are not launched into time like boats on the river. They create temporal order by their own way of being."[29] A donkey *is* donkey-being-time, and a horse *is* horse-being-time.[30] Even sentient beings and Buddhas are equally times.[31] Therefore, in the oneness of being-time, everything or every being is primordially equal, albeit distinctive, if all conceptualizations and categorizations of them are stripped off.

In this conception of temporality, time is concrete, specific, and "experienced." As Dogen points out, "[a]t the same time the mountain was being climbed and the river being crossed, I was there. The *time* has to *be* "in" me. Inasmuch as I am there, it cannot be that time passes away."[32] This is to say, time does not have independent existence or "life" that is detached from concrete beings, activities, or events; time and being are not separable. What being-time means is that—to borrow some terms from Heidegger—a concrete "being-in-the-world" is "temporality," and "temporality" is, specifically, "being-in-the-world."[33]

27 "Uji," 56.
28 Joan Stambaugh, *Impermanence is Buddha-nature* (Honolulu: University of Hawaii Press, 1990), 50.
29 Christian Steineck, "Time Is Not Fleeting: Thoughts of a Medieval Zen Buddhist," *KronoScope* 7 (2007): 38.
30 See "Uji," 57, note 63.
31 See "Uji," 51, 52, and 56.
32 "Uji," 50.
33 Notice however that Heidegger's terms "being-in-the-world" and "temporality" tend to assume Da sein (literally means "being there," but refers to humans' existence, or presence) as the centre of discourse, whereas Dogen talks about everything being-in-the-world and being temporal without assuming a centre of discourse.

Obviously, Dogen's understanding of time differs radically from Aristotle's and Newton's conceptions of time—both separate being and time. According to Aristotle, "time is the measure of change" (*Physics*, Chapter 12), but "time is not change," because a change "may be faster or slower, but not time ..." (*Physics*, Chapter 10). To illustrate, the falling of a leaf (a change) can be faster or slower, but time itself cannot be faster or slower. For Newton, real time, or absolute time, is like an empty container: "Absolute, true, and mathematical time, of itself, and from its own nature, *flows equably without relation to anything external, and by another name is called duration*: relative, apparent, and common time is some sensible and external (whether accurate or unequable) measure of duration by the means of motion, which is commonly used instead of true time; such as an hour, a day, a month, a year."[34] To understand Dogen correctly, one must be careful not to objectify or reify time as if it were a "cosmic womb" or a "cosmic receptacle," so that pine trees and so on are pieces of furniture stored in the receptacle.[35] For if time were objectified as a whole, pine trees would then be considered to be *in* the whole, or to be only *part* of the whole—pine trees (as beings) would not be "identical to" time. To Dogen, however, since "[e]ach time is without exception *entire* time,"[36] pine trees are entire time, so are bamboos, rats, and so on respectively. Thus, in the sense of being temporal, every being is entirely equal.

The verb "is" in the statement "time is being and being is time" is philosophically very significant. It (the word "is") is not used in the sense of attributing a property to a subject, as in the proposition "The rose is red." Rather it is used in a sense that signifies identity, similar to the "is" in the proposition "Two plus two is four." Being and time are distinct yet paradoxically identical to each other. They are distinct, in the way that "two plus two" and "four" have different senses; they are identical, as "two plus two" and "four" are identical—referring to the same quantity. All pine trees, bamboos, rats, tigers, mountains, and seas are manifesting time, yet each manifests time in its distinct way, just as blossoming flowers, flowing rivers, and chirping birds all manifest spring in their own unique ways. It is clear that this identity of being and time is markedly similar to the identity of *Atman* and *Brahman*.[37] There is, however, a crucial difference between them. While both *Atman* and *Brahman* (in one interpretation) are taken to be permanent entities, being and time, in Dogen's view, are seen as impermanent or impermanence.

---

34 Scholium to the Definitions, *Philosophiae Naturalis Principia Mathematica*, 1687, emphasis added. In *Sir Isaac Newton's Mathematical Principles of Natural Philosophy*, Florian Cajori, trans. (Berkeley: University of California Press, 1934), 6.

35 Dogen's conception of time is not even what Newton called "common time" like an hour, a day, a month, or a year. Although Dogen by no means denies the importance of common time (see Steineck, 39), he seems to think that knowing the "twelve hours of your day" [in the traditional Chinese timing system, one day was divided into twelve hours] is not knowing the true nature of time: "Although you never measure the length or brevity of the twelve hours, their swiftness or slowness, you still call them the twelve hours. As evidence of their going and coming is obvious, you do not come to doubt them. But even though you do not have doubts about them, that is not to say you know them" ("Uji," 48–49).

36 "Uji," 50.

37 Compare this idea of equality with the Christian idea that everyone is equal in the face of God.

## IMMEDIATE NOW

According to Dogen, time, in the Buddhist way of living, is not to be understood in a spatial sense as a linear process consisting of past, present, and future. As he puts it, "[p]ast time and present time do not overlap or pile up in a row."[38] A linear conception of time, for Dogen, is not concrete and real time. This conception of time is an abstraction that is detached from the living process of being (to-be, or becoming). In our lived reality we do not experience the past or the future; we only experience a continuous present, the "immediate now." To put it differently, the past is realized (recollected) as the past only in the "present"; the present is realized as the present in the "present"; and the future too is realized (anticipated) as the future in the "present." In Dogen's words, "As the time right now is all there ever is, each being-time is without exception entire time.... Entire being, the entire world, exists in the time of each and every now. Just reflect: right now, is there an entire being or an entire world missing from your present time, or not?"[39] When we are completely fused into the activity we are doing, be it listening to a piece of music, cultivating land, carving wood, and so on, without distinguishing "now" and "then," or "I" ("the interior") and "others" ("the external"), there is nothing lacking. Our doing is the entire being, and also the entire time.

Contrary to our everyday understanding of time, Dogen suggests that one "should not only come to understand that time is only flying past," since time, if so understood, would "have to leave gaps."[40] The being-time "after" a bird's flying by is ontologically equal to the being-time "before" the bird's flying by. There is no gap or separation between them.

To understand Dogen's view on the immediate now, let's consider the following scenario. A three-year-old little girl is going to a playground to play. She is not going to wait till she gets there to play. She plays all the way to the playground, picking up a wild flower here and there, watching ants attentively beside the road, flirting timidly with a bee, and generally wandering around aimlessly. She plays and enjoys herself *each and every immediate now.* She is "fused into" the present or "attuned to" the world—a state of *to-be* that is remarkably similar to Daoist Zhuangzi's wandering in the world. In this scenario there is no duality between the subject and the environment, nor is there a duality between the present (the time along the way to the playground) and the future (the time there at the playground), nor is there a duality between the means (going to the playground) and the end (playing there). The way the little girl behaves is very different from the way adults behave. Adults often separate means (present) and end (future) and treat the present as less valuable. Working time, for many adults, sadly means a chore relative to their free time. It is common to hear people say that they're going to do something or other when they make enough money, or when their kids are grown, or when they retire.

---

38  "Uji," 51–52.
39  "Uji," 50.
40  "Uji," 51 and 53.

"Fusing into the present" here, however, is different from "being attached to the present." The former is based on the practice of forgetting the imagined substantive self or of "dropping off body and mind." The practice is ultimately rooted in the acceptance of impermanence as the true nature of reality. On the contrary, when one clings to every moment and indulges oneself in sensual pleasures right now and right here, it only discloses that one does not want to accept change, or that one is clinging to an ego that Zen Buddhism tries at all costs to dismantle.

### DOING PHILOSOPHY
*Dogen's "Immediate Now" and the Conception of Time in the "Ecclesiastes"*

There is a passage in Ecclesiastes (3:1–8) that expresses a conception of time that is very close to Dogen's view on time: "There is a time for everything, and a season for every activity under heaven; a time to be born and a time to die ... a time to love and a time to hate, a time for war and a time for peace." This passage seems to be basically in line with Dogen in *accepting the impermanence of all human affairs*—though unlike Ecclesiastes, Dogen's view on time is not confined to human affairs. The rest of Ecclesiastes 3, however, departs from Dogen and makes a divine ascending which puts the impermanence of human affairs in the perspective of an eternal God. How is it that the author of Ecclesiastes can believe in God and impermanence at the same time? To what extent can the doctrine of impermanence be a common ground for interreligious dialogue?

### RANGING

To fully understand Dogen's view on time or being-time, we need to first understand his conception of *"kyoryaku,"* translated by Kasulis as "ranging,"[41] Waddell and Abe substitute "seriatim": "The entire world is not changeless and immoveable, nor unprogressing and unregressing—the whole world is passing seriatim [*kyoryaku*]."[42] However, according to Kevin Schilbrack, the word "seriatim" may not be ideal here, for it is part of Dogen's goal to reject the understanding of linear time, thus the term "seriatim" seems "an unhappy choice."[43] Kasulis's translation seems more appropriate as it better captures the double meaning that *kyoryaku* contains: "dwelling" and "continuous."

According to Dogen, each time (being-time) keeps its distinctive nature: "various times" do not "get in each other's way,"[44] and all dharma stages "[dwell] in their

---

41  See Kasulis, "The Zen Philosopher: A Review Article on Dogen Scholarship in English," *Philosophy East and West* 28:3 (July 1978): 370.
42  "Uji," 54.
43  Kevin Schilbrack, "Metaphysics in Dogen," *Philosophy East and West* 50:1 (January 2000): note 22.
44  "Uji," 49.

suchness."[45] But the "dwelling" of time does not mean "past time and present time ... overlap or pile up in a row,"[46] for example, spring is spring, not summer. The "present" or "immediate now" is neither linear nor stagnant. It is not the instant points portrayed in Zeno's flying yet motionless arrow. It is rather endlessly moving: all dharmas "[move] endlessly up and down."[47]

For Dogen, the emphasis on the "dwelling of time" does not cut off the present from the past or future. Dogen puts it figuratively: the time climbing the mountain or cross-ing the river [past] "swallows up" (negates) as well as "spits out" (affirms) the time of the splendid vermilion palace [future].[48] Waddell and Abe explain this point nicely in a footnote in their translation of the "Uji": "The present time swallows all past time and being and all future time and being and also spits it out. Hence, there is a constant merging of past and future in the present."[49] In other words, time is nonlinear, multi-directional, and totally dynamic. The etymological study can help clarify what may be in Dogen's mind when he talks about *kyoryaku*. *Kyoryaku* contains two parts "kyo" and "ryaku," with the former referring to the warp threads of a textile, and the latter meaning "to run to and from between different point along the woofs." Thus, the idea of *kyoryaku* can be illustrated by the activity of weaving cloth on a traditional loom in China and Japan. The weaver has to constantly "run through" the warps to make a piece of cloth. Any warp-woof crossing point on the cloth dynamically links to other points both horizontally (synchronically) and vertically (diachronically).

---

**DOING PHILOSOPHY**
*Dogen and Heidegger on Time*

What Dogen says about the continuity of time is remarkably similar to what Heidegger says about time. Consider the following passage from Heidegger's *Being and Time*: "Temporalizing does not signify that ecstasies come in a 'suc-cession.' The future is *not later* than having been, and having been is *not earlier* than the present. Temporality temporalizes itself as a future which makes pres-ent in the process of having been."[50]

---

To illustrate this dynamic nature of time, Dogen wrote one of the most puzzling pas-sages in the "Uji" about "today," "yesterday," and "tomorrow": "it [being-time] passes from today to tomorrow, passes from today to yesterday, passes from yesterday to today,

---

45  "Uji," 52.
46  "Uji," 52.
47  "Uji," 52.
48  "Uji," 50.
49  "Uji," 51, note 17.
50  *Being and Time*, John Macquarrie and Edward Robinson, trans. (San Francisco: Harper, 1962), Section 68, 401.

passes from today to today, passes from tomorrow to tomorrow, this because passing seriatim ['ranging'] is a virtue of time."[51]

This passage completely defies our ordinary understanding. One might say it is sheer nonsense. What can we make of this passage? How is it possible that time can pass from today to yesterday? What does it mean to say that time passes from today to today, and from tomorrow to tomorrow?

All these questions are natural and understandable, given that we all unwittingly presuppose that time is a linear process, running from the past to the present, and to the future. Based on this presupposition, then, it is inconceivable that time passes from today to yesterday. In the same manner, it is hard to see how time could pass from today to today, and from tomorrow to tomorrow.

To understand Dogen's point, the key is to see today, yesterday, and tomorrow as indexicals (like "this," "that," "here," "there," "now," and "then") that we use to characterize being-time, and the meanings of these terms can only be determined in relation to some reference point—in this case, being or to-be. What you call "yesterday," "today," and "tomorrow" depends on what day it is. Thus over twenty-four hours, you can pass from one "today" to another.

I think Dogen's point is that today, yesterday, and tomorrow (or past, present, and future) are not like three fixed pillars. As conventional or provisional designators, they have no self-essence, and their very beings rely on and interpenetrate one another. In other words, every moment of time, when not being objectified, is distinct yet completely equal ontologically. Any day can be called "yesterday," "today," or "tomorrow." No moment is superior to any other moments, and there is no obstruction at all between any two moments. Dogen would ask: does winter obstruct spring from arriving? Does night prevent day time from coming?

To recapitulate, Dogen sees time as consisting in endless coming and going immediate nows, with no permanent entity or identity running through the immediate nows. Time, in this view, is neither a static "now," nor a flying "past." Any present now connects to any other times ("past" and "future") by "swallowing up" and "spitting out."

### PRACTICE AND ENLIGHTENMENT

According to Dogen, when one has cast off body and mind, one is enlightened. But enlightenment is not a once-and-for-all state or activity; it goes on continuously in everyday life. True Buddhas (the enlightened) "are realized, fully confirmed Buddhas—and they go on realizing Buddhahood continuously."[52] "[E]nlightenment continues on without end."[53] Nor is enlightenment an externally oriented searching, for "[t]o learn the Buddha Way is to learn one's self."[54] Therefore, for Dogen, practice itself is enlightenment, and it takes place only in the Now.

51 "Uji," 51–52.
52 "Genjokoan," 40.
53 "Genjokoan," 41.
54 "Genjokoan," 41.

We have already seen Hui Neng's view on the oneness of practice and enlighten-ment in the Platform Sutra—"The very practice of Buddha, this is Buddha."[55] But for Dogen, Hui Neng's teaching may still be misunderstood. For example, Hui Neng's doc-trine of "seeing into one's own nature" may imply separating "seeing into" from "one's own nature"—a separation of practice ("seeing into") from enlightenment ("one's own nature"/Buddha-nature). As Hee-Jin Kim points out, Dogen "severely criticized the idea of 'seeing into one's own nature' (*kensho*) and went so far as to regard the Platform Sutra as a spurious work and not the words of the sixth ancestor ... From his [Dogen's] own standpoint, the activity of seeing was itself one's own nature."[56]

To illustrate this oneness of practice and enlightenment, Dogen uses the analogies of fish swimming in the water and birds flying in the sky:

> Fish swim the water and however much they swim, there is no end to the
> water. Birds fly the skies, and however much they fly, there is no end to
> the skies. Yet fish never once leave the water, birds never forsake the sky.
> When their need is great, there is great activity. When their need is small,
> there is small activity. In this way, none ever fails to exert itself to the full,
> and nowhere does any fail to move and turn freely. If a bird leaves the sky,
> it will soon die. If a fish leaves the water, it at once perishes. We should
> grasp that water means life [for the fish], and the sky [for the bird]. It must
> be that the bird means life [for the sky], and the fish means life [for the
> water]; that life is the bird, life is the fish. We could continue in this way
> even further, because practice and realization, and for all that is possessed
> of life, it is the same.[57]

While we may be inclined to accept Dogen's statement, "water means life [for the fish], and the sky means life [for the bird]," we may not be equally inclined to accept his next few sentences: "It must be that the bird means life [for the sky], and the fish means life [for the water]; that life is the bird, life is the fish." We cannot help but ask why it is that the bird means life for the sky and the fish means life for the water. For we all think that the sky and the water can exist whether there is any bird flying or fish swimming. But this questioning fails to see Dogen's point.

An example may help to explain what Dogen wants to say here. When a pianist is playing a piece of music, where does the music reside? It does not hide in the piano nor does it lurk in the pianist's fingers. It lies in the pianist's actual *playing* of a piano. The actual playing of the piano brings forth both the nature of the piano and the nature of the pianist. Similarly, according to Dogen, the *swimming* reveals and defines both the fish and the water, in that the notion of swimming has no independent being apart from the configuration of fish-swimming-in-water. In this sense, the fish and the water are fused into the conception of swimming. Likewise, the *flying* reveals

---

55  Section 42, also see Section 13.
56  Hee-Jin Kim, *Dogen Kigen—Mystical Realist*, 56–57.
57  "Genjokoan," 43–44.

and defines both the bird and the sky. In the "beginning" (before the subject and object bifurcation) was the event, not the isolated fish and bird on the one side and the water and sky on the other side. In flying, the bird's "self" and the sky's "self" are dissolved into each other. Similarly, in swimming, the fish's "self" and the water's "self" completely interpenetrate. In a manner of speaking, the water realizes itself in the swimming (of the fish), and the sky realizes itself in the flying (of the bird). Dynamically and existentially speaking, the bird does mean life for the sky, and the fish life for the water. Without the bird the sky is only a "dead" sky—its meaning and significance are not presently manifest; without the fish the water is merely "dead" water—its meaning and significance are not presently shown. Dogen uses these analogies in exactly such dynamic and existential senses.

In utilizing the analogies of fish swimming in water and bird flying in the sky, Dogen seeks to show that practicing the Buddha Way and realizing the Buddha Way are one. Without practice, Buddha-nature remains an empty potential, even if everyone is endowed with it (see discussion on *Bussho* below). In other words, *the authentic self is not potential but actional*. It is the actional *kyoryaku*—i.e., that which occurs continuously in each moment of Now. Practice realizes Buddha-nature, just as the fish's swimming directly and immediately realizes the fish's nature *and* the water's nature. It is *not seeing but becoming* Buddha-nature that matters. Every action matters, no matter how apparently insignificant it appears. There is no Buddha-nature without action, just as there is no swimming without the fish, no flying (broadly construed) without the bird. Life is action, and action is life. In this sense we can call Dogen's Zen a unique philosophy of action.

Following Dogen's view of the oneness of practice and enlightenment, it is now easy to see the point of the seemingly puzzling fanning *koan* at the end of *Genjokoan*:

> As Zen master Pao-ch'e of Mount ma-yu was fanning himself, a monk came up and said, "The nature of the wind is constancy. There is no place it does not reach. Why use a fan?" Pao-ch'e answered, "You only know the nature of the wind is constancy. You haven't yet grasped the meaning of its reaching every place." "What is the meaning of its reaching every place?" asked the monk. The master only fanned himself. The monk bowed deeply.[58]

The monk's question in the *koan* follows the same logic as the question that Dogen had wrestled with in his youth: If everybody already has Buddha-nature, why practice? For master Pao-ch'e and for Dogen, the wind's *reaching* every place means action (fanning), and by analogy, "everybody's already having Buddha-nature" shows itself in action (practice). For Dogen, there is no Aristotelian duality of potential and actuality, no Mengzi's sprouts of moral goodness waiting to be cultivated to their fruition in the future, there is simply and straightforwardly action.

---

58 "Genjokoan," 44–45.

**DOING PHILOSOPHY**
*The Moon on the Waters: What Is Enlightenment Like?*

Dogen describes enlightenment by adopting the image of the moon (dharma)
on the water (man). In the first place, he says, "it [enlightenment] is not like
the moon on the water"[59] and then in the second, he states, "The attainment of
enlightenment is like the moon reflected on the water."[60] Is Dogen then making an obvious contradiction by saying A and not A? If not, why not? You may
find Waddell and Abe's notes 7 and 13 on these passages helpful.

## BIRTH/LIFE AND DEATH (*SHOJI*)

Let's now turn to Dogen's view on birth/life and death, which is intrinsically linked to
his understanding of temporality.

Death in the ordinary sense means the final destiny of (this) life. This ordinary
understanding of death is derived from the view that birth and death are completely
dichotomous, each occupying a place at one end of a bounded time line. Living signifies
the process from birth to death (see illustration below).

*Ordinary understanding of birth/life and death*

This ordinary conception of death presupposes that one has an enduring identity
(at least within one's lifetime). Many hold that this identity would be terminated at the
point of death *in the future.* Others believe that this identity endures past death in the
form of resurrection or an immortal soul.

But according to the Buddhist doctrine of no-self, there is nothing permanent or
independent in this life, nor is there anything permanent that precedes birth or survives
after death. In this regard, Buddhism differs sharply from views like the immorality of
the soul in Plato's *Phaedo*, the *Atman* of the Upanishads, and the personal resurrection
in the New Testament. Following this doctrine, Dogen maintains that it is a mistake to
think that one passes from life into death because that would paradoxically presuppose
a permanent agent. Dogen states:

---

59  "Genjokoan," 41.
60  "Genjokoan," 42.
61  The dotted line after the death-point symbolizes some kind of immortality—of the soul or otherwise.

It is a mistake to think you pass from life into death. Being one stage of time, life is possessed of before and after. For this reason, the Buddha Dharma teaches that life itself is as such unborn. Being one stage of time as well, cessation of life also is possessed of before and after. Thus it is said that extinction itself is undying. When there is life, there is nothing at all apart from life. When there is death, there is nothing at all apart from death. Therefore, when life comes, you should just give yourself to life; when death comes, you should give yourself to death. You should neither desire them, nor hate them.[62]

The type of mistaken thinking is given further exposition in a previously quoted passage (about firewood and ashes) from *Genjokoan*. The error in this way of thinking is exactly the same as the error in believing that there is some enduring substance that remains unchanged when firewood turns into ash, or that there is some entity or state that stays unaltered when winter turns to spring. In the case of life and death, the error consists in the belief that there is an agent ("I") passing from life to death. But, according to Dogen, there is no substance or permanent entity underlying any of these happenings.

In denying that there is a permanent agent underlying any change, however, Dogen has not abandoned the basic Buddhist tenet of causal connection or interdependent-arising. Firewood and ash, as well as winter and spring, have "before and after" conditions, and so do life and death.

Consistent with Nagarjuna's view of the identity of samsara and nirvana, Dogen insists that "birth-and-death itself is nirvana" and one's present "birth-and-death itself is the life of Buddha."[63] The world of impermanence (samsara) is itself the world of nirvana—when the truth of impermanence is accepted and embodied existentially. It is like following the flow of the cosmic river, letting go of any mental or physical attachments. In this profound acceptance of impermanence, there is no more yearning for an eternal life or for anything that is imagined to be permanent, nor is there any hatred toward reality. With such an approach to life and death, one would adopt a middle way. In Dogen's words, "you will neither hate one as being birth-and-death, nor cherish the other as being nirvana. Only then can you be free of birth-and-death."[64] This middle way attitude toward death also resonates well with Daoist Zhuangzi's view on death as evident in these words of Zhuangzi: "If you act in accordance with the state of affairs and forget about yourself, then what leisure will you have to love life and hate death? Act in this way and you will be all right."[65]

There are three common attitudes toward death: (1) escapism—indulging in bodily pleasures, (2) fatalism—committing suicide or doing nothing and waiting passively for the coming of death, (3) eschatological faith—living a moral life in the hope that

---

62 "Shoji," 106.
63 "Shoji," 106.
64 "Shoji," 106. Dogen suggests that the way to foster this middle attitude is by letting go or dropping off both one's body and mind (see "Shoji," 106–07).
65 *Chuang Tzu, Basic Writings*, Burton Watson, trans., 56; see also 76, 81, 83, and 113.

the soul or the person will continue to exist after death. But, for Dogen, these attitudes are all wrong-headed: (1) holds onto the ego-self; (2) fails to accept the responsibility of being human; and even (3) reveals a trace of the impulse of self-preservation or a vestige of egoistic concern. All these attitudes stem from a failure to accept the reality of no-self. Dogen maintains that the right attitude towards life and death is to live an ego-less and compassionate life, facing each moment calmly and non-dualistically: "If you refrain from all evil, do not cling to birth-and-death; work in deep compassion for all sentient beings, respecting those over you and showing compassion for those below you, without any detesting or desiring, worrying or lamentation—that is Buddhahood."[66]

## BUDDHA-NATURE (BUSSHO)

In the *Bussho* fascicle, Dogen quotes from various Chinese Buddhist texts and com-ments on them. The fascicle can be divided into two parts. Part I[67] contains a general discussion on Buddha-nature, and Part II[68] analyzes many particular *koans* about Buddha-nature from Zen patriarchs or Zen masters. Our exploration will focus on Part I (interested students could read Part II and refine their understanding of Part I).

As we have seen in previous chapters, human nature was a key issue in Mengzi's Confucianism, and Buddha-nature (mind/heart-nature) was a central issue in Hui Neng's version of Chan Buddhism. Although Dogen follows the general doctrines of Buddhism (i.e., emptiness, no-self, and non-dualism) in his treatment of Buddha-nature, his understanding of Buddha-nature itself has its distinctive characteristics.

In the beginning of *Bussho*, Dogen quotes a key statement from the *Nirvana Sutra*: "All sentient beings without exception have the Buddha-nature." But he boldly reinter-prets it in an innovative and non-dualistic way. As Dogen sees it, the statement may be misunderstood as implying a dualism that treats "sentient beings" as the subject/means and Buddha-nature as the object/end. It is also sometimes taken to imply that there is a duality between "sentient beings" and "other beings" ("non-sentient beings"). Dogen deliberately misreads "without exception have" (*shitsuu* 悉 有) as "entire being," but this bold and innovative reading interestingly better conveys the true message of Mahayana Buddhism upon which Zen Buddhism is based—entire being *is* the Buddha-nature and Buddha-nature *is* interdependent-arising or impermanence. Let's lay out the traditional reading and Dogen's reading of the statement from the *Nirvana Sutra* more clearly:

> *Issai shujo shitsuu bussho* (一 切 众 生 悉 有 佛 性)
> Traditional reading: All sentient beings without exception have (*shitsuu* 悉 有) the Buddha-nature.

> Dogen's reading:
> All beings/entire being (*shitsuu* 悉 有) [is] Buddha-nature.
> (Entire being = Buddha-nature; Buddha-nature = entire being)

---

66  "Shoji," 107.
67  "Bussho," 59–67.
68  "Bussho," 67–98.

The traditional reading of Buddha-nature is susceptible to dualism, in that it can be read as positing all sentient beings as substances or entities, and Buddha-nature as an attribute of sentient beings, just as we imply in saying "Snow (an entity) is white (has the attribute of being white)." This is typical Western essentialism traceable from Aristotle, via medieval philosophy, to Descartes (think of his wax example). Such an essentialist reading can take three forms.

One form is to take Buddha-nature as some *thing* that inherently exists in humans or even in all sentient beings. According to this view, known as the "Senika heresy,"[69] the permanent ego, or the soul of a person (like *Atman*), is like the host of a house. While the house can be destroyed, its host can just run away intact. In the same way, the soul of a person will survive when the physical body of the person dies.

Another way to posit a substantive Buddha-nature is to see it as a seed. "When this seed receives the nourishment of Dharma rain, it begins to sprout; branches and leaves, flowers and fruit, appear, and the fruit contain seeds within them."[70] According to this view, just as a seed (a potentiality) when properly nourished will sprout and branch, get leaves, flowers, and fruit, Buddha-nature (a potentiality) will likewise realize itself when adequately cultivated. This understanding of Buddha-nature is immediately reminiscent of Mengzi's view of human nature (review the *Mengzi*, 2A6 and 6A8).

A third way to posit a substantive Buddha-nature is to see it as a fruit or an outcome that will come naturally in a future time. Those who hold such a view say "all [enlightenment, or realization of Buddha-nature] comes about spontaneously, as a matter of natural course."[71] This view implies that the outcome (enlightenment) comes naturally without serious *present* practice. The pie in the sky will naturally fall on you!

Dogen's creative (mis)reading of the *Nirvana Sutra* text dismisses all three substantive readings of Buddha-nature. First, in Dogen's "All beings/entire being [is] Buddha-nature," "all beings/entire being" is not posited as a substance, and "Buddha-nature" is not posited as an attribute of that subject. Rather, according to Dogen, the expression says "all beings/entire being" are in complete identification with "Buddha-nature." The expression is to be understood as "Entire being (impermanence) [is] Buddha-nature (impermanence)"![72]

Secondly, Dogen attacks the seed analogy in the understanding of Buddha-nature, for it is hopelessly dualistic. It separates practice (cultivation) from realization (fruition) and it renders present practice secondary and devoid of value in itself. To Dogen, "seed and flower and fruit are each, individually, the unbarred [Buddha-] mind itself.... the roots, stem, branches, twigs, and leaves are each equally the Buddha-nature—living the same life and dying the same death as the same *entire being*."[73]

---

69  "Bussho," 63.
70  "Bussho," 64–65.
71  "Bussho," 66.
72  Unlike Hui Neng who seems to speak of Buddha-nature only as humans' nature, Dogen stresses that Buddha-nature is the nature of all beings/entire being, not just that of sentient beings. "The words *entire being* [*shitsuu*] mean both sentient beings and all beings [including non-sentient beings]" ("Bussho," 61). Therefore, for Dogen, there is not even a tiny trace of dualism between human beings and any other being.
73  "Bussho," 65.

Thirdly, Dogen criticizes the view that enlightenment or the realization of Buddha-nature will come naturally in the future. He interprets the clause "If the time arrives" (*jisetsu nyakushi* 时 节 若 至) as meaning "the time is already (*nyaku*) here, and there can be no room to doubt it."[74] Therefore, for Dogen, there is no dualism between present and future; there is no excuse for delaying practice.

Dogen's reinterpretation of the old text here allows him to retrieve and revive the true spirit of Buddhism, including the idea of non-dualistic thinking and of impermanence. In the traditional reading, language can become "a clothing that hides truth" whereas in Dogen's reading it becomes a "window" towards the truth.[75] No wonder Kim calls Dogen "a magician or alchemist of language."[76]

In the *Bussho* fascicle, Dogen also clarifies the meaning of "entire being." He proposes four ways in which "entire being" can be characterized:

1. "an infinite number of miscellaneous fragments."
2. "a single, undifferentiated steel rod."
3. "not large or small."
4. "a raised fist."[77]

According to Dogen, the first two characterizations violate the basic tenet of inter-dependent-arising. Entire being cannot be an amalgamation of an infinite number of fragments or objects, or the world would not be causally linked. Entire being cannot be a single, undifferentiated steel rod either, or the world would be changeless or motion-less. For Dogen, the third characterization—entire being is neither large nor small—is correct, for entire being is beyond any conceptualization. Conceptualization can only fix or reify entire being; it cannot realize being.

Better than the third characterization of entire being is the fourth one: entire being is "a *raised* fist." A raised fist signifies an action, a movement, a concrete living reality. Compared with Nagarjuna, Dogen's characterization of ultimate reality (emptiness or interdependent-arising) is clearly more vivid and lively.

With Dogen's identification of entire being with Buddha-nature, a complete identification of being, time, and Buddha-nature is obtained: "Time = Being = Buddha-nature." Compared to the identity of *Atman* and *Brahman*—both of which are believed to be permanent and independent—Dogen's identification of being and Buddha-nature is a revolutionary accomplishment: it brings temporality into the very nature of every being or entire being.

---

74  "Bussho," 66. Here Dogen read the character *nyaku* as "already" instead of "if."
75  David R. Loy, "Language against Its Own Mystifications: Deconstruction in Nagarjuna and Dogen," *Philosophy East and West* 49:3 (July 1999): 257.
76  Hee-Jin Kim, "The Reason of Words and Letters: Dogen and Koan Language," in William R. LaFleur, ed. *Dogen Studies* (Honolulu: University of Hawaii Press, 1985): 63. For more comprehensive discussions of Dogen's skilful manoeuvring of language, see David R. Loy, "Language against Its Own Mystifications: Deconstruction in Nagarjuna and Dogen," *Philosophy East and West* 49:3 (July 1999), 245–60, and Steven Heine, "Koans in the Dogen Tradition: How and Why Dogen Does What He Does with Koans," *Philosophy East and West* 54:1 (January 2004): 1–19, especially 5–10.
77  "Bussho," 64.

## DOING PHILOSOPHY
*Can Chan (Zen) Be Rationally Studied?*

Now that we have explained Hui Neng's Chan and Dogen's Zen, we need to be aware of two contrasting attitudes towards Chan/Zen. In the 1950s, there was a famous debate between a well-known Chinese philosopher, Hu Shih (1891–1962), and D.T. Suzuki (1870–1966), the best-known Japanese Zen scholar, on how to understand Chan. Hu Shih argues that Chan can be understood only in its historical setting:

> The Ch'an (Zen) movement is an integral part of the history of Chinese Buddhism, and the history of Chinese Buddhism is an integral part of the general history of Chinese thought. Ch'an can be properly understood only in its historical setting just as any other Chinese philosophical school must be studied and understood in its historical setting.[78]

Hu Shih maintains that, contrary to Suzuki, Chan is *not* "beyond the ken of human understanding," nor is rational or rationalistic way of thinking useless "in evaluating the truth and untruth of Zen."[79] In sharp contrast, Suzuki insists that to understand Chan from a historical point of view is to treat it from outside, not from within.

> Zen must be understood from the inside, not from the outside. One must first attain what I call *prajna*-intuition [which is beyond rational or rationalistic thinking] and then proceed to the study of all its objectified expressions. To try to get into Zen by collecting the so-called historical materials and to come to a conclusion which will definitely characterize Zen as Zen, Zen in itself, or Zen as each of us lives it in his innermost being, is not the right approach.... Hui Shih, as a historian, knows Zen in its historical setting, but not Zen in itself. After he has exhausted Zen in its historical setting, he is not at all aware of the fact that Zen is still fully alive, demanding Hu Shih's attention and, if possible, his "unhistorical" treatment.[80]

Can Chan be rationally studied? Can "seeing one's Buddha-nature" be explained in words? In understanding Chan, who is right, Hu Shih or Suzuki? Could they both be right? How?

---

78 Hu Shih, "Ch'an (Zen) Buddhism in China: Its History and Method," *Philosophy East and West* 3:1 (April 1953): 3.
79 Hu Shih, 3.
80 D.T. Suzuki, "Zen: A Reply to Hu Shih," *Philosophy East and West* 3:1 (April 1953): 26.

Recall that in Chapter one, we have Eknath Easwaran who refuses to characterize the Upanishads as philosophy texts and Joel Kupperman who regards them
as philosophy (as well as religious) texts. Now it seems that similar interpretive
issues we have seen in the study of Upanishads have resurfaced here in the
study of *Shobogenzo*. Why do you think the same interpretive issues do not
seem to go away?

## CONCLUDING REMARKS: THE INFLUENCE OF *SHOBOGENZO*

Dogen is probably the best-known religious thinker and philosopher in Japanese history. The Japanese are proud of this great Zen master. The Japanese philosopher Tanabe
remarked that he was "impressed by the depth and accuracy of Dogen's speculation"
which "strengthened [his] belief in the Japanese people's capacity of thinking."[81] As
the founder of Japanese Soto Zen, Dogen's influence on Zen in Japan is peerless. Soto
Zen has been and still is the biggest Zen sect in Japan. It has attracted thousands of
Western practitioners since early in the twentieth century. Dogen's insights on being-
time, life-death, and on practice-enlightenment have profound implications for how
we should live, including how we should treat others as well as the environment. Over
the past thirty years, Dogen has become the most renowned and most studied figure in
Buddhist history in the West, and the *Shobogenzo* has also secured a place among the
masterworks of the world's religious and philosophical literature.

## WORKS CITED AND RECOMMENDED READINGS

1. Norman Waddell and Masao Abe, trans., *The Heart of Dogen's Shobogenzo*
   (Albany, NY: State University of New York Press, 2002).
2. Reiho Masunaga, trans., *A Primer of Soto Zen—A Translation of Dogen's
   Shobogenzo Zuimonki* (Honolulu: University of Hawaii Press, 1971).
3. Masao Abe, *A Study of Dogen: His Philosophy and Religion*, Steven Heine, ed.
   (Albany, NY: State University of New York Press, 1992).
4. Masao Abe, *Zen and Western Thought* (Honolulu: University of Hawaii Press,
   1985).
5. Hee-Jin Kim, *Dogen Kigen, Mystical Realist*, revised, 3rd ed. (Somerville, MA:
   Wisdom Publications, 2004).
6. T.P. Kasulis, "The Zen Philosopher: A Review Article on Dogen's Scholarship in
   English," *Philosophy East and West* 28:3 (July 1978): 353–73.
7. Kevin Schilbrack, "Metaphysics in Dogen," *Philosophy East and West* 51:1
   (January 2000): 34–55.
8. Hee-Jin Kim, *Dogen on Meditation and Thinking: A Reflection on His View of Zen*
   (Albany, NY: State University of New York Press, 2007).

---

81  Tanabe Hajime, *Shobogenzo no tetsugakushikan* (Tokyo: Iwanami, 1939), 11, as quoted by Steineck, 36.

# How to Live
# a Human Life

The ten Asian philosophy classics introduced in this book contain a rich array of spiritual insights that are at once diverse and multi-layered. In mining these insights, different individuals may focus on different elements. One may come to appreciate different elements at different times. Whichever the case may be, it is clear that these classics all strive to address the issue of how one should live as a human being—that is, how to live a *human* life.

It goes without saying that a human life is not simply a biological life, for if so, a human life would be no different from a dog's or an aphid's life, nor is it merely a social life, such as that of ants or bees. This is something that the ten Asian philosophy classics all agree on. But merely saying what a human life is *not* does not really help us understand what it *is* or *should be* like, or how an individual *should* live. In addressing the nature of the human life, the ten classics do not come to a single conception of the ideal human life. Instead, they present us with diverse, but overlapping, visions of the ideal human way of being in the world.

The Upanishads argues that a human life is one in which an individual realizes his or her ultimate oneness with everyone and everything else, which crystallizes in the identity of *Atman* with *Brahman*. The ego-centred life, or the illusionary life, must be replaced by an authentic life of Big Self (*Atman* or *Brahman*). The Dhammapada agrees that the ego-centred life is not an ideal human life, but it revises or reinterprets the ideas in the Upanishads (e.g., *Atman* and *Brahman* being immortal and the caste system being rigid and hereditary) that it sees as inconsistent with the ideal of a non-ego-centred life. The Dhammapada maintains that the permanent Self, whether taken as ego, *Atman*, or *Brahman*, is illusory; therefore, an enlightened one will live a selfless and compassionate life.

The Upanishads and the Dhammapada both emphasize moral cultivation and spiritual liberation. However, neither tradition implies that the social-political dimension of life is not important, although they seem to agree that social and political concerns are secondary to human beings' ultimate concern—namely, the yearning for spiritual liberation. In sharp contrast, the *Analects*, the *Mengzi*, and the *Xunzi* are concerned centrally with state-ruling and self-realization in various social contexts. The ideal human life they envision is one that is deeply embedded in the social context of families and states. In such a human life, one is required to cultivate the sprouts of moral goodness innate to one's nature (*à la* Mengzi) and to channel one's desires (*à la* Xunzi) accordingly, in an effort to bring about universal social harmony, evidenced by harmonious relationships within families and nation-states and peace in the whole world (*tian-xia*).

In presenting its unique understanding of human life, the *Daodejing* shares the social-political concerns of the Confucian classics, but it also warns people of the problems that Confucian doctrines of humanness (*ren*) and ritual propriety (*li*) may cause. According to the *Daodejing*, there is too much artificial interference in Confucianism; authentic human existence, in contrast, should be natural, spontaneous, and gentle (*rou ruo*) rather than "pushy" or contrived.

Compared to the perspectives of the *Analects*, the *Mengzi*, the *Xunzi*, and even the *Daodejing*, the approach of the *Zhuangzi* is radical, for it advocates transcending social-political concerns, evening out all man-made value differences, and going with the flow of nature. It is a way of life that is characterized by spontaneity and joy, fully in tune with nature, as fish in water.

Although the Platform Sutra and the *Shobogenzo* both come from the Mahayana Buddhist tradition (represented especially in Nagarjuna's *Fundamental Verses of the Middle Way*) and both promote a selfless and compassionate human life, they each have a different emphasis. The Platform Sutra emphasizes the application of the *spirit* of meditation in daily activities, whereas the *Shobogenzo* stresses the indispensability of literal sitting meditation (*zazen*).

In grappling with the Asian philosophical classics, I have come to appreciate the diversity of the moral visions they represent. (And I hope you have come to a similar discovery.) At the risk of simplifying things, I will highlight three very important insights I have gleaned from them.

The first insight is that an ego-centred life (though tempting and attractive) is not worth living, for such a life is not free, joyful, or fulfilling. It is a life of ignorance of one's true nature, a life rife with fears (of death, for example) and worries. The true Self (*Atman*, Buddha nature, or one realizing humanness or *ren*) is paradoxically no self (ego). A drop of water "fears and worries" about its existence, but when it merges with the ocean, it becomes infinite and free. Similarly, we cannot ultimately be free from fears and worries until we (progressively, perhaps) lose our "selves" in a family, a community, a society, the whole of humanity, and even the entire universe (symbolized as *Brahman*, Heaven, Dao, or Buddha-nature). This may be seen as a process of evolution—from a small self (an ego) to a big Self, and then to no-self at all. To be sure, not every individual can completely reach the highest level or the perfect realm of no-self, but it is the point of reference to which the Asian philosophy classics look in order to set their moral compass.

While the first insight is expressed in spatial terms—going from small self (small "space"), big Self (big "space"), to no-self (infinite "space"), the second insight can be articulated in temporal (or "atemporal") terms. To live a human life involves engaging every moment in every daily activity. That's why Chan/Zen masters often say the essence of Chan/Zen is "chopping wood and carrying water." Your life is the totality of your moment-by-moment living, and your happiness lies in your being-in-the-present-moment; immortal life is not an endless linear process, but one timeless moment after another. Ultimately, happiness consists in not taking some periods of our life as merely means to an end (and thus as inferior) and other periods as the true end (and hence as superior). There is no slack in our being-authentically-human at any moment.

The third insight I have gained is that, ultimately, one can only rely on oneself in the realization of an authentic human existence. To realize *Atman*, to practice *ren*, or to penetrate no-self, gurus and teachers may help. Skilful means (*upaya*)—such as rituals—may help, but eventually a spiritual ascension (whether you call it enlightenment, realization, transformation, illumination, or anything else) depends exclusively upon each individual's self-effort.

# Selected (Non-Ranked) Journals
# on Asian Philosophy

1. *Asian Philosophy*
<http://www.tandf.co.uk/journals/journal.asp?issn=0955-2367&linktype=1>
2. *Contemporary Buddhism*
<http://www.tandf.co.uk/journals/titles/14639947.asp>
3. *Dao: A Journal of Comparative Philosophy*
<http://www.kutztown.edu/academics/liberal_arts/philosophy/dao.htm>
4. *Harvard Journal of Asiatic Studies*
<http://www.hjas.org/>
5. *Journal of Asian Studies*
<http://www.asian-studies.org/publications/JAS.htm>
6. *Journal of Chinese Philosophy*
<http://www.wiley.com/bw/journal.asp?ref=0301-8121>
7. *Journal of Chinese Religions*
<http://isites.harvard.edu/icb/icb.do?keyword=k7027&tabgroupid=icb.tabgroup41942>
8. *Journal of Indian Philosophy*
<http://www.springerlink.com/content/102937/>
9. *Philosophy East and West*
<http://www.uhpress.hawaii.edu/journals/pew/>

# Selected (Non-Ranked) Graduate Programs in Chinese Philosophy

University of California, Riverside
The University of Hong Kong
The Chinese University of Hong Kong
City University of Hong Kong
National University of Singapore
Duke University
University of Connecticut
University of Hawaii
University of Utah
University of Toronto
University of Indiana
University of Oklahoma
University of Oregon
San Francisco State University
State University of New York at Buffalo

For selected (non-ranked) Graduate Programs in Asian Religions or Asian Studies Programs, see <http://www.h-net.org/~buddhism/GradStudies.htm>.

# Useful Websites

Manyul Im's Chinese Philosophy Blog
  <http://warpweftandway.wordpress.com/2009/11/08/welcome-to-the-group-blog/>
Chad Hansen's Chinese Philosophy Page
  <http://www.hku.hk/philodep/ch/>
The Useless Tree: Ancient Chinese Thought in Modern American Life
  <http://uselesstree.typepad.com/>
The Columbia Society for Comparative Philosophy
  <http://www.cbs.columbia.edu/cscp>
The Society for Asian and Comparative Philosophy (SACP)
  <http://www.sacpweb.org/>
International Society for Chinese Philosophy (ISCP)
  <http://www.iscp-online.org/>
ASIANetwork—A Consortium of Liberal Arts Colleges to Promote Asian Studies
  <http://www.asianetwork.org/>
International Society for Comparative Studies of Chinese and Western Philosophy
(ISCWP)
  <http://sangle.web.wesleyan.edu/iscwp/index.html>
Association of Chinese Philosophers in North America (ACPA)
  <http://www.acpa-net.org/>
A useful link on Dogen's Zen
  <http://hycadventures.com/page17.php>

# A Very Simplified Note on Pinyin Pronunciation

(Some of these "equivalents" are as close as English speakers can get—but not very close.)

a as in the a in far
ai as in the ie in die
ao as in the ow in now
e as in the u in luck
i as in the ee in knee
o as in the o in off
ou as in the ow in snow
u as in the oo in mood
c as in the ts in hats
ch as in chew
q as in the ch in teach
x as in the sh in she
z as in the ds in heads
zh as in the j in jam

# GLOSSARY OF KEY TERMS

(The interpretation of the terms listed below is based primarily on the classics introduced in this volume.)

*Atman*: The enduring Self, the true Self, or the true master of an individual that is "behind" experiences; the true knower "behind" all knowing; not to be confused with the ego-self or individual *jiva* self; it is identical with *Brahman*—the ultimate foundation of reality.

BEING-TIME (*uji*): A Zen Buddhist idea that completely identifies time with being—time *is* being and being *is* time. Time is not understood as a container that holds beings.

BIRTH/LIFE-DEATH (*shengsi*, 生死; *shoji*): In Buddhism, since there is no substantive self, there is no "birth" (creation) of an individual nor his or her "death" (annihilation). There is only change, which can be conventionally or provisionally described as birth or death—the "birth" of a sprout (from an oak seed) *is* simultaneously the same as the "death" of the seed—the only difference lies in (human) perspectives.

*Brahman*: In the Upanishads, it refers to the impersonal absolute Being of reality, or a state of awareness devoid of any opposition and duality; it is not to be confused with the totality of objects; it is identical to the true nature of an individual, or *Atman*.

BUDDHA-NATURE (self-nature): An empowerment concept symbolizing the capacity or potential for enlightenment that is assumed to be endowed in every individual human being, or even in every species in the world; it is not a substance hidden inside an individual but purity or freedom (for Hui Neng) and impermanence (for Dogen).

CHAN (禅, *dhyana*): A transliteration of the Sanskrit word "*dhyana*," meaning "meditation"; it also refers to a dominant Mahayana Buddhist school that is integrated with Daoism and (to a lesser degree) with Confucianism. Its Japanese equivalent is *zen*.

COMPLETED/FIXED MIND (*cheng-xin*, 成心): A state of mind/being that fixates on an egoistic, narrow perspective or prejudice, and judges everything from this perspective and imposes this perspective on things; a state of mind that does not adjust itself when things have changed.

CONVENTIONAL TRUTH: In Buddhism it is a truth that is based on language and everyday habitual experience which tends to see one's self as permanent (in some sense) and essentially separate from the rest of the world; it does not capture the ultimate reality, which is suchness, as-it-is, impermanent, interdependent, or empty. According to conventional truth, the discourse of "I," "my," and "mine" still can be necessary and useful, but according to ultimate truth no substantial "I" should be assumed in this discourse.

DAO (道): A term that literally means "path," or "to guide," or "to speak," and by extension means "principle," "law," and so on. The term is shared by all ancient Chinese philosophers. For Confucius, it primarily refers to social order; for Laozi, it denotes the material reality, its patterns, right ways of operation, ethical guides, and so on.

DELIBERATE EFFORT/CONSCIOUS ACTIVITY (*wei*, 为): To do things consciously and deliberately, regarded as a unique characteristic of being human by the Confucian philosopher Xunzi, but seen as unnecessary and destructive (as doing so may lead to coercive behaviour) by the Daoists Laozi and Zhuangzi.

DHARMA: A term for natural law, patterns, social, and religious duties; it may be called the Hindu or Buddhist counterpart of the Chinese *dao*. In Buddhism, dharma also refers to Buddha's teachings or doctrines.

EMPTINESS (*shunyata*): The most important concept in Buddhism, symbolizing the true nature of reality (including human beings) without substance (*svabhava*); it is also translated as interdependent-arising, suchness, or as-it-is-ness; understanding emptiness leads to enlightenment; not to be confused with absolute void or non-being.

ENLIGHTENMENT (gradual vs. sudden): In Buddhism, it means coming to understand the true nature of the world, including one's self. In Chinese Chan, particularly in the Platform Sutra, there is a debate between two interpretations of enlightenment—the gradual and the sudden. The gradual approach emphasizes literally sitting in meditation and practicing in order to reach a non-dual mental state; it emphasizes that enlightenment is a process. The sudden approach stresses conducting daily activities in the spirit of non-dualism; it sees enlightenment happening in the timeless present.

EXTENDING AFFECTION (*tui-en*, 推 恩): The Confucian idea that love or care starts within the family, between parents and children and between siblings, and then extends to relatives, friends, people in the community, and the general public. Although those closer to an individual (particularly those who are consanguineously related) may receive love or care with priority and more intensity, those not consanguineously related to an individual are also to be loved and cared for.

FIVE AGGREGATES (*skandhas*): According to the Buddha, a person is not an entity or substance (thus there is no self, *anatta* or *anatman*), but a conditioned existence that is composed of five elements—form/body, sensation, perception, volition, and consciousness. But these five elements themselves are not to be seen as ultimate entities, either. As the Buddha's follower Nagarjuna has argued, the five elements themselves are devoid of self-nature (*svabhava*).

FOUR SPROUTS (*si-duan*, 四 端): The four innate moral faculties that Mengzi believes to exist generically in humans—the heart of compassion, the heart of disdain, the heart of deference, and the heart of approval or disapproval. According to Mengzi, these four hearts, when properly cultivated, lead respectively to benevolence/humaneness (*ren*, 仁), righteousness (*yi*, 义), propriety (*li*, 礼), and wisdom (*zhi*, 智).

HEART or MIND (*xin*, 心): A concept in Chinese philosophy that denotes the source of thinking, emotion, and moral conscience. According to Mengzi, heart has four innate moral sprouts.

HEAVEN (*tian*, 天): In pre-Confucius texts, *tian* is often associated with *di* (帝, the Lord or Supreme Ancestor Spirit). In the *Analects*, *tian* is used in the sense of the Lord as well as in the sense of sky or Nature. In the *Mozi*, *tian* signifies a personal god. In the *Mengzi*, *tian* is not anthropomorphic or personal, but Nature with moral inclinations or tendencies. In the *Xunzi*, *tian* is neither personal nor moral, but brute Nature.

(HUMAN) NATURE (*xing*, 性): A concept that figures prominently for the Confucians Mengzi and Xunzi. Mengzi argues that human nature is good in the sense that humans generically have four sprouts, or innate moral potentials, that, if properly cultivated, can lead to moral perfection (sagehood). Xunzi uses the concept *xing* to refer to humans' natural senses and instincts that (according to him), if not regulated with rituals, lead to bad social consequences. Thus Xunzi calls human nature bad (*e*, 恶).

HUMANNESS (*ren*, 仁): Arguably the most important idea in Confucius' teachings, signifying the moral ideal, the most fundament virtue, and the defining character of *junzi*, or exemplary persons. *Ren* has been translated into English in a number of ways: "benevolence," "goodness," "humanity," "perfect virtue," and "authoritative conduct or persons." *Ren* is to be realized in concrete situations. Thus, Confucius offered no fixed formula for how to practice *ren*, but he did provide specific examples and give general guidance for it.

INTERDEPENDENT-ARISING (*pratîtyasamutpâda*): The idea that the Buddha (Gautama) realized upon enlightenment that everything is always changing and based on conditions, and that nothing (including one's self) is permanent or independent. It is stated in a paradigmatic expression: "If this, then that; if not this, then not that." Nagarjuna in his *Middle Way Treatise* interprets interdependent-arising as an equivalent to emptiness.

JUNZI (君 子): Literally "lord's son," but used by Confucius to mean exemplary person who cultivates humanness on the inside and follows ritual propriety on the outside, and who is not necessarily a "lord's son"; translation of this term varies: gentleman, superior person, or noble man; the opposite personality is called the petty person or *xiaoren* (小 人) who is egocentric and narrow-minded, and who indulges in sensual pleasure.

KARMA: Moral causality in Hinduism and Buddhism—what one sows is what one will reap; the Buddha seems to *internalize* karma by focusing on the intention of an action and its consequence rather than the outward action itself. Logically, the idea of karma working autonomously seems to exclude a personal, divine God who is in control of each individual's life in terms of reward and punishment.

MIDDLE WAY: A way of life initiated by the Buddha that avoids extreme views, such as hedonism and asceticism, substantialism and nihilism; it was further expounded and made prominent by Nagarjuna in his famous Mahayana *Madhyamaka* treatise *Mulamadhyamakakarika* (*Fundamental Verses on the Middle Way*).

MIND (*mano*): The Buddha sees the mind (*mano*) as a faculty along with other sense faculties: eyes, ears, nose, tongue, and body. The eyes, the ears, the nose, the tongue, and the body all have their respective objects: material form, sound, smell, taste, and tangibility. The mind has ideas and concepts as its objects. Moreover, unlike the eyes, the ears, the nose, the tongue, and the body, each of which focuses on its own objects, the mind can intervene in the faculties of seeing, hearing, smelling, tasting, and feeling, and it can shape the performance of these faculties significantly. Both ignorance and enlightenment hinge on the mind.

MOKSHA: Liberation from the cycles of life and death when one realizes one's true nature, *Atman*, which is also identical to *Brahman*, the ultimate nature of reality; a Upanishadic counterpart of the Buddhist idea of nirvana.

NIRVANA (Pali: *nibbana*): Literally means the "blowing out" of a fire, and symbolically means extinguishing the fire of craving or attachment that is caused by ignorance of one's true nature of no-self. When one is in *nirvana* one is enlightened.

NO-ABIDING (*wu-zhu*, 无住), NO-FORM (*wu-xiang*, 无相), NO-THOUGHT (*wu-nian*, 无念): Notions used by Hui Neng in the Platform Sutra. All these three terms describe a state of mind, or state of being, that is similar to the state of nirvana. One in such a state is not bothered by dualistic thoughts, nor attached to forms, nor resistant to admitting change.

PU (朴): An uncarved piece of wood, symbolizing simplicity and undifferentiation (no value distinction or social hierarchy), a social and psychological state that is considered to be ideal by the Daoist Laozi.

RECTIFYING NAMES (*zheng-ming*, 正名): A Confucian political strategy that emphasizes behaviour in accordance with the duties prescribed by one's social position.

RITUAL PROPRIETY (*li*, 礼): Codes of correct conduct or right procedures for doing things in Confucianism; true *li* has to do with inner attitudes and emotions, and is not sheer formalism.

SAMSARA: Literally means "going around." In the Upanishads, it signifies the unsatisfactory cycles of life and death of embodied existence (*avatars*) of an eternal Soul or Self on the basis of merit and demerit (karma). In Buddhism, it means the suffering cycles of "giving birth," of an attachment and its demise. To liberate from *samsara* is called *moksha* in Hinduism and *nirvana* in Buddhism.

SELF-NATURE (*svabhava*): Believed to be the permanent, unchanging, and self-sufficient essence of a thing or person, regarded by the Buddhist as the cause for all kinds of attachments; the opposite of the Buddhist idea of emptiness or interdependent-arising.

SHENG (生): A dominant Daoist idea that sees the world as an endless process of "giving birth," "producing," "growing," or "evolving"; not to be understood as creation *ex nihilo*, but as self-producing.

TRANSFORMATION OF THINGS (*wu-hua*, 物化): Things transform endlessly into each other as *qi* (energies) takes different forms; there is no entity or substance in the world, only constant processes of transformation. Life and death are ontologically equal as they are phases of transformation.

ULTIMATE TRUTH: Truth in Buddhism about what is ultimately there as-it-is (thusness, interdependent-arising, or emptiness) without the prejudice of conventional view and the reification of language; one is enlightened when one realizes the ultimate truth.

WANDERING (*you*, 游): A way of life advocated by the Daoist Zhuangzi that is carefree, happy, and *dao*-following, like the free, spontaneous swimming (*you*, 游) of fish.

WU (无): Depending on the context, it can mean a prohibiting or warning "don't" (as in *wu-wei*), "absence," "no-object-ness," or "not-taking-form/formless"; not to be confused with Parmenides' non-being.

WU-WEI (无 为): Not-doing-things (in a coercive way), a general Daoist *de* (virtue) that one (especially for a ruler) has to cultivate through knowing *dao*; not to be misunderstood as simply "doing nothing."

YIN-YANG (阴 阳): A paradigm of opposite yet complementary forces or energies that the ancient Chinese philosophers in general adopted in their explanation of change in the cosmos and in human affairs.

YOU (有): Depending on the context, it can mean "existence/existing," "presence/presenting," "form/taking form." *You* is the opposite of *wu*. According to Laozi's *Daodejing*, *you* and *wu*, like *yin* and *yang*, complement and transfer to each other.

ZAZEN: Sitting meditation, a Zen practice that is particularly emphasized by Japanese Zen Master Dogen in his *Shobogenzo*.

ZEN: The Japanese equivalent to the Chinese word Chan (禅), a transliteration of the Sanskrit word *dhyana*, meaning "meditation" or "meditative state."

ZI-RAN (自 然): A term that figures centrally in Laozi's *Daodejing* and Zhuangzi's *Zhuangzi*, which can be translated as spontaneity or naturalness. It describes the ideal state of human *being*, different from brute Nature, or Hobbes's imagined primitive "state of nature."

Loy, David R. "Language against Its Own
  Mystifications," 308n75
loyalty, 107, 145, 260n2
loyalty and faithfulness, 148, 188, 247
loyalty or conscience (*zhong*), xiii, 85, 87,
  107, 108
lust, 54

Ma-wang-dui (Ma-wang-tui) silk
  text, 154
Madhyamika (Middle Way) teaching of
  emptiness, 263
Mahavira, Vardhamana, 28
Mahayana Bodhisattva ideals, 282
Mahayana Buddhism, 53, 58, 260, 263,
  273, 278, 286, 289, 306
  integrated into Chinese thought, 261
*Mahayana Buddhism* (Williams), 63n11
*Mandukya*, 4
manifesting suchness (*genjokoan*), 287
"Man's Nature Is Bad," 234
Mara's bond, 44, 53
Mascaro, Juan, 32
Materialists (*Cârvâkas*), 33–35
"me," 40
meditation, 3, 35, 41, 43, 46, 62, 229
meditation (*ding*), 275
meditation and wisdom
  unity of, 275–76
meditative school (*Yoga*), 27
Mengzi, 99–100, 120, 232, 256, 265
  all humans can become sages, 269
  concern with state ruling and self-
    realization, 312
  follower of Confucius, 124, 306
  on hatred and virtue, 96
  heart is innately good, 272–73
  on heaven, 234–35
  influence, 151
  life attitude, 234
  moral cultivation, 272, 276
  obsessed by need to lessen
    desires, 240

philosophy has religious
  dimension, 151
political philosophy, 147–49
sprouts of moral goodness, 246, 249,
  266–67, 273, 287, 303
theory of human nature, 125–32
thought experiment, 127, 129–30
venerated as "Second Sage" in the
  Confucian tradition, 125
*Mengzi*, xi, xiii, 90, 123–51, 286
"Mengzi and Xunzi" (Van
  Norden), 246n65
Mengzi-Gaozi debate on human
  nature, 133–35
mental states, 205
mental training, 36, 43
"meta-seeing," 268
metaphysical Self, 12
metaphysics, 5
Michael, Thomas, *The Pristine
  Dao*, 205n29
middle way, 35, 57–58, 65, 78, 305
Middle Way school 58, 82
Mill's utilitarianism, 111
mind, xvi, 29, 31, 34, 36
  Buddha's understanding of,
    37–38
  polluted mind, 36, 38–43
  pure mind, 44
  straightforward mind, 264, 281
  training the, 41
mind-matter dualistic school
  (*Sankhya*), 27
"mine," 40
*ming* (illumination, clarity, or
  light), 210–11
Ming Dynasty, 282
Mo, Di, xiv–xv, 116, 126, 139, 184–85, 188
  on continuity between heaven and
    humanity, 235
  first opponent of Confucius'
    teachings, 138
  Xunzi's criticism, 254–55